PASEANDO

"OUT" FOR A WALK

John Rock

PASEANDO

Copyright © 2010 John Rock

All rights reserved. No part of this publication may be reproduced, stored in any information or retrieval system, or transmitted in any form or by any means electronic, mechanical, photocopying, recording or otherwise without permission in writing from the copyright owner.

ISBN: 978-1-4466-8167-1

For

All Humanity
My Fellow Travellers

Contents

Chapter 1: Letting go an accent—1

Chapter 2: London in the sixties and seventies—11

Chapter 3: Facing the truth—17

Chapter 4: Women who wanted—27

Chapter 5: Escape from Iraq—41

Chapter 6: A small world—57

Chapter 7: New York, an unlikely destination—61

Chapter 8: From celebrations in Israel to complications in Algeria—73

Chapter 9: Mexican money—87

Chapter 10: Heading to Sydney—97

Chapter 11: Settling in Sydney—113

Chapter 12: Loving and hating India—117

Chapter 13: Meeting Charles—129

Chapter 14: India calls again—135

Chapter 15: Enlightenment in Luzon—147

Chapter 16: My love lost—159

Chapter 17: Getting my life back—171

Chapter 18: Treading water and the quest for knowledge—181

Chapter 19: Checking out the boyfriend—191

Chapter 20: Flying around—197

Chapter 21: Living positively—217

Chapter 22: Letter from Lesotho—223

Chapter 23: Bali to Malawi—239

Chapter 24: Stopping work—255

Chapter 25: Tales of a summer in Europe—261

Chapter 26: Manila to the Mekong—273

Chapter 27: Glimpses of Estonia—279

Chapter 28: Ten "mirrion"—285

Chapter 29: The "Z" and "U" of Africa—293

Chapter 30: Q and A—303

Chapter 31: The wrong solution—311

Chapter 32: Looking to the future—317

Chapter 33: Dreams—321

Chapter 1 Letting go an accent

I have lived in Australia more than half of my life, and certainly most of my adult life, and for me it is home. I never expected it to be. But I certainly did not intend staying in the country of my birth, England. When I was in my early twenties I was a convinced European and I thought I would end up living somewhere on the continent. I was offered a position in Brussels once. I liked the sound of the job. It was with Monsanto developing a market for a new plastic coating material, before Monsanto became unfashionable due to genetically modified food. But my mother was dying of cancer, and I used that as the excuse for not taking it.

I confess that I have let the unhappiness of my childhood influence how I feel about the environment in which it took place. I know that I am unfairly harsh in my judgment of England. I can appreciate the pretty lanes in early summer, the country pubs and the history. But whenever I go there I feel the suffocation of my upbringing clawing at me and dragging me down. Once I left I no longer had to be the son of a middle-class family, with a distant father who managed the local Boots the Chemists shop, and a mother who did not work and who was always there, and whom I adored. I could just be "me". But I waited until she died before I left.

On May 14th 1944 I was born in the upstairs front bedroom of a typical two-up-two-down semi-detached house in a bland suburb in the west of Birmingham. There had been a long gap between me and my other sibling, my sister Jean who was born before the war in 1937. I have always assumed that the uncertainty of war was responsible for such a large gap. Inevitably, I suppose, my elder sister exercised an uninvited and unwanted parental role towards me.

I have few recollections of my early childhood, and those I have are confused between what I really remember of that child and the anecdotes that others have told me about him.

As I look back through my mind's eye, I have difficulty in recognising him or relating to him. How did that child become me? He was born into a very pedestrian English family, rising from a working-class background to the middle class. I don't think he was a good-looking child, not cute, rather ordinary, but eager to please, and with a mischievous wit. He was lonely, and in some strange way remained so for the rest of his life. He did not do what most bo.ys do. He never climbed trees or played football or cricket. He hardly even had any friends. He avidly read travel books, dreamt about far away places and designed his own cities.

This young boy was bright, performed well at primary school and then won a scholarship to the best secondary school in the region.

My father was not a man of great passion, in either beliefs or interests; in fact it was difficult to get him to express an opinion on any serious matter. I never once heard him comment on any news item or political issue.

He was the youngest of what I gather was a highly dysfunctional family. His parents died before mine even married. His mother, so my own mother told me, was sweet and gentle, whereas the father was a bad-tempered tyrant. My father's elder brother, George, would have been 15 years older than my father. My father wanted to be an engineer, but he was not allowed by his elder brother to study engineering, and so was sent to study to become a pharmacist. George paid for his education, which is why he was the final arbiter on my father's career, the repayment once my father started to earn money to be made to his parents rather than to him. My father contracted pneumonia while he was doing his pharmacy apprenticeship in London at the end of his studies. Amazingly, considering there was no penicillin in the early 1930s, he recovered.

Before he went to London he had met my mother through the old Waverlians club, established for the school they both attended. She was banned by her father from going to London to see my father, despite his illness. London was an evil and dangerous city. At the time she was well into her twenties, and took the enormous decision to defy him. Once my father started to recuperate he returned to Birmingham where both families lived. Even though my father was penniless and could not work, George decreed that he must continue to pay back the student loan to his parents. My mother described how she had to give him the money even to have his haircut.

My father had two sisters. One was beautiful and kind. She fell in love at the age of 22. Her father forbade the relationship, she caught tuberculosis and, as my father described it, lost the will to live and died. The other never married. She was a mean, shrew-like woman with tendencies towards religious mania. She was for me the archetypical spinster. My mother hated her, partly because she had refused to put the heating on when my father returned to their family home after his illness in London. She died in a religious institute at the age of 64. My father was the only one at her funeral to shed a tear.

My father was a distant figure, remote rather than aloof. He managed the same local branch of Boots the Chemists for over 25 years. I was never sure whether he refused to move or whether the company did not choose to offer him a promotion. In the early days he had a male assistant, but for most of his working life he had no male colleagues. He went to work every morning, coming back at lunchtime for his "dinner", the cooked meal of the day. He then slept for half an hour and went back to work. In the evenings he would fall asleep in front of the television. He did not chat. He worked every Saturday and once a month on Sundays on "rota", when he worked in the afternoon from twelve to one. Most Sundays he put on an old discarded suit, forgoing a tie, and either dug the garden or repaired or serviced the car. He was a reasonably competent mechanic, no doubt; after all he always had wanted to be an engineer. But to his great regret I did not share this interest with him, and this was simply another fact that divided our lives. He was not a sportslover; in fact he had no interest in sports at all, never playing nor watching it. In that alone I followed him.

I find it rather strange that he had no friends of his own, no mates to whom he could talk and share his thoughts with. His social contact with other males was always in the context of the husband of a friend of my mother, or a brother-in-law. He did not seem to miss having a male confidant; it was, I suspect, something that never developed as a young man and was simply not part of his experience or need. He never went anywhere without my mother, with the exception of the Boots managers' dinner once a year when wives (there were no female managers in those days) were not invited. He never seemed to develop the art of conversation, and in later life after my mother died was extremely gauche in some of his relationships, causing considerable hurt to those who were his closest support.

My mother was the eldest of four siblings, all born within five years of each other. She was warm, kind and loved by everyone who knew her. She apparently had no ambition for herself, dedicating her time to the family, accepting for the most part whatever my father decided was best for us all. She was never harsh or spiteful and nursed her pain silently and stoically. For people did take her for granted and on occasion abused the generosity of her love and friendship.

My mother's family was really the only family I knew. My grandparents lived around the corner after they were bombed out of the house where they lived in the industrial part of the city. My grandfather was a short-tempered Victorian man with a glass eye as a result of an accident at work. My grandmother was wonderful. She was warm, plump, caring, with a spicy sense of humour and amazing patience and loyalty towards her rather difficult husband. She outlived my mother by several years. It must be hard to see a child go first.

My mother had two brothers who lived in the same city and we saw their families on Sundays on a fairly regular basis. We would exchange visits for the ubiquitous afternoon tea.

My mother's sister moved to London where her husband lived; they had met on holiday in Torquay. They had an adopted son, Mike, some 18 months younger than me. Apart from him I was the youngest of the five cousins in my generation. My London uncle was a short-tempered man with short, curly reddish hair. He was a successful but uneducated timber merchant. Frankly I never liked him much. Mike and I had little in common, and we were thrown together often as we spent many holidays together, both in London and later at a seaside bungalow in Pevensey Bay in Sussex. This was a luxury, for few of my friends had the opportunity to take a holiday at all, let alone visit London and go to the seaside. It was on a visit to London when I was about 10 years old that my father took me out, just the two of us, the one and only time in all the years of my childhood. I remember that we needed to go to the public toilets, near Southwark Cathedral. On the wall there was a warning about "venereal disease". "What's that?" I asked my father. "Don't worry, you haven't got it!" was the only answer I got.

For many years as I was growing up we rented the beach house at Pevensey Bay for a month every summer. It was built right on a hill of stones, just at the back of the beach. You could hardly get closer to the sea. At night I would listen to the noise of the waves grinding the stones, and fall asleep with the sea in my head. I loved it. My mother and her sister got on very well together, and the times we spent together were harmonious and relaxing. Even the fact that my cousin and I had so little in common did not seem to matter. Then my father and uncle would join us for two of the four weeks, and they were the two weeks I enjoyed much less, with far more stress and tensions. My father would fall asleep on the beach, and my uncle would taunt me over my cousin's far superior skills at hitting a ball. This was no doubt to compensate for his inability to perform well at school. That indulgence in pretending my cousin was something that he was not, and baling him out time after time, in the end cost my aunt and uncle the comfortable assets they had acquired, with my aunt left virtually penniless when my uncle died. My cousin died at the age of 52 from liver cancer after a long battle with alcoholism.

It is true that academically I did well. But this was never spoken of in our house. My parents were probably afraid of offending my sister. So there was no praise or recognition. Only many years later in Australia when I came top of the year in psychology and won some prizes, did my father recognise my achievements. He simply said, "I wish your mother was here to see this now".

This was the family I grew up in. I rarely think about it, never reminisce unless others force me to, and for the life of me I cannot see any relevance or connection to the life I have led. There must be of course, I just choose to not see it.

I was never allowed to have a bicycle, it would have been too dangerous. My cousin in London had one, and I used to borrow the bicycle and make circles of eight around the two plum trees in their small suburban garden. I once sneaked out along the side passage to the road between the houses that served as access to the garage, but never dared to break the rules and go for a spin in the cul-de-sac where they lived.

I adored animals, but I was not allowed to have a pet. The closest I managed to get was a tortoise called Timmy. Timmy loved strawberries and basking on the lawn in summer downpours. When it rained less heavily he would head for his box. One spring towards the end of his hibernation there was an early warm snap followed by a frost. Timmy did not survive it.

Once, a small black-and-white cat appeared in the chemist shop that my father managed. There was brief talk about keeping it, since my father was very fond of cats. I remember once at the beach house he cradled a neighbour's cat in his arms and fed it butter and sugar on his finger. We kept the black-and-white cat one night, but it must have committed some awful social gaffe, for it disappeared the next day and my sister and I never knew what happened to it.

When I was a young teenager, the next-door neighbours had a dog. It belonged to their son who went away to agricultural college and so was not able to look after it. He was called Buster and he was mainly whippet, white and slim like a greyhound, with a speed to match. Most days after school I took the dog for long walks.

Buster and I went everywhere together, disappearing on expeditions for hours at a time. We walked to the bluebell woods, down the riverbed that was called Watery Lane. We walked though old streets with crumbling houses, and passed estates at the edge of town with modern large homes, looking warm and comfortable inside as the evening drew in and the lights were switched on. Buster obeyed me completely. He would never run into the road, and came as soon as I called him. He walked to heel and would "stay" even when I was out of sight, although I did catch him shuffling after me on a few occasions.

I guess he ran and sniffed and realised many of his dreams on those long walks. I used to look and observe and think and even talk to myself. I used to enjoy being on my own. Or did I just enjoy not being in the places where I would have been otherwise?

The secondary school that I won the scholarship to attend was an English Public School that was founded in 1552 in Birmingham by King Edward VI. It had the most hysterical school song that included such phrases as "here's no place for fop or idler", "never mind the cheers or hooting, keep your head and play the game" and "never stop to rub the shin". I was never really happy there. Maybe it was part of being different, of not liking sport and as a result of that, never being valued by the mainstream of other boys.

My parents operated from a mixed dogma of Victorian conservatism and overprotection. Together with the disallowed pet and bicycle, I was not even allowed to have the smallpox vaccination that all the other children had. My parents asked for an exemption on the basis that I would never go anywhere that I might get smallpox. Of course I did, and that meant that I had to have the vaccination as an adult, which has far more side effects and is in fact much more risky. When the cousin of the daughters who lived next door, and who lived in the next street, caught polio, my parents were very concerned and made sure that there was no contact whatsoever with the neighbours in case my sister and I caught it.

Most children of my age went to the kids' cinema on Saturday mornings. When I heard about it, I was intrigued and wondered what it would be like. It seemed to me that it was somewhat decadent and not the sort of thing decent parents would allow their children to do. In fact the first film I ever saw was when I was about 13 or 14. It was the Glen Miller story, and he died of course at the end of the movie, in a plane crash. It was a premature and sad death and I did not enjoy the film at all. It took a very long time for me to develop an appetite for films after that. Only later at university did I start to go the cinema, but even then not often.

My escape from my life was to be vicariously involved in the lives of others through reading. When I was just nine or ten I used to read about children who went to live in other European countries and attended school there. In my teens I read every one of the *Fortnight in ...* series. I became an expert in every place from Madeira to Finland. I started to long for somewhere else to be.

As a young adolescent I did of course have sexual fantasies. They should have told me something at the age of 14, but it took a little longer for the penny to drop. I had a small notebook with a metal spiral binder. In the notebook I had practised my rather doubtful artistic talents by drawing male genitalia from all sorts of angles and in a variety of states of excitement – big dicks, smaller dicks, large heads and bulging balls. I considered this book as private and was horrified when my father confronted me with it, having taken it from my bedroom without my knowledge. It is still a mystery to me as to what on earth my parents were doing rummaging around in my bedroom, for this gem was hardly left in an obvious location. The indignation I felt about the invasion of my privacy was short-lived, as I was suddenly facing a far more serious situation. On a Wednesday afternoon, my father's half-day at the pharmacy, I was bundled into the back of the car, my mother in the front seat, in order to confront the headmaster with my handywork. It is still not clear to me what my father thought this would achieve, but my mother managed to persuade him to relent when we were about halfway there and turn back home. I have no recollection of what happened after we got home. But I remember everything before that vividly.

The subject would not arise again with my father for another 14 years. But my relationship with him, virtually non-existent in any case, was never to recover.

Meanwhile I continued to be totally absorbed by thoughts of travel. I remember at the age of 17 going with my parents by car to Switzerland. A picnic for me had up until then meant cowering in the lee of the car while a howling gale blew on a country road, rugged up and eating tomato and cucumber sandwiches and drinking milky instant coffee out of a thermos flask. A new world was revealed to me seeing a Swiss family sit down for a picnic at a table with a neat red and white checked table cloth, on top of which was a feast of garlic chicken, salami, lavish salads, a variety of cheeses, fresh crusty bread and a bottle of wine. I realised I had been born in the wrong country.

Almost despite the experiences of my youth, I would eventually grow up to experience myself the travel I read about and so longed for. I would hold interesting jobs, feel accomplished, satisfied at times, and I would experience many of the emotions of the human condition. But I would never have simple, unconditional, uninhibited fun. I never did and probably never will. There was always a brake to be applied to fun and spontaneity, a need to retain control. This need to be in control has been a dominant factor in the rest of my life. As I look back, there have been some aspects of my childhood that I have been able to throw off and overcome. But I also believe that the influences of one's early life are so great that it is not easy to discard them all and consign them to the garbage bin.

In many ways I should not be so ungracious. I never went hungry, I was well clothed. My father only laid hands on me a few times; I mean this literally as opposed to slapping me for misbehaving. He once accused me, probably quite justifiably, of answering my mother back. I was sitting on a dining chair in front of an easy chair with wooden arms. He put his hands around my neck and ordered me to apologise. His force pushed the chair back so that it leant on the arm of the easy chair behind it. He had strong hands from all the work he did on our old car. I felt them tight around my neck and I was frightened. I thought he might actually throttle me so I apologised, but I never forget.

I also recollect a time at the beach house in Pevensey Bay, when I was only 9 or 10 years old. At the end of lunch during the less pleasant period when my father was with us, I was angling for some more of some delicacy that had been served for lunch. I said I was hungry and would like some more of whatever it was I wanted, I frankly can't remember. My father told me that if I was hungry I could eat dry bread. I protested that this is not what I wanted. At that point my father grabbed me, made me sit in his iron grip on his knee and told me I would be there until I had eaten the dry bread, since I had claimed to be hungry. I thought I would be clever and threw it on the ground; we were sitting out in the garden. I figured that would get me off the hook. But no, he picked up the dry bread and forced me to eat it with all the grit and dirt from the garden still on it. Sometimes he was frightening and, I felt, even cruel.

I struggled during those teenage years with my feelings of being different and not fitting into the school environment. I used to hang out with other boys who were also marginalised for some reason or other, for example, for being nerdy or bad at sports. Later I befriended Australians, Jews, Mauritians, Iraqis – anyone who seemed more or less normal yet like me was "not quite in the mainstream", someone who hinted at another life. I was alone, isolated and frightened, and tending towards feelings of inferiority and hypochondria, a legacy that I have never managed to entirely shake.

This manifested itself in my teenage years through phobias of various sorts. I was terrified that I was dying from cancer or that I would catch some dreadful disease from unclean people. This often bowel gripping fear virtually ruled my life from my early teens into my mid twenties and beyond. It was debilitating. One day when I was about 14 years old, travelling on a rattling train from Eastbourne to London, I found I was not able to relax enough to pee. That fear has been with me ever since, but has transferred to aircraft. Even 40 years later I still find it a challenge sometimes to pee on an aircraft. The problem became generalised and for several years I found it difficult to pee if there was anyone else around. I had to stop having school lunch so that I could use the toilets while the others were in the dining room.

This was all conducted in terrible loneliness. My mother was the only person who had any idea of these plagues in my head, and she was powerless to do anything about it. She was my only confidante, the place where I went when I needed help, for I knew my father would not countenance such nonsense. My closeness to my mother was such that my father had always been able to use it against me. Even when I was younger, as a punishment I was not allowed to see her. Once when he banned me from seeing her, I was so bereft that I kicked in the panels under the banister railing along the landing outside my bedroom. I was frightened and I wanted to see my mother, but he still would not let me.

I now recognise that my fears were symptoms of depression. Teenage depression was of course not known in those days, but it has more recently been recognised and documented, and perhaps more importantly, subjected to treatment. The problems I experienced eventually led to my being nervous and lacking in confidence, and I started to perform less well at school. I did worse in university entrance exams than I could or should have, and while my friends were being accepted to Oxford and Cambridge, I was rejected by the only university where I had the emotional security of home as a base, Birmingham. The confidence to go to another university away from home was beyond me at the time, although it is of course now quite clear that is exactly what I needed. I learned later that the headmaster of my school, affectedly called the Chief Master, had written on my application that I was unsuitable for a university education. He had never met me, never even spoken to me, but had the power to sign me into oblivion with the stroke of a pen. Such was the greatness of the English Public School system – over 400 years of history and experience. I have resented the "establishment" ever since.

In the end I obtained an external BSc (Hons) in chemistry from London University, which compared to most of my friends was a disgrace. It would not be for another 15 years, when I was earning distinctions and high distinctions eventually coming top at the University of Sydney in second-year psychology, that I began to believe that I was not so stupid after all.

It was during the university holidays that I finally managed to do some real travelling. Armed with a three-foot high ex–US army tent and a mate, I set off in my Mini Minor to Turkey and Greece in 1964, Morocco and Algeria in 1965, and in 1966 to every Eastern bloc country including the Soviet Union. The invisible shackles were beginning to loosen.

During one of the practical chemistry sessions at university I remember trying to win the attention of a fellow student by saying, "Eeyah!" in the unattractive local vernacular. He laughed at me, and I vowed that it was time for a makeover. A new person, a new place and a new accent.

It was in Tangier that I learned in a telegram that I had passed my BSc with honours, far better than I ever expected. After a short while I was working in London, my offices based first in Mayfair and then in Knightsbridge, requiring me to travel all over the world. I rented a flat in a fashionable part of London, I drove an MGB, and I was still barely more than 22 years old.

The nervous adolescent had staggered hesitatingly into adulthood, his horizons finally beginning to broaden.

ooOOoo

How strange this world of dreams. It is my world and then yet again it is not. There are times when I can see that it is me, and then times when it is someone like me acting in a different and strange world. There are people I know and can identify. Then there are also people I have never seen in my life. Who are these people? Do they exist, or have I myself created them, as would a god or a writer? Or have I met them before, but just cannot remember? Are they real people who do not live in the conventional, general-consensus world, or are they people I knew in some other existence? Who knows? Maybe they have no physical existence, maybe they exist only as stirrings of a neuronal pulse in my brain. And who is to say that my whole world is not as such?

And why do I stand there in my school uniform, wearing a school cap, years after I should have abandoned it? Many times I relived the anxiety of the impending exam, only to find that it was already over – 20 years before.

Chapter 2 London in the sixties and seventies

Being in London I began to feel happy, but the job did not come immediately. Before I left on the trip to North Africa in July 1965 I had not lined up a job. This was partly because I wanted to wait for my university results and partly due to simple procrastination, which is not an affliction that I commonly suffer. When I returned to England in September, tanned a deep brown and full of stories of the bazaars of Fez, Meknes and Marrakech, I had to look for a job. I knew only that I wanted to work in export.

In those days jobs were not hard for graduates to find, but I was looking for something specific. Most graduates were already placed; I had left it rather late. I chose, somewhat reluctantly, the Tube Investments Graduate Program. They had an export division for their manufacture of metal tubes and I had my eyes on getting into that division once the three-month general training program was over. I joined late, several weeks after the other graduates on the scheme. It was not one of the happiest periods of my life. Part of the training program was about becoming familiar with metal. This included working on lathes and other foul machines, the names of which my memory has mercifully obliterated. There were on-site visits to noisy factories with massive tubes rolling out of ovens, spewing toxic gases from their ends. The Tube Investments empire was enormous and included all sorts of factories. Some factories I found close to Dickensian, their enormous wheels and belts looking like something out of a history of technology museum, and I was shocked at the conditions under which people worked. When I was advised that the competition to get into export was intense and that I was not to be offered a place, I was angry. I was offered, and virtually had to accept, a domestic sales position with Raleigh Cycles in Nottingham with the vaguest of hopes that from there I might eventually get into their export department.

I found lodgings in Nottingham with another graduate in the house of a pleasant but fussy widow. The arrangement was for full board, and after enduring the torture of the induction program during the day, I then had to suffer typically English overcooked food, accompanied by a cup of milky tea.

Fortunately about this time an advertisement appeared in the newspaper for an export representative for a fine chemicals company at their offices in London. I applied, had just one interview and was offered the job. Who knows what would have become of me if this opportunity had not occurred. Not only was I the last to join the Tube Investments Graduate

Program, but I was also the first to leave. I had been there less than three months, more than enough.

I was a little surprised that the fine chemicals company would employ someone of my age (I was 21 at the time), and have enough trust in me as to provide me with airline tickets and travellers cheques (there were no credit cards in those days) and send me off into the wide, wide world. It is true that there was a training period, much of which entailed my working as the Technical Coordinator answering all sorts of queries from all over the world. Maybe they took a risk, but it worked to our mutual satisfaction.

I progressed well, gained a good reputation quickly and was only limited by the fact that despite some time at the technical centre in Loughborough in Leicestershire, I really knew very little about the technical application of the products I was selling such as azodicarbonamide and methyl methacrylate.

This did not turn out to be a major disadvantage in that there was a whole technical department to responsible for that , and my forté turned out to be languages, situational analysis and developing relationships with our distributors all over the world. I had always had an interest in languages, but my parents had discouraged it, pointing to the certain fact that linguists never make as much money as scientists do. I just seemed to have a facility for languages. I have never ventured into non-European languages, although I would be interested in learning Japanese, but I do speak three European languages completely fluently and get by well enough in another three.

My territories started modestly with Switzerland, Scandinavia, Spain and Portugal. Soon added were France, Italy, Eastern Europe, Benelux, the USA, Canada, South America and the Middle East. In those days when travel was not anywhere near as accessible as it is now, it was quite chic when I was invited to a party on a Saturday night to have to decline on the basis that I had "to be up early for a Chicago flight the next day".

By the time I hung up my passport for a while in 1975 when I stopped working in export, I had been sent, all expenses paid, to 65 countries on every continent. I loved my job, especially the travel. While many of my colleagues when travelling would frequent nightclubs and bars, for the most part I spent my evenings walking. I would have dinner and then set out to discover the cities where I was staying. Rarely did I have dinner appointments and so most evenings were my own. I walked and walked, through old quarters, along river banks through city centres that had been abandoned by their daytime inhabitants. Milan, Moscow, Madrid, Mexico, Malmo, I knew them all.

As a result my expenses were very low compared to those of my colleagues. My first boss took me aside after my first trip and told me in no certain terms that to put in low expenses was unacceptable as it set a precedent that the rest of the team would not be prepared to live with. I invested the extra money I saved by establishing a modest but international wardrobe, and by setting up a bank account in Switzerland so that I could circumvent the personal foreign currency limit of 50 pounds per person per year that existed in the UK for several years during that period.

I was at my happiest heading down the M4 on the airport bus towards Heathrow and horizons beyond. I never became bored with or tired of the travel. I tried to make sure that I spent weekends away in places that I either had not visited previously or that I really liked.

I was just as much at home relaxing on the beach at Copacabana, having coffee on Hamra in Beirut, listening to polkas and watching the prostitutes in hotel bars in Warsaw, being lashed with laurel leaves by an ex–pop star in a sauna in Helsinki or falling down ski slopes in France, Sweden and Norway.

But my home base was London in the days of Carnaby Street, one of the richer belles époques of that city. Sharing a flat was one quick avenue into a social life, helpful given I was away for almost half of the year. I lived on the north side. The first place I had was at the back of Oxford Street over the road from Selfridges. The flat I enjoyed most was in Hamilton Terrace in St John's Wood, a wide avenue of Victorian houses; we rented the top floor of such a house, two friends from Birmingham and I.

But there was of course still Birmingham. My sister had married a wonderful guy called Doug a few years earlier, and by then they had two sons. In 1966 they emigrated to California because the silicon chip industry there, which was Doug's specialisation, offered far more opportunities than in England. During the same year my mother had fallen ill, lost an enormous amount of weight and finally was operated on for what my father told us was an ulcer.

In 1969 I went on a long business trip to South America and managed a day or so in Senegal on the way there, and took holidays in the Caribbean, California and New York on the way back. I was away for three months. On my return I noticed a sharp deterioration in my mother's health and confronted my father.

He told me that my mother in fact had cancer of the stomach, but that he had decided that she should not be told. He feared it was coming back again. My sister and her family had decided after three years in California to return to England, and I was sworn by my father not to tell them about my mother's condition until they were settled, not to tell anyone else in the family at all, and certainly to never mention it to my mother. This was very hard on everyone concerned but my father seriously thought that he was doing the right thing. When my mother died in February 1971 the rest of the family was furious that they had not been told how ill she was, although surely they must have worked it out. The hardest part was that my mother had to die playing this game of secrecy, although visits to oncology departments must have made it clear to her she had terminal cancer. We were all condemned to silence, and I was too young to know that I should have defied my father and not let my mother die so mentally and emotionally alone.

During the last few months of 1969 and in 1970 visits to Birmingham were painful, but I drove up the M1 often on weekends when I was in the country. I held my breath for what I was going to see, the deterioration, the hopelessness, all suffered in silence. A bit more weight lost, less ability to keep down a meal. Again leaving the country was always my best escape. It still is.

And then after a week in Brussels in the grip of ice early in 1971, I called their number from Heathrow when I arrived, as I always did, and Doug, my brother-in-law, answered the phone. I knew immediately that if he was there something had happened, and I feared that the end was close.

My father somehow had failed to take in what was happening. He was apparently shocked when on the day before she died she did not recognise him. It seems as if that was the first moment that reality finally sank in. He had been telling us during the previous months that she had been doing well, but as that was not my observation I had called her doctor directly and he had confirmed that this was not the case. The slight weight gain was simply due to an increase in the size of the tumour.

I shared her last moments with her; just my sister and I were in the house at home where she died on a cold February morning. My father had had to go out on an errand for a short time. And while he was out, while Jean sat with her, she stopped breathing. I was of course not shocked or surprised by her death, I was just empty. I walked through silent frozen parks after we had lodged the necessary papers in the right offices. It seemed so normal to deal with all that, it was mundane and could not be reconciled with the enormity of what had happened. The funeral took place, but I can remember nothing of it.

When it was over I went straight back to London that very afternoon, knowing that with her passing a part of me had gone for ever. Since then there has never for me been a real sense of family. My mother held our family together, and without her it fractured. I tried to do what I could to ease my father's pain by telephone calls and weekend visits. This fell to me completely when after a few months my sister and her family returned to live again in the USA, where they have remained to this day (divorced now, of course!). Never having enjoyed the friendship of other men, my father was very isolated, lonely and extremely sad. It was not easy for me to bring much comfort since there was so little my father and I had in common, and so much history that could be forgiven but not quite forgotten. There were things that would divide us even more of which he was still at that time blissfully unaware. But despite our differences, I always tried to keep close, more perhaps because I know that is what my mother would have wanted me to do than for any other reason.

My mother's death was the very thing that unlinked me from England. She was a wonderfully kind and gentle person, and I say that in the full knowledge that many boys think the same of their mothers, but in this case there are many who are more objective than me and who would agree with my assessment.

I was really on my own now. Well perhaps not quite, but the door of the cage had been wrenched off, and I was able to float on the wing, ready to migrate.

ooOoo

I rewrite history. Or do I? My mother died in 1971, on 17 February. Even after neatly 40 years in my dreams she lives. But she is never really available to me. She is often in a house. I know where it is, it may even be our house. But I do not call her and I do not visit her, and to my sadness, she does not try to contact me. Sometimes I pass by and I know she is there, but I never go in.

Chapter 3 Facing the truth

While the place of family in my life changed abruptly with the death of my mother, what I have come to feel are my real family, where I really belong, had started to emerge years earlier. The origins of that process were really only clear to me in hindsight.

It was warm and comfortable in the tea shop, with a pleasant background buzz of conversation. One of the advantages of being a student is that even in the middle of the afternoon on a weekday, there were breaks in the lecture schedule that enabled us to enter the lives of shoppers and other townsfolk, just living their lives. It was quite dark at our table, towards the back of the café. I savoured the piping hot Russian tea, sweet and full of lemon. It was cold outside and we were still dressed in our winter coats. I was glad to be sitting next to Mahmad, my friend from Mauritius. We passed the time chatting away; then, as the conversation turned towards sex, I started to feel a little uncomfortable. I had never really let it enter my conscious mind that I was very sexually attracted to him. But I knew it at some subliminal level. Suddenly Mahmad ventured the opinion that what he understood by "queer" was someone who never had sex at all. This he found worse than a man who had sex with another man.

I felt a surge of redness creep up into my face despite all my endeavours to prevent it. I was burning with embarrassment and hoping to hell that nobody would notice in the darkness of the café.

For a while I had been somewhat uneasy realising that my feelings for Mahmad were not quite "right". I ached to be with him, close to him. How, I cannot remember, but I had one day managed to comb his hair for him, and felt an immediate surge of blood, this time not to my face! It occurred to me that this was strange, but the feeling was too compelling, too wonderful, to not embrace it. The fact was that I was totally infatuated with him. He never knew, of course.

There had been throughout my teens many signs that I was different. These had worried me at some level, but I had never acted on them. I had always been very shy with girls, I never felt comfortable going out with a girl. I felt that something was expected of me that I was either unwilling or incapable of providing. When I was 18 years old and had been out with a few girls, sex had only gone as far as open-mouth kissing. I had never enjoyed it and certainly avoided taking sex any further. At the same time I was dismayed by the fact that all my friends were talking about their sexual exploits and I seemed to have been left out. On the one hand I wanted to be a sexual being, yet I did not want to have sex with any of the girls I knew.

One of them was Barbara, a friend of my cousin, whom I had invited to some event where I needed a partner. We started to go out and I really enjoyed her company. Her mother had died and her father was convinced that we were having a raging affair. She laughingly recognised that I was terrified of such a happening. She was, of course right, but she did not realise that it was her brother that I was attracted to.

Another was Anna, the stunningly attractive daughter of Jewish communists politically involved with Bulgaria. I met her soon after leaving university, just after I took the export job with the chemicals company in London. She had been working as a part-time filing clerk in my office. I found her interesting and exotic, and invited her out, as it seemed to me to be the thing to do. My standing in the office soared, as all my male colleagues salivated over her extraordinary beauty and her voluptuousness. She had the most perfect breasts and I was the envy of others who incorrectly imagined that I was intimately involved with them.

But my heart was really not in it. I know that she would have gone to bed with me if I had asked. And no doubt that was the very reason that I never did ask. Indeed I was the one who terminated the relationship. I felt guilty that Anna never understood the reasons for the rejection. That rejection would have hurt her, and she deserved to be reassured that it was not a problem with her, but a problem with me. But I did not even really completely understand that myself at the time.

It would be several months later that the truth would force itself into my reality and no longer be ignored and denied. I went to Switzerland on business. It was winter. Our agents in Switzerland had their head office in Basel, and so that is where such visits always started. I had flown into Basel on the Sunday afternoon, and went out for a meal in the evening.

As I approached a crossing, and waited at the red light, I became aware of a young man looking at me. This was more than just a casual glance that one accords fellow pedestrians as one waits for a red light to change. It was an intense look, directed with intent and enquiry. He was extremely good-looking, with black hair, high cheekbones and piercing blue eyes. He was wearing a light beige raincoat, tied tightly at the waist. My guess is that he would have been perhaps Slavic rather than Swiss. My heart skipped. The light turned green and we both crossed the road. I walked down the hill to the right and noticed that he was following at a discrete distance.

I was both excited and terrified. I stopped and looked in a few shop windows. He stopped and looked as well. I wanted him, but in the end terror overtook desire. I went into a restaurant, to escape, but more than half hoped that he would follow. He did not. I ate quickly and without appetite and then set about scouring the streets to see if I could find him again. This time desire had the upper hand. But sadly he was nowhere to be found. I had missed my opportunity.

About a month later I was in Copenhagen, and decided that the time had come to revisit this problem. I went into one of the many porn shops and looked through the wide range of pictures and magazines. There was absolutely no doubt now. It was the gay porn and that alone that interested and excited me. I found a guidebook with the address of a gay coffee shop in Gothenburg in Sweden, my next stop and to where I was leaving the next day.

Spring by this time was edging towards us, and the nights were getting lighter. From my habitual walking in the cities where I stayed on business, I knew Gothenburg quite well. The coffee shop I was interested in was quite a way away, maybe 45 minutes walk. When I got there I found that fear again was playing its card and I could not summon the courage to go in. But on the Friday night I was returning from a late evening walk, and shortly before the hotel where I used to stay, the Rubinen, I passed through a tiny park on Kungsgatan. Sitting on one of the park benches was a young man smoking who observed me as I walked past. I turned and saw that he was still looking at me. I took a couple of steps back and sat on another bench facing him across the path, and took out a cigarette. I pretended not to be able to find a light. In an instant he was there with a light and a smile. Once having established that I did not speak Swedish, he said, "I am Sven. Do you have somewhere to go?" I told him I was staying just up the same street at the Rubinen Hotel. We left together in that direction.

At last I understood what sex was about. It was the wildest discovery I had ever made and I just revelled in him, the touch of him, the smell of him. I kissed him furiously, deeply and completely. And then passion completely overtook me. I devoured his sex, and he mine until we both came. For the first time in my life I knew what everyone was talking about.

Afterwards I suddenly felt dirty and that what I had done was wrong. The Hotel Rubinen was a sound Swedish functional hotel. The rooms were modern, spotlessly clean and rather small. On the top floor there was a bar, and I invited Sven up for a drink. I learned that he was in the catering department on board a merchant ship that was in dock in Gothenburg for a couple of days. We chatted in the bar for a short while and the feelings of distaste at myself dissipated as I let my eyes move over him. They quickly turned again to lust, and he hardly had time to finish his drink before I had dragged him down to my room again. We repeated the experience, which was just as wonderful for me the second time as the first.

There was only a single bed in the functional Rubinen, and in any case Sven had to be back on board, and he left. In the morning I looked in the mirror and saw what I already had felt. My face was raw with the abrasion of his beard. I had kissed him in passion with such power that his heavy stubble had torn at the skin on my chin. I felt horror that I could have stooped so low, that I could have indulged in something so awful. However wonderful it had been, and I acknowledged that it had been exceptionally wonderful, I vowed I would never have sex with a man ever again, it was wrong. A vow that I never kept.

It was Saturday and I got up and had breakfast and then went for a quiet stroll through the city. Almost unconsciously I found myself walking towards the gates of the port. By lunchtime I wanted Sven again so badly that I had quite forgotten my vow of a couple of hours earlier. I did not know which ship he was on, and in any case I could not clamber on board. I was not even permitted to wander freely around the port. I realised with the first pain of lost love, or at least sex, that I would never see Sven again. But clearly the time spent with him had changed my life for ever. And he would never know the role he had played in that.

After that experience my life had a totally different point to it. I wanted to make up for lost time, and I did. I went out for a while with a Chilean in London. I cruised Kings Road in my MGB with the roof off, examining the sweep of the wrap around mirror I had fitted especially. My overseas visits now had a different goal for the after-dinner stroll. I was on the prowl. I was young, I had a hotel room to go to, and I had a lot of sex. Only occasionally did I go to bars, but often I would pick up guys out walking, at the beach, wherever. I enjoyed it all, fucking and being fucked, and had a particular talent for and pleasure in taking large cocks deep into my throat and working until the guy could hold off no longer. I never had an English boyfriend as such, although there were a few English guys I had sex with, but mostly they were not English, even in London itself. Particularly memorable was an Italian waiter I used to visit in his flat behind Harrods, after a long day in the office and before he went out to work. He used to turn me on so much that I hit the wall behind his bed when I came.

The fact is that most gay men do have a lot of sex; this is borne out by studies that suggest that they have more sex than any other group of people. This is likely rooted in the immediacy of male sexuality when in a male–male context. Just like most gay men, many of my sexual contacts have been anonymous and often in public places such as parks, beaches, public toilets, cinemas, even once in a cemetery. I have never been good looking enough to wait for someone to pick me up, and so have tended to be the hunter, the one that makes the first move. Nobody likes rejection, and somehow I always found it more satisfactory to go to a beat (a place where gay men go to meet each other), such as a park, fairly late at night, where the people there are there for one purpose only, rather than spend a whole evening and a lot of money in a bar or club while guys eye each other waiting for someone younger and better looking to turn up.

To some that endeavour may seem sordid. Following a man into a public toilet and fucking there, or joining a man in a cubicle in a toilet on the other side of the world and letting him fuck me through a hole in the arse of my pants, might seem depraved. But it is simply giving expression to the drive for sex without inhibition or reservation. Gays have always had to dismantle the mores that society, and especially religion, have tried to shackle them with, because their very essence is outside of society's mores. You either reframe your own values, deny your sexual being, or live a life of terrible guilt. There are many who never quite manage it, and through guilt suffer incredible problems of low self-esteem, often leading to mental illness and sometimes psychosis. I am not one of them. I make no apology for liking sex, having sex, and not feeling the least bit guilty about it. It is perhaps just surprising given the environment in which I grew up.

Monogamy in gay relationships is relatively rare, and I suspect it might not be that common in straight relationships either. If it were left to men, whether they be straight or gay, I suspect they would all be sexual opportunists. In the life of a gay man it is of course left only to men, and that is why there is as much gay sex happening as there is. That is not to say that the relationships between gay men are not committed, or are in any way more frivolous or of less value than straight relationships. But they are generally different as far as monogamy is concerned. I know many couples who have been together for more than 25 years, and some close to 40 years! Their relationships are as secure, as loving and as committed as any heterosexual relationship. It is simply that a sexual act for most men, at least in my experience and that of the many gay friends with whom I have discussed the subject, can be separated from love and from personal, mental and social commitment. Monogamy is not necessary for devotion, and while it tends to be seen as making people feel more secure in a relationship, it is not a guarantee of that security.

For some of these reasons I do not agree with the fight for marriage between same-sex partners to be recognised by the state. Marriage implies a relationship that I feel is not the same as the one that same-sex couples have. It tends to place constraints and expectations on them that are inappropriate in a same-sex context. I am not even sure it makes sense any longer for heterosexuals either! On the other hand committed same-sex partners should have accorded to them all the legal, tax and other rights that heterosexuals enjoy. Inheritance, superannuation, medical insurance and government medical schemes should all be consistent between gay and straight couples. Furthermore the argument that the interests of a child may be best served by being brought up by a competent male and female parenting partnership, should not negate the right of same sex couples to have or adopt children. If such an arrangement be called same-sex unions, that is fine, as long as these relationships are formally recognised.

When I have really been infatuated with a guy, I have tended to want to only have sex with him, at least for a while! But infatuation should not be confused with love. And so what do I want from a lover? I need to know that I am the only one he wants literally at the end of the day. For, maybe because of my own insecurities, I have always had the unpleasant tendency to want to possess my lovers, for them to be mine. I have found threesomes to be quite a workable way of accommodating my need for both variety and security. But insensitivity to the needs of one's partner can also create tensions in three way sex. Threesomes are often not equilateral triangles.

Part of the excitement of sex for me is in the hunt, and I always have been aware of a raised heartbeat and awareness in anticipation of what might be whenever I am on the prowl. But for me the hunt without a catch would be an awful frustration. And while raw sex is great, I am at my happiest when I can make love to a man, caress and kiss him, nibble his ear, nuzzle his nape, gently play with his nipples, lick his chest and stomach, and gradually make my way lower until passion takes over completely. After, I like to gently kiss his brow, hold him in my arms, to keep him safe and secure from all the evil in the world, and fall asleep to the slowing of his breathing that tells me he has already succumbed to his dreams. I want to give a man pleasure. I want to give him all of myself. Intimacy and affection was not as far as I can remember a big part of my upbringing, yet strangely for me it is a driving force in my adult life. An enormous part of my life has been about the tireless search for all this.

When my mother died at home on that February morning, on his return a short time later and at my mother's side my father told me that he wanted to express my mother's dying wish that I would get married and have children, as they both thought it was the only way I would ever be happy. At that time I had already been living for two years with João, my Portuguese lover. My parents of course knew him and liked him, but they apparently did not know we were lovers. I just did not know what to say to my father and so I said nothing.

I had met João just before I left for South America in 1969. When I got back he was sick in hospital with hepatitis. We went away together in November in the MGB all around Central Europe and to Venice and the South of France. We had a good time, but when we got back to England he wanted us to live together. I was reluctant to do so, but in the end it was so difficult to find a flat to share with others that I relented and we moved in together into a flat near Earls Court.

João was a very handsome man, with a stupendous body, all the more surprising since he never did any sport or exercise to maintain it. He was slightly shorter than me, had a hairy chest, was well proportioned with a slim waist, narrow hips and a very nicely shaped arse. His dick, without being enormous, was more than acceptable. I enjoyed having sex with him. He was kind and sociable, but there were so many parts of my life, the life in my head, that he could not share. I was very fond of him, but I never loved him, and that caused hurt to him in the long run. I had not been out for long when I met him, and I did not want a commitment with one man, and I know that he was more ready to settle down than I was. But I was young and randy, I had missed out by starting late, and I wanted to play the field.

His family came from a small community north of Lisbon. They were viticulturists and owned a 600-year old farm that produced an excellent red wine, which was sold through the local cooperative. This gentle, very good-looking young man, who in London was rather submissive and passive, became the elder son at home, expecting his mother and sisters to run around after him all day. They did, too.

I remember sitting in the main room of the house, which was a massive dining room with little seats built into each window that overlooked the valley to a village called Matacães ("mad dogs"). Downstairs was the powerhouse of the house, the kitchen. The men rarely ventured in, but one afternoon we went there when João's mother held a snail party for the women of the village, the focus of which was an enormous bowl of small cooked snails, which they merrily attacked with small pins. They were tasty but far too fiddly to spend an afternoon at it.

João had many good connections in Portugal. One day we were invited to a house at the coast in Porto Novo that had been rented for the summer. There was a bracing romp in the cold surf of the Atlantic as an appetiser, followed by a lavish lunch of what looked to me like a whole fish market tipped on the long trestle table around which sat 20 or more lawyers, doctors and others of the wealthy classes. At the end of the meal half a dozen of the cutest kittens were produced, and they danced over the debris picking for themselves some of the morsels that were left.

Another family had made all their money in Angola, not unusual in those days. They had the good taste to convert it into wonderful antiques and their home was like a museum. The collection was so valuable that a cleaner was considered too risky, so that the wife, to her constant complaining, had to dust and clean. They used to rent a summer house in Ericeira, and we would often go and spend the day at the beach with them. Their son Carlos once came and stayed with us at our flat in London. We were a little taken aback when he told us that he had been to Soho, and by mistake went into the wrong cinema. The film was about two men and two women who walked down a road together and then the men went into one building and the women in another. The men started having sex with each other, and so did the women. Carlos confided that he thought that people like that should be put to death. A few years later I heard that he married a woman not to his father's liking as a result of which the father cut him off from his considerable inheritance and vowed never to speak to him again.

My favourite was João's younger sister, São, who was kind, warm, gentle and very patient. Her beau was in the army as a career soldier fighting the insurgencies in Africa. She was terrified of losing him to war. She waited for him throughout the years of those wars, and in the end they married. I only once met her again, in London when they came to see João in hospital, some 16 years later

My friends were far more accepting of my homosexuality than I might have feared. I should have known them better. The flat near Earl's Court where João and I lived when we returned from the trip at the end of 1969 was right on the Great West Road. It was terribly noisy and not in an area that we particularly liked, but as the rental market was still fairly tight we put up with it. Fred, a close friend from my school days in Birmingham with whom I had previously shared the flat in Hamilton Terrace, had, in the meantime, married, gone to live in New York, divorced and returned again to London. He wanted to share a flat with me again, pointing out that I had only known João a short while and so why did I feel more allegiance to staying with him than moving in with Fred? I explained that it was not just a flatmate arrangement but that we were lovers. He hesitated only a few seconds before suggesting that we needed then to look for a flat with a double room for me and João, and a single room for him.

That is exactly what we did, and we found a superb flat in Kensington Court, right behind Kensington High Street in one of the trendiest and most pleasant parts of London. The flat was on the top floor of a Victorian building served by a cranky old cage lift. Our phone number was part of the 'WEStern' exchange, and that was about as fashionable as you could get! By this time, to my great sadness, under pressure from the operating divisions of the fine chemicals company I worked for, the export office for the whole corporation in London had been closed and the export functions returned to each manufacturing division. If I had wanted to retain my job, I would have had to relocate to Loughborough. I was far too committed to my life in London and so left, and then joined the export department of another chemicals company, this one based in Knightsbridge almost opposite Harrods.

I used to walk to work though Kensington Gardens and Hyde Park, and often used to walk home stopping at the toilets at South Kensington tube station on the way. That sometimes led to delays and some frivolous but enjoyable sexual encounters.

After a couple of years Fred was moved by his company to Amsterdam, and I decided it was time to buy my own place. It would have been nice to stay in Kensington, but that was way outside my price range, and I bought a very pleasant ground-floor flat in Highgate in North London. João and I moved in not long after my mother died. I suffered another change in jobs for almost the same reason as previously. The office in Knightsbridge was to be closed and my job was to move to the very part of the country near Birmingham that I had striven so hard to get away from. Again I left the company.

This time I had to change industries, and ended up working for a small company in the graphic arts equipment field. It was my job to develop the export business. It was not ideally what I wanted, but I had a mortgage and bills to pay, and at least I was going to visit some new and interesting countries.

ooOoo

It is not surprising given my work that so many of my dreams are about flying. But not all of them are. There is one old often-repeated dream where I am driving a car. There is a labyrinth of highways and I find it hard to find the right one. Sometimes they soar high into the air, passing over lower levels. I find it scary to drive along those highways and it happens that I take the wrong lane and end up having to cross over a high bridge, turn around and come all the way back again. High up in the air I feel vertigo, and am relieved when the highway descends and joins the other lanes at the lower levels.

Not recently, but a few years ago, I used to try to find my way from London to somewhere, possibly the town where I was born. In fact in the waking world I used to drive that route often, and even now I can rehearse it in my mind's eye faultlessly. But in the dream I am not at all sure of my way, and the streets are unfamiliar. Then out in the country there are green fields, and traffic lights at crossroads where there seems to be no need for them. On-ramps come in from the side from nowhere in particular, and I press forward not really knowing whether I am on the right road.

More familiar in feeling yet not in memory is a part of London where I am with João. The pavements are very narrow as the buildings come nearly to the road itself. There is a pale light to the city, almost an Agfa sepia light. The streets are hot and dusty. We live together in a small and rather old flat. But it is not the one where we really lived.

Chapter 4 Women who wanted

Being gay does not mean that I do not have good relationships with women, on the contrary I do, but just not sexual ones. However, before I started having sexual relationships with men, I felt threatened by women, largely because I felt that I was not able to deliver what they expected of me. That is not to say that I have never been to bed with a woman. I have, but only one, when I was quite young, and it was not a very satisfactory arrangement. To start with she was playing games with me, trying to make the man she had been dating and the one she really wanted jealous. That was alright, because I was just experimenting too. I met her at a party in London, where we both arrived early. As the other guests arrived neither of us felt that we were having a good time and so I suggested going somewhere else. "Where?" she enquired. "How about my place?" I ventured. It was after all only about half past eight. "Fine". And so off we went. I made it clear once we reached my flat that I wanted sex, and she simply said, "If you go to bed with me now, I will never see you again". That was a risk that I was prepared to take and so I fucked her. I did in fact see her again several times, but after a very short while her strategy worked, and I was more interested in men anyway, and so we parted both having achieved what we wanted out of the venture.

Since then I have never wanted to go to bed with a woman again. There are some women I find incredibly beautiful, but I just am not sexually attracted to them. This has from time to time created some problems, especially where my work was involved; the times were such that having it known that I was gay was not a very good idea if I wanted to retain my job. That was the reality in the 1960s and 70s. In many countries it still is. Indeed in some countries such matters are still a matter of life and death, literally.

The first time a problem arose was in London. Working in the office with me was a young English girl married to a French guy. She handled all the administration for shipping overseas the products we sold. We knew each other quite well and had been on overseas trips together, especially for international fairs. She knew most of the customers from these events including a sleazy man from Beirut, who clearly was consumed by his desire for her. He once made up a little poem about her, running after her saying (her married name was David), "Ah, Madame David [pronounced Daveed], pour qui mon amour est tellement livide". This was delivered with the ponderous accent of a person whose mother language is Arabic, rendering a potentially romantic compliment into a lascivious, lecherous blasphemy.

Michelle was a discrete person and she knew that I was gay, but never let on to anyone else. Then a secretary was employed, Maree, a charming, gentle and very kind young mother returning to the workforce as her children reached school age. She was quietly spoken, efficient and while not a stunning beauty, a very attractive woman. She often had hinted that she would like to see the flat where I, unattached at the time, was living. A straight friend of mine lived there for a while, but he was often out with his girlfriend.

Eventually I relented and invited Maree and her husband Darren around for dinner one night. I had met Darren a couple of times when I had dropped Maree off after work as they lived in North London more or less on my way home. He was pleasant enough and not bad-looking, although very straight-acting and, I felt, a potential homophobe.

The evening they were invited I prepared dinner and was awaiting their arrival when the phone rang. It was Maree. Darren was not able to come and she had come by tube: could I please pick her up at the station? This came initially as a surprise, but I assumed that he had suddenly been taken ill. I was wrong. I am almost certain that he was never invited by Maree in the first place and that she had always intended coming on her own. Colin, my straight flatmate, was out, and as the evening progressed, Maree made it clear that she was more than ready to go to bed with me. In fact she was extremely keen to go to bed with me. I felt embarrassed, useless and unworthy as I circumvented her advances and poured freezing cold water on the passion that was engulfing the flat, at least from her side. I felt clumsy and even guilty that I could not respond to what was clearly an enormous compliment. I regretted that Colin had been out for the evening. I suggested taking her back to the tube station, and she could hardly do anything but accept.

The next morning at work, she looked awful, depressed, embarrassed too, and the air was tense. Michelle asked me later that day when we had a quiet moment what had happened. It seems that she had more or less guessed the basic facts of the evening. She told me that Maree was very depressed because she thought that there was something wrong with her, that she was just not attractive enough. Michelle told me that for Maree's sake I needed to tell her that I was gay.

I am really glad that I followed her advice. Maree and Darren's marriage was on the rocks. They did not have sex any longer and would have separated, except that they both agreed that for the sake of the children, who were seven and nine years old, they needed to stay together until such time as they felt that to separate would do them little harm. One might question whether the environment they created by their decision would be the right one in any case, but it was their decision and on the face of it a rather selfless one. Meanwhile Darren had said that he wanted to pursue sexual relationships outside their marriage and that he expected Maree to do the same. The fact that they were going to remain together for the children should not mean that they both should abandon their sex lives. Darren had managed to find his share, it seems, but Maree was far less confident and uncertain about how to embark on a sexual adventure outside marriage.

Maree had not had sex with anyone other than her husband for many years, in fact since their marriage some 10 years previously. In the meantime she had had two children, her husband had signalled that he did not want sex with her any longer, and she must have felt very insecure, not at all sure whether she was still a desirable woman, vulnerable and more than a little frightened.

In the routine of her daily life she did not have many opportunities to meet suitable candidates for an affair. In any case she would not have a relationship with a married man as she thought that it was not a moral thing to do. She finally thought that through her work she had found a single man, in a world separate from her other social circles, and that I would make an ideal person to rekindle her sex life.

Imagine then, after making the first move with trepidation, fear and a great sense of insecurity when her self-esteem had been badly shaken, what it must have felt like for her advances to be rejected. She questioned whether she was sexually desirable, she was depressed and very anxious. When I explained the situation to her she was exceptionally relieved. It was after all not at all due to her deficiencies as a sexual being, but rather that she had aimed at the wrong target. I tried to reassure her that indeed she was a very attractive woman, I could recognise that as an objective gay man, but gay man I was, and that was the limiting factor.

She respected the confidence with which I had entrusted her, and never divulged my secret. I have no idea whether she found another suitor.

***

The man who owned a company I worked for in London was close friends with the man who owned the company that represented us in the USA. That office was in New York, and that is where my visits to the USA for that company always started and finished. It was a family business of very conservative and stereotypical New York Jews. The daughter and son-in-law of the owner were involved in the business in the way that it is hard in these cases to differentiate between family and business. They were about my age, and I am sure that the owner felt that they would make far more companionable dinner partners for me than he would. The daughter had invited along a friend of hers to make up the four. Her friend had recently gone through a divorce and was, I was led to believe, somewhat "damaged" as a result.

I cannot remember the name of the restaurant where we went, but I do remember that the address was No 666, possibly Fifth Avenue, for that was emblazoned on the building, and it was expensive.

The girlfriend was a little shy and nervous, and not particularly interesting. So I was both surprised and dismayed when the daughter and her husband got up at the end of the meal and the daughter suddenly said, "We really must go as the babysitter cannot stay late and we have to get back to our apartment to our children. The check is taken care of, but you two love birds are more than welcome to stay here for as long as you like". They left.

We talked for a little while, and then the girlfriend told me that she lived only a few blocks walk away, but that she felt uncomfortable walking alone at night, and would I mind accompanying her to her apartment. I had no option, and the walk allowed me time to think through a strategy should I require one. After just 5 or 10 minutes we were in front of her apartment. She invited me up, hinting that she did not have to get up early the next morning. Again this was an invitation to perform in a play in which I was bound to fluff the lines.

I thanked her for her very kind invitation, but went on to explain with feigned embarrassment that there was a little problem. I told her that I was on a course of antibiotics to treat a dose of the clap that I had contracted on my previous overseas trip. That might have been true on some other occasions, but it certainly was not true at that time! I said how embarrassing it was to have to confide this to her, but that in honesty it was the right thing to do, and I hoped that she would understand.

I am certain that she would have told her friend, the owner's daughter, and it seemed to be so sad that in those days of 1970 there was more honour in having a dose of the clap than to be homosexual. Certainly when the message got back to the two owners, they would have undoubtedly felt that this was just the consequence of being a red-blooded male with a healthy appetite for women. They would welcome the news far more than they would have done to know that a homosexual was working in their midst. And the girl was able to save face and thank her lucky stars that I was enough of a gentleman to spare her the same fate as me, a load of embarrassment and a course of antiobiotics.

***

The former Yugoslavia was never an easy country to get around. I remember in 1964 driving the full length of the Autoput, the motorway that stretched almost the whole length of the country. It sounded impressive, but the reality was that it consisted of one lane in each direction of large concrete blocks, uneven enough to cause occupants of cars to nod every second for hours and even days as they drove at an appropriately modest speed, necessitated by the surface rather than any other limitation, from one end of the country to the other across the flat interior.

In subsequent years when travelling on business it was even more stressful. I once arrived in Split one evening (after flying from Tel Aviv to Rome and then Munich in an ever-decreasing circle), to start a grueling visit to our customers in almost all four corners of the country. Most of the week was taken up trying to get around. There was an overnight train to Ljubljana, a plane to Zagreb and then Belgrade, a hire car (which I had to drive) to Novi Sad, a bus to Skopje, and finally another overnight train to Belgrade. This was in the company of a bear-like man from our local agents who grunted away at my side, nudging me in the ribs to gain my attention, the length and breadth of Yugoslavia. I even had to share a bedroom with him once, and a wagon-lit twice. Had we only booked ahead of time, we could have done the whole trip by plane. One might argue that JAT internal flights were risky, but they generally arrived, even if not quite at the time predicted. Flights were in my book a better option than overnight trains, or even worse, buses.

A couple of years later we had changed local agents to another company, and I was to meet their representative, Mrs Madirazza, who normally lived in Zagreb, on Monday morning at her hotel in Belgrade where our visit was due to start. The previous week I had been trying to do some business in East Germany. I was not prepared to actually stay in the East, and so booked a hotel in the West and crossed over to the East every day, changing my nice hard deutschmarks into the required daily minimum of ostmarks, most of which had to be thrown away as there was nothing to spend them on. It was a particularly unsuccessful week, and I was later advised that there was no way I was going to make any progress as long as I was not staying in the East. Going back to the comfort of the West every night was not very well appreciated in the East. It suggested that I was not altogether serious about wanting to do business with them, and maybe faced with the options, they were right. On the other hand there were some great gay bars in West Berlin, and thanks to one of the guys working in one of the bars it was overall a good fun week for me. I felt at the end of it that that was what mattered most for me.

Rather than spend the weekend in Belgrade or Berlin I decided to split the difference and went to Vienna. I trekked out to Shoenefeld Airport in East Berlin on a special bus that took West Berliners to Shoenefeld for their cheap flights to places like Beirut. While West Berliners were not allowed to go to the East, they were allowed to get to the airport and in that way get some desperately needed hard cash without being seen to compromise a principle. My flight was a "special" Interflug flight that operated that day and never again from Berlin to Vienna. They were repositioning an aircraft to fly from Vienna to Leipzig for the duration of the forthcoming Leipzig fair. Interflug was the dour East German airline that operated only Russian equipment, in this case a Tupolev 134 that at first sight looked like a fighter with a passenger cabin attached, the wings swept downwards in a threatening leer. How my travel agent had found out about this flight, I cannot imagine. There were few others who knew about it, and in fact we were just four passengers. No announcements were made, the four of us sat in the front row, and the crew came up and had a casual chat about the safety features, and then sat down too. There was no service.

Vienna was also predictably a good fun weekend. The beauty of Vienna as a city is well known to be offset by the unpleasantness of the Viennese. They are generally arrogant, superior, and while fun-loving, exceptionally conservative. Except, that is, for the gay guys who manage to combine a certain pretentiousness with a rewarding base interest in sex. One gets the impression that the Viennese have difficulty fitting work in between a demanding schedule of drinking coffee, eating enormous Wienerschnitzel that hang over both sides of the plate, and feasting on lashings of whipped cream to get to rich dark chocolate cakes.

Sated, I arrived in Belgrade late on Sunday night. Rather than stay in the business hotel where Mrs Madirazza had booked, I decided I would opt for a bit more luxury and booked into the Intercontinental on the other side of the river. I caught a taxi the next morning for our eight o' clock appointment in Mrs Madirazza's hotel. I asked for her at reception, and was told that she was in the breakfast room. I wondered how I was going to recognise her. However, as I pushed open the door and peered across the smoky breakfast room, scanning the local business travellers preparing for a week of hard work with a strong coffee and a cigarette to fortify them, it was very clear. There was just one woman. She looked up and smiled. Mrs Madirazza was young, blond, tanned and very beautiful.

She had our Belgrade visits mapped out for the next three days. On Wednesday afternoon we were to fly to Zagreb. Knowing from experience the problems with air bookings I asked if we already had reservations. No, we didn't, but the Belgrade office would get onto it. I requested that they attend to it as a matter of some urgency, not particularly wanting to travel on either the bus or the train again.

Mrs Madirazza explained that she was finding it difficult to get back to work having just had two wonderful weeks holiday on the Adriatic coast with some friends, swimming and sunbathing. That is where the tan came from. She dropped into the conversation rather quickly that she was divorced and had an 11-year-old daughter, being looked after by the grandmother during her absence in Belgrade.

We finished up the first day of work at Mrs Madirazza's hotel. She suggested that we have dinner together and then possibly retire to her room where she happened to have a bottle of whisky with her. The way one does. I excused myself saying that I was very tired from the previous week's hard work (I forgot to mention the late nights out at the gay bars), and thought that I should get an early night to be prepared for the next day. She seemed a little surprised and disappointed.

I was glad that I had had the foresight to stay in a different hotel. Mrs Madirazza, was at 28 years old, only a year or so older than me. She was away in a town with a foreigner where no-one knew her and where she could enjoy a certain anonymity. A small adventure under such circumstances would have had very few risks attached to it: nobody would know, there would be no gossip, no repercussions, no family or friends to avoid.

The next day we made some visits, and then after lunch we were walking through the modern and austere business area with its boxy and intimidating communist-era buildings. She pointed out the street kiosks selling papers and magazines, and asked me if I had noticed the provocative magazines that were available for sale, depicting busty women in brief or no attire. I confessed that I had not noticed. She took up the point.

"Actually, I notice that you never look at women passing in the street".

She was clearly very observant. "Don't I?"

"No, you don't! And I find that is quite unusual. Men always notice a pretty girl walking down the street, but not you. I wonder why?"

There seemed to be little point in denying it, and in any case I liked Mrs Madirazza – she was bright, intelligent and full of energy. "Well, the reason is that I like men".

"You are a homosexual?"

From that moment on we had a wonderful time. Mrs Madirazza had never met a gay guy before and she was fascinated. She wanted to know all about my life, not in an intrusive way, but in a way that she could make sense of it. That evening we went out to dinner together in the old steep part of Belgrade where the Danube and the Sava rivers meet. It is the only part of the city with any charm, and there were lots of restaurants and cafés, with tables outside taking advantage of the early summer evenings. Business was brisk and we arrived a little late. The only table that was available was one where a young couple was already seated. They motioned that it was fine if we sat down at the same table, and indeed the empty plates suggested that they had already eaten.

Mrs Madirazza and I of course were speaking English, and they Serbian. Almost as if we were invisible the couple ignored us while they were getting quite heated, looking longingly into each other's eyes, with impatient squirming, and fingers intertwined and twisting. I leant across to Mrs Madirazza and said, "God, I wish these two would go home, get their clothes off and get on with it!" Shortly after they did indeed leave with a polite nod as a goodnight.

The next morning we went to the local Belgrade office and again I pushed the issue of the arrangements for the flight back to Zagreb. I was assured that indeed seats had been booked. The flight was due to leave at ten that night. This seemed to me rather suspiciously late and I demanded to know what sort of aircraft it would be. They called JAT and relayed the information to me that it was to be a Boeing 707. "Impossible", I protested, "they don't have any 707s" It was checked again and they assured us that indeed it was a Boeing 707, but did mention that it was a "special" flight. This made me both curious and a little concerned.

When we reached the airport I finally understood what had happened. JAT had chartered a Boeing 707 from an American company for the summer season to operate charters between Yugoslavia and North America. This flight was a special flight in that it was a repositioning of the aircraft to Zagreb ready for a charter flight overnight to Toronto. The flight was called and we walked across the tarmac to board by the forward stairs. At the foot of the stairs a stewardess was waiting to welcome passengers and direct them up the stairs. I heard a slight groan from Mrs Madirazza, and as I turned I recognised the stewardess. She recognised us and said in perfect English, "Good evening again. Did you enjoy your evening down by the Sava?" She had heard and understood my comment about their need to go home and hop into bed! I hope that she had.

***

There is one other woman whose story I will tell, although the thought of matching her daughter with me must have lingered only a second in her mind. She was too smart to think that it might ever work. And although she herself was seeking a man to marry, she equally knew that I was not that man. I met her first in her native Romania, but the week or so that led up to that encounter contained some adventures of its own.

I had changed jobs and my first overseas trip with the new company was to Eastern Europe, accompanying a more senior person as part of my induction. Ian was a revolting man. He was a sleazy slob who worked only in Eastern Europe and made no secret of the fact that one of the perks of working in this otherwise barren environment was the inexpensive and easy availability of women. I was feeling a little seedy that Monday morning as I had spent the weekend in Hammamet in Tunisia with an Italian gay friend of mine. We were supposed to be investigating establishing a business renting holiday villas, based on the very successful business he had built doing the same thing on the Mediterranean coast of Italy. We both found a local guy each to give us another perspective on the tourist trade. The flight back to London arrived late.

By the time Ian and I arrived in Warsaw most of the next day had gone, but it was early enough to go to the bar of the hotel and have a drink watching the girls and listening to the unidentifiable palm court music. We then went to a restaurant for dinner, and I announced that I was tired and walked back to the hotel, while Ian said that he would stay for a few drinks and to see what might develop. We agreed to meet for breakfast at eight ready for our first meeting with the state purchasing office of chemicals, Chemolimpex.

I was ready waiting in the breakfast room at the appointed time, but Ian did not appear. I called his room, but there was no answer. I ate breakfast wondering what I should do next. I rang again, but there was still no answer. I went to his room and knocked on the door. No answer. Gingerly I turned the handle and was quite surprised to find the door was unlocked. I went in and there he was unconscious on the bed in a deep, not really sleep, more a coma. I called his name and eventually had to shake him into a more or less waking state. It was almost nine and it was clear we would miss our appointment. Quite unfazed, he stood up, and then suggested we needed to talk to prepare for the meeting while he got ready. He did not shower, simply put on another shirt and a suit. I have never seen such disgustingly dirty underpants, and recoiled in utter distaste. It was almost enough to turn me straight.

He had arranged to go to Budapest for the weekend; I am not sure why, but can only imagine it was a personal agenda. I flew on a bumpy, scary flight in an Ilyushin 18 turboprop of the biblical LOT, the Polish airline, straight to Sofia in Bulgaria where our next meetings were arranged for the Monday morning. A weekend without that disgusting creature! I settled into the hotel, stretched out in my glorious solitary space, and in the afternoon went for a walk near the hotel where I noticed a young guy walking along. We glanced at each other, a microsecond too long, and then renewed after a moment or two, as I had so often done in the past. I slowed right down and looked intensely into a shop window. He passed me and then stopped and looked in the next window. It was going to happen.

He was from Cuba, and spoke a little English. He was on a government visit, staying in the same hotel as me, but under constant surveillance inside the hotel by the guy he shared a room with. He managed to be "lost" for half an hour and came to my room where we had sex. He explained that he could not stay then, but that he had managed to make contact with some local gay guys and he invited me to go with him on an excursion with them into the country the next day. I wondered how he had managed to escape for a whole day, especially since he was so nervous about being seen with me. I think it was to do with my being a westerner.

I met him in front of the hotel the next morning and indeed some gay Bulgarians turned up with a car and we set off to visit some friends of theirs in the country. One of the guys spoke some Italian and I conversed with him. The property was quite isolated, on the top of a hill and not overlooked at all. It belonged to an older guy who had had some kind of artistic career, and seemed to be quite unmoved and unaffected by the apparent constraints that the communist government was reported to apply to dissenters and misfits such as gays.

I was quite surprised that the gay guys had as much freedom to do what they wanted and go where they wanted as they obviously did. The fact that our host wandered around in the garden without a stitch on, quite drunk, with the invitees acting in just the same way as gay men the world over acted when they got together, was both a revelation and a relief. It was a pleasant day with good fresh salads and meats to eat, and plenty to drink. By the time we got back to town it was late afternoon. The guys with the car invited me to their house and we chatted some more before I headed off to the hotel. The Cuban had had to leave and report in before this. He was married and had a child whom he adored, but clearly from my own observation was far more gay than straight and had obviously married for self-preservation.

Waiting for me was a curt message from Ian who had obviously expected me to be at the hotel waiting for his arrival with the appropriate thankfulness and respect. We met the next morning and he expressed surprise that I had been out. I simply said that I had had a pleasant day out and about. Our first appointment was with the trade section of the British Embassy. Ian had met the officer previously and the conversation drifted to how things were going in Bulgaria. The resident expert stated that things had just got tighter and tighter with contact with foreigners almost impossible. "There is no way one would ever be invited into someone's home", he affirmed. At this I leant forward and spoke. "That is not always true", I said, "in fact I was invited to someone's house last night and had a very pleasant and relaxed time". They both looked at me in amazement, my statement having raised more questions for them than it answered. But I said nothing more and an air of mystery veiled the conversation.

Our next stop was Bucharest. Tarom, the Romanian airline, much to my surprise had equipped itself with western aircraft, in fact a BAC-111, not really my favourite and long since an aeronautical dinosaur. We stayed in the main business hotel of those days, a comfortable and busy place. We were aware that there was a woman called Maria Alexandrescu who represented several western chemical companies and assisted them in trying to do business with the state purchasing office, and who had an office in the same hotel. She had a reputation for two things: her excellent connections and ability to facilitate sales, and her enormous breasts.

As we sat in the open bar a woman swept past, an enormous prow surging ahead of her. "That has to be Mrs Alexandrescu!" Ian observed. I agreed that she seemed to have the attributes. After a few minutes she swept back again. "Mrs Alexandrescu!" shouted Ian. She stopped, turned abruptly towards us and with a broad smile said with a deep enquiring tone, "Yes?" We explained that we were interested in talking to her about our extensive phosphorus-based range of industrial chemicals, and were keen to meet with her. "Well, how about dinner this evening?" she asked. We said that would be fine. She suggested that to make a foursome she should bring her daughter along.

It was a good, fun evening. Maria had a personality as large as her bosom. Her daughter was still a student and lived quietly in the shadow of her mother. We were expected to dance together and I lived up to my obligations. Maria was wearing a provocative dress with buttons down both sides of the front with two bobbing suggestively on her nipples. She seemed to enjoy having them shake and wobble, the buttons, that is. On asking us how we had known it was her when she swept past the bar, Ian told her that we had heard about her bosom. She laughed generously and let her buttons ripple to reinforce the credibility of the story.

Mr Alexandrescu never made an appearance either in person or in conversation.

Maria spoke very good English and had managed through her business to travel extensively to the West. These visits were ostensibly for technical training that enabled her to represent foreign companies effectively.

It was not unknown that Eastern bloc regimes allowed such people to operate even though at first sight it seemed a contradiction in what they stood for. There was also the example of Herr Pachtinger and his buxom wife who had an office in the Hotel Rossia in Moscow, and two Mercedes cars (equipped with drivers also employed by the KGB), and who represented foreign companies selling graphic arts equipment. He had been asked by the Soviets to contact the company I worked for to investigate our products, which they were interested in purchasing. He made a lot of money, but his role was to make sure that they did not buy a pup. If he had made one single mistake his next visa would be denied and he would have lost everything. He was there to keep the foreign salespeople honest. I arrived in Moscow once just as his flight arrived from Frankfurt. I could not believe all the baggage he had, much of it gifts for his contacts. I could never even manage to get a table in our own hotel if we arrived after seven, but he could get a room at the much busier National Hotel at any time of the evening. Frau Pachtinger explained to me once that the head waiter's gold watch was one of the reasons that it was so easy for them.

I suspected it was the same with Maria Alexandrescu. She had a lot of freedoms and advantages as long as she kept her nose clean and helped the Romanian state–buying juggernaut to locate the best suppliers and kept them honest.

It was a pleasant surprise, although in hindsight not altogether unexpected, when several months later, in the middle of a dull and depressing November afternoon in my office in London, the telephone rang, and there was Maria Alexandrescu on the line.

She had just arrived and was on a three-week visit for technical training for one of her other British principals. I was not quite sure at first that I had heard her correctly when she said, "John, I am here just for three weeks, and in that time I have to find a husband. I wonder if there is anything you can suggest to help me?" I was quickly turning over in my mind the exact nature of her question. She was maybe 15 or 20 years older than me, and I imagined that she was not suggesting a quick trip to the altar with me. But just to be on the safe side I said, "Well, I don't know really. You know I'm gay". By this stage I had become a bit more open about my sexual orientation. "Yes, I know", she said quickly, "but I just wondered whether you know anyone who might be suitable". She explained that she was thoroughly fed up with her life in Romania and wanted to move to the West. She could simply have overstayed her visa, but then neither her mother nor her daughter would have been allowed to leave and she would never see either of them again. She clearly was not going to do that. On the other hand if she married, she would be allowed to leave and her mother and daughter would be allowed to go with her. I was at a loss to suggest anyone. The single men I knew were all of my orientation.

Several months went by and Maria called me again. She told me that she was back in London, this time permanently, and that she had indeed managed to find a husband through an agency that arranged such matters. She confided that she did not have any real expectations that it would be a good relationship, but was delighted to say that the man she had married was wonderful and that she loved him. Her daughter and mother had arrived and they were all living in her husband's house in South-East London. She invited me and João to their house for dinner. I accepted of course. Her husband was indeed a wonderful man: he seemed kind and generous and a thoroughly decent human being. I think they really loved each other. I could hardly believe her luck, and I suspect, neither could she.

Chapter 5 Escape from Iraq

Most of my travel up to this time had been in the western hemisphere, either Europe or the Americas, with the possible exception of Israel and Turkey. But with the change of jobs in 1971 there was the prospect of more new destinations in the Middle East and beyond. Several of those trips took me to Iran.

The best thing about Tehran in those days was the bazaar. When I first went there it was the furthest east I had ever been. I was breaking new frontiers and the bazaar epitomised the exotic that I had demanded from such a distant city. Frankly some of the streets in the area near my hotel were disappointing in how conventional they looked. They were upper-class residential areas, neat and clean with trees in the streets, and they just did not look, well, foreign enough for my taste. But the bazaar was different. It had eastern goods, textiles, ceramics, metalware and jewellery, and a smell and look about it that excited me. It had foreign-looking people with different clothes. I was satisfied.

The next best thing was the caviar. I was interested in eating in a local restaurant but found that more difficult than I had envisaged. There just did not seem to be any in that area. It was in fact on a subsequent trip that I did finally manage to eat in a local restaurant, but it did not serve any caviar.

Belinha was a friend of Clarissa. They both worked at the Portuguese embassy in London. Clarissa was a close friend of João. Belinha had met her Iranian boyfriend Massoud in London and they were engaged to be married. I had met Massoud briefly once in London; João knew him slightly better. For some reason Massoud had been obliged to return to Tehran several months before they were to be married. Belinha was going to live in Tehran and I often wonder what happened to them, for this was in the days of the Shah when Iran was a different place.

Belinha asked me if I would take a present for Massoud from her, a jacket she had bought for him. She gave me his phone number. I called a few times from my hotel and only after several attempts did I finally get Massoud on the line. He was expecting my call and seemed pleased to have someone in town who was in a way a contact with Belinha. We arranged to meet one evening at my hotel and then go and eat together.

He arrived with a cousin and a friend. The cousin had a car and I suspect that is why he had been invited. I gave Massoud the present with which he was delighted. I requested that we eat in an Iranian restaurant. This created both surprise and I suspect some disappointment. The

Iranians were hoping for something European; however, they agreed and we went in the cousin's car to a busy, rather modest restaurant, full of noise and life. There were long tables full of people eating and illuminated by the ubiquitous fluorescent lights, one of the curses of the developing world. The tables and chairs were simple, the floor bare concrete and none of the plates matched.

Neither the cousin nor the friend spoke any English at all, and so I sat next to Massoud. The Iran of the days of the Shah was relatively liberal and copious quantities of alcohol were served. To such an extent in fact that Massoud and his compatriots quickly became a little inebriated, and shortly afterwards dead drunk! The meal was after all not very memorable. But what was memorable was the fact that as Massoud got more and more drunk he became increasingly friendly. He put his arms around me and called me a true and great friend.

I have always found it a little embarrassing when this sort of thing happens. I have never had a problem with men putting their arms around me, as long as they were gay and I knew the rules. But in this case I attributed the apparent affection to alcohol. Massoud confided, "Jooohn, you are a dear friend, I loove you", as he clasped me in his arms again. This surprised me given that I had only ever met him briefly once before in London.

The meal was very inexpensive and I paid the bill. This was followed by protests (not preceded by them), along the lines that I was a guest in their country and they should have paid and that I was just too generous. I justified my generosity by explaining that my company would in fact be paying through my expense allowance. I walked and they staggered from the restaurant to the car. With horror I realised that the cousin was going to drive and that I was going to sit in the front seat. I examined the options. If I refused they would be even more offended, and in their state the deep affection might turn rather quickly into an antipathetic emotion. In any case I had no idea where I was and there would be nobody who spoke English. Getting out of there would be a little complicated, so I gritted my teeth and got in the car.

To my great relief in only about 5 or 10 minutes of weaving across the streets and slewing around corners, we stopped in front of a house that Massoud announced was his cousin's. Massoud got out and beckoned for me to do the same. I did not delay. Then he said that to regain his honour I must let him buy me a drink at the Hilton Hotel. I agreed and he called a taxi. To my relief the cousin and friend had been ditched.

Tehran is built on a steady slope with the Hilton at the northern and higher end of the city. It was a cold night and there was snow from a fall several days previously laying 30 centimetres or so deep around the Hilton. We ordered a cup of coffee, which seemed to me to be a very sensible idea. Then Massoud looked at his watch; it was about 10, and he suggested that we should instead go to my hotel for a drink. I was staying at a far more modest establishment than the Hilton, called the Park Hotel, and I was not even sure there would be a bar open there. It was a good half-hour's drive along a wide avenue down the gradual slope to the Park Hotel.

I asked for the key to my room, and enquired whether there was a bar open. Before the receptionist could answer, Massoud suggested we go to my room and get a beer through room service: it would be more comfortable and less trouble. I was not sure where this was going to lead but already had some idea. I agreed. The beer was ordered and delivered, and Massoud stretched out on my bed, laying on his back with his arms behind his head. His eyes were closed, but I knew that he was very much awake, and indeed not as drunk as he had been.

I could see that he was not going to make the first move, but rather give me every sign that I should do so. I said, "You know, Massoud, you have really beautiful hair". Immediately he said, "You can touch it if you want to". So I did, and the rest is history. I have been to bed with straight men in Kuwait and Beirut, under circumstances where fucking a man is alright if there are no women around. They were what in Australia we call a dud root, that is to say, not very good in bed. But Massoud was different. He had been there before, I could tell.

After the peak of the passion had expired, and the blood had drained back to our brains, a confused bundle of words rushed out, from which I gleaned that Massoud still was not quite sober. "I never did this before. I hope you are clean. You are clean, aren't you? (In this case he had fucked me.) You must not tell Belinha. Belinha knows all about me, I said I would not do it again. I have changed. Please promise me you will not tell her. You are clean aren't you, you know, you haven't got anything, have you? I won't do it again".

I did not tell Belinha. And I did not tell João. It was the easy way out; I hope I did the right thing.

Next I headed for Kuwait, which is the way the route normally took me. My memories of Kuwait are diverse. But the first thing I think of is the heat. A pounding heat once caused me to sweat so much on a 10-minute walk to a meeting with the British Consular Trade Office that I stopped and bought a new shirt halfway. The one I was wearing was soaking wet.

I remember one night having dinner outside by the pool at the Sheraton with a business contact from Lebanon called Fawzi, a Palestinian who had taken shelter in Beirut, and who had been drawn to Kuwait by the prospect of work and money. He drew my attention to a group of Kuwaitis at a neighbouring table, dressed in their long white flowing robes and head dresses. He pointed out that the water glasses at this hotel and most others were a light-brown colour rather than clear glass. The reason for this he said was that if anyone were to add whisky, it would not be noticed. He told me that he had been watching the group and that they had a bottle of whisky secreted under their robes, and that they were pouring whisky slowly into the water glasses under the cover of the table.

Shortly afterwards, there was a hell of a crash and sound of breaking glass, followed in a few seconds by the strong aroma of whisky carried into the still hot air of the night. Possibly because their consumption of the whisky had led to a less tight grip on the bottle, it had slipped from the robes of one of them and crashed onto the tiles around the pool, spilling the amber liquid all over the floor. Kuwait is of course a dry state, and so not surprisingly the heads of the other diners turned towards the group. The waiters rushed forward sweeping the glass and spilled liquid away with such an efficiency that it seems they had been expecting this accident and that it had happened on various previous occasions. The smell of whisky lingered a little longer and then gradually dissipated. The diners turned their attention back to their meals.

My dinner colleague smiled, and then said that if that had been a foreigner, someone like him, a Palestinian living in Kuwait, they would have been expelled immediately from the country or worse. As they were local boys, no action would be taken at all.

A brief interlude of pleasure was provided by two guys from an airline who were staying at my hotel. I met them at the pool, looking spectacular in their Speedos. One was Pakistani, the one I really fancied. The other was Lebanese. I ended up in bed with the Lebanese, although I actually don't think he was really gay. In countries as socially repressive as Kuwait he probably figured that having sex with a man was one better than doing it on his own. I had had a similar experience in Beirut with a young Lebanese guy hanging around the pool, who was almost certainly more straight than gay. He stayed with me for several days, but one night I had plied him with too much alcohol to relax him, as a result of which he relaxed so much he wet the bed. I had to admit to housekeeping that it was indeed my accident, as I doubt they would have appreciated knowing the truth. They pretended to be understanding. He helped to pass the time but was not very good sex.

Some of the local Kuwaiti men did not seem to me to have well-developed interpersonal skills as we understand them in the west. I had a meeting with one such man, the manager of a printing company that almost certainly would have belonged to his father or uncle. I was talking to him about equipment used in the photographic processes prior to printing. The factory was a little way out of town in a new area of light industry. It was hot and dusty, the streets were not marked, and the taxi had great difficulty in finding it.

The manager was young, very good-looking sporting a thick moustache and beard of strong black hair, and arrogant as he sat there in striking white robes. The only thing I recollect from the conversation was his saying that Kuwaitis are so much brighter than the English (which is what I suppose I was in those days even though now as an Australian it comes as bit of a shock to say it). The evidence he offered for this was the fact that we were speaking in English and that I could not speak Arabic. I chose not to debate the logic of his argument or the conclusions he had reached.

My only other encounter with native Kuwaitis was of a rather different nature. I was walking along the street in the city one night after dinner as I often used to do. A car drove past slowly and I looked inside. There was a young Kuwaiti driving. He stopped and smiled, and motioned for me to get in the car.

Now I am sure you will be thinking, "My God, he would have to have rocks in his head to go and get in". But I was prepared to take the risk as I was feeling very horny. So I opened the door and got into the car. We headed out of town, rather to my surprise. Since he spoke no English, I had no idea where we were going or what was planned. The road was initially quite well lit with a yellow light exaggerating the yellow colour of the dusty and sandy roadside. We had been travelling for 20 minutes or more and the buildings had become more sparse and then virtually disappeared at the same time as the streetlights.

We were now in a desert kind of landscape, with poor stony land off both sides of the highway. I began to be a bit concerned. Nobody knew where I was; I could just disappear and no-one would have any idea what had happened. But logic also whispered that there would be little point in just picking up someone to kill them. I was concerned but not panicking. I was not as scared as the night I picked up a guy in Copacabana in Rio; we went back to his place, did what we did, and then just as I was about to leave, he pulled out an enormous knife with a huge blade. He of course heard the loud intake of air expressing my extreme and urgent fear. He burst out laughing, and said, "Did you think I was going to kill you? The lock on the front door is broken and I have to use the blade to push the catch back". I felt a bit stupid.

Suddenly the Kuwaiti slowed down and drove off onto a sandy track, an unmade road leading off to the left into the desert. After a few hundred metres I saw a collection of tents and a few men walking around. My escort stopped the car short of the tents and got out and walked towards the men. I stayed in the car wondering what was going on, with my concern hardly having abated.

He came back and motioned for me to follow him. We went into an empty tent, just the two of us. Although he was wearing the traditional headdress, he was wearing jeans rather than the long robes. He unzipped them, pulled out his cock, and the performance began. Figuring that whatever was to follow, I might as well enjoy each moment, I played my part to perfection. In all honesty an encore would not have been called for.

The big question was after the seed had been spilled, what would happen to me next? My host walked out of the tent, motioning me to follow, and we both got into the car. He headed back down the dirt road onto the main highway back towards Kuwait and drove me right back to the place where he had picked me up.

However, the most significant meeting in Kuwait occurred at the airport as I was departing for Baghdad. As I went through passport control a dark, short and very sophisticated-looking man placed a green passport on the counter. One of my idle pastimes in airports is to try and guess the nationality of people. One has to do something, for heaven's sake. I could not recollect seeing a green passport quite like that. I stepped a little closer to him so that I could see better, and was rather surprised to see that he was Mexican. I wondered what on earth a Mexican was doing in this part of the world, especially heading to Iraq. There was a wait before the plane took off, and so once through the control area I initiated a conversation with him. It was really subtle, along the lines of, "What on earth is a Mexican doing here?"

It turned out that Dr Cueva was a specialist in allergies. He had been invited to Kuwait by the Kuwaiti government. With the new-found wealth from oil of that country, money had been invested in trying to provide a better urban environment for the people. To provide some shade in the street and break up the steely heat of the summer furnace, they had planted trees. Unfortunately it appeared that an amazingly large percentage of the population was allergic to those trees. Preferring on this occasion to request the assistance of a less-aligned country, Dr Cueva had been invited to Kuwait to see if he could suggest what exactly was the nature of the problem and what they should do about it.

I subsequently met his wife and family in Mexico City where they lived. He told me that many years before when he was lecturing at the medical school in Mexico City he had had as a medical student a young Argentinian. This particular student, whom he assessed as very bright, was better known for his subsequent non-medical activities. He was Che Guevara.

The flight to Baghdad was in a medium-range British-built tri-engine Trident. The Iraqis had bought it from the British in the days some time previously when they enjoyed cordial relations. It could not really have been that old, although its lack of care made it seem much older. I wondered what contact they had with the manufacturer nowadays and whether the service and spare parts had been properly managed.

There was a group of women wearing the veil travelling on the aircraft. A man accompanying them carried their passports. I wondered how they managed passport control under the veil. The plane smelled of that Middle Eastern smell that I have never quite been able to identify, a strange cross between cumin and camels. It was musty, not really unpleasant, but certainly not the sort of smell I had ever associated with an aircraft.

The flight was uneventful, and we cleared passport and customs controls in Baghdad without any problem. It was late on a Thursday morning, and the weekend was just beginning, Friday being the holy day. Dr Cueva and I were staying at the same hotel and so we decided to catch a taxi together. We then agreed to have lunch together, and after checking in set out down the street. We found a small restaurant still open, and as it was getting a little late for lunch, decided to settle on it before we missed lunch altogether.

The menu was written of course in Arabic, but with a translation in what I can only call European. It was not in any particular language but was in Roman script and had words that most Europeans would have been able to make some sense of. There was one item however that we were not sure about. "Testis", said Dr Cueva, "I wonder what that could be". I had my suspicions, and said, "Well you are the doctor, what would your guess be?" We decided that the only way to be sure was to order it. Sheep's balls in fact turned out to be far nicer than I had ever imagined, as long as you are used to eating offal, which I am.

We then went for a walk down the street. It was a mixture of the buildings one might associate with a Middle Eastern city, but with bold and highly symbolic monuments to glorious goals. The leader of Iraq at the time (1971) was a certain Major General Ahmed Hassan al-Bakr, who was later succeeded by Saddam Hussein; both were from the Baathist Socialist Party. The Baathists were very anti-Israeli, pro-Soviet and anti-West. The regime was highly oppressive and not to be trifled with. Our hotel had an enormous banner strung across the front. It read in English: "Death to Zionism and all Jews".

As we strolled down the street suddenly two military cars screeched to a halt right in front of us, and the uniformed occupants rushed out and grabbed two men who were on the pavement. Dr Cueva and I, not wanting to be part of an international headline, rushed into the nearest shop. It was a bookstore. The two men were bundled into the cars and they sped off. The owner of the bookstore was visibly very shaken. He spoke a little English. We asked him who they were and what all that had been about. He said that it was nothing, just nothing, but we could see from his eyes that he was terrified.

We had little appetite for further walking that afternoon, and returned to the hotel. The next day was to be a holiday, and no work would be done. My work contact had already left a note to the effect that he would pick me up on Saturday morning for a meeting at the British Embassy. Dr Cueva had some contacts with the American pharmaceutical company Upjohn, and it had already been arranged that they would pick him up on Friday and take him sightseeing in Baghdad. He very kindly invited me to go along too. I accepted and we agreed to meet the next morning.

That evening after dinner in the hotel, I took a walk as was my habit. A few blocks from the hotel in a street with small businesses and buildings laid back from the road by different distances, all closed, I noticed a young man walking the other way down the street. He glanced at me and I held his gaze. I knew the game well enough to think that he might be gay. He walked past and I turned, and as I did I saw that he had also turned around. I changed direction and walked after him. He stopped very briefly so that I caught up with him. He continued to walk and without looking at me said, "You must be very careful". He had a deep husky voice. "I must go now but I can be here tomorrow night at this time". I said to him that was fine, and he told me he would wait in front of a certain building, which he pointed out. He then told me not to wait if he was not there but to just keep walking until he arrived.

The next morning Dr Cueva's contacts from Upjohn arrived, introductions were made, and we set off sightseeing. There were two local Upjohn men. The one who was driving was short, dark and well dressed, and clearly the more senior of the two. He delivered a whole load of rhetoric about how wonderful Iraq was, especially the current regime of the Baathist Socialist Party. The other man, who sat in the back with me, was to my surprise a redhead. He added his support parrot-like to what the driver was saying.

Our first stop was the magnificent gold-domed mosque of Kazimayn. It was a most impressive building from the outside. The driver explained that in Iraq only Muslims were allowed to go inside the mosque. However, since Dr Cueva could easily pass as an Iraqi with his swarthy complexion, as long as he kept quiet, nobody would question him. So the driver said that he would accompany Dr Cueva inside the mosque, while the other man, the redhead, would remain with me. I said that it was fine if they both wanted to go into the mosque, I would be quite happy strolling around the square. But the redhead insisted on staying with me.

As soon as the other two were out of earshot, he turned to me and explained that he could not go into the mosque anyway as he was a Christian. He told me that everything he had said in the car was a lie, and that the regime was a disgusting and oppressive dictatorship. Iraq had always been an open and liberal country with high education standards and a diverse ethnic mix, but now as a Christian he was being persecuted and he feared for the safety of his family, and wanted desperately to get out of Iraq. It seemed that was not very easy to do. He told me that he did not trust his boss, that he gave lip service to the regime as it was the safest thing for him to do, and that I was not to reveal the conversation that we had just had.

I went off on my own walking around the square. It was already stifling hot. I took a couple of photographs of the buildings in the square and the mosque. Suddenly a uniformed man – I assumed that he was a policeman – grabbed hold of me and tried to rip the camera out of my hands. He was shouting and seemed extremely angry. While I did not check it at the time, I am sure my pulse rate was very elevated.

The redhead ran over and there followed a fiery discussion in Arabic. It seems that photography was more or less banned in Iraq. A mosque could hardly have been considered as militarily sensitive, but the policeman interpreted it as a "public building" and as such it was off limits for photographs. Somehow the redhead managed to persuade the policeman to just let me and the camera and film go. Later in the day we passed a beautiful old home with wooden overhangs onto the street, a classic of its style. I asked if I might sneak a photo from the cover of inside of the car. I was told in no uncertain terms that I could not.

Overall the day was pleasant enough, but I felt a little out of my environment and was looking forward to meeting my date for the evening. After dinner I walked to the appointed place right on time. My friend was already waiting. It seems that an Iraqi waiting could be waiting for anyone, and so would not arouse suspicion. But a foreigner waiting was likely to be waiting for an Iraqi, and that meant that that Iraqi could well get into trouble. He walked off up the street and I fell in beside him. He did not speak and when I tried to start a conversation, he just said, "Later!" We walked for 10 minutes or so and then turned along the banks of the Tigris river. There were fewer people here and obviously he felt a bit more relaxed. He talked a bit but was clearly waiting until we reached our destination before talking very openly. His English was fair, not fluent but good enough to be able to have a serious conversation. After a further 10 minutes or so we reached a street a block or so from the river, and he led me through a gate and along a path to what looked as if it might be a garage converted into a small flat. He unlocked the door and went in. He locked the door again from the inside.

At last he relaxed. I learned that his name was Hashim Agajhani. He was, like the majority of Iraqis in fact, a Shia Muslim, unlike the powerbrokers who were all Sunni. He felt he had more in common with Iranians than with the Iraqi government. He had thick strong hair that even sprouted in an exceptionally virile fashion from the lower part of the shaft of his cock.

After we had had sex, we sat and talked in low tones. He told me that he saw absolutely no future in Iraq, not only as he was gay but simply because he felt a general sense of oppression and hopelessness. He told me that he had applied to go and live in Australia, but that he had not heard anything back. He explained that Australia did not have an embassy in Iraq – the nearest one was in Beirut – but that applications were handled through the British Embassy in Baghdad. An Australian would go from the embassy in Beirut on a visit to Baghdad and working out of the British mission would hold immigration interviews.

Hashim had already had such an interview and at the end of it his understanding was that he was going to be accepted for migration to Australia, and that they were supposed to send the formal advice directly to him. Then he would need to go to Beirut, complete the administration and leave from there. The problem is that nothing from the Australian Embassy in Beirut would ever get delivered in Iraq. It would be intercepted by the secret police, as did any mail coming from another country, especially from the embassy of a Western country. Even going to the British Embassy for the interview was risky. That would also mean that the police would have opened a file on him, even more of a reason for getting out.

It was already several weeks after the date by which he would have expected an answer. He was extremely miserable about the future. He saw Australia as his last opportunity to get out, his salvation. He said that failing that he would rather go to Iran than stay in Iraq. I told him that I was going to Beirut after Baghdad and offered to follow up the matter on his behalf with the Australian Embassy there. We discussed how I could get a message back to him. He suggested that as his address and name were already known to the police, it would be better to use the name and address of his cousin. And as I was also going to Egypt, it seemed a better idea to mail any letter from there; it would excite less interest than even Lebanon. He gave me his cousin's details.

By now it was around midnight. I stood up and told him that it was time for me to go. Hashim became most alarmed and said that under no circumstances could I leave now. A westerner out at that time of night would be certain to excite the interest of the police, and who knows where it might lead if I was picked up. No, I would have to wait until after the sun had come up. Then it would be safer. I remembered the incident on the footpath outside the bookshop the day we had arrived, and the banner across the front of my hotel. I decided to do as Hashim suggested. I had an appointment at 9.00 a,m, the next morning with the local agent to go together to the British Embassy, but figured I would have enough time for a shower and to get ready, even if I was going to be rather tired. I snuggled down with Hashim again and we both slept a little.

Around half past six the sun was already up and the heat of the day was building. The sky was pale with the dust and heat in the air. The city looked a little like a sepia photograph as I walked back to my hotel, taking the same route along the banks of the Tigris that I had the night before. The air was still and already with promise of another scorching day of 40 degrees. I knew well enough if I was stopped not to say where I had been.

But the walk was uneventful, and I went straight up to my room and got ready for my meeting. I have always tended to take room keys with me when I go out, and so there was no need to stop at reception. In some strange way I never want people in the hotel to know where I am. Besides it saves having to stop at reception and ask for the room key.

I cannot recollect how my company had located this sales agent. Usually people would have contacted us after seeing our name in a trade publication or at an international exhibition. It is just possible that he could have been recommended by the British Trade office in Baghdad. My reason for being there was to investigate whether or not he would make a suitable person to represent my company selling Graphic Arts equipment in Iraq, and whether indeed there was a market worth spending time trying to develop.

Neither can I recollect his name. Somewhere I still have some books he gave me of his work, full of black-and-white photographs. For above everything else he was an artist. He had a thin face, dark skin, long and straight black hair and a very intense manner. He wore heavily tinted glasses. I did not particularly like him, but he was certainly interesting. I learned in due course that he was a Kurd, and that he had been very politically active on behalf of his people, trying to get Iraq to give more autonomy to their northerly region. For his trouble he had been arrested and thrown into gaol.

He was waiting for me in the foyer when I came down from my room, and immediately we walked out to his car. Once we had started to move, he said to me, "I do not want to know what you did last night, but while I was waiting for you there was a discussion at reception as to whether you had returned to the hotel last night. They were not quite sure, it seems. If in fact you did not, then you should realise that while you will yourself not be in any danger, if they find out where you were and who you were with, then that person will be in serious trouble".

He went on. "This hotel is under constant surveillance by the secret police. Every phone call you make from your room is monitored. If you take a taxi, the taxi will be required to make a report of where you go. If you want to take a taxi somewhere, go out into the street and hail one there. It is safer".

I wondered whether everyone in Baghdad was paranoid or whether all this was true. I let the officer in the Trade section of the British Embassy make up my mind. He welcomed us and ushered us into his office. Our prospective agent thanked the officer for the fine cocktail party of the previous week. It was obvious that he was a fairly frequent visitor to the embassy and had close relationships with the Trade Office. The officer asked him if he had had "a visit" after the cocktail party. He said that he had, as usual. He laughed, and said that every time he came to the embassy he "had a visit". He said that he just told the police every time that it was part of his business, and that he needed that contact with the Trade section to enable him to access goods that Iraq needed.

I got a chance to ask the officer on his own whether all the stories that I was hearing about the regime were right. I was assured that they were and told to exercise extreme caution.

The next day I left Baghdad on an MEA (Middle Eastern Airlines, the Lebanese airline) flight to Beirut. I had not tried to contact Hashim again and I was a little concerned about him. I could not believe that we had been followed to his place, and I doubted that they could know where I had spent the missing night. By the same token I have to confess that I was a little nervous going through passport control and customs when I left. I felt much more at home on the MEA plane, and Beirut, a city that I knew well and loved, seemed like home.

As soon as I was able I called the Australian Embassy in Beirut and made an appointment to see them. I explained that I had met Hashim and that I was acting on his behalf. Obviously I did not explain the nature of the meeting, but simply said that I had met him through some business contact in Baghdad. I was surprised at how open they were with me. They looked up his file and told me that indeed his application had been approved, and they had sent that notification to him by mail, with instructions to bring his passport to the embassy in Beirut where all the necessary paperwork would be processed. They expressed surprise that they had heard nothing from him.

I explained the situation in Iraq. I was somewhat taken aback that they seemed to know so little about how things were there and the fact that their modus operandi was so problematical in many ways. They told me they would hold the paperwork there. If I could get a message to him to travel to Beirut, on his arrival they would process it, and he would be able to fly on to Australia within a few days.

My stay in Beirut was short on that occasion, I hardly had time to go and sit in the fashionable coffee shops of Hamra and watch the world go by, one of my favourite pastimes, coupled with a stroll along the corniche towards the Phoenicia Hotel, or a quick visit to the sauna in the Continental Hotel, and the groping hands of its patrons. I left a day or so later to Cairo with the intention of writing a letter to Hashim from there.

The flight surprisingly left 20 minutes ahead of time given that all the passengers they were expecting were on board. Next to me on the flight there was a Swiss businessman. Although the flight was short we chatted about what we were doing. He told me that he was heading to Baghdad after Cairo. He was going to stay in the same hotel as I had.

I asked him a favour. Would he be so kind as to mail a letter for me? The only condition was that he should mail it outside the hotel, not leave it to be mailed from reception. I explained roughly what it was about, without providing the details of how I had met Hashim. He kindly agreed.

I took a sheet of paper and wrote in very clear writing: "I went to see your aunt in Beirut, as we had planned. She has the package there you are waiting for. She said you must go to Beirut to collect it. She will keep it until you get there." I addressed it to the cousin, as Hashim had asked. I sent the same letter a few days later from Cairo, but I do not believe that letter was ever delivered. But the one that the Swiss man took was, even though the envelope was addressed in English and not Arabic.

After Cairo I flew to Tripoli via Benghazi with Libyan Airlines, an adventure in itself, and the next day I flew on to Tunis. Just a few days later I was back in London working at my desk, and it almost seemed like a dream. I had said nothing to anyone, least of all to João, who would probably not have been too interested in the story.

A couple of weeks had gone by, when my father called me one evening. A telegram had arrived for me. To avoid potential problems of having to explain more than I needed to João, I had given Hashim my father's address in case he wanted to contact me. My father read the cable to me. It said: "ARRIVED IN BEIRUT. I CANNOT TRAVEL. MY PASSPORT NOT VALID FOR AUSTRALIA. PLEASE CALL ME AT HOTEL. NUMBER 66 43 29 ROOM 24 HASHIM". My father commented that he did not understand it and enquired if it was really meant for me. This was an invitation for further explanation, but under the circumstances I declined to react to the prompt for more information, but assured him that it was for me and that I knew what it was about.

I called the hotel in Beirut straight away. I did not manage to get Hashim right then but I left a message as to what time I would call back. The next time I spoke to him he told me that he had received the letter that the Swiss man, true to his word, had mailed in Baghdad. I later discovered that it almost did not get delivered to Hashim. I think that he really did not believe that I would help him and he forgot to say anything to his cousin about the possibility of a letter arriving for him at his cousin's address. But one evening he was talking to his cousin, and he mentioned that he had received a few days before a weird letter in English about an aunt and a parcel in Beirut. Hashim realised that it was meant for him, and as soon as he read the letter made plans to leave.

The next day he went to the British Embassy and obtained a visitor's visa in his passport for the UK. It was a wise precaution to get that visa as it turned out. He then booked a one-way flight to Beirut. The next afternoon he packed what he needed, took with him the little money he had, and left. He had checked into an inexpensive hotel. He went the next day to the Australian Embassy and everything went fine until they looked at his passport. It seems that the passport had major restrictions on its validity. It was valid only for travel to other Arab countries and a few nominated countries in Western Europe such as Germany and the UK. It was not valid for travel to Australia or any of the other likely transit ports in Asia.

The Australian Embassy advised him that until the passport was amended with validity for travel to Australia, he could not leave. They suggested that he go to the Iraqi Embassy to get it validated. The Iraqi

Embassy of course would do no such thing, and as he had no desire to return to Iraq, and indeed it might have been very dangerous for him to do so, he was stuck!

I told him that I would try and reason with the Australian Embassy myself and I would call him back. I called the embassy in Beirut and managed to speak to someone about the situation. They were adamant that he could not travel with a passport without validity. I explained that he could not get that validity but they could offer no suggestions.

At this stage I decided that if the worst came to the worst I would have to bring him to England. He could not be left languishing in limbo in some seedy hotel in Beirut, not being able to move forward and not being able to go back. I felt responsible for him in the sense that I had been instrumental in his going to Beirut, and in any case there was nobody else in a position to help him. I would send him a ticket and then bring him to London. I figured that a solution might be easier once he was there. But one hurdle I had to jump was to tell João what was happening. He was not terribly amused, and frankly I do not blame him. He had every right to be very angry with me. João was above all a gentle man with a kind spirit, and while he saw it quite rightly as my problem and not his, he generously said he would accept whatever solution was required, even if Hashim had to stay with us for a while.

I called Hashim and gave him the news and told him that we would not leave him languishing in Beirut and if necessary I would bring him to England. There were still a few things I wanted to try. I was not sure what more I could do. I called Amnesty International to see if they could make any suggestions, but they were not able to assist.

I then remembered a Jewish guy with whom I had worked previously. His name was Zacky Douek. He and his wife were both PhDs, and I used to call them The Doctors Douek. Zacky had been born in Cairo, was intelligent and very street-wise. I called him and asked his advice. He thought for a second or two and then said, "There is only one thing he can do. Go to the market and find someone who will forge his passport. It is not difficult, he just needs it to be amended to include travel to Australia and other Asian countries. There is bound to be someone in the market in Beirut who is capable of doing a job like that".

I tried calling Hashim's hotel in Beirut but he was not there. I sent a telegram with Zacky's suggestion. I tried the hotel the next day, but I was told that he was no longer staying there. I had no idea what had happened to him.

A week or so later I left for a business trip to the US. When I returned I called my father. He informed me that a strange postcard had arrived for me from Bangkok, written in poor English. He told me that it said: "On Pan Am flight to Sydney. Thank you for my freedom".

I found out later that Hashim had come to the same conclusion as the advice given by Zacky, and he had managed to get his passport forged for validity to travel to Australia.

I only saw Hashim once again, and that was in Sydney quite a few years after his arrival. He was well settled. He had a reasonable job and was living with a man quite a bit older than him. The man was kind and considerate and clearly was very fond of Hashim. Hashim looked after him and while it did not seem from the outside to be an ideal relationship, in fact it met most of the needs of both of them. Eventually Hashim would live alone in the house they then shared, the man's house.

Hashim told me that he was extremely content. Even though I have now lived in Sydney myself for 30 years, I have never seen Hashim again and I have no idea where he is. I found a telephone number that I believe to be his, but there is never any answer.

Chapter 6 A small world

The hypothesis of six degrees of separation was first proposed in 1929 by Frigyes Kanthy in a short story called "Chains". It postulates that anyone on the planet can be connected to any other person through a chain of acquaintances with no more than five intermediaries, hence the six degrees of separation. If each person knows 100 people and each of those knows 100 people, and so on, 100 multiplied by 5 gives 10 billion, a very rough approximation of the population of the world today. Actually if we all knew 93 people then the calculation would bring us only marginally above the estimated current world population of 6.5 billion.

On a personal level all of us have experienced examples of coincidences that occur in our lives, but on the international stage such coincidences can be all the more remarkable. It was during this period that I went several times a year to Spain, which was one of the largest markets for the products my company sold and where we had a strong market domination that needed to be secured by providing a lot of service and support. It was on one of these visits that a quite unusual coincidence occurred.

I am not quite sure why I changed from staying at the Hotel Colon. It was right in the part of Barcelona that I loved, the old town bordered on one side by the elegant avenue Las Ramblas, on the port side by the Paseo de Colon, and stretching right up to the Plaza de Cataluna. Close by were all the restaurants I liked, sometimes hard to discover in the first place and then to find again in the labyrinth of narrow streets without cars, the Barrio Chino, the Chinese Quarter, as it was known. In later years it became a haven for robbers and thieves and a centre for drug dealing, or so I was told. I tended to believe it since the gay life had moved away altogether, up town to the other side of the Diagonal that split the city into two, a wide scar of an avenue that separated not just old from new, but order and style from history and imperfection.

It was in the Hotel Colon that I first discovered Zumo de Naranja. Orange juice for me had always been a processed, manufactured drink, and even so rather a luxury in relatively post war England. It was full of sugar, preservatives and artificial colouring. It would not surprise me if it even had artificial flavouring. It was certainly a very long way from an orange branch in a sun-blessed grove. But Zumo de Naranja was exactly what it said it was, the juice of freshly squeezed real oranges. There was a myriad of such simple pleasures that the English were not even aware they were deprived of.

After work a stroll along the tree-lined Ramblas, with the throngs of people strolling and sitting, chatting and laughing, was restorative. There was one particular small square with modest galleries and columns, where I might stop at a café and either have a coffee or an aperitif. As a lady *d'un certain age* is also allowed, it showed signs of the passage of prior years, some cracks and peeling paint, stonework that had lost the sharpness of its edges. For me the glory of the square was the palm tress that stood there stoically, seemingly oblivious to all the traffic and noise around them.

On a Sunday morning in the Plaza de Colon in front of the hotel and with the cathedral behind they danced the Sandana in large circles, joined hands held high from outstretched arms, with a slow and rhythmical music. In those days of the Franco era it was one of the few expressions of the Catalan culture that could be found.

The Hotel Colon did have two major disadvantages for all its wonderful location. The noise from the square penetrated every room, and in those days it had no airconditioning. I suspect these were the reasons that I abandoned it for a quiet modern hotel in a side street on the other side of the Plaza de Cataluna.

While the Colon was a hotel full of light, the Continental was more somber and discreet. The bar had low lighting above dark smoked glass, and was furnished with heavy brown leather sofas. Many countries have a peculiarly individual smell, one that often defies identification into its component parts. For me Spain had a mélange of what might have been Ducados cigarettes, freshly ground coffee and a men's cologne of mediocre calibre. The bar at the Continental left me in no doubt that I was in Spain.

I often used to go there after work and before heading out for dinner. One night I got talking to an American woman. I was 24 and she would have been close to 50. She lived in a small studio in San Juan in Ibiza. She had come to Barcelona to see her son off on the plane back to the USA after spending a holiday with her. She told me that her husband had died unexpectedly of a heart attack a couple of years previously in California where they lived. She had had a wonderful marriage and could not imagine life in the same environment without him. Against all of the advice and in some cases pleading of her friends, she had decided to embark on a complete change. She had always wanted to paint and so she packed up and left California for Ibiza.

I found her fascinating and suggested that we might have dinner together, to which she readily agreed. I was captivated by the courage and strength that this woman had exhibited in facing the reality of her circumstances, and creating a new life rather than live in the shadow of the memory of the one she had lost. Indeed she had learned to paint, and had become integrated into the artistic life of San Juan. She had found a kindred soul with whom to share her intimacy. I wondered if her son was as enthusiastic about his mother's evolution as I was.

But the coincidence I want to recount occurred during another stay at the Continental. As I was heading up to my room in the lift before going out to dinner I noticed that there was a rather shy English girl, maybe in her late twenties. We started to talk, and she explained that she worked for a publishing company and that she was in Barcelona on business. It was clear that she had not travelled much and she seemed to be at a loose end. I know that sometimes it can be lonely in the evening in a strange city, and eating on your own is for many a miserable experience. I suggested that she might like to join me for dinner, explaining that I was going to a local restaurant I knew and that the food was good and reliable. She was pleased I had invited her and accepted after just a slight hesitation.

We walked across the Plaza de Cataluna and into the narrow streets of the old town. The restaurant I chose was very pleasant, with neat, white starched tablecloths tightly stretched over small tables. It was always busy and cheerful. We were shown to a table for two; Jane sat with her back to the wall and I sat opposite. I noticed that on the table to my left was an attractive young couple speaking Italian. I wondered if they were on holiday or business.

The evening passed by pleasantly enough. After the main course a group of three students came around and sang to a guitar accompaniment at each table. As is often the case, as they passed it broke the ice and people on adjacent tables started talking to each other. We got talking to the Italian-speaking couple. They said they were from Madrid. It seemed strange to me that two people from Madrid should speak Italian, so I surmised that the story was a little more complicated than that. The man went on to explain that his wife was really from Tangier. This did not explain at all to my satisfaction therefore why they were speaking Italian, which had nothing at all to do with Morocco. There was going to be still more to this story, I knew. It seemed to me most likely that they were Jewish and so I took a punt.

"Do you by any chance know the Azagury family?" I asked of the woman from Tangier.

She replied, "Most certainly, and in fact one of the sons married my best friend two years ago".

"And I was invited to the wedding", I said.

It was true. I knew another Azagury brother, David, from university. I had happened to be in Tangier on holiday at the same time David was there for the summer break and he had invited me to his brother's wedding. I felt that it was not appropriate for me to go, and in any case the timing would not have been ideal as I would have had to stay on a few more days in Tangier to be able to attend, instead of leaving to drive east into Algeria, which was my plan.

"And are you from Madrid originally?" I asked the man.

He laughed. "No, I am from Istanbul".

I now began to suspect why Italian rather than French or Spanish was their common language. There was a significant Jewish community in Turkey that for some reason spoke Italian, and I can only presume was originally of Italian descent.

"Oh! Do you by any chance know Armando Boton?" I asked the man.

"Armando! Yes, my father knows him very well through business".

Armando Boton was our agent in Turkey and I knew that he was Jewish. There was always a fair chance that the community would be small enough for everyone to know each other.

The woman did not know Armando Boton, and the man did not know the Azagury family. So I knew someone each of them knew without the other knowing them, one in Tangier, and the other in Istanbul. The English girl seemed giddy with excitement at the international labyrinth she had fallen into.

ooOoo

I am able to stir my brain into conversations in French and Spanish when the occasion requires it. And the occasion is not necessarily precipitated by my being in France or Spain at the time. Now here is the rub. My characters speak to me in French and Spanish, and that is why I answer them in that language. But I never know what they say, just that they say it, in no language at all. I just know the meaning and I have to respond. For how could I manufacture a fluency greater than the one I have? My words are real. On waking I can tell you the words I used, but not theirs.

Chapter 7 New York, an unlikely destination

The first time I went to the USA was in 1969. I remember having cocktails at the top of the Fairmont Hotel, looking across the San Francisco skyline and thinking that I could easily have plonked myself there permanently. I would have bought myself a Ford Mustang and been real cool. I still have pangs of nostalgia when I see an old Mustang.

Over the years I gained the maturity to look a bit further than the glitter of that moment at the Fairmont, and I have come to intensely dislike the central tenets of the American Way. I have many American friends whom I love dearly; it is just the country they are from that I have a problem with. Many of them share my views. I find it a harsh and unforgiving society, capable of serving those who are fortunate very well indeed, but offering little help to those who are less so. I guess that if you are fortunate, and I would have been if I had lived permanently in the USA, and you are not affected by others' misery, life can be pretty good there. But if, like me, you see yourself as being part of a wider society whose overall wellbeing affects all parts of society, then it is hard to cope with. The majority of Americans struggle financially while the wealthy continue to make their money often at the expense of the majority. I remember once meeting a waiter at a hotel where I was staying in Barbados; we were almost literally swept together by a tropical storm one night. He came to my room for shelter and comfort, of sorts. He wanted to go and live in America because he thought he would earn a lot of money and be wealthy. I tried to persuade him that not only was that not guaranteed, but that at least in his own country, he was a Barbadian he would not end up a second-class citizen as he almost certainly would have in the USA.

I find the inequity of American society obscene and it has been made even more so since companies started to provide stock options. How can the wealthy be taxed so little when there are people who cannot even access reasonable healthcare? Should the individual be allowed to act unimpeded on the stage of life, or should the individual be encouraged to act in a way that recognises that she or he is part of a social context? For example, I will never have children, but I believe that my taxes should in part go towards the education and care of youth, for without them there will be no future, albeit a future in which I will not figure anyway. There is a word that is anathema in the USA that comes to mind: socialism. I would consider myself very much a socialist given that I see myself as existing as part of a social whole rather than as simply an individual.

Furthermore, I do not feel part of the materialism that has swamped the western world, led by the USA, and that is now gradually ruining many of the wonderful aspects of life in other parts of the developing world. People get mixed up between the play and the stage. The stage is simply the context for the play: where you live, the money you have, the clothes you wear, the job you do. The play is what life is all about: who you are, your interactions with other people, the way you play the cards that are dealt to you, your value system and whether you live and act by it. For me it is the play that is important. There surely is nothing in life beyond relationships. However, I fear that for many the stage is where they concentrate their energies.

Given my views on the USA, it might seem very strange that I ended up living in New York for a year. The circumstances that brought that about depended on a bit of fate.

After my mother died and my sister and her family returned to the USA, I spent as much time with my father as I could. I would drive to Solihull, for they had moved to the other side of the city from where I was born when my father retired several years earlier, at least every month for the weekend. But at the same time I was living with João, and as I was travelling a lot in those days, my weekends were precious. I tried to balance competing priorities, and probably did none of them justice.

Dot and Gerry had been friends of my parents. Dot and my mother were very close friends. Gerry had worked for Boots as a sales area manager, and was the original point of contact of the friendship with my parents. But the friendship that blossomed was primarily between Dot and my mother. As my father found it difficult to converse with other males, when Gerry came around when I was a teenager at home, I in fact spent more time talking to him than my father did. He was dashing and well travelled, and I found him fascinating.

But Gerry died almost at the same time as my mother, and Dot retained a friendship with my father, more out of a sense of loyalty to my mother than anything else, I suspect. Her son also lived in London and on a few occasions my father and Dot travelled to London together to visit their respective sons. I once drove Dot back to the Midlands after one of the visits and when she stayed on longer than my father.

On the drive north she initiated the following conversation.

"João is very nice, isn't he?"

"Yes, he is".

"A very good-looking man".

"Yes, he is".

"Maybe a bit effeminate, don't you think?"

"Oh, I don't know".

"Come on, John, you two guys are on together, aren't you?"

"Yes, Dot, you are right".

"Well, don't tell your father, he would never understand".

Dot was of course right. She was well aware of my father's conservatism. My London cousin Mike swore that my father knew that I was gay and said that he had had a conversation with him about it. But he hadn't. He just thought he had. My father was so naïve that the conversation would have been in two totally different dimensions, and my cousin just would not have realised.

However, in 1972 I decided to halt the relationship with João. That decision was partly to do with my liking João but not loving him, and partly to do with the fact that one night after a long day's work in New York I had met Marty in Harry's Back East.

I had perhaps always known that my relationship with João would not last for ever, and indeed I had been reluctant to live with him in the first place. I had had a relationship the previous year with Karl, a German guy I met in Tenerife where I went with my father after the death of my mother. I visited him often in the small village outside Heidelberg where he was a medical student. It was fairly easy for me to drop into Frankfurt with my schedule flying around Europe. He wanted me to go and live in Germany, and while I thought about it and even went once for a job interview, I decided that was not what I wanted and called the affair off.

But Marty was different, and I decided the time had come for João and I to split up. These are never easy times, and I felt very bad about telling João it was over. I also felt a sadness because even though I was the one to initiate the break-up, he had been an important part of my life through some very difficult times including my mother's death.

I said something to my father in a telephone conversation when João moved out about the sadness I felt, and the truth of the nature of our relationship suddenly must have dawned on him. For, Dot rang me the next morning, a Sunday, and told me that my father had called her, that he had realised "the situation" and was going around to see her to talk about it. She said, "John, I will do my best for you. Stay by the phone and I will call you". I did as she requested and an hour or so later she called. She told me that my father was terribly upset; she had tried her hardest to explain. He was going to call me, and I should not let on that we had spoken.

About half an hour later the phone rang.

"I am terribly upset".

"I am sorry to hear that. What's wrong?"

"I did not realise until our conversation yesterday. It seems that you have become a lesbian".

While my friends and I have laughed many times over this story, it does demonstrate the extreme naïvete of my father. He wanted me to leave the wicked city and take up the priesthood. I found this surprising from a man who never ever went into a religious institution apart from weddings, funerals and for sightseeing purposes. In subsequent years he appeared on the surface to accept my being gay. But Dot told me much later, after his death, that it was simply a front, and that he never understood it and never accepted it.

Nevertheless, I was his son, and when I left England, first to go to New York and then to Australia, even though he never asked me not to go, I could see that it crushed him, all the more since my sister had returned to California with his only two grandchildren, and with no hope of any more. Now that I was leaving he must have felt utterly alone. He tried not to let it show, but I still feel the sadness of that moment.

So, how did fate cause me to go to New York to live? I liked staying at the Holiday Inn way over on West 59th street, because the rooms were enormous and I was able to bring back any trade I might have encountered in the city jungle. There had been several over the frequent visits I made to New York in those days, including one very camp number who worked at Castro Convertibles and who embarrassed me by forgetting his umbrella in my room, and after I had gone to work, returned to the hotel and explained to reception that he had slept with me the previous night and needed to retrieve the umbrella he had left in the room.

Marty was altogether different from the parade of bed partners that had hitherto enjoyed the welcome of the Holiday Inn. He was intelligent, and had integrity, a great sense of humour, and a lack of that New York abrasiveness that grated so. I was intrigued. We saw each other for dinner and fucking every night until I left, and then again when I returned. He was a professor of law at Brooklyn Law School, and enjoyed long university holidays. We rather quickly drifted into a relationship, initially for the most part at a distance.

He came to the UK whenever he could for the next two years and I was often in New York. He accompanied me on a business trip to France, Netherlands, Germany, Turkey and Lebanon. Beirut was particularly interesting for a young Jewish lad who at that time had travelled little. He wanted me to take him to Syria, but I baulked at that.

I had once before been to Syria, by road through the Beka'a Valley, later to become well known for its fighting and desolation during the civil war. I went with Joe Damgagian, the salesperson of our local agents; he was an Armenian who had a wife called Claire who adored him, and who suffered from a smell of stale perspiration and a bad squint. We left before dawn and stopped just after Zahleh in the early morning at a café for piping hot coffee and Lebanese snacks of cheese and pastries. It was cold and foggy at that height and we needed to restore ourselves. The border was austere and threatening with its obvious high security, and the road into Damascus revealed many of the characteristics of Eastern bloc countries, with dour buildings and enormous symbolic posters showing the glory of socialism depicting muscley handsome men producing heavy industrial goods. The old market was more pleasing with artisans in their small ateliers working the crafts of hundreds of years, timeless and yet totally in the moment. The air was heavy with the noise of metal pounding against metal, and the sparks of products painfully taking their form. There was the occasional whirring of an old sewing machine, operated of course by men. Electrical wires, more recent intruders, hung dangerously festooned across doorways. There was the smell of strong black coffee with cardamom seeds.

But despite all this peaceful industry I was aware of a lack of predictability; I felt a warning to beware. That evening I was waiting for Joe in the bar of the hotel where we stayed, with the only other customer being an Indian reporter from a prestigious Indian weekly magazine who was waiting for a man he was going to interview. The man entered; I sat quietly as he looked around nervously. They talked in English, and it was quite clear that the visitor was high-ranking in some Palestinian organisation. Just as their conversation was getting interesting, turning towards aspects of the Lebanese civil war, Joe entered the bar. Joe Damgagian hated Indians, it seems, and decided to get stuck into the reporter, taunting him and insulting him, referring to him as a chapati. The Palestinian fled, and both the Indian and I were furious.

The journey back to Lebanon was uneventful but Joe told me that on some occasions they just shut the border and he had sometimes been stranded days at a time in Syria not able to get back. I was just not going to take Marty into that sort of politically charged situation, especially with an American passport and a very Jewish family name. So we remained in Beirut on that occasion.

I had been negotiating for almost a week over an installation of equipment at a major printing company, Dar Assayad. It was not an easy week. I would go about my normal business in the day and then as soon as the sun went down, and just as we were thinking about dinner around seven a rather oily old letch with heavily tinted glasses (the same one who wrote poems about Michelle David) would call me at the hotel speaking in heavily accented English. "It is Monsieur Michel. You must come immediately to Dar Assayad". I would take a taxi and spend the rest of the evening waiting for something to happen. It was summer and Beirut was a pleasant relief from the 40 degrees of the torrid Gulf summer. Beirut was in those days the centre of all Middle Eastern commerce, a place where those from the more conservative Gulf States would come to enjoy the cooler weather and more frivolous atmosphere and all sorts of pleasures denied them at home. Tea or coffee would be served in the Dar Assayad office, and men in flowing white robes and lavish headdresses would chat away in Arabic, a language I found harsh and guttural, often sounding as if they were arguing, but in fact they were not. I sat there inert, not understanding, not participating, wondering why I had been summoned.

Then finally Nasri or Monsieur Michel would start talking about the "deal". Nasri was the technical man who in many ways had the final say. I had a very weak stomach for bribes, but had already brought myself to ask Nasri, as diplomatically and honourably as I could, whether his consultancy in this matter should be financially compensated, and he had said not.

Finally our impending departure back to London forced the negotiations to their culmination. I had already been told by Monsieur Michel that the president of the company, Mr Bassam Freiha, wanted to offer me some gold cufflinks, very expensive, I assumed in exchange for my dropping the price. It would be my personal reward. Did I like gold cufflinks, very expensive? I told them that I was totally ambivalent towards cufflinks, very expensive, or anything else, but that in any case such issues would not be in any way connected to the business under discussion. We were leaving on the Saturday morning, and the deal was struck finally on the Friday night, but being a newspaper, they wanted to take photos of the handshake, and that was arranged for the next morning. I protested that the flight was leaving shortly after the time they wanted the meeting. Not to worry, they advised, Mr Bassam would send his Mercedes to pick up Marty from the hotel and pick me up from the offices and take us straight to the airport for the flight.

That Friday evening, once the deal was signed, Joe Damgadjian, performing what I considered an odd role for a salesperson, called at my hotel to ask for the commissions that needed to be paid to appropriate stakeholders and interested parties. He said that there was the salesperson from the competing supplier of equipment who had generously retired from the negotiation on the basis that he would receive an appropriate sum. I said "no". And to my astonishment Nasri was also on the list. I was annoyed that it now looked as if he was asking for his cut, especially when I had already approached him. Again I said "no".

I was disappointed as I quite liked Nasri and I had felt I had some bond with him since a few nights earlier we had been stopped in a roadblock set up by the army trying to address the Palestinian problem, which was already erupting. We had been ordered out of our car, and stood together with our legs apart, elbows on the roof and our hands behind our heads. I said to Nasri that I did not have any identification with me, which was in fact illegal. He admitted that he had forgotten his papers too. It was late and the last thing we wanted was to spend half the night trying to clear ourselves. Nasri addressed the officer sternly. He apparently told him that I was an important overseas visitor and guest of Dar Assayad, and how dare they cause me the humiliation of making me stand there against the car with my hands behind my head. The ploy worked and we were allowed to proceed.

The next morning at the offices of Dar Assayad I graciously accepted some very cheap gold plated cufflinks, and good to their word, the Mercedes rushed us to the airport, and then the driver arranged for an escort rapidly through check-in, immigration and on to the plane, which was about to depart. We were supposed to be on the MEA flight to Paris with a connection to London. It was therefore quite a surprise to us when they announced the flying time to Milan. They had facilitated us onto the wrong flight. But the flight eventually was destined to go to Paris, and although we missed the connection we did eventually arrive back in London.

Shortly after we returned to the UK we set out in my MGB driving across Europe, right down to the toe of Italy and across to Greece. Marty started to turn a nasty shade of yellow even before we got to Italy, and I had to nurse him through hepatitis through the rest of the trip. We stopped and rested in Corfu for two weeks while he got over the worst of it, but the trip was not at all what it had been designed to be.

We once had a January break in Andalucia, driving through the winter mists across frozen landscapes, with white villages appearing through the fog as the sun warmed the land. I recollect piping hot garlic soup in Cordoba to fortify us for the visit to the Grand Mosque, and strolls along the Mediterranean shore in a January sun, which while thin, was balmy compared to London.

In the summer of 1973 we flew to the Seychelles when there were only two hotels on the island of Mahe. It was an unutterable paradise in those days, and I have never returned in case the spell be broken. The discovery of the island with its deserted beaches, and cool passes in the centre of the island with amazing views down to the shore, was made possible by hiring an open Mini Moke. We went to two of the other islands, Praslin and La Digue, the latter really a Robinson Crusoe destination. I am not a very good sailor and the boat ride between the two islands was rather rough. I sat in front of the sick room contemplating going in and laying down, until I saw the most enormous spider I have ever seen, the size of my hand, crawl into the room around the door jam. I decided I was safer on deck. The postman was on our boat and came to the shore with us on the tender. He stood in the water and called out the names of the islanders who had mail. They stepped forward, collected their letters, and then he left back on the boat, and La Digue settled back into itself. There was no electricity or paved roads, just the silence of paradise interrupted by the occasional coconut dropping to the ground.

Having a transatlantic relationship, even with our joint abilities to make the crossing, was often difficult. But then I was approached by a company with its headquarters in New York, who wanted me to set up a distribution network for the international sales of their graphic arts equipment. They made me a ridiculously low salary offer. I countered, they accepted, and I was suddenly on the path out of England, although in the opposite direction to the one I had always imagined. I knew the time was right to go, but as I set off I had lurking just below my consciousness the feeling that this was not where I really wanted to go.

Given the feelings that I had developed about the USA, it was always going to be unlikely that a relationship with Marty would work long-term. Not so much because of him, but more because I just could not see myself as being a New Yorker, certainly in the way that he was. But that is the wisdom of hindsight, and in the moment, I had a lover who was good company, and who fucked me as often as I wanted. (He had some anatomical complication that required our relationship to operate that way around, and if I am honest he did it well.) The future would take care of itself.

He lived on East 80th Street in an apartment that was on the third floor. If I stood more than a metre from the window I could see no sky at all. I worked for a miserable company located at the back of La Guardia airport. This meant that I had no practical option other than to drive to work. The adjustment from my MGB to Marty's humungous Pontiac

Catalina, which I suspect might have been an early model for an aircraft carrier, was one that I never managed. Every time I drove over Brooklyn Bridge my heart was in my mouth in case I hit another car or a pillar on the bridge. Trying to park the wretched piece of mechanical shit in the evenings was worse. It took me up to an hour sometimes to find a parking spot, driving down 80th, up 81st, down 82nd, from Park Avenue to 1st and then all over again.

I hated the job. The company was a very unprofessionally managed private company owned by a Jewish family. It was well known that you needed to catch the boss between 8.15 and 8.30 am if you wanted to have a useful conversation. This was the narrow window between the valium starting to work and taking over completely.

I survived only because I had a job that was very different from the others, and because they had no idea how to take me to task without appearing to lose dignity. It was probably my accent that intimidated them. Managers were expected to work on Saturday mornings to show that they were dedicated to their jobs. I simply told them that I worked the whole of the weekend and every weekend when I was travelling, and that was half of the time, and that when I was in New York there was no way I was going to the office on a weekend. I was the only manager to escape.

The year that I spent in New York – at least that was where my toothbrush charger was – was full but not satisfying. I just never settled down into being a New Yorker. I hated the rudeness of the people in the stores and the suspicion everywhere. There was a general assumption that everyone was a potential nut, thief, drug addict, whatever, and should be kept at a distance. If you smiled at them, it would lend weight to the argument that you must be recently escaped from a high-security mental institution.

We did not go out much, not to the theatre or cinema, we made only the odd excursion to Queens at the weekends to see Marty's parents. We once went to Fire Island, and the smell of promiscuity excited me. But it was only a whiff in the air that I experienced, something that I always regretted in some way.

Marty was not Jewish by belief, but rather by tradition or even habit. I cooked only kosher meat, which his mother bought, and I used to send him on an errand out of the kitchen every time I wanted to pop a little cream into some exotic sauce that I was making to go with a meat dish. He would drag me 15 blocks in howling blizzards because orange juice was on special. I enjoyed being with him, but I was not having fun.

To bring my presence into the apartment we redecorated the bathroom with silver-and-blue wallpaper, a very art deco look. When I smoked dope I used to stand there for what seemed like hours, my dick in my hand, staring at that wallpaper trying to remember what I had gone in there to do.

Social life in the city tended to revolve around the Brooklyn Law School group. It was usually rather boring. We were invited one night to dinner at Sutton Place; one of his colleagues had married well. I insisted that we take some wine, and of course that was given to me at the store in a brown paper bag. When we arrived at the front door of the very upmarket and expensive apartment block, the concierge looked at me in a very dismissive way and said tersely, "Deliveries around the back".

When these people made a return visit to us, they were intrigued by a lithograph of mine hanging in the hallway.

"Oh, how interesting, what is it?"

"It is the start of the revolution in Leningrad, given to me in Moscow by some one I worked with there." There was an audible intake of horrified air.

"We are very 'ant-eye' communist. My wife has written a book about how awful East Germany is".

"Oh, really, when was she there?"

"She has never set foot in any of these countries and never will. None of our money will ever go to a communist regime".

More uplifting was the wife of another of the Brooklyn professors. The conversation over dinner one evening turned to university politics and became boring for those not involved, and the wife (born in France of Russian Jewish parents) and I started speaking French. Whether this is what set her off on the track, I do not know. But she revealed an amazing story of how her parents disappeared at the start of the war, and she and her brother were left with nowhere to go and nothing to do, except to try and save themselves.

They were 19 and 20 years old. They joined the Resistance, believing they had nothing to lose. This very ordinary, middle-aged, overweight woman with plastic daffodils in her garden in middle-class Queens, who would not arouse any interest in a suburban supermarket (perhaps her main strength in hindsight), went on to describe jumping off trains and rolling down grassy banks to get across the Vichy line; being arrested by the Germans, but then released because they could find nothing; acting as a courier; and so on. She survived (as did her brother) and she met Milt when he was part of the occupying forces in France at the end of the war, and transitioned into a suburban house wife in Queens. When I told Marty how amazed I had been by the story, he told me that as far as he was aware she had never revealed this to anyone in the circle before, and that he was astounded.

I felt that my salvation in New York was my friend Ernst whom I had met in Paris many years earlier. As I recollect it, we got into the lift at the hotel where we were both staying, pressed buttons for different floors but both got out on the same floor. He had left his native Switzerland and then lived with Roger in New York. It was the contact with another European that I relished. In those days they had a modest apartment in Jersey City, a far cry from the comfortable home they now have in Garden City Long Island. But I remember Sunday morning soufflés cooked to perfection, and a European feeling in what was otherwise a desolate New Jersey urban dump.

I travelled an enormous amount, which brought some further escape from New York, and at least solved the problem of my not having residency and a Green Card at that stage, although once we did make a trip to Montreal to avoid overstaying my visa permit. The Green Card was to happen just in time to be too late. My work would take me that year twice to South America, twice to Japan and the Far East, several times to Europe, once to Africa, and once to Australia and New Zealand, that trip being the one that finally sealed my future in New York.

But before that we took a holiday in Israel.

Chapter 8 From celebrations in Israel to complications in Algeria

Fred, my close friend from school days, married Marianne in August 1974 in a small town on the Mediterranean called Nahariya, five kilometres south of the Lebanese border in Israel. This was his second marriage; the first also took place in Israel, but was an unmitigated disaster. Both Fred's mother, Blanka, a wonderfully vivacious and very direct Viennese woman whom I adored, and I agreed that the first wife's mother was more of a catch than the daughter. I was to join Marty, who was already in Israel, for this second nuptial.

For me it was a three-day journey starting in Mexico City with nights in New York and London. I claimed when I arrived at the wedding that no other guest had come a longer distance and spent three days getting there. In New York I stayed the night at the house of Marty's parents, which happened to be in Queens and much closer to Kennedy than going all the way into the city to our apartment (alright, Marty's apartment!).

They had kosher toothpaste. I knew about the plastic covers on the sofa in the hardly used sitting room, and about the two sets of plates and cutlery. I had once warned my father, who stopped in to New York to see us on his way back from visiting my sister in California, not to ask for milk in his tea, which they always served after the main meal. But in that case they had pre-empted me by providing some non-dairy milk especially for him, thus ensuring the kosher qualifications of the household were upheld. I had managed to answer with a straight-face questions like, "Do they celebrate Thanksgiving in England?" and "Do you have cheddar cheese in England?" I even never commented on the fact that they called Yiddish, the language of their Russian-born parents, Jewish. But as I stayed overnight at their house in Queens I could hardly believe that people could be so vulnerable to commercial exploitation as to pay a significant premium for kosher toothpaste. They made their first excursion outside the USA to Mexico City and were so terrified that they would get some stomach bug that they only ate bananas and drank milk. They were as sick as dogs for the whole week they were there and saw nothing at all of Mexico City.

It was kind enough of them to pick me up at Kennedy and then deliver me back the next morning. They were good people. I had been the lover of their son Marty for three years. I doubt that they ever imagined we were lovers. His sister knew, and in fact it was to her apartment in Israel where I was headed. She lived with her sabra husband Gingie (so named for the rather unusual ginger hair he had as an Israeli-born boy) north of

Tel Aviv in Ramat Aviv in a new apartment complex. Marty was already there, and I was joining him for both a holiday in Israel and to attend the wedding. Marianne's parents lived in Haifa, which is why they were to be married in Israel.

The first few days we spent in Ramat Aviv. Gingie was a slob, lazy, ugly and a litter bug of unimaginable proportions. We were horrified watching him throw litter out of the fourth-floor window of the apartment they could afford only because Marty's sister was a teacher and had saved money in New York before they left to live in Israel. Otherwise they would never have managed to live in such relative luxury. Empty cigarette packs, paper, fag ends – straight out the window and no longer his problem.

From Ramat Aviv we took a bus up north to Nahariya for the wedding. It was late starting because the rabbi, for some reason, was very late in arriving. The guests sat down at the tables surrounding the *huppa* where the ceremony was to take place. The mistake was made of putting food on the tables before the ceremony started. As a result most guests had their noses so firmly into the delicacies laid before them that they seemed hardly to acknowledge or even notice that there was a wedding ceremony taking place when the rabbi finally did arrive.

I have always tended to embrace informality over pomp. But this wedding even stretched my capacity to not be shocked. It was a rabble rather than a serious event attended by caring friends and relatives. As the couple were combined together in binding matrimony and the glass duly stamped on by the groom, few noticed. There was a general buzz of animated chatting between mouthfuls of food, while the wedding party was totally ignored. It was I suppose a truly Israeli affair.

It was late by the time that the festivities were over, and we counted ourselves lucky to manage to get a cheroot (a group taxi) back to Tel Aviv at such a late hour. The highway back to Tel Aviv passed within a block of the apartment in Ramat Aviv. It was empty and dusty with not a blade of grass to be seen, there was just a mustard colour in the streetlights silent and utterly peaceful. Yet, during the wedding in Nahariya the Israeli navy had slipped up the coast and delivered a massive attack on the villages just a few kilometres away over the border in southern Lebanon. It was a wonder we had not heard it. The attack, which was of course a few years before Israel occupied that area, was to counter several cross-border mortar attacks on communities close to the border on the Israeli side.

In those days every conversation turned eventually to Israel's security. I passionately defended the right of Israel to exist at that time when neighbours were threatening to throw every single last Israeli into the Mediterranean. I now do the same thing for the Palestinians, who equally deserve to have their homeland. This has been rendered almost impossible by the establishment these last years of Jewish settlements throughout the territories that should be Palestine. It is a policy of the Israeli government that could so easily have been halted by the US government if it had so chosen. It always seemed strange to me that modern Israel was populated mainly by survivors of World War Two or people who had left the countries of their birth to live a life without persecution. They were often the butt of stigma and discrimination, and were forced to be humble. Yet, possibly as a reaction to the humility forced on their parents, the offspring of these people are in my view arrogant. I suspect their arrogance pre-dated the military successes they had in the two wars they fought with their neighbours, but these would have reinforced that attitude. I think they have developed a superiority, a disdain for the Arabs, and persecuted not only the Arabs, but also the Bedouins who had lived in these lands since the beginnings of time. The Israelis have forgotten who they are, and when a country forgets its history, it loses its way.

Israel in 1974 was almost always on a war footing. We hired a Ford Escort to drive around Israel for a couple of weeks, and we often stopped to pick up soldiers who were returning to service after a short break with their families. They were not grateful; it was their right and expectation that the community would get them to wherever they were supposed to go. Another day we had to escape a tank roaring down the road towards us, by driving off the road onto the verge to let it pass. We might have felt a little indignant, but careering tanks have a certain imperative about them.

It intrigued me that the Israelis apparently seem to not hold their land in very high regard. It is one of the most littered countries I have ever seen. One might have thought, given how hard they have fought for it, and the amount of blood that has been spilled to create it, that they might be gentle and loving with it. But no. I had a conversation with a couple who had been born in Europe and emigrated to Israel as children. We were on the beach at Eilat and it looked like a garbage tip. When I mentioned this, they said, "Look, see our son there playing in the water. He is 15 years old. In two years more he will be going to the army. Who knows whether he will live or die. Because of that we spoil our children. We do not discipline them enough. But if he were yours, what would you do?"

I am not sure how the uncertainty of life in Israel and discipline, urban pride and responsibility are connected; I did not see their argument as being in the least bit logical. But then I have always found Israelis strange.

They will rush around, trampling you, pushing you out of the way as if a second's delay might cost them their life. Then if you ask them how to get to a particular place, they will walk 10 minutes out of their way to make sure you find it, and then almost push you under a bus as they rush off again.

Israel is one of the most amazing countries in which to tour. It holds in Jerusalem the crucible of three of the world's major religions. History that is embedded in much of humanity is everywhere. The old city of Jerusalem is one of the most amazing places I have ever seen. I was fortunate enough to go there in 1968 when it was still possible for westerners to visit the Dome of the Rock, the third holiest site of Islam and a stunningly beautiful mosque with a wonderful blue dome. Walking streets such as the via Dolorosa, treading (more or less) the same paths as Christ brings history alive for me. Gethsemanee, Bethlehem, Nazareth, the Sea of Galilee, the River Jordan – the names send electricity through my veins.

On a later visit to Israel I attended the bar mitzvah of the son of close friends at the Wailing Wall. As we drove to the Sea of Galilee through the West Bank, there was a lone Arab sitting on a donkey at the side of the road. He was dressed in traditional Arab dress, and he looked just as if he had been cut out of the Bible and placed there by the tourist authority.

But apart from the ancient history, there is also Israel's modern history, although many would argue that very little has changed in terms of the conflicts that have existed thousands of years. In 1974 we drove along the road that follows the border with Jordan from the southern end of the Dead Sea, past Sodom to Eilat. Between the road and the border was a broad furlough of carefully moulded sand, wide enough that it would be impossible to cross it without leaving a trace of some sort in the perfect shape of the sand. The military patrolled the strip constantly, so that they would have known within a very short period if someone had crossed over from Jordan in an attempt to get into Israel. Nowadays of course the situation has gone way beyond that.

Marty and I stayed on the shores of the Dead Sea at Ein Geddie. We floated in the highly concentrated salt of the lower end of the sea, finding it physically almost impossible to stand on the floor as the sea was so dense and buoyant. The floor of the sea was sharp with crystalised salt, and our bodies were so slimy and slippery that even a good long shower left us feeling dirty.

We tried out the health spa with reputedly therapeutic mud baths. It was messy, not at all pleasant, and frankly I could not tell any benefit at all, either in the way I felt or looked!

On the other hand Masada, the rocky outcrop at the foot of the Dead Sea, where the Jewish zealots lived for several years in defiance of the Romans before they committed suicide en masse, was an amazing experience. Not only because of its extraordinary history but also because its superb views to the Dead Sea, Jordan and the surrounding landscapes. Another visit there nearly 20 years later was a shock. The southern end of the Dead Sea had almost become a lake as a result of the amount of water that has been taken out of the River Jordan flowing into the Dead Sea. It looks as if the Dead Sea is getting deader. And if the politics of the region can ever get away from oil, there is plenty of scope for conflict over water, although the Turks would hold the cards in that case.

The road through Sodom, almost a pilgrimage for me although there seemed to be nothing there, followed the border with southern Jordan down to the port of Eilat. In the distance stood the Jordanian port of Aqaba. South of Eilat is Sinai, and in 1974 the whole peninsula was in the hands of the Israelis. They had taken it during the Six-Day-War in 1967. We headed down the coast staying at *moshavim* (like a kibbutz but with a commercial charter) in Dahab and Nuweiba. I could see how the Red Sea got its name. On the other side of the Gulf of Aqaba lay Saudi Arabia, deserted and mysterious. In the evening as the setting sun fell over Sinai, the mountains on the Saudi side became a deep red colour, contrasting with the deep blue of the gulf. It is also one of the few places I know where it is possible to just stroll into the sea and be surrounded by tropical fish and coral.

In the evenings we talked well into the night with the many Israelis we met at the *moshavim* about the political situation. The conversations were vibrant, well informed, and conducted with both compassion and passion. Israelis saw their existence as precarious, as in those days their country was a defender.

We made an excursion into the interior of Sinai in a four-wheel drive with a tour guide who had befriended some of the Bedouin nomads who lived there. Their worldly possessions appeared to be in a small pile on the floor. The guide produced water and tea, and a few plastic cups. Somehow they managed to kindle a fire from some dead branches. They were probably totally unaware that they lived in Israeli-occupied territory, and after all what did it matter?

The Sinai landscape is so arid and inhospitable that the Americans used it to make films about the moon. For me these areas, as well as other arid places such as Central Australia and the Sahara, have an eerie, almost spiritual beauty. I was astonished to see ibex in the distance standing on a rise looking curiously at us. I wonder what on earth they ate, as there seemed to be nothing with a leaf on it for miles.

But there is always life of some form and in some way. Even on rocks recently created by volcanoes on the coast of Hawaii I have seen plants growing within an amazingly short period.

The Straits of Tiran may not mean much to people younger than 50, but these narrow straits, between what was Egyptian Sinai and Saudi Arabia at the neck of the Gulf of Aqaba as it reaches the Red Sea, allowed Egypt to control access of Israeli shipping to their only port south of Suez, Eilat. In 1951 Egypt blockaded the straits so that Israel lost their only non-Mediterranean port. Later, when Egypt nationalised the Suez Canal this prompted the war in 1956 that saw the closure of the canal, with Britain and France acting in war in concert, and then the Six-Day War happened 11 years later in 1967, followed by the Yom Kippur War in 1973.

We drove down to the town at the point, Sharm-el-Sheik, past the Straits of Tiran, and stayed in a modern temporary hotel of sorts. It was like a giant plastic cube that clearly could easily be removed if and when the Israelis agreed to go. We drove around the point along a forlorn road through low sandhills until we were facing the Egyptian shore looking across the Gulf of Suez. On the way we saw the carcasses of rotting tanks from previous wars – Egyptian tanks, of course. Then in the distance we could see the flares on the distant Egyptian coast of the fledgling Egyptian oil industry.

We turned back towards Israel and thought of Moses. This part of the world has history, both ancient and modern, and is still unfurling its miserable account.

From Eilat we headed across the Negev, climbed a steep precipice to Beersheva, and passed by what looked to me as if it had to be an installation of the Israeli nuclear industry. Later that day we went to Gaza. The gap of frontier land into Gaza – one could hardly call it a border – was forlorn and full of foreboding. The town was poor, with old broken buildings, people poorly dressed, streets full of rubbish; yet poor though it was, there was not the oppressive feeling of isolation that it has more recently endured. There were no bomb craters or rubble where people and homes used to be. In some strange way it did have dignity, a sense that however precarious, the place was theirs. We of course were driving an Israeli car, but even so we were welcomed everywhere we went, even if the local population were rather surprised that we were there at all.

We handed back the Ford Escort, and headed to London. After a day I had to leave Marty to find his own way back to New York, and he was sick with some bug he picked up somewhere on the trip. I took everything off on one side of the room, packed again, changed passports (I had two British passports for this very purpose), got dressed and got on a plane to Geneva. After a short transit, I caught a Swissair flight to Algiers.

It was just a few days before the opening of the World Fair in Algiers. I was part of a British Board of Trade mission. Britain was to have their own building at the fair, and there were a dozen or so exhibitors of all sorts from different industries. We managed to be part of it through our British subsidiary based in Thetford in Norfolk. I always felt it was a little risky given the mother company for which I worked in New York was Jewish-owned and quite publicly so. The mother company could not participate as the Americans had decided to totally boycott the fair. This might have been something to do with their displeasure with some of the other participants. The Cold War was alive and well, and Algeria was very much in the Pan-Arab and Soviet spheres.

As a precaution before the British subsidiary signed up, I checked with the Board of Trade (BOT) in London as to the existence of a "Black List". I had tried to do that in the USA, but they seemed to be totally unaware of the existence of such a thing. The British, always practical about these matters, had a staff position devoted to administering the list and answering enquiries. The current incumbent sounded like a bright young woman just out of Oxford.

"I would like to check whether my company is on the Arab Black List of companies they will not deal with".

"Connecting you". There was only a slight pause and the phone rang again a couple of times.

"Good morning, Black List". I explained what I wanted to know.

"Can I have your full company name and address please?"

She looked it up. "You are on the list in a couple of the Gulf States, but certainly not for Algeria".

When we landed in Algiers, I was not entirely confident this was going to be an easy trip, and it turned out that I was quite right. Most of the BOT delegation was on the same plane, including the engineer I took with me from our British company. The whole trip had been pre-booked and pre-paid through the BOT. In fact a very nice young girl called Sandra from the BOT, totally unsuited for the demands of the job, had arrived a few days earlier and met us all at the airport.

We had prepaid hire cars, one car for each company, for the most part two people, which were going to be necessary as we were staying at a beachside resort just outside Algiers on the western edge of the city. The exhibition site was a good 45 minutes away by car on the eastern side of the city. The first problem, Sandra confided in me, was that there were no cars available. They had all broken down and could not be repaired because the government would not give a licence for the importation of spare parts on the grounds they did not have enough foreign exchange. We went by multiple taxi to the location of the car rental company. They opened the door on what looked like a vast hangar of broken down cars all waiting for parts. They were Romanian-manufactured Fiats. The owner shrugged his shoulders; there was nothing he could do about it.

They offered us instead a much smaller number of chauffeur-driven VWs. We wanted them just to give us whatever VWs they had instead of the Fiats, but they would not budge. The VWs only came with drivers. We had little option but to accept.

By the time we arrived with the drivers and the VWs at the hotel where our accommodation had been arranged, it was late afternoon. The hotel was virtually on the beach, and was very pleasant, with one-storey bungalow accommodation, all white in the Mediterranean style. We were advised that our rooms had been given to an African delegation that had arrived unexpectedly, and the hotel staff were sorry to have to point out that such government visitors always had to take precedence over other guests. Even if the other guests had already paid for the rooms in advance? Yes, even then!

They had made alternative arrangements at a hotel a couple of kilometres away. We clambered into our chauffeured cars, and went to have a look. As we might have expected the accommodation was diabolical, and not at all acceptable for people trying to work for 19 days at an exhibition, or any other decent human being for that matter. We returned to the original hotel, where our luggage to the dismay of the hotel staff was piled up in reception. We told them we would move it only once they had found us acceptable accommodation. When I say "we told them", I mean "I". This should really have been handled by Sandra, but there were two problems with that. The first is that women are not taken at all seriously in this society, especially if they are young and as slim as a willow tree bending in the breeze. And the other was that she spoke no French (or Arabic) at all. The BOT possibly totally destroyed this poor girl's career and confidence in one fell swoop. As I was the only person who spoke decent French, and being the sort of person who finds it difficult to not take charge in a vacuum (or in any case, many would argue), I spoke on behalf of the rest of us.

But by the time midnight had come and gone, we had to go to that appalling other hotel for the night, or else sleep on the floor. The next morning we were due to start working on mounting our stands for the exhibition that was due to open in three days. But we did not. We went instead to the British Embassy and demanded to see the head of the

Trade section, who had supposedly organised everything on behalf of the BOT. The head of the section was busy with some meetings and then was to have lunch with some totally unimportant person. We could try and come back later. We did, and His Exemploriness turned up the worse for wear in the mid-afternoon. It was clear that he was not in the least bit interested. He simply demanded that we go and work at the exhibition site, pointing out that the President, Houari Boumedienne, was going to visit the British stand on opening day, and that he certainly did not want to be embarrassed by our not being ready in time.

Meanwhile, one of our group was a Swiss citizen and he called their embassy, where they did everything they could in their power to help us get accommodation. The British never did anything. But in the final event, we had to compromise. The hotel was quick to offer me and my engineer a room in the good hotel. They figured that if they could shut me up, the others would be sidelined though their inability to communicate. But to their astonishment I told them. "All or nothing". In the end they found about half of us rooms, and promised that the rest would be given rooms over the next few days as they became available. That was the best deal I was going to be able to make, and so we reluctantly accepted.

The day of the opening came and amazingly the stands were ready enough to pass muster by Boumedienne as he swept quickly by surrounded by his protectors and political entourage. He was not only president, he also held the position of Prime Minister and Minister of Defense, so he was not a man to be trifled with. He had started off as a colonel supporting Ben Bella who won the war of independence against France.

When I first visited Algeria in 1965 at the end of my university studies Ben Bella had just been thrown out of power by Boumedienne in a bloodless coup. At that early stage, not long after the end of the Algerian war, there were still French soldiers there. This was provided for by the cease-fire and referendum on independence that left France assisting in the reconstruction of the country that had been devastated by the war. There were well over a million deaths, and close to two million refugees by the end of the war. That was the trip when I had driven with a friend to Morocco in my faithful but clapped out Mini Minor. We had been from the north to the south of that wonderful country. We had watched nomads wander out of the desert on their camels on market day in Goulimime, an outpost of the French foreign legion way down the coast past the mysterious Sidi Ifni hiding over the hazy mountains at the back of the Atlantic. We had marvelled at the tall noble Blue People, named for the colour that their indigo-dyed robes gave to their skin. And we had also avoided the only other presence of foreigners, a Swiss television crew making a documentary. They must have felt the same about us.

We had driven over the unmade road through Tizi-n-test and the pass over the High Atlas mountains to Marrakech. And we had felt that a visit to the coast of the Mediterranean would hardly be complete without an excursion into Algeria. We arose from our tent, which we had pitched in the municipal gardens at Oujda, much to the surprise of the gardeners who started work there a little earlier than we had envisaged, and set off for Algeria. Unfortunately just after we crossed the border, near Tlemcen, a tube from the radiator must have burst, but the temperature gauge did not alert us to any problem and the engine boiled dry. There was nothing to do but wait until it had all cooled down and then add water and see if the block was cracked. It wasn't; we had caught it just in time. So we limped slowly into Oran to repair the tube on the radiator. Then we went for a swim at the beach where we met some young French people. One was part of the French Army support I mentioned, doing his national service in the army. The rest were his mates from university who had come to visit for the summer. They all lived in an apartment in the centre of Oran that had as its only piece of furniture a massive refrigerator full of beer and soft drinks. We were grateful to be allowed a place on the floor to sleep for a couple of nights. They all slept on the floor, and we simply grabbed a bit of parquet between them.

My next excursion to Algeria had been from the east, from southern Tunisia in 1967. After a wonderful week on the lotus-eater's island of Djerba we drove inland through the desert stopping at oases in Tozeur and Nefta. In Nefta there were fish swimming in rivers, and rich palm groves. A few steps away was a relentlessly arid desert. We cleared customs and immigration in Nefta and then set out towards the Algerian border. That was manned at the border itself, unlike the Tunisian side where they sensibly allowed themselves the comfort of manning the border at a considerable distance in the comfort of the oasis. The sandy unmade road was suddenly surfaced. At last real sand dunes! The Hollywood image of the Sahara had been upheld.

And as Boumedienne swept by I was brought back to the Algeria of 1974. A rich country that had never really managed to acquire the peace and prosperity it aspired to. The trouble is that there was and still is no consensus on what is the right path to that goal.

We then embarked on the 19 days of the exhibition, a marathon in such events. It started every day at one in the afternoon, and went until 10 at night. In the morning I would get up and go for a stroll along the beach. Then our drivers would take us across the city to the exhibition site; we would have a quick and exceptionally mediocre lunch and be ready for the doors of the exhibition to open.

I have to confess that there was very little interest in the goods of the company for which I worked. The most popular of the British stands were the guys selling dry-cleaning equipment. There were many local entrepreneurs who thought that this might be a good new business to get into. As a result of the low traffic on our stand I became extremely bored, but it did allow me to wander around the rest of the exhibition. It seems that we were well placed having our own British exhibitors building. To start with it had a usable toilet. This became the envy of other nations that were stuck in the International Building where the facilities were appalling. We made an offer to the Canadians and the Brazilians to use our facilities, which they took up instantly. The Brazilians rewarded us all with paper bags of ground coffee, which broke in my suitcase on the way back to London, meaning I had to have everything washed or dry-cleaned.

There was the odd bit of fun, such as when for some unrevealed reason the secret police arrested and dragged off some visitors from a nearby stand. You never knew who the secret police were as they wore civilian clothes.

It was also interesting to see the more politically provocative stands, namely Black South Africa, Palestine and communist Chile (Allende, the democratically elected communist president of Chile, had been deposed by a US-backed coup the previous year, almost to the day). They were simply political statements, the stands having no goods to sell, as what they represented did not exist as entities. It was presumably in protest at these stands that the USA pulled out of the exhibition altogether.

By 10 at night we were tired and hungry. Our drivers picked us up, and instead of going back through the city we used the road skirting the villages south of the capital. In one of those villages we stopped and had dinner. This was usually the spicy Algerian sausage called *merguez*, made from lamb or mutton. We would relax and have a beer, and agreed that it was by far the best time of the day. We were also aware that the drivers were pissed off because they wanted to go. One night they got so fed up with waiting for us that they told us they wanted to go. It was well after midnight, but we were having a nice time, so we ignored them. They got in their cars and went.

This left us potentially in a difficult situation. Our briefcases and all our possessions were in the cars. I do not think we even had enough money to pay the bill. The villages were at least 20 minutes drive from where we were staying. So we had a small council of war between the half dozen of us in the predicament, decided that there was little we could do, and ordered some more beer. We had hardly given the matter much more consideration when, after an absence of about an hour, they mysteriously reappeared. Perhaps they had wanted to make some money on the side and had subcontracted themselves for another job, thinking that we would have dispensed with their services for the night by then. For the rules were, as we found out a couple of nights later, that they were only allowed to drive the cars if we were in them, or if they were driving to or from picking us up.

It was about this time that I sat on my bed one morning and glanced in the mirror. What I saw nearly turned me to stone. How could I have forgotten it? I turned to the table in the room to make sure that it looked the same in direct rather than mirror image. It did. It was a plastic bag in which I had put some shoes – a pretty green and blue bag from a famous store in Israel, with writing in Hebrew, unmistakable, in large bright green letters. I wondered how long it had been there, and whether the maids would have recognised it. I thought probably not. But how on earth was I going to get rid of it? Plastic bags of such excellent manufacture present a real challenge of disposal. Should I screw it up and place it in the paper bin? It refused to be screwed up small enough, and just kept unfurling slowly in the bin. I doubted that setting fire to it would have worked very well either. I thought of dumping it in one of the public areas of the hotel. At least my passport did not connect me to Israel, as I had most certainly left that one in London. Perhaps sneaking it into the exhibition and leaving it there might have allowed more anonymity, but then you never knew where the secret police were.

In the end I borrowed a pair of scissors from a fellow traveller, cut it up into lots of small pieces, placed it in another bag and left it in the waste paper bin.

The days seemed to go by so slowly. I enjoyed my morning strolls along the beach. One morning I noticed a young man who appeared to be staying in a tent at the back of the beach, pitched on the sand. He invited me in and we had sex. It was a pleasant interlude in an otherwise tense time.

The only salvation was the group of people I was working with. They were very good company. We had one thing in common – we all were involved with British companies that aspired to export, often to "harder" places like Algeria. I remember one guy who was really angry that his company had been taken over by another. He had lived in Gloucestershire in a very pleasant environment. His daughter was at school, doing very well, and his wife had a part-time job. He was not young enough to retire but too old to find another job easily. The new company forced him to move to Manchester. He realistically had no alternative, especially as in those days pension funds were not transferable. He was bitter and I understood why. Twice I had left companies because they wanted me to move to places I did not want to go to, and it would happen to me one more time years later when I refused to go to Melbourne. This guy also went through some interesting calculations about what percentage of a person's salary was used up making it possible to earn the salary in the first place. He included location of house, reliability and type of car, clothes, lunch and even drinks in the pub after work. It came to a surprisingly high figure.

One night I was fast asleep in my white bungalow by the sea — it would have been about three — and my phone rang. It was reception. They told me there was a man to see me. (Normally that might have sounded like an interesting proposition, but I knew that there could have been no tryst involved in this situation.) They put him on the phone. It was our driver. He told me there was a terrible problem and that he must see me immediately. It had to do with the police.

Now, given all of the things that had happened at the exhibition with arrests and so on, and the fact that I knew enough about this country to want to avoid problems with the police, I was concerned. I was also aware that I had been seen as the troublemaker when we were fighting for our accommodation. And I also had the plastic bag from Israel at the back of my mind.

I said I would be there in a few minutes. I dressed quickly in some shorts and a T-shirt, then knocked on the door of the closest British neighbour. I told him quickly what had happened and asked him to make sure that I came back to my room, and if not to alert the British Embassy, not that realistically I had great expectations of them given their track record to date.

At reception the driver was waiting, nervously smoking a cigarette. He led me outside out of earshot of the hotel. He explained that they were only allowed to use the cars if they were either picking us up or we were in the cars. It seems that he had decided to take the car on some jaunt of his own after he had dropped us off at the hotel. There had been an accident, and the car was in a ditch somewhere, badly damaged. He wanted me to say that I was in the car at the time, and that we were there on "my business". It seems that where the accident had occurred was not by any stretch of the imagination on the way to drop either me or the car, so he could not have claimed that he had dropped me off and was taking the car back.

I had no idea how much of this was true. Had anyone been injured? Was he drunk? I told him that I was very sorry, but he was on his own. I

85

was not with him and would not say that I was. He looked worried and angry. But witnesses to accidents in some countries, especially where there was a death involved, are jailed or held by the police until the trial. I am a nice guy, always keen to help, but there are limits.

The next day we were intrigued as to who, if anyone, and in what car, would pick us up to take us to the exhibition. The driver turned up, looking rather sour, driving another VW from the hire company. Somehow he had managed to tell them a story that avoided him getting the sack.

It was about halfway through the exhibition that the problems with Air Algerie surfaced. It became apparent that as people went to reconfirm their flights, it was done without any consideration as to whether there were actually seats on the plane or not. All flights were grossly overbooked. They decided to have a system at the exhibition where you would take your ticket and be given a final, absolute reconfirmation. People involved in the exhibition would be given priority. This was to be done with all flights, including our Swissair flight back to Geneva. We managed to reconfirm that flight without too many problems, but the Air Algerie flights, most of them to Paris, were a disaster. People waited for hours for their confirmation and then were never quite sure whether this time it would work or not.

By the time the last few days arrived, we were all itching to get out of Algeria. There were stories of a meningitis epidemic sweeping Algiers. The cook at one of the other hotels had died. I wondered how it was transmitted, always having been a bit of a hypochondriac.

At long last the exhibition closed, the stands were dismounted and we were more than ready to head to the airport. It was a predictable mess. The first thing we saw was a guy who was supposed to have left several hours earlier on an Air Algerie flight to Paris. He had had a reconfirmed guaranteed ticket. The flight had left. He hadn't.

The procedures were bureaucratic, tedious and lengthy, but our Swissair flight at least had not been overbooked. We clambered aboard the DC9 up the back stairs, almost hugging the cabin crew who had only just brought the aircraft in from Geneva.

There was a sigh when the doors were shut, and silence as the plane taxied to the end of the runway. When the wheels lifted off the ground there was an enormous cheer of pure delight.

Chapter 9 Mexican money

Once I returned to New York there was a heavy schedule of travel lined up. Probably the largest and most important market for the company I worked for was Mexico, and it figured frequently on the itinerary. Although my relationship with Mexico spans well over 30 years, now is as good a point as any to talk about some of the experiences I have had there.

The first encounter was on holiday in 1968 at the age of 24 on my first discovery of North America. I had headed south from New York, stopping in New Orleans, taking in the world fair in San Antonio, Texas, which included as its far-reaching and expansive international component a representation from Taiwan, and then headed to Mexico City. How was I to know that I needed to get a Mexican Tourist Card from a Mexican consulate before I could travel? I found out only once I was at check-in at the airport in San Antonio. I was going to have to go and get the Tourist Card the next morning as it was already late afternoon and too late to get one that day. In those days I had not established my little horde of money in a Swiss bank, and I was restricted to just 50 pounds a year in cash to spend overseas. Even all that time ago it did not go very far, so I was concerned about the extra costs of staying in the USA for another night and getting in and out of town. The look on my face must have told the check-in clerk that I was somewhat dismayed by the news that I had to delay my flight. I was also concerned about the waste of time; there is precious little to do in San Antonio whereas I perceived that there would be far more to see and do in Mexico City.

The check-in clerk went way beyond the bounds of duty. Mind you, remember that in 1968 there were very few foreigners travelling around the USA, even when there was an international fair going on. In fact foreign students who managed to get a student visa so they could work were often called for the draft, and unless they left the country very fast might have found that their working holiday ended up in Vietnam. This limited the student visitors considerably.

The check-in person was a cheerful, slightly buxom lass; she was blonde, confident and brimming with health the way only young Americans in those days could be. She asked me to wait a moment while she made a call. I heard her part of the conversation. "Hi Randy (could anyone really have a name as provocative as that or did she know him more intimately than it seemed from her tone of voice?), Sheree here. You remember that ticket I got for you in April? Well, I need a favour from you now". She asked him to come and fetch me from the airport, give me a bed for the night, look after me until she could pick me up the next morning, take me to the consulate and drop me back at the airport in time for my flight the next day and for her to start her shift.

And he agreed without Sheree having to insist too much. Within a half-hour he came and fetched me, and I was suddenly immersed in a youth culture I had only glimpsed occasionally on American television programs. He shared the house with a few mates. They were chummy without necessarily being friendly, kind without being attentive, and beefy rather than fit. They had large thighs, ample buttocks, and while I felt no sexual attraction, I recognised a rather exciting smell in the air of old socks, waiting washing and testosterone.

The place was untidy rather than dirty, and I was welcomed without ceremony, essentially absorbed into what was going to happen anyway. They were slightly interested in me and the world beyond, but not in any way that would change their lives. We went out for some fast food, and they insisted on paying, referring to the obviously considerable favour Sheree must have done for Randy, and accepting the need for payback without compromise. They did indeed look after me. The next morning they breakfasted on what I considered a strange mixture of tastes for breakfast that included very sweet things as well as peanut butter. Sheree picked me up as she promised, and I went weak at the knees to find she had a Mustang. I was so grateful to her for turning a disappointment into a small adventure and an insight into a youth culture so different from anything I had experienced. She took me to check-in, and this time everything was in order.

I arrived in Mexico City a day late, and by late afternoon I had found a small but modest hotel, checked in and, armed with a map and tourist information, set out to plan my time in Mexico City. It was going to have to be planned more effectively to ensure that the lost day did not impinge on my discovery of the city. As soon as I headed into the street the seasonal late afternoon storm hit, and I went into a bar to shelter and plan my visit. As I was pouring over the map, a young man came up and engaged me in the normal first questions of "Where are you from?" "Is this your first time in Mexico City?" "When did you arrive?" "When will you leave?" "What is your job?" He was around my age and spoke quite good English. I had no illusions that this might turn into a sexual adventure and neither did I want it to; he was pleasant enough but not my type and fairly obviously straight, but it seemed to me that a bit of company might be quite pleasant. He made some suggestions about how I should approach visiting the city, and then suggested that we could meet the next evening, go to his house for something to eat, and then go out and see Mexico City after dark. I did not probe what that might entail, but although it would no doubt not be exactly my cup of tea, the visit to his home sounded interesting, and I thought that the rest of the night would look after itself.

The storm, like a rush-hour affliction that occurred most evenings, was sharp, and accompanied by very heavy rain and lightning and thunder that was nursed by the mountains that surrounded the city. Shortly after it abated we each went our own ways. The next day I climbed the pyramid at Teotiuhacan, and walked all over the city, disappointed at the relative lack of colonial architecture, but impressed with the Paseo de la Reforma, which in those days was a very elegant avenue. My friend, true to his word met me at the same bar we had met at the previous evening, and we set off to his parents' flat.

His mother was a slab of a woman, slightly suspicious of me and rather more matter of fact than welcoming or friendly. She seemed to warm to me a little after I demonstrated my appreciation of the tortillas she had prepared by eating a healthy number of them. We did not stay long, leaving in a taxi for what turned out to be a long ride to a place I had no hope of locating relative to any part of the city I had been before. This was not a feeling I particularly enjoyed. We were met by another of Carlos's friends at the door. It was a huge kind of club. We climbed the broad main stairs to a massive room with a bar at the centre and tables situated around it. They were already full, and we had some difficulty in finding space at a small table. The music was loud and the place so busy that you could barely see from one side of the room to the other. As soon as we sat down three girls approached and sat with us. They appeared to be either working for the club, or paid the club a fee to work. Drinks were ordered. Whiskey seemed to be more popular than tequila. The girls started to work their charm, and Carlos and his friend were getting into the mood, exploring hands pointing the way the evening was likely to end up. I began to wonder what the expectation was of how much of the bill I was to be footing. I was on a very tight budget largely because of those exchange controls in force on the export of sterling in those days. I was feeling increasingly uncomfortable and decided I needed to escape. But it was not going to be easy. I could hardly say, "Well, I am going now".

So I planned my exit. After another 15 minutes or so and another round of drinks, I excused myself to go the toilet, which happened to be right at the other end of the room, and whose access was pretty much hidden by the crowds. I went into the toilets, waited a minute or so, and then quietly walked out, around the back of the bar and down the large staircase to the exit. As fortune would have it some people had just arrived in a taxi. I rushed forward and jumped in the back seat, and in seconds we were speeding back to my hotel, the name of which I had never revealed to

Carlos. I was confronted with two emotions. I felt guilty about leaving them with the bill for two drinks, especially after Carlos had invited me to his home. But the overwhelming feeling was one of relief and liberty I felt about escaping from a situation that at best was not at all what I wanted and at worst might have ended up costing me a small fortune, or even worse.

The next day I took an evening flight to Acapulco. The sun had started to set as we flew over the steep mountain ranges between Mexico City and the Pacific Coast. The shock of the heavy coastal air hung heavily after the altitude of Mexico City. It was already dark as the taxi sped north along the coast road from the airport, past the luxury pink hotel of Las Brisas, and I basked in my first experience of a balmy tropical night. I felt the magic of the warm, still and humid air envelop me, and I stretched out in the back of the taxi feeling like a film star, with the sensation that something special was happening. The palm trees and tropical vegetation and the sparkling of the Pacific Ocean seduced me, and I have never escaped from their charm. Acapulco, for all its ugliness in the light of day, and despite the fact that since then I have experienced far more wonderful destinations, still holds a special place in my heart because of that magic moment.

The next few days delivered the gentle rustling of the wind in the palms, tequila cocktails on the beach, a cruise around the bay at sunset, and the famous dive from the rocks at La Quebrada. From 40 metres above the surf, the divers jump, timing it so that hitting the water coincides with the tidal surge into the inlet, for otherwise they would be dashed against the rocks.

I felt a very long way from Birmingham.

***

My next visit to Mexico was on business. My main contact then was a young Englishman who had gone to Mexico City and met and married the vivacious daughter of a Lebanese family who had lived in Mexico for many years. He of course spoke fluent Spanish and English, an ideal combination for a commercial career in importing and exporting. He was more or less a salesman for the company in Mexico that represented the company I worked for at the time, the manufacturer of fine chemicals products.

We got on very well together, and he invited me to his house one evening for dinner. We were about the same age, and to be honest I found him rather attractive, so I was quick to accept. The house was a large two-storey home in a suitably well-heeled suburb. The main entrance was in the centre of the building, and served as a large space for entertaining. There were several large and comfortable chairs, a couple of sofas, and a huge sweeping staircase descending into the centre of the area from the floor above. My colleague served us a whisky each, and we sat on one of the sofas chatting about Mexico, waiting for his wife to appear. I was not quite sure what to expect. I did know that when they married, as a wedding present her mother gave them a "his and hers" Ford Mustang, one each. This was in the epoch when these cars were at the zenith of their appeal. I was slightly envious.

Rather more than fashionably late, his wife finally made a grand entrance, sweeping with great gushing down the curved staircase. She had bright red hair, and was wearing glasses that might even have made Elton John wince, with huge black-and-white zebra-striped frames. She surged towards me, and extending an exhuberant hand towards to me proclaimed in accented English "Good evenin, I am so please to mit you". She had that husky voice that is the mark of the Mediterranean woman and is in its way most seductive. She was not quite the image I had in my mind of the sort of partner my English colleague would have chosen. I was fascinated and a little enthralled.

We were joined at dinner by an Italian friend of hers who worked at the Italian embassy. We had to accompany her back to her residence at the end of the evening, not because she did not drive; indeed she came in her own car. Rather the concern was the danger to which she might be exposed between stopping in front of the locked gates of her home, and opening them and getting through them to safety. We successfully supervised that operation. It is sad to reflect that this scenario of taking precautions to ensure one's safety is one that would play itself out in many of the world's cities in the years to come in many of the world's developing, and in some cases developed, countries.

The pharmaceutical division of the company I worked for used the same company to represent them as the division for which I worked. Before leaving London I had checked with them whether there were any issues they wanted me to follow up. They mentioned that there was an issue of an outstanding debt of a considerable sum of money. Maybe I could chase that up, and perhaps go and see the customer who owed the money. And indeed I did take the matter up with the company representing us in Mexico. "It is out for collection", they told me. "Good", I replied, "when could I go and see them?" "It is out for collection", they repeated. "Yes, but I promised the pharmaceuticals people in London that I would go and see them."

The man sighed slightly, and then said, "I don't think you understand what 'out for collection' means in Mexico. We have exhausted all avenues of recovering the debt normally, and now it is in the hands of a company that does collections. They will turn up one day and seize at gunpoint whatever they can to the value of the debt. The goods are then disposed of, and you will get half of the value. It is most unadvisable for you to go anywhere near them". I agreed.

Another evening we had an appointment with a customer who we were unable to see during the day at his office. We pulled up in the street, a very elegant street with massive houses quietly slumbering behind high walls. These were lined with menacing shards of broken glass looking more like decoration than the security they were intended for. We rang the bell. Dogs, a large number of them, started to bark, sounding as if they had not been fed for weeks. After a while a servant of some sort came to the gate and let us in, quite a procedure in itself.

In the background was a huge mansion, but we were to be shown into a smaller building, closer by, and clearly built simply to receive visitors. There were several reception rooms in an open plan, all on different levels, a few steps up or a few down. Each one was comfortably and expensively furnished, and the polished wooden floors covered in exquisite Persian carpets. I do not even recollect the conversation, only that our host was pleasant, totally lacking in pretension and very matter of fact about the business discussion we conducted. We drank a coffee, had a short meeting, and without delay or ceremony we left, so that he could return to who knows what luxury in the main mansion. I do not think I have seen such wealth before or since.

And yet, increasingly in Mexico City, the poverty that abounds stands in disgusting juxtaposition with obscene wealth, as indeed it does in so much of the world, and not just the developing world any longer. Some estimates put the number of children living and working in the streets of Mexico City at very hard to believe 1.9 million (Sydney Morning Herald, 20 November 2003). Whatever the number, it is a disgrace, not just for Mexico but for humanity.

Travel takes us away from our own comfortable suburbs of intimacy and complacency where, even if there are disparities of comfort, we manage not to see them because they are part of the pattern of our lives. Travel places us in different places outside our milieu, in areas beyond our intimacy, so that if we dare to open our eyes we see the tremendous injustices of the world. Apart from a very few countries the divide is sharp, even dangerous in the long run for those who live on either side of it.

Many find it hard to cope with the poverty in under-developed countries. People wearing rags and covered in dirt; maimed and disabled people waving amputated limbs and thrusting awful sores under your nose; those living on the street: they all cause distaste and averted eyes, because the pity for them is just too hard to digest. Beggars force their intrusion, knowing that the very revulsion they generate is the key to getting people to ease the guilt of their own comfort and wellbeing by donating. The beggar attempts eye contact, and the potential donor avoids it, pretending not to see despite a horrified glance that encapsulates the whole misery in a split second. A bandaged stump, covered in flies, challenges the good fortune of passers-by. Yet, in many countries it is an industry, and westerners often just do not know the rules of the game. I have noticed at times, when I have been reluctant to give for fear of creating more problems than already exist, that there are local people who have discreetly dropped a beggar a few coins. Have they the ability to differentiate between the really worthy and needy in a way I cannot? Or are they also easing their consciences, just like me?

In the East the belief in the laws of action and reaction and *karma* help the fortunate to accommodate the less fortunate without feeling they should interfere, although of course compassion and sympathy are allowed. The belief is that the misfortunes of this life are payment for the wrongs committed in a previous life, and mortals should not seek to change the will of God or divine retribution. On the other hand good fortune has been earned and should be relished rather than shared. It is of course a very convenient rationalisation, and should not justify the inaction indulged in by many of the blessed levels of society. Maybe a closer reading of the scriptures, whatever they are, would reveal something requiring us all to do more about the appalling poverty that exists in this world.

I suspect that some of the root causes of inequity and the consequential poverty are institutionalised by the policies of bodies like the World Bank and the International Monetary Fund, not to mention the need to provide greedy shareholders overseas with more and more returns on the money they have invested. Or the policies of governments made in fear of trade sanctions threatened by the strong and powerful, particularly the USA, and the protectionist tariffs and quotas placed by European countries, as well as the USA and others, in order to protect often inefficient producers and manufacturers.

I find that as long as I personally do what I can when I can, I am able to cope with the evidence that I have not done enough, and neither has the rest of the world.

***

Señora Genoveva Rivera was a fine and elegant woman when I knew her, a product of the Mexican upper classes. But this lady was not just a social butterfly; she was what one might call a "goer". I had heard about her before I met her, about a visit she had made to Drupa, a huge annual printing and paper exhibition in Dusseldorf. It was an exhibition that industry players from all over the world attended. Not because it was useful in any way at all, really, but because if you did not go it would be assumed that your organisation was about to go broke. As a result there were no hotel rooms to be had for a distance of 30 to 40 kilometres from Dusseldorf. Many people had to stay in private houses therefore, often with a buxom Frau making sure that there was no hanky panky going on between any of the guests, and that all rules of decency and decorum were observed.

Señora Genoveva Rivera was forced into these circumstances on one such visit, but was quite taken aback to find that a bath was charged as an extra to the bed and breakfast, and at considerable cost. This was not only an abuse of the situation, but suggested perhaps, she thought, that taking a bath might not have been a daily occurrence for the indigenous population. She was not at all amused by that appalling speculation.

But I first met this impressive lady in her native Mexico City. She ran the company that represented in Mexico the company I then worked for. The company had been owned and operated by her husband. One night, she recounted, she was playing bridge with some friends. She suddenly stood up from the table, placed her cards face down on the baize and said, "My husband has just died". And he had, at that very instant, in an air crash.

Her friends had all pleaded with her to either sell the company or get in a manager, but no, Señora Genoveva was made of more than that. She decided to run it herself. To be honest, I am not sure that she was that effective. She certainly did not have all the technical knowledge of the products for the printing industry that she sold, but she was most personable, highly energetic, very well connected, and an absolutely dreadful driver.

We drove from customer to customer apparently oblivious to the traffic and the chaos to which she in no small part contributed. She was indifferent to the blaring horns directed towards her or to the shaking of fists as she cut cars off, happily chattering away to me, in a totally different world. The back seat was always occupied by her constant companion Max. Max was a highly excitable yappy little terrier of some type that barked at every male within range. Except me. "I do not understand", she confided, "Max, xhe [you know that guttural sound in Spanish, the *jota*, reminiscent of trying to clear a hair of some sort from your throat] xhate men. But you, I don' know. Xhe like you. Very estrain". I did not bother to go into a theory I was fairly sure would have explained it. I had after all had a similar experience with Mrs. Madirazza in Belgrade identifying the difference between me and other men she had met.

The three of us had a pleasant few days driving around Mexico City and seeing customers. The best part of the day was when we returned to her home at lunchtime where the maid had prepared some wonderful home-cooked Mexican dishes. This was nothing like the commercial Mexican restaurants and the popular image of Mexican food. Right to the bottom of every *ceviche*, this was fine dining. It was capped by chocolate chicken, what sounds to be an absurd combination, but in fact works very well.

One morning, Señora Genoveva explained that she needed to make a personal rather than a business call, and asked me if I minded. I could of course go with her if I liked. It was a question of visiting a young widow whose husband had tragically and considerably prematurely had a heart attack without any warning, and dropped dead. She needed to pay her respects and deliver condolences.

The widow was in her late husband's office on the 18th floor of a 20-storey office block. We were shown into the office. It was a beautiful room with dark wooden panelling, some fine paintings and a large curved heavy desk, behind which she sat, looking in some way very small against the grandeur of the setting. Dressed in black and her eyes visibly swollen from weeping, she could not have been much more than mid- thirties in age.

Señora Genoveva pulled a chair right up to the desk, and then lent across seizing her trembling hand. She said, "We widows must stick together", provoking another outpouring of grief from the new member of the club. Señora Genoveva retreated enough to take a neat white handkerchief from her handbag, and sniffing quietly, dabbed at her eyes in this moment of awful sadness. For quite a few minutes they remained in this pose, with Señora Genoveva between light sobbing herself and leaning across to the new widow with a reassuring hand on hers, mumbling about the awful shock and sadness of the situation and how it reminded her so much of her own awful loss.

After a few minutes I noticed Señora Genoveva sneak a furtive glance at her wristwatch, in an almost imperceptible movement. "Well", she said as she leaned back, still dabbing the eyes, "This won't do. We must leave you as I am sure that you have many people to see and things to do. You know I am always here for your support". And with that we abruptly took our leave.

In the lift down I said to a now totally recomposed Señora Genoveva, "How sad, I wonder how she will cope". "Oh, don't worry", she said, "She will be alright. See this building, her husband left her the whole lot, all 20 storeys. She will be fine".

During a more recent visit to Mexico City in 2000 I was shocked to see how seedy the formerly trendy Zona Rosa had become and how what used to be the most elegant boulevard in North America, the Paseo de la Reforma, had broken pavements, derelict buildings and a sense of abandonment.

There was no money available to repair the considerable damage of the major earthquake that had occurred several years previously, and the cracks in the pavement created suddenly and with the violence of the moving and smoking earth stand starkly as a reminder of the power of nature over the constructs of man. In previous years I had always stayed in the Zona Rosa at the Hotel Aristos just off the Paseo de la Reforma. I would eat as early as I could, generally a light meal that was much easier to digest at the altitude of Mexico City. Then I walked through the Zona Rosa, past the smart restaurants, sometimes popping into a general store that seemed to be a gay pick-up place. The wealthy and the gays have retreated to more inaccessible locations. From Nairobi to Rio, from Lilongwe to La Paz, it is no longer safe to be abroad at night, as the poor attempt to deliver to themselves what their governments have failed to do, more equality in the division of wealth.

Chapter 10 Heading to Sydney

The last long trip of 1974 took me first to Japan, where I arrived on a wet Saturday night, with my fly broken during the flight and jammed in the down position, my luggage not having made the connection in Chicago I had planned in order to get an extra hour in bed, and confronted with the entire management of our Japanese associates to repay past solicitudes I had provided for them in New York. I recovered my poise and luggage the next day and prepared for some hard work in Tokyo. This was followed quickly by a visit to Kyoto and Hakone as payback for the entertainment I had provided them in New York. I got the better deal. Our Japanese associates both were suppliers of goods my company sold in the USA, and distributed our products in Japan. When the senior managers from Japan had visited us in New York, I had taken them to dinner and generally entertained them. In Europe this is what we did, and I was astonished that none of my work colleagues was prepared to be involved. We were a little early for dinner and so we popped into a bar for a drink. It was on the west side of midtown and turned out to be a strip joint. I was not from New York, so how could I be expected to know? Not only was it a strip joint but it was not a very high-class one. A tarty-looking broad was moving languidly from foot to foot, her tits bobbing about, just out of synch with the music, complaining in the most profane way that the management had not paid her what she was owed. From a grammatical point of view the Japanese would have learned that fuck can be a noun or a verb, and fucking an adjective as well as a present participle.

Whether this reinforced the view of the depravity of American society, or whether they actually enjoyed it, it is hard to say, but at least they seemed to have appreciated the effort I made, and my visit to Japan was payback time. I was treated royally, and I was afraid to ever mention what I liked in case it just appeared. I was taken to superb restaurants and they applauded my insistence on eating only Japanese food. They offered only the slight criticism that I did not make quite enough noise while eating.

I was taken to the temple at Senso-ji at Asakusa in Tokyo having expressed an interest in seeing it. The guy who accompanied me there told me that he did not have any religious belief. Yet when we got there he went through the traditions and said his prayers. When I asked him why, he replied that he had a daughter, and given that one can in any case never be sure, it was like an insurance policy.

I was keen to buy a telephoto lens for my camera, and they went with me to make the choice. I wanted the right lens to make sure it fitted; I wanted it to have a long focal length lens, but one that was not too heavy. Unfortunately given the confusion in many Asian languages between the letters "l" and "r", the conversation became confused. Light, right, long and wrong meant that the real meaning of the answers to my questions evaded me.

These people were extremely kind to me and carefully listened to and were pretty right in assessing my interests, at least my cultural ones. The visit they arranged to a customer in Kyoto was quite unnecessary from a strict business perspective. In the late afternoon once the visit was over, believing (and this bit they did not get quite right) that I might enjoy a bit of sexy girls show, they took me to what they called "flank Japanese stlip show". The room was packed, mine being the only foreign face, with a small horseshoe shaped stage jutting at waist height into the crowd. There was a series of vignettes all of which followed a similar pattern. The lights were dimmed and a girl would come out and dance. Clothes would be removed. In some cases a discrete little basket with a towel over it was placed on the floor. This contained some flesh-coloured testimonies to the accomplishment of the Japanese plastics and rubber moulding industries, I suspect based on moulds of European or African original models. The girls demonstrated some inventive ways these mouldings can be used. Then at the end of the "artistic" part the lights were turned up, and there followed what could best be described as a biology lesson. The girls bent backwards and forwards pulling open for all to see, and in some cases for 100 yen coins to be inserted into orifices that the men in the crowd seemed to be inspecting for the first time, such was their intense curiosity. My hosts kindly pushed me closer to the stage every time someone left and there was a space closer to the action, in case I also needed such instruction. They were not to know that they were not doing me a favour. Afterwards my hosts sought my opinion about the whole experience. I told them truthfully that I was astonished that the front door stood under a large Shinto sign of a temple.

The next day they took me sightseeing in Kyoto. It was wonderful – the palaces, the temples, the old buildings – and even in the warm gentle rain it was one of the most magical days of my life. In the late afternoon we got back on the *Shinkansen*, the bullet train, and headed north. But I got off the train at a small station with one of my hosts, who put me in a taxi to head to Hakone in the mountains, before he got back on the next train and headed home. I was met at a wonderful old hotel by the son of the owner of the Japanese company. The hotel was a large rambling mansion in the Japanese style, with most un-Japanese massive rooms. It was still pouring with rain, and we had a late dinner and chatted. His father had founded the company and adopted the trappings of a modern, rather western way of life. The son had, however, despite the so-called benefit of an American university education, and much to his father's surprise and apparent displeasure, elected to live a traditional Japanese life with *tatami* rather than western furnishings.

We talked about the violent history of Japan in juxtaposition with the aura of peace, tranquility and beauty that is the modern face of the country. He ventured that part of the reason for this aura was face-saving as a result of their defeat in World War Two. Although we drove through the mountains the next day, the misty weather and rain prevented me from seeing Mount Fuji, which had been a large part of the reason we went to Hakone. That evening I flew to South Korea.

In those days Seoul was pretty much a small hick town with no tall buildings to speak of. It was poor, and I have a recollection of going to a factory with a dirt floor, and a smell of garlic and poor food. The change when I returned nearly 30 years later underlined what an amazing metamorphosis South Korea has experienced as it turned into a wealthy country.

After a few days in Seoul I headed again for the airport. Flights were delayed and the departure lounge at Seoul airport was packed. There was a delay of an hour on my flight to Taipei with Cathay. There was little choice of seats in the departure lounge, and it was therefore fortunate, even providential in hindsight, that I sat next to a guy about my age. As is so often the case, gay guys have often an ability to identify other gays, and we were both keen to talk to each other. He told me that he was from Melbourne and worked for the ANZ Travel Service. ANZ is an Australian bank, and his work required him to travel overseas from time to time. He was heading for Taipei on the same flight as me, and then as coincidence would have it we were both going to Hong Kong.

Unfortunately our conversation was cut off by the intrusion of some Americans who were sitting close by and who clearly thought that they would reduce their boredom by getting in on our conversation. Rob, as his name turned out to be, and I were not sitting anywhere near each other on the aircraft, but we did have a chance to exchange the names of hotels where we were staying in Taipei with the hope that we might be able to meet.

As soon as I had checked into my hotel, around eight in the evening, I called Rob at his hotel and he was expecting my call. He jumped into a taxi and came around to my hotel. At last we were able to chat more openly, unencumbered by noise, other passengers and clothes.

I had an interesting few days in Taipei. I was visiting a company that had expressed an interest in distributing our products in Taiwan. I was keen to go out and see a few of the larger potential customers, but they saw things differently. They wanted to make sure that my company was an honourable one and suitable to do business with. This was rather difficult for them to ascertain since they had learned of us through the US Trade Department, and had no way of knowing much about the company at all. In such cases they pin everything on the company's representative. The logic goes that if the person representing the company is honourable, then so must be the company itself. From my experience this is a very risky strategy.

However, it meant that instead of letting me loose on their customers, they wanted to get to know me. To do that we needed to spend time together, doing things like sightseeing and eating. This suited me fine, although I must have enough of a dose of Protestant work ethic in me to have made me feel a little guilty. The best part was the visits we made to the temples, with the throwing of what looked like wooden segments of an orange. Whether they fell on the floor pointing in the same direction or opposed was an indication as to whether their prayers would be answered.

In Hong Kong Rob and I saw each other again. I was to arrive in Australia for the first time in less than two weeks. Although he was from Melbourne he knew the Sydney scene quite well. He suggested that a good place to go was Enzo's wine bar on Oxford Street in Paddington.

I arrived in Sydney from Jakarta on a wet Saturday morning. A friend and flatmate from London days met me and guided me around the wonderful city of Sydney for most of the weekend. The first opportunity to pursue my own agenda was Sunday evening. I arrived at Enzo's about a quarter to ten. It was packed. I bought a drink, and hardly had a chance to take two mouthfuls when they announced that it was about to close. This was November 1974, and in those days the licensing laws were far more strict than nowadays. Somewhat dismayed I turned to the guy standing next to me, and asked if that was it for Sunday night entertainment. He assured me that the night was still young and that everyone would go on to a club called Capriccio's. He kindly offered to show me where it was, a 15-minute walk towards the city along Oxford Street. His name was Moises, I learned, and he was from Chile.

As we left Enzo's a Chilean friend of Moises was walking past the wine bar. Enrique was strikingly good-looking; tall and slim, he had dark brown wavy hair, brown eyes and just about the most engaging smile imaginable. He had a rather deep and husky voice. Whether Moises was just being Chilean or whether he noticed my extreme interest in him, I do not know, but he rather forcefully suggested that Enrique should join us at Capriccio's.

I do not remember how long we stayed there, but I suspect not that long. Enrique came back to the Hyatt Kingsgate with me and stayed the night. I saw him every moment I could for the rest of my stay. During that week my feelings intensified and by the time I left I had become totally infatuated with him. Not only have I always liked dark men, but there was the added mystique of speaking Spanish with him. In those early days I actually spoke better Portuguese than Spanish, but my Spanish rapidly improved.

We started to write to each other and it was with great anxiety that I waited for the mail every day. I left Sydney towards the end of November and by the time I had spent a week working in New Zealand, a few days in Fiji and Hawaii to relax, and returned via a trade show in Chicago to New York, it was well into December. The weather was grey, cold and miserable. Even Christmas in Puerto Rico did not help. The Spanish environment and the destruction of Darwin on Christmas Day by cyclone Tracey kept Enrique and Australia foremost in my mind.

Enrique turned up at a point in my life where I was unhappy. I had been living in New York for getting on for a year, and I knew that I was just not going to make it there. I now quite enjoy going back to visit New York, knowing that my stay will be just for a few days. There is always a very different relationship to a place depending on whether you see yourself as living there permanently or for just a while. Expats have a wonderful relationship with a place in the sense that they can enter into the life of the community yet remain aloof to any negative aspects. They know that one day they will simply leave it all behind. It was the thought of living permanently in New York that filled me with an awful depression.

While I did enjoy Marty's company, his intellect, his sense of humour, living with him was another matter altogether. He had grown up in New York and was a product of it. We got on better when we were in another environment such as Europe. Even the sex was not enough to keep me in the relationship. After all, I had hardly demonstrated an ability to be very monogamous in those days.

It was easy to see how the thought of being in Australia with Enrique could be so appealing. I decided that that is what I wanted. While Enrique wanted it too, I think he doubted that I was serious about my intentions. He had planned a trip to see his parents in Chile in March. My job of setting up a network of overseas agents and distributors for my company would make it easy for me to make Chile part of my travel schedule.

But first I wanted to investigate what I needed to do to be able to go and live in Australia. I called the consulate in New York. I was devastated to find out that immigration had just about been halted. The economy was suffering badly, unemployment had increased and the Lucky Country had fallen on hard times. Or hardish! In Australia even hard times are much easier than in any other country. The bottom line was that the consulate held out little hope of my getting residency. I felt that the bottom had fallen out of my world. I called the New Zealand consulate thinking that New Zealand may be an easier way of getting into Australia, but even though they were a bit more optimistic, it would be years before I could achieve my dream of living in Sydney with Enrique.

Many of my friends would call my obsessive tenacity a major personality defect. On the other hand it has served its purpose on occasions. I decided to call the Australian Embassy in Washington to see if I could get a better answer. In speaking to a lady from the embassy, she remarked that I seemed exceptionally keen to go to Australia and asked if I had ever been there. I told her that I had been there the previous November, just three months before. She then asked what passport I travelled on.

She went on to explain that at the end of 1974 there had been a change to the Australian Immigration Act. Prior to that date British citizens had been allowed free entry into Australia, but after that date they would require visas and were subject to the same rules as everyone else except New Zealanders. So, in a sense I was unlucky because if all this had happened a few months earlier, I would just have been able to walk in and stay.

On the other hand there was a glimmer of hope. There were of course many residents of Australia travelling on British passports who had left Australia on holiday or whatever during the latter part of 1974, and who now needed a visa to get back home. It was decided to cater for this situation by allowing British passport holders who had an exit stamp in their passport during the last six months of 1974 to convert this into a migrant's re-entry visa during the first six months of 1975.

This seemed to me to be far too easy, but on the basis of what she said, the next morning instead of going to work, I called in with some excuse and headed for the Australian consulate on Fifth Avenue. There was also a complication. For some reason they did not stamp my passport when I left Australia, but they did stamp it when I arrived. I felt that this situation weakened my position somewhat as it revealed the fact that I had not really have been living there and had just gone on a trip, which was not the intent behind the rule. But I would give it my best.

I explained my understanding of the law on British citizens and told them that what I was looking for was a migrant re-entry visa. When they heard the story, as I expected, they told me that it was not quite as simple as that. However, I should fill out an application form and they would decide what they would do. I should go back in the afternoon, when they reopened after lunch.

I have to confess that I was anxious, apprehensive and doubtful. I went for a walk in Central Park wishing the agonising minutes of wait away. I returned just after they opened, and approached the counter.

"This morning I was talking to somebody about migr—".

"Name", barked the woman at the counter.

"Rock, John Rock".

"Here's your passport". She handed my passport to me over the counter.

"What do I do now, what is going to happen?"

"Happen? Nothing. You have your visa, and that's it!"

I almost felt dizzy. I walked out in a daze, opened my passport and stamped there on page 24 was a migrant re-entry visa, valid for entry before 30 June 1975. No interview, no medical, just the visa. I could have left that day!

After that things fell into place rather smoothly. I would meet Enrique in Chile, take holidays due to me for a week or so, then I would leave Chile with Enrique and get off the plane in Brazil where I had work to do, while he continued his trip to Europe. I would then go back to New York and go to England and meet him there at Easter.

I needed to go to England for two reasons. The first was that the application I had had for a green card for residency in the USA had also been granted. That had not been easy to obtain, and while I had no intention of living permanently in the USA, it would have been stupid not to have gone through with the process. The visa was to be issued in my supposed country of residence, the UK. For the year I had been in New York I had been travelling so much that it appeared that I had just popped in from time to time. I was not really legally resident anywhere.

The other reason was that my company wanted me to work on assignment at their UK location in Norfolk for a while. This could hardly have suited me better. I planned to leave to live in Australia in May after Enrique got back from his trip and to give him time to find a place for us to live together.

There was still one minor complication. Enrique, like many boys from a Catholic background, felt very guilty about his sexual orientation. (Many call it a sexual preference, which is utterly inaccurate. Preference implies choice, and for most of us there is no choice. We are attracted to people of the same sex, and it is a non-negotiable part of our total being.) He had not been back to Chile since arriving in Australia some three or four years previously. It might be assumed that his reasons for leaving Chile were political, but the truth was that he could never imagine the freedom to live his life there as he wanted.

To please his parents and to make sure that they would die under the happy illusion of his heterosexual bliss, he wanted to marry. He had in Australia a very good friend, Aileen. She was Chilean, had blond hair, spoke much better English than Enrique, and had been having an affair with a Spanish girl called Maria. Maria had gone back to Spain and Aileen planned to travel with Enrique to Chile and then to Europe to see Maria. Aileen and Enrique would marry in Chile. Aileen was a very close of Enrique, and being Chilean herself understood his wishes, and so agreed to assist him by going through with the marriage.

I had tried to persuade Enrique that this was a flawed plan from many points of view. But a brief fling with a Chilean in London a few years previously had taught me that logic was not something that rules the lives of most gay Chileans.

The wedding ceremony was due to take place a few days before my arrival in Santiago. I was not happy about it, but could not do much about it either. How often we all find ourselves in that situation!

My trip started off in Mexico City and then I went to Panama on the Friday night. The flight from Mexico to Panama was considerably delayed, and then due to the heavy freight it had taken on board, the plane was too heavy to accommodate all the fuel necessary to fly direct to Panama, given the high altitude of Mexico City. We flew first to Acapulco and used the denser atmosphere at sea level to get airborne with the necessary fuel.

The flight was so late arriving in Panama that Serafin Mitrotti, my work colleague in Panama, had long since left the airport where he was to pick me up, and gone home. I had no idea in which hotel I was booked, and so had to make my own arrangements. In the morning when I called him he was distressed that I had had to stay in such a poor quality hotel in a very doubtful part of town. He had believed that the hotel was going to send transport to pick me up. He decided to punish the hotel, and me, by insisting that I go to stay at his house for the weekend.

I tried to get out of it, as I hate such obligations and would much rather have spent the weekend getting to know Panama and taking a trip to an island close by for a little swimming. But Serafin would not hear of it. He called the hotel, blasted them for their incompetence and ruined any chance I might have had of staying there.

Instead, we sweltered away the weekend visiting friends of theirs, including some who were preparing for a wedding. The climate of Panama is very humid, and most people seemed to live without airconditioning in those days. The weekend was in every way stiflingly tedious.

Serafin worked for Kodak, and they had access to the duty-free zone. I took the opportunity to buy a projector as a gift for my sister in California. It was made to US standards and electricity supply. When I left Panama I flew to Bogota, and predictably they wanted to either charge me duty on the projector or to leave it at the airport and collect it on my departure. The trouble was that I was not leaving Colombia from Bogota, but taking an internal flight to Cali and from there to Guayaquil in Ecuador. This was a complication that in the end was only resolved by the airline shipping the projector back to New York at no charge to await my eventual return there. In fact to my surprise that part of the arrangement worked perfectly.

But by the time we had sorted out all of those details it was getting rather late. I had a reservation at the Tequendama Hotel where I usually stayed. However, I was carrying with me a thousand US dollars in cash that Enrique had asked me to bring for his parents. He would pay me later, but was concerned that if he brought it into Chile he would be more likely to be searched, and the money possibly confiscated. Knowing how dangerous Bogota can be I was a little nervous about travelling around late at night on my own even by taxi. Fortunately there were two Germans recently arrived from Frankfurt via New York who got out of customs at the same time as me. They were also staying at the same hotel. I suggested we take a taxi together and as they had not been to Bogota before they were glad to accept my suggestion.

On the way into the city the taxi driver asked me if I had a reservation. I told him that I did. Even so, when we arrived at the hotel he said that he would wait for me "just in case".

I walked up to reception and gave my name saying that I had a reservation. They half-heartedly looked through their lists and then told me that there was no room for me. I insisted that I had a reservation but it made no difference. There was one young guy at reception, who I am sure was gay and that is why he confided in me, who leaned across the counter and whispered that they had given my room to someone else as the hotel was overbooked. It seemed that the only hotel with any rooms was quite a way away in a rather suspect part of what was an undoubtedly suspect city. He asked me how I got to the hotel, and suggested that if I could find the same taxi driver he would be more likely to be safe, since he had brought me there in the first place without mugging me. The taxi driver from the airport certainly knew there were problems with accommodation that night and had correctly anticipated the fact that I would need to go elsewhere.

Needless to say I arrived without any problems. However, the people I was working with did confirm that the area where I stayed was a rough neighbourhood, and that caution was essential. Colombia has been a violent country for as long as I can remember, and carrying a large amount of cash is never sensible.

When I left Bogota I took a morning flight to Cali, and spent the day there waiting for the evening flight to Guayaquil. Cali had a reputation as a drug city even back then. It was quite hard for me to imagine that this pleasant town nestling in hills, with a few neat modern buildings in the centre and walks along tree-lined streets, could be home to such violence. I chatted to a teacher for a while, sitting in a peaceful park near the town centre, then headed back to the airport.

The common stereotypes of Ecuador revolve around the high Andes, or maybe the Galapagos. Guayaquil is quite different from both of them. I strolled through the town centre the night I arrived, in tropical rain rotting and decaying the streets. The columns of the galleries along one street were falling apart from the continuous assault of rain and lack of money to stop the disintegration. In those days it was a wretched old port town that time had passed by.

About this time there had been political upheaval in the neighbouring country of Peru. The police in Lima had been on strike for a while. The government finally got fed up with the situation and ordered the army into the police barracks to bring an end to the strike. The images of tanks breaking down the wall of the police barracks shocked. In response, in the centre of Lima there were riots led by students, as they often are. Students tend to be more idealistic and passionate and have less to lose than other more established members of society with all their trappings of family and jobs. At least in those days they did.

The centre of the city of Lima was sacked, left smouldering and raw. The government imposed a curfew from nine at night until six in the morning. I arrived two days later on an Air France flight from Guayaquil. It was a couple of hours behind schedule, which meant that it arrived after the curfew had started. There were not many passengers getting off in Lima, but all of us who were given a "*Salvo Conducto*", a safe pass, which entitled us to travel during the curfew on the route indicated, in my case from the airport to the Hilton in the city.

I walked out of the airport into the fresh night air. The place was almost deserted. There was one taxi standing in front of the terminal. I approached him and told him where I wanted to go. He asked to see my "*Salvo Conducto*", and I asked him if he needed one too. He nodded and showed me his. I climbed into the back seat, and we headed out of the airport. He told me that the main road to the city had a huge number of checkpoints and that it would take a long time to get through. He suggested that it would be much faster to take an alternative route where there were fewer roadblocks.

He was right, but there was also a danger in his strategy. Rather than roadblocks there were soldiers under trees stopping any odd person who was out. They were sometimes hard to see, and indeed I read in the newspaper the next day that a tourist had been shot dead in the back of a taxi because the driver had not seen a soldier and therefore not stopped.

Some of the soldiers were very young. There was one who stopped us who would not have been more than 17 or 18 years old. He demanded our identity cards and passes. I handed my passport and pass to the driver to hand to the soldier. The soldier got quite irate and demanded my identity card. The taxi driver tried to explain that I was not Peruvian, that I did not have an identity card, and that my passport was like an international identity card. He seemed most doubtful, but finally put his suspicions aside and let us pass. As we came closer to the city I saw some soldiers hitting a man with the butts of their rifles. He was facing against a wall, with his hands and feet spread out, and they were hitting his knees with their rifles to spread his legs further apart.

When we arrived at the hotel the foyer was a scene of utter chaos. It was past midnight by this time, and as many guests had not been able to leave the hotel was packed. Rooms were not ready, hotel guests were sitting wherever they could find space until a room could be made ready. The crew from the Air France flight was there too. Suddenly there was panic as a woman, clearly quite drunk, smashed a bottle and ran around the foyer screaming and threatening anyone who came near her. Eventually she was overpowered and the scene returned to a lower state of chaos. By the time I managed to get into bed I was exhausted.

In the evenings I used to watch the traffic from my room as the hour of the curfew came closer. I was intrigued by how fine everyone seemed to cut their bolt to safety. At five minutes to nine the streets were still full of cars, and then suddenly at nine they were deserted as if spirited away into thin air.

The flight from Lima to Santiago was in the afternoon. I got to the airport early to make sure that I got a seat on the left-hand side of the aircraft to see whatever I could of the Andes. When there was an announcement asking me to report to the counter and I was told that my seat had been changed, I became a little testy. But I cheered up when I found that the Air France crew in recognition of camaraderie had upgraded me to First Class. The views in the latter part of the flight were excellent, and the food and wine set me at ease for my arrival in Santiago to be reunited with Enrique.

After the wedding Enrique and Aileen had gone to stay at the apartment of Aileen's grandmother in the centre of town. The rooms were spacious with high ceilings, but there were only three bedrooms. One was reserved for the live-in maid. Before I arrived, Enrique and Aileen shared a room of course, as these were supposed to be their post-nuptial days of bliss, and the third room was the grandmother's. But my arrival required a certain rearrangement. Aileen shared her grandmother's room and I shared with Enrique. I could hardly have shared with either the maid or the grandmother. It did strike me that the grandmother would surely have found this arrangement bizarre to say the least.

This was fine by me, but I had to hold my passion as Enrique was terrified of making any noise that might suggest the truth. We arranged to go to Vina del Mar the next day for a few days, just the two of us together, by the ocean. Again I could hardly imagine what the grandmother would make of that. In the morning I was surprised to hear German spoken in the house. It suddenly all made sense. Aileen's family were German immigrants and still spoke German together. That explained her blond hair and more European looks, and the fact that she was far more comfortable speaking English than other Chileans I had met.

The few days Enrique and I spent in Vina del Mar were wonderful. The first day I don't think we even got out of bed. Subsequent days we ate out, went to see The Merry Widow, and enjoyed being together, just the two of us. The curfew at Vina started at two in the morning, later than in Santiago. These were the days of Pinochet and even with the iron grip he had on power he was not confident enough to lift the curfew entirely. But the curfew had been relaxed from the early days when it was virtually from dusk to dawn.

Back in Santiago I had some work appointments. Chile was politically charged still. In some quarters there was enormous resentment at the overthrow of Allende. He was after all a democratically elected head of state. As the country was in a mess, partly because of the excesses of the government no doubt, but equally as a result of CIA-inspired factors that had ruined the economy, Allende would almost certainly have lost the next election. But he was removed by a US-supported coup, and replaced by a vile military dictatorship.

On the other hand there were many who saw Pinochet as the saviour of Chile. He had rescued the country from disaster. Thirty years after these events the divisions in Chilean society remain and the wounds still smart. I remember my business contacts telling me of months when no work had been done during the Allende regime. There were just parades in the streets and the shouted rhetoric of the unions and the workers.

Then friends of Enrique told me that even during the Allende years it was the wealthy who prospered and flourished. It had been possible in those days to buy a house by the ocean in Vina del Mar with just a thousand black US dollars cash. Only the wealthy were able to raise that sort of money. They cleaned up in the property market.

On the last Sunday we went to Enrique's parents for lunch. It was a modest one-storey house in a pleasant middle-class suburb of Santiago. We ate *empanadas*, *pastel de choclo* (a delicious savoury corn pie), and other Chilean delicacies. Enrique's mother was like a little bird, short and a little dumpy but hopping around, so happy and welcoming. She called me *"El Gringuito"*, a term of endearment based on the fact that *"gringo"* in Chile embraces all foreigners, not just North Americans.

His father was sombre, and Enrique looked a lot like him. The wedding farce seemed to have succeeded; I am sure they did not suspect anything.

One afternoon in the flat in town, I was summoned by the grandmother to the sitting room for a chat. Enrique and Aileen were not around. She spoke to me in German. She said, "Don't think I am so stupid as to not know what is going on around here. As for you, I know he is very good-looking, but you could do much better".

A few days later Enrique, Aileen and I left together on an SAS flight. There were stops in Buenos Aires and Montevideo, and then I got off the plane in São Paulo and they went on to Madrid. By the time they had done some sightseeing in Europe I had returned to New York and left for London, where I met them again.

The British are a pragmatic lot when it comes to diplomatic issues. They understood very well that not all countries like each other. So for businesspeople like me who travelled a lot they were quite willing to issue two fully valid passports so that one could visit countries that did not like each other. Examples in those days included Israel and most Arab countries, Guatemala and all communist states, and many other examples. I kept one passport for "normal" countries including Israel, and one for Arab and communist states. I used the latter one sometimes for Europe to get a few stamps in it just so that it would not seem too obvious that it was restricted. In fact one evening that passport caused me to be taken out of line from the ferry to Ostend from Dover on a trip to meet Karl, the German boyfriend, in Bruges in Belgium. I was interviewed at length by the British immigration officials on my departure from Dover. They wanted to know why I just went to all these "odd" countries.

Obviously the Australian migrant re-entry visa was in my "normal" passport. On this trip I was to be taking to London I was to process my American green card. Having an Australian migrant re-entry visa dated only a few weeks earlier in the passport might have invited some quite reasonable if embarrassing questions. But if I turned up with a passport that had only Arab and communist stamps in it, in 1974 it would no doubt also have raised a few Yankee eyebrows. Another approach was required.

I hired a car on arrival at Heathrow. I was purposefully cheerful and joked with the staff in the office in the hope that I would be remembered by them. I drove to the house of some friends with whom I stayed a couple of nights before Enrique arrived. Half an hour later I called the airport and told them that I could not find my passport. They put me through to lost property, but nobody had found it. I called the car rental office and asked if I had left it there. They remembered me, but there was no sign of the passport. Although I was tired, having flown through the night, given that it was Friday and my appointment with the US Embassy was for Monday, I had to make my arrangements that same day. I called the passport office at Clive House and explained my dilemma. They asked me to go there straight away and they would try to help.

I gave them all of the details of the attempts I had made to locate the passport. It was registered as lost, and they issued me with a temporary one with a validity of just one year instead of five years with the ability to renew for another five, which was the norm in those days. Apart from the validity it was the same as any other British passport. I did not mention that I had a second one, and they did not notice! So, when I walked out of Clive House I had three valid British passports.

The next Monday I had the cursory medical somewhere at the back of Marble Arch and then went to the US Embassy in Grosvenor Square. I was somewhat disgusted that they would not accept in payment, which had to be in US currency, any $50 bills as there had been a spate of forgeries recently. The transaction was straightforward. When I next entered the USA, on my special new passport which had easily passed muster, I would present all the documentation and the green card would be issued.

Enrique and Aileen returned to Australia and I to New York where I duly obtained my green card. I stayed a week, finished up all of my affairs and prepared to leave. My company wanted me to go back to England to finish the project I was working on, and then they agreed to pay my fare to Australia if I would do a week's work for them at a trade exhibition in Sydney in late May. I accepted and made all the flight plans.

The only thing that I regretted was the state Marty was in. He had taken my leaving very badly and I felt awful about subjecting him to so much unhappiness. He stopped eating and even started to vomit blood. I was appalled at what I had brought about. Even today when I think back I feel that the way I treated him was one of the low points of my life. I really think that if we had been together in another place it might have been different. We were certainly well matched emotionally and intellectually. And the sex was good too. I wanted to remain friends with him, and it might have been possible had it not been that he met another guy a few months after I left. Marty and he are still together after 30 years and for that I am happy. But he and I did meet once since I left, in 1980, when I was in New York on business. The lover caused Marty a great deal of anguish over that meeting, even though he was there too, and it was decided that Marty would not have any more contact with me.

I returned to London and called the Passport Office to tell them that my passport, the "normal" one, had turned up in the house of the friends where I had been staying. I told them it looked as if the cleaner had put it away for safekeeping in a drawer not realising it was mine. I took the "special" one in, gave it back to them and they cancelled it. It had served its purpose.

I completed the work in Norfolk for the US company in a few weeks, and on 12 May set off to the airport. I de-hired the car and made my way to Terminal 3 (Terminal 4 had not been built then) for my British Airways flight to Sydney. Take-off was late at night and the terminal was empty, rather forlorn and foreboding. I did not feel lonely but I did feel alone. For the first part of the flight my thoughts took me back. Back to England, to my father who was alone, to my mother whose death cut any desire I had to remain in England, to my life so far.

After leaving Bahrain as the sun had come up for the next day I started thinking of Enrique and the new life that awaited me in Australia. I had travelled so much that it was in some ways no big deal for me. It was in just another journey. I have never felt a sense of belonging specifically to one place, and so to leave London or New York to live in Sydney was just staying in the world.

The plane touched down in Sydney at half past six on the morning of 14 May 1975. It was my 31st birthday.

ooOoo

I also go to New York. I check into a room in a high-rise, a dark brown building high in the sky with a view down to the busy street below. One of the first things I do is call Marty. Usually he is not there and I leave a message and hope that he will call me back and we can meet. In fact I never do get to meet him. I sometimes manage to speak to him, but we never meet.

Chapter 11 Settling in Sydney

The next few years of my life were of consolidation. It was hard for me almost starting over again in Australia. I found it difficult to get a job. There was virtually no export of manufactured goods; the exports were all geared towards resources and primary produce in those days. There was certainly no export of chemical products; Australia was rather a large net importer.

I had little option but to get a job in domestic sales in the chemicals industry where at least I had some product knowledge, given that the job market was very tight in the mid- to-late-1970s. Then I found that the fact that I had not had work experience in Australia and was already 31 years old was a problem. I had a couple of jobs until finally I got a position I really wanted, NSW Sales Manager of a large American petrochemicals and plastics manufacturer based in Sydney but with production operations in Melbourne.

Initially Enrique and I lived in a rented flat in the Kings Cross area of Sydney, just close by St Vincents hospital where he worked as a pharmacy orderly. In years gone by Kings Cross had been well known for its coffee houses and continental atmosphere, but that had all changed and it had become the area of strip joints, the naughtiest place in the southern hemisphere! After a few months I found a flat to buy in the coastal suburb of Coogee, just 10 minutes walk from the beach, and I started to feel more established and settled. I had no friends when I arrived, and Enrique's friends quickly became my friends. His English was not very good and all of his friends were from either South America or Spain, the bulk from his native Chile. It was inevitable that we would speak Spanish together and when we were out socially. During the first three years of my life in Australia I only spoke English when I went to work or out shopping.

The only travel during that period was for holidays. It was an opportunity to explore areas of the Pacific I did not know very well, such as New Caledonia, Fiji, Tahiti and American Samoa. I also made visits around Australia, and started to appreciate the extraordinary beauty of this country. I never could have imagined beaches five miles long with pounding surf, superb fine sand and hardly a soul to be seen. I loved visiting the temperate and sub-tropical rainforests along the coastal fringe, and going off on dirt roads just surrounded by bush with hardly any sign of the footprint of man.

I fell deeper and deeper in love with Sydney. Not only is it a spectacular city with its harbour and beaches, and the stunning impact of the Opera

House, the Harbour Bridge and the city centre buildings reaching towards the sky, but it has a vibrant cultural life and surely one of the best restaurant scenes in the world, representing every immigrant population, at affordable prices. I loved the laidback and informal way of life, the earthy sense of humour and turns of phrase and personal expressions. I adored the climate and the fact that for a large part of the year one can enjoy a beach culture. Living in Sydney can be like being on holiday at least every weekend. The first time I saw Fred, my school-time friend, when I returned to London on a holiday and he asked me when I was "coming home", it suddenly struck me that there had been a great change in me. His words jarred. I said to him, "Sydney is my home now, I will never live in England again". I took out Australian citizenship as soon as I possibly could.

But as positive as my relationship with Australia was, my relationship with Enrique was not so secure. I had been smitten by his looks and the exoticness of having a Latin lover. He also had a huge cock. And I met him at a time when I hated living in New York and I was vulnerable to change. I am not even sure how much of my feelings were about Australia and Sydney rather than him. In truth we were not really sexually that compatible, and I was more ambitious than him; I wanted a life beyond the Hispanic gay community of Sydney and its petty infighting. I felt that I was drifting gradually away from him, and maybe in response to this Enrique became difficult and petulant. He moved out in 1978 after three years together, and I saw very little of him after that.

By this time work was going really well for me, I had been promoted to National Sales Manager, and travelled all over Australia on a regular basis. During one period I flew to Melbourne every week for months on end as we were unable to locate a suitable manager for our office there. I started an undergraduate course at Sydney University in psychology, just because it interested me, but although I was obtaining high distinctions and came top of the university in second year, I discovered that the subject that really fascinated me was philosophy, which was the minor subject that I took alongside psychology. Although I did the course in the evenings after work, it did create some tensions with my employer. However, when I came top in second year they offered to pay my fees for third year. I declined the offer.

In 1977 I was so sure that I wanted to stay in Sydney that I sold the flat in Highgate that had been rented since I left London, with the intention of investing in a property in Sydney. I decided that I would only buy a house in which I would want to live myself, and had at the back of my mind that in a few years I would like to move from the flat into a house anyway. I had lived in flats ever since I left my parents' house more than 10 years previously.

The real estate agent became very frustrated with me as I rejected property after property. Finally he said, "Please, just tell me what your ideal is. Maybe I have not understood, what do you really want?" I said to him, "My ideal? You know that area on the cliff up on the hill on the south side of Coogee Beach; to have a place there overlooking the ocean would be my ideal".

As it happens the previous day exactly such a property had come back on the market after a sale had fallen through. The vendor was a recently widowed woman who decided to move to a flat and the intending purchasers for whatever reason had pulled out at the last minute. I went to see it. It was a small, freestanding brick cottage looking straight out over the ocean, nestling into the cliff over the brow of the hill. It was exactly what I wanted, even though it was not in very good condition. It was November and just coming into the Christmas season when it is hard to conduct business in Australia, and so the widow was under pressure to sell. I offered her 10% less than the price of the previous sale; she accepted, and so I bought my house on the cliff by the ocean.

I let the house for a couple of years before I moved in early spring 1981. I had to evict tenants, take them to court for the damage they had done to the house, and live in it while it was repaired. Today the house is more than twice as large after three different extensions and additions. It now boasts three floors with balconies and every day I look out at the ocean and thank my good fortune for the beauty of my house and the location where I am so fortunate to live.

ooOOoo

One of the strangest recurring dreams is about houses I own. I have been to all of them many times. There is one located high on a cliff overlooking the ocean. In fact I really do live in such a house, but the dream one is quite different and not in the same place at all. It has a far more Mediterranean feel about it; it is a small neat house. I have no idea what it is like inside, but there are other houses cheek by jowl. Then down at sea level there are two other houses I live in, one next to the other. I live in one and am renovating the other. In some dreams I am trying to make the two houses into one, but somehow I have difficulty in integrating the two homes. One has a better view, but people around are always building houses that tend to obstruct it. So I try to build up higher. The ocean here is open and wild, even though the shore is very built up. Sometimes I go for long walks along the ocean front.

There is another house where I live. This one is an enormous single-storey home of strangely shaped rooms. There are many bedrooms, but none of them has a door. The living area is open plan and so large you can hardly see from one side of the room to the other. It has large comfortable furniture, almost like the foyer of a hotel. I am not sure that I really like this house.

In another part of town (which town?) there is a large rambling house I own. I forget that I own it, and then suddenly I come across it again. From the outside it is austere but not very imposing. It is a vast mansion, with sweeping staircases and scores of rooms with old dusty and decaying furniture, furnishings of deep reds and chintz, old worn carpets, and high cobwebbed ceilings. The house is abandoned, part of it in such bad condition that it is falling apart. The stonework is broken, the stairs are unsafe. I have to climb several staircases, high up towards the roof to reach the furthest parts of the house. This part of the house is utterly uninhabitable.

I walk alone through the rooms, which are dark and sombre. I am not aware of any natural light in this house. It is not clear whether it has windows or whether the drapes are heavy and permanently closed. While it is neither friendly nor welcoming, in some strange way I feel at ease here. I am vaguely aware that I probably will never make it my home, but think that with some money spent on it I could sell it and make quite a profit. But the amount of money I would need to spend is considerable, and I do not have the cash to do it. When I wake up it is hard to realise that in fact I do not own this house. The feeling that I do endures several minutes into the waking state and I abandon the house with sadness.

Chapter 12 Loving and hating India

Overseas travel after Enrique and I broke up was still confined mainly to holidays. But with a minimum of four weeks paid leave for Australians who have worked for a company for more than one year, and with the public holidays over Christmas and the New Year, there is still the opportunity of making some long and worthwhile trips. So it was in the summer break of 1979/80 that a friend of mine from work, Gerrard, and I decided to go to India.

India changes people in a way that no other country I know ever does. My personal relationship with India is a love–hate one. The hate relates to the extreme frustration in trying to get things done, the noise and dirt, the relentless beggars. Then suddenly the most beautiful experience is revealed, whether it be the strange serenity of the sanctum sanctorum of a temple in Mahabalipuram, the magic of the Taj Mahal, or the beauty of the setting sun viewed from a palace balcony in Mysore. It is impossible to observe India impassively. You are destined to become part of it, and it part of you.

A good place to start the experience of India is Calcutta, and that is exactly what we did. But before that we acclimatised ourselves to a different pace in Burma.

Burma in those days had not opened itself in any way to the world. The cars were ancient; the buses made of wood, dating from before the Second World War and constantly breaking down. Before dawn the streets were full of joggers, as the government had decreed that jogging was good for people.

Rangoon, as it was still called then, was a charming city with some of the friendliest people you could find anywhere, good-humoured and keen to stop and have a chat without any strings attached. In the People's Patisserie, a coffee house serving exquisite pastries that was a favourite haunt for tourists, we selected a table and then waited for someone to take our order. Eventually a rather elegant older lady came across and asked us if she could help. We placed an order with her for some coffee and pastries. She brought them in a few minutes. We asked her where the bill was. It turned out that it was self-service and that she had simply taken our order, paid for it, and delivered it out of kindness. We were severely embarrassed, paid her the amount on the bill and thanked her effusively. Another day we asked someone in the street how to get to a place we heard sold books on Burmese history. Rather than explain, the person took us there, a good 15 minutes walk away.

The temples in Rangoon were havens of tranquility and beauty. In a small and unpretentious temple in the city the day we arrived, a young man approached and asked if he could talk to us for a while to practise his English. After half an hour he suddenly looked uncomfortable, apologised for taking so much of our time, thanked us profusely for our patience with him, and left. To not be asked for some money under these circumstances especially when the disparity in wealth between us was so great has stuck in my memory all these years.

But the most beautiful of all temples was for us the Shwe Dagon, the largest temple in Burma. It is covered with gold leaf so that it can be seen from jets passing over at 37 000 feet, glinting in the sunlight. I remember tinkling of bells, spraying of water, and an atmosphere of serenity, grace and beauty. The city's markets were full of unidentifiable products, smells of dried fish and spices, and shy smiles. In those days the choice of places to stay was very limited indeed. We opted for the YMCA, which was basic but adequate. Visas were only given for a maximum of seven days and the only way of entering Burma was by air from either Thailand or India. This meant that the number of tourists was easily controlled. In fact you could do nothing without Tourist Burma, and so in a very subtle way they were able to totally control you. There could only have been a maximum of a thousand foreign tourists in Burma at any time, since that was the maximum capacity of all flights in a week. You had to purchase all train, bus or plane tickets through Tourist Burma, as well as book all accommodation, but you could only do that once you were in the country.

When we arrived in Mandalay, a little shaken by the experience of a Burma Airways Fokker, the local Tourist Burma people were there to meet us. We were easy to recognise and to control, as our white faces stood out easily in the crowd.

The Tourist Burma representative came up and greeted us as we walked across the tarmac. How long did we want to stay, and what sort of accommodation would we like? How would we be leaving? It was only possible to book the next flight sector once you arrived at your destination. This was partly because it made it easier to control you, and partly because there was no electronic booking system. The Burma Airways booking system was a list on a piece of paper kept in a drawer at the office of the airport of departure. You might wonder how it was possible to get on at the last minute. Tourists had a higher priority than anyone but military, so there were always seats, even if it meant that someone else got bumped off a flight.

Mandalay represented a lot of walking, and heat and dust. There seemed to be temples and *stupas* dotted all over this sprawling town on the banks of the Irrawaddy River. We stayed in an exceptionally modest place that was rather like a doss house. On the second morning we awoke before dawn and made our way through the streets. It was cold at night, and people were sleeping in the streets in rugs and warming themselves against fires they had lit to make tea. We reached the station in 20 minutes, and the train on which we were booked to go the hill station of Mamyo, was already in the station waiting to depart.

We asked the inspector to help us find our seats, as the train was crammed full, and entirely in the dark, the sun still another hour off rising. There were no glass windows, and old wooden blinds had been drawn to keep out the early-morning cold. This added to the darkness and made the job of locating our seats that much more difficult. Eventually our seats were located, although they were already occupied by opportunists who must have hoped we would not turn up. Good-humouredly they made way for us. The seats were uncomfortable wooden slats, but at least we had seats. As our eyes became accustomed to the dark, we saw there was a sea of humanity packed into the train, quietly waiting to start its slow climb up the escarpment into the hills not more than 50 kilometres away. Eventually the train shuddered into life. Progress was slow because the train used a zigzag motion to go forward, changing the points and reversing to beyond the next points, and gradually climbing the steep hill. As the sun came up and a little warmth crept into the morning, the shutters at the windows were raised and we were able to better appreciate our fellow passengers. It was impossible to move through the carriage without stepping on the shoulders of those sitting on the floor.

Conversation was difficult, but eventually an older man with some English (probably from the time of the British Raj) acted as a go-between to all the people who wanted to know where we were from and where we were going, and if we had any plastic bags or medicines that we did not need.

Almost in answer to their prayers a medicine man appeared selling some magic elixir, promising long life and good health. He stood on the top of a seat, and had a well practised and polished patter that made his audience laugh. We declined to make a purchase, but many people made an investment in their health.

After four hours we reached the small old British hill station of Mamyo. This time Tourist Burma were absent, but really we could hardly do much more than go back to Mandalay without them. They had our tickets for Pagan where we were going in a couple of days time.

Mamyo was a delight: cool, green and utterly peaceful. Transport was by horse and trap. I was too big to fit in the carriages and used to sit on the back with my legs dangling. We decided to stay in Candacraig, an exact replica built during the Raj of a house in Aberdeen carrying the same name. Our room was enormous and had a superb fireplace. At night our houseboy constructed a huge fire and we sat there after dinner sipping diabolical Burmese gin, staring into the flames and thinking of Christmas in just two more days.

The days were warm, and we took a horse and trap at a leisurely pace to see some waterfalls, and then to the botanical gardens, which were in surprisingly good condition. There we met a young man who spoke excellent English, and who accompanied us on a walk through the park, talking of all the problems of the Shan states to the north and of the excesses of the military government.

The next day we left by jeep back down to Mandalay to catch our flight to Pagan. The elderly man at reception at Candagraig used the ancient telephone to call us a taxi to take us to the marketplace from where the jeeps leave to Mandalay. But no taxi arrived. The receptionist rang again to give them a bit of a hurry on. He was a fine gentleman, having been trained in the past how to serve the white man. We heard a torrent of invective delivered from the ancient apparatus into the ear of the poor receptionist. It seemed that things did not work quite like they used to in the old days, but he was not about to let the side down and admit that there was anything wrong. He absorbed the abuse with a stiff jaw, replaced the receiver, and with a forced smile advised us that the taxi was on its way. There were probably only two motorised taxis in the whole of Mamyo, so we just had to take our chances.

Pagan is built on the banks of the Irrawaddy. In the surrounding area there are still about 5000 of the many thousands more of pagodas that were built there between 1044, under the reign of Anawrahta, and 1287, the year Kublai Khan launched an attack on Pagan that ended its glory. We found a small house to stay, and walked down the steep sandy path to the mighty river, avoiding the water buffalo straining to haul water up from the river for the use of the villagers. I was sad to learn that subsequently the military removed the village and the villagers, leaving just the thousands of temples. Magnificent though they are, there is a limit to how many temples one person can assimilate. I was glad when I had had enough and it was time to head back to Rangoon. There was one moment of tension just after the plane took off and headed out over the plains, bumping along as the thermals caught the flimsy machine in the heat of the late afternoon. We stopped climbing and then embarked on a steep turn and headed back to the airport again, much to the surprise of the flight attendant who was sitting next to me, as nervous as I was. But it turned out that there was nothing sinister in all this. A small jeep drove out to the aircraft. A package about the size of a suitcase was loaded on board, and then we took off again for Rangoon.

We decided to splash out for the last night in Burma and stay at The Strand Hotel. In its day it would have ranked on the same level perhaps as The Peninsula in Hong Kong or Raffles in Singapore. It looked as if not much had been done to it since the British left in 1948. The notices in the room dated from the early 1960s. We ignored the dirt and run-down appearance and headed for the bar thinking of a Singapore Sling or a gin fizz before dinner. The bar, empty of people, had a few broken heavy leather armchairs strewn about in no particular order. Above the bar was a long shelf about five metres long. There was one bottle on the left, one on the right and one in the middle. We ordered a beer. After a rat scurried across the floor we decided it was time to move on to dinner.

The dining room was a long room with fans suspended from the high ceiling. Only one or two of them worked. We were shown to a table by a young man wearing what might once have been a white uniform. It now was worn, with holes in it and in some places heavy stains where the curry must have escaped its battered metal tureens. Dinner was served on what was left of an original English dinner service. It was cracked and chipped and no doubt seething with bacteria.

We had thoroughly enjoyed our allotted seven days, and the time had come, having slowed our pace and expectations, to confront India. The Burma Airways aircraft that was to take us to India was hardly a year old, yet there was bird shit encrusted on the wing so badly it looked as if it might have been camouflage. The ovens to heat the food did not work, and my chicken was not even lukewarm. I imagined the salmonella festering away inside and decided to go hungry.

When we landed in Dacca in Bangladesh for a stop to let passengers on and off, we did not expect to have to spend the afternoon there. But the plane was already late, and the loadings were light enough that they decided to wait another hour or so until the departure time for the return flight from Dacca to Rangoon. Then they would take the passengers going from Dacca to Rangoon with us to Calcutta so that they did not need to stop in Dacca on the way back, and thus save the landing charges. Burma Airways operated like that.

An establishment at least in practice restricted to Europeans and Anglo-Indians had been recommended to us as a good place to stay in the centre of Calcutta. It was called The Fairlawn, and was well placed near the New Market, and the Indian Museum, only a few steps from Chowringhee, a main artery in the centre of Calcutta. Because our flight was so late arriving in the unlikely named Dum Dum airport in Calcutta, by the time we had reached the centre of the city the Fairlawn was booked out. We were warned that it was going to be difficult to find a room so late, and they sent us off to the only place they could recommend some 15 minutes away. The hotel occupied the top few floors of a seven- or eight-storey office building. There was just one room available. It was more expensive than we had anticipated, but market forces prevail, and it was close to midnight: there was no alternative but to pay the ransom. The room had a simple padlock to close it, and no curtains or lamp shades, and its beds looked crumpled and dirty. I extracted a long black hair from the pillow suggesting that the bedding had not been changed since the room had been previously occupied.

"No, no, clean, Sir, clean", came the insistent reassurance from the hotel employee, delivered with a certain shaking of the head from side to side as only the Indians (and it seems me) can manage. It is all to do with keeping the neck utterly still and moving the head from the jaw. It does not, as many foreigners interpret, mean "no", but rather "I understand or I have heard". Don't ask me how it is that I can perform this unusual movement, but I can.

I stuck to my guns and insisted that new bed linen be provided. Our room boy reluctantly stripped off the bed clothes, went into an adjacent room, and reappeared a few minutes later with other bed clothes bundled in his arms. To this day I am convinced that he simply swapped the bed clothes with those on a bed in another room. I slept with a towel I had brought with me covering the pillow.

The next day we took up residence at the Fairlawn with a certain amount of relief. Just to pass through the heavy gates from a street where people lived, rose in the morning and washed their teeth with bamboo stalks – for the Indians are always clean however poor their facilities – was like entering an oasis. There was still a general buzz of noise and traffic in the distance, but there were trees and bushes in a garden, and seats in the shade to relax. We were greeted by the proprietor.

"Mrs. Smith. My husband is British you know", suggesting satisfaction that this marriage had delivered her from what might have been a less advantaged life. "Of course, I am Armenian of origin", she continued, lest we should fall into the error of thinking she might be Indian. "Let me show you around the house. I have decorated it entirely myself, you know". We examined all the frills and trinkets that adorned every window, alcove and horizontal surface.

"How extraordinary", we offered in encouragement. She smiled her appreciation, and continued the tour with explanations interspersed by the house rules. Dinner was included, that event to be announced by one single loud blow to the large bronze-coloured gong in the hallway. The Indian staff were all dressed in what looked like either the regalia of an outmoded maharajah or the entire stock of a fancy-dress-hire company. The maitre d' had a rather lavish headdress; the waiters looked somewhat less breathtaking, but all were equipped with white gloves. The waiters and the guests never looked at each other. The etiquette required that those of us born of more privileged race should ignore those born to serve us. But those born to serve were not that pleased with the status quo judging by the bad-tempered way they slammed down the plates in front of us. The meals were plentiful, mainly curry and potato, with a hint from time to time of bony meat of some sort that gave its name if not its flavour to the dish.

In the mornings we awoke to the noise of the laundry and ironing service retching and coughing, showing skilful clearing of the throat and nose in a mucosal symphony, down in the courtyard as they went about their daily chores. The odd rat sharing the dining room with us did not deter our enthusiasm. We were well satisfied with our stay.

Calcutta is not a city about which one can be ambivalent. I defy anyone to go into the streets of an evening and not feel something. It could be fear, elation, disgust, panic, excitement, even claustrophobia. But as you enter this seething mass of humanity, feel something you will. I love the sound of the Indian music distorted through overloaded loudspeakers, the smells of perfume and incense, the colours of the saris, the buzz and excitement of the Indian bazaar, especially as it comes to life at dusk. And I have to confess to you that I have an awful weakness for Indian men, with their dark eyes, their black drooping moustaches, fine features and jaw lines, their slight build with often a touch of black curly hair on their dusky chests.

And so at Calcutta we entered India. We visited temples, including the Parasnath Jain temple and grand buildings from the British Raj, the most impressive of which I found to be the domed marble Victoria Memorial. We saw a dead body being carried on a stretcher through the streets of Howrah on the way to its cremation. We walked through the Maidan along the banks of the Hugli river, often referred to as the lung of Calcutta, the only place through which it can breathe. We saw the Writer's Building on Dalhousie Square, once the headquarters of the British East India Company that for so long had dominated life in this part of India, often cruelly and ruthlessly.

It was winter, and many of the inhabitants of this city suffered all sorts of respiratory afflictions. This required a large amount of expelling of the consequent mucous without using disgusting things like handkerchiefs. A well-placed finger and thumb each side of the nose accompanied by a short sharp blow from the lungs was far more effective. It did mean that if you were on the street when a bus went past, it was wise to make sure that you did not get caught in this process of clearing airways. These habits were no doubt at least in part to blame for the high incidence of tuberculosis both in Calcutta and our next destination, Nepal.

The difference between Kathmandu and Calcutta is far more than the time change of just 15 minutes between the two might suggest. That time difference by the way was just enough to cause a tremendous misunderstanding about whether an airline office should have been open or not. It is the sort of time difference that is so small it can slip by without you really being aware of it. I once spent two days in Bulgaria thinking that the local time was two hours different from what in reality it was. So you can imagine how 15 minutes can appear to be neither here nor there. Until you discover that an office you needed to visit has just shut.

The more modern part of Kathmandu is pleasant enough, as long as you do not mind being gassed by the smoking traffic in the small streets. But the old city is like walking back into a medieval world, with its narrow streets and ancient buildings. When we came back to Kathmandu we stayed right in the middle of this experience in what is called Freak Street. In those days it was very hippy, and quite one of the most unusual places I ever saw.

We hired bicycles and crossed the valley floor to Bhaktapur. I felt like I was in a time machine, entering another world of several hundred years before, a peaceful existence untouched by modern hands, where sound was deeper and colours more vivid. But then again it might have been due to the dope that I had bought from a cute 10-year-old at Lake Fewa a few days earlier.

This feeling of being in another time I experienced several times in Nepal. It probably was the dope. Gerrard had gone beyond dope in those days and was heavily into Cadbury's chocolate. The stuff they made in India was not a patch on the Tasmanian or Bourneville products, he assured me, but it was good enough to satisfy his addiction. I thought I would be rather more "local" and opted for the dope. The stash of *gunja* that this kid sold me was both enormous and potent. The first joint I smoked at the lakeside hut where we stayed in Pokhara, eight terrifying hours to the west of Kathmandu on a dangerous fog-bound road, was so strong I couldn't even get up off the bed. One day we walked out in the country climbing a low range of mountains near the town. The road gave way to a steep path, and we were soon walking through simple villages of mud houses with a panorama of magnificent peaks spread out before them. We climbed to the top of a small mountain from which the whole of the Annapurna range could be seen. We sat there for an hour or more just staring at the magnificence of the mountains. I smoked another joint. The effect on me is often that I get halfway through a sentence and then forget what it was I was going to say. Gerrard was well aware of what it did to me and I remember seeing his neck stiffen as a lady and her son climbed on to the top of the mountain. She was employed by the Australian mission in Kathmandu. I knew that Gerrard was talking in such a way as to avoid my entering the conversation, fearing that as I suddenly came to a halt in the middle of a sentence possibly accompanied by a lot of giggling, she would realise I was stoned. Eventually I seized my opportunity, started to say something and then petered out halfway through with a smile on my face, leaving the woman looking a little puzzled. Gerrard gave me a sideways look of death.

One evening back in Kathmandu I needed to change some money. This was a rather lengthy process that required the filling out of some rather daunting forms, well at least if you were stoned. I asked Gerrard to help me as I did not think I was capable of doing it on my own. Halfway through the process he was suddenly seized with an urgent craving for Cadbury's and rushed out leaving me standing in the moneychanger with a half-completed form in my hand. I will never know how I managed to conclude the transaction, but then again they were probably used to stoned westerners acting as silly as farts trying to change money. I reluctantly left behind what I had not consumed when we finally left to go back to India.

One day we walked to a temple. We stayed on the other side of the river, not wishing to intrude in the cremation that was taking place. I remember the man sitting at the side of the burning body waving to us and cheerfully explaining that this was his friend, and that he was happy to be seeing him on his journey to the next world.

At another temple there was blood on the steps that led up to the top where there was a small shrine. When we arrived we were somewhat relieved to find that it was from the sacrifice of a chicken. Such considerations of religion prepared us for our next stop back in India, Varanasi. The flight there was superb. As the plane took off from Kathmandu and turned in a tight circle to climb out of the valley, we were treated to a vista of the whole Himalayas crowned by Everest itself, in clear sparkling sunshine.

Varanasi is a holy city on the banks of the Mother Ganges. It is where devout Hindu pilgrims come every year to be cleansed by bathing in the waters of the holy Ganges, a city of narrow streets winding between old painted buildings and overhanging balconies leading down to the terraces on the river banks – the *ghats* where most of the religious activity takes place. This is the holy city of the Hindu religion, the streets full of barely clad men and fully clothed women seeking to cleanse themselves of sin by bathing in the Ganges. We took a boat along the river watching life and death on the *ghats*. For to die in Varanasi will lead to breaking the awful cycle of birth and rebirth, *samsara*. The boatman told us that it was an amazing fact that even with all the bodies floating down the river, many not fully cremated as poor families could not afford the necessary wood, the waters of the Ganges were so sacred that they were sterile. We were doubtful.

In the narrow streets there were many holy men, *saddhus* or *sannyasins*, ascetics who have given up all worldly possessions and values to prepare themselves in old age for the transition to the next life. Varanasi is steeped in religious study and practice, and features a centre of learning of the ancient language of Sanskrit that dates back to the dawning of time in the stories of the epic poems of the Ramayana and the Mahabharata. For me Varanasi is the quintessential Hindu India.

Our next destination was to be the centre of Moghul Islamic India where the Taj Mahal is located. But, as so often in India, the journey was less than straightforward. We were supposed to fly first to Kujaraho to see the erotic temples. India is the home of the *kama sutra* after all. We boarded the Indian Airlines Boeing 737, and I was quite relaxed listening to the beautiful, soporific Indian music as we waited on the runway. My stupor was brought to an end by the realisation that as there was simply no traffic at all at Varanasi airport; there was a problem delaying our take-off.

"What time do we expect to arrive in Kujaraho?" I asked the flight attendant. She gave me a time that had already passed several minutes ago. I asked a different question.

"When will we be leaving for Kujaraho?" She looked at me earnestly before revealing, "There is a slight [slipping her head sideways in that Indian way] snag". The slight snag was that the aircraft had totally broken down and a replacement could not be found for several hours. In compensation we were treated back in the departure lounge to tea and hard boiled eggs. As many eggs as we wanted.

Khajuraho airport did not have the sophistication of runway lights, and so we went straight to Agra. There Indian Airlines generously paid for a night in a five-star hotel, in a room that was more expensive than our habitual accommodation by a factor of 20. Notwithstanding the apparent luxury, I was poisoned by the dinner and for the only time in India I was as sick as a dog. Normally in India I used to enjoy, and I use the word advisedly, constipation. Everything is relative, and when travelling around constipation can be infinitely easier to manage than its opposite affliction. We never did get to Kujaraho. I slowly recovered from my gastric attack and we investigated Agra instead.

My first view of the Taj Mahal was at night. There were no tourists; the moon shone on the white dome, and so it looked like pearlescent magic. The Taj is of such beauty, such perfection in shape and dimension, that all I could do was stare at it speechless. It is unknown who was the architect of this mausoleum for the Mumtaz Mahal, the wife of Shah Jahan. The sad irony is that family devotion did not span the generational gap, and he was imprisoned by his own son, Aurangzeb, for the last eight years of his life.

From Agra we took the train to Jaipur in Rajasthan. We had not realised that bedding, including a mattress, had to be provided by the travellers themselves, not the train. We turfed out the occupants of our reserved seats, and suffered the hard bench of the so-called bed until dawn. Jaipur is a pleasant town full of history, fine monuments and parks, with a hill overlooking the city. It was the festival of the kites during our visit, and the skyline was a mass of kites fluttering away above the buildings. We saw a wedding procession, admired the astronomical observatory, hired bicycles and cycled to the Amber Fort.

But the most impressive site is surely the Palace of the Winds, a superb building five-storeys high and made of pink marble. It was built for the women of the maharajah's harem, providing them with a kind of window onto the outside world. It was in stark contrast to the pervasive smell of urine that hung around Jaipur.

Delhi was the last stop on that particular journey. Gerrard is somewhat shorter than I am, and that made him far more accessible to people in the street wishing to sell something or just be generally annoying. He was accosted one day in Delhi by a professional ear-cleaner. This man came up and mumbled at Gerrard. Inevitably, Gerrard angled his head and tried to decipher the message. It was of course an invitation to improve his hearing by using the very thorough and professional ear-cleaning services of this young man. He even had a scrappy and well-used notebook with testaments to his expertise. Many were probably elicited under pressure, and others were no doubt ironic, but whatever, they were all entertaining and amusing. He even had sophisticated equipment, like ear-buds, which had probably only been used on one or two people before!

This reminds me of my rather naïve shock a couple of years later, in the south of India this time, where a street seller had spread his wares on a large, not very clean blanket neatly set out on the pavement. He sold used false teeth. There they were all lined up, not graded as far as I could see.

Prospective customers would try a few pairs until they found one that fitted.

I am sad to say that one of my most treasured memories of India was a restaurant where we ate every night. The waiter was from Poona, and was without doubt one of the most striking men I have even seen in my life. He described a dreadful life, his departure from Poona intended for him to earn enough money to support quite an extended family. I used to lament to Gerrard that I wanted to scoop him up in my arms and take him to Sydney to rescue him from all this, of course without a selfish thought in my head.

The Red Fort in Delhi was for me less impressive than the Great Mosque, and the Indian Parliament seemed like the one tradition that the British left that really was worthwhile. In retrospect the railway system for all its faults is very impressive too. However, my favourite Delhi is the maze of small streets near *Chandni Chowk* (Silver Street), with artisans and shops of all sorts selling everything from metal buckets to fine damask cloth. When I returned in 2004 and again in 2008 I was delighted to find that its charm was intact.

Like I imagine most visitors to India, I was glad to be leaving by the time I got to the airport, but in the sure knowledge that I would be back soon enough. That's what happens when you get bitten by India.

ooOoo

Maybe the most intimate dreams are about sex. The wonderful freedom to have sex with anyone we want to, without having to wait for their reciprocation. How many men, I wonder, who want to believe themselves or portray themselves to be totally straight, have been betrayed by their sexual fantasies in dreams? For them such dreams would certainly not be worth remembering! I do not infrequently dream that I am able to suck my own penis. These are wondrously pleasurable dreams, but unfortunately I always wake up before I ejaculate. I feel horribly cheated. This made me wonder about the ability to be able to choose a dream experience at some stage of future human development, rather like putting on a video. Except that instead of observing the story, you would be the story, the scriptwriter, the director and the actor.

Chapter 13 Meeting Charles

Does one really meet the people who are important in one's life simply by pure chance, the result of a random process? That would be a rather non deterministic view of the world. I have often felt that there are certain happenings in my life that I have had complete control over; I make choices that lead to outcomes that I am totally responsible for. Yet there are others that seem in hindsight to be so fantastic that they create the sensation that they can have hardly been by chance. It feels as if the basic facts of my life were destined to happen anyway. How I then deal with them has been up to me. It was as if I had been dealt a pack of cards, and then it was up to me how I played the game. How I played the game in some fundamental way matters. Whether I would be accountable only to my fellow travellers on this planet, or whether it would be to a higher order of things, has never been clear. This is totally unscientific, impossible to prove either one way or the other; it comes down to either an insightful intuition or a total illusion. I still do not know which, even though I have given such matters considerable thought and attention over the years.

If someone had said to me when I was younger that I would spend most of my life in Australia, I would have laughed at them. Not in England, but for heaven's sake, Australia? I don't think so!

But Australia is where I landed. It felt as if somewhere it was written that I would end up here. In the same way I feel that it was destined that I would meet Charles, whose life was such a major influence on mine.

One lunchtime in 1980 I decided to alleviate the boredom of my office on the 17th floor of the Union Carbide building in the centre of Sydney, by taking a little midday excursion to a rather sleazy lunchtime pick-up place called Platypus. In the darkness there, I met a somewhat pushy young man. Pushy because he decided that he wanted me, and literally pushed some other guy who was showing me some attention, out of the way. It turned out that he was very turned on by guys in suits.

We left together and I invited him to my place for the next evening. He accepted. I gave him my address; he gave me his name: Charles. He arrived a few minutes late with a bottle of rosé wine in his hand. He did not want to have sex in bed, but wanted me to fuck him on the carpet in the lounge room.

The next time he came around he stayed the night. To my surprise he brought with him a photograph album and we sat in bed the next morning, a Sunday, looking at photographs of his family taken in the village they came from, Batroun, on the Mediterranean coast north of Beirut. Charles was Lebanese but with Greek blood on his father's side. In fact his surname was derived from the town in Greece where his father's family came from. His real name was Khalil, but he changed it to Charles when he took Australian citizenship.

His elder brother and sister had come to Australia several years previously and established themselves and their families. He had a married sister still living in Beirut. At home in Batroun had been living his mother, two sisters, a younger brother and Charles. The father had died some years before. The younger brother, John, the one who shared the whole family's allocation of good looks with Charles, had become active fighting in the civil war in Lebanon in the mid 1970s. The mother became increasingly anxious about his safety, indeed the safety of the whole family, and she decided they should leave. The first step was to take the boat from Jounieh, the port in Beirut that remained in Christian hands throughout the civil war, to Cyprus where they remained for several months before obtaining their residence as refugees to Australia.

None of those five really ever wanted to come to Australia, for they were not economic refugees, and had it not been for the civil war, they never would have come. They had a good life in Lebanon until the civil war started. There is an enormous difference in the way you feel about a country depending on whether you emigrate there willingly or reluctantly, and whether it was your decision, or one that was made for you, in Charles's case by his mother.

In Batroun they lived in a large house by the sea. Charles was a student and not much more than 20 years old when they left. Behind him he left his friends, his whole life, and he did not want to go. He even left his name behind. They lived, the five of them, in a two-bedroom flat in a lower middle-class suburb of inner Sydney. The mother and two sisters shared one room, and the two brothers the other. No wonder he wanted to share with me that morning in bed the life he used to have in Lebanon rather than talk about the one he had come to in Sydney.

I knew Beirut well, and this was a great subject of commonality between us. We talked about the villages in the mountains where everyone used to go in the afternoon to escape the heat and humidity of the summer. People would eat a *mezze* at a large table under the cool of the trees and trailing vines, and late at night head back to the city. We talked about Hamra and the corniche along the front opposite the hotel where I used to stay. He was surprised when I told him that one morning in that hotel for breakfast I had ordered *foul*, a traditional heavy bean and garlic soup.

I remembered the start of the problems in Lebanon. I had been there just before it all began. Maybe the fact that he could talk to me about his life there, and I knew the places where he had whiled away time as a student such as the cafés of Hamra, were part of the reasons that he was attracted to me. To him I was neither Lebanese nor typically Australian, and he liked that. Both Charles and I adored Fairouz, the Lebanese singer with a melodic and mournful voice, but we both came to prefer the voice of her less well-known sister. We both spoke fluent French and sometimes in company where that was required, we did so, just as naturally as we did English.

I was 36 when I met Charles, established, a businessman, more worldly than most people Charles had met in Australia, and he was interested in me. Charles was 28, incredibly handsome and exactly the sort of person I was bound to fall in love with. He was almost as tall as me, with thick, strong what I call black hair, but which he insisted was very dark brown. He had big brown Middle Eastern eyes, almost almond-shaped, a proud strong nose, beautiful olive skin, and a smile that melted my heart. As if made to order for me he had a chest covered in black curly hair, a five o' clock shadow that sent shivers down my spine, and a thick full moustache that I used to love to nibble. I loved to hold him in my arms in bed, cuddle him and then slowly enter him and fuck him gently until we both came.

I did not become immediately infatuated by him, in the way I had been with Enrique. It was a fire that started slowly and built up over a period of weeks and months. We saw each other two or three times a week, and soon I was introduced to his family. His relationship with his family was complicated. There is a large Lebanese community in Sydney, and apart from brothers and sisters Charles had more cousins in Sydney than I could imagine was possible for a family to have.

On Sundays in particular, but also on Saturdays, they used to visit each other. The best strategy I quickly discovered was to leave home early and call in on relatives or friends. If the first family had already left, you went to the house of the next until you found the poor ones who had got caught. The first ones to receive visitors were trapped. They themselves could not leave, and so inevitably they would end up having 20 or more visitors to whom they would serve Lebanese coffee (Turkish in fact) with at least cakes and pastries, and sometimes more substantial sustenance. It would always seem wise to have a tray or two of *kebbe*, a bowl of *tabouleh* and a bucket of *hummous* hidden away in the kitchen. It also meant that their houses all had to be equipped with enormous entertaining areas, and they had to be able to produce 20 or more chairs for people to sit. Of course the Lebanese probably did not think about this in the same way I did. I would either have left early, or hidden the car and pretended I was out when the first knock at the door came.

Charles was an incredibly social and outgoing person, always the centre of attention. He had a wonderful sense of humour, and a husky voice that I used to love listening to even when he spoke Lebanese, which I did not understand at all. He had a great sense of fun, and was an incredible dancer, especially in Lebanese dancing. One New Year's Eve we went to a Lebanese function. Part of the entertainment was a belly dancer who had a male dancer to accompany her. He was so useless that Charles could stand it no more, got up on the stage, pushed him out of the way and danced with the belly dancer. He brought the house down.

The family ordered his life. In return he was looked after and would never have starved. But the price was sometimes very exacting. He had to attend family get-togethers and do what the family asked. His eldest sister had been the first to come to Australia. Her husband was a pleasant happy-go-lucky man, but without much ambition or ability. At one stage he bought a petrol station and ran that. The sister had in the meantime a very close relationship with a dentist, comfortably off, and with the degree of sophistication the family would have preferred for their daughter. This is the reason why, although he was also married, the family tacitly approved. It went on for years. Strangely enough that same sister was incensed when her best friend, an Egyptian dentist, had an affair with the youngest brother, John, neither of whom was married at the time.

The dentist friend of the eldest sister was instrumental in getting the family to insist that Charles become a dental technician. This would have been one of the last things Charles would have wanted to do, but he had little choice. He completed the course and while he was still apprenticed, the dentist set him up in a business attached to his own dental practice, paid him a pittance and made a fortune out of his work. Charles hated the job with a passion, and when he left to join a more established practice there were ructions within the family that created waves that took a long time to dissipate.

Charles was talented and made a success of everything he did. He used his talents as a dental technician to make jewellery. He made a beautiful ribbed gold ring for me from gold of his own, and I wore it as a wedding band; I still do and will until the day I die. He also made some tiny facsimiles of male genitalia from dental amalgam, which could be worn as a charm on a bracelet by any woman bold enough to do so.

His mother was a powerful woman. She had severe diabetes, and produced extraordinary hysteric symptoms when required. These might include partial paralysis of an arm, for example. But I got on very well with her. My voracious appetite and willingness to try any food at all meant that I was always a grateful guest at the dining table, and a welcome one too. In the end I believe that she came to understand how much I loved her son. It was an unsung bond that united us eventually in some strange way.

Periodically she went back to Lebanon for months at a time. I used to look forward to those times as the pressure on Charles reduced. There is no doubt that the hold the family had over him was an irritant in our relationship. It made it hard for him to live with me, and in fact he did so permanently only after leaving dental work altogether and starting his own restaurant, *Chez Nous*, in Bondi, when he could justify to the family that it was more sensible to stay at my place than drive so far back to his mother's flat. When he was summoned, he had to go irrespective of what other plans we had made. I had great difficulty in understanding this, and felt that he should stand up to them and establish his independence, his right to do what he wanted with his life. But the family made the stakes very high. It was unwritten, but his interpretation of the rules was, "all or nothing". Later, much later, too late, he came to feel that the family cared about the family, but not about him.

In 1983 the company for which I worked sold the assets of the business to a joint venture between Exxon and Mobil. I was the Australian Sales Manager, a job that I really enjoyed and that was quite well paid. The last thing on my mind was to change jobs. But when the sale of the company was announced and I was told that my job would be available for me, but in Melbourne, I knew that I would resign. Yet Charles said to me at that time, "Why don't we go to Melbourne?" I did not think he was serious, but afterwards it crossed my mind that he saw it as a way of living his life without being beholden all the time to the family, yet at the same time retaining his relationship with them. For the third time in my business life I was going to have to change jobs, not because I wanted to, but because my employer wanted me to go and live somewhere I did not want to.

In fact my career changed abruptly and strangely as a result of a phone call I made that, again, seemed almost bound to happen. The reality is that it was not at all logical to make that call, and was contrary to my usual mode of behaviour and the way I do things, but despite that I did. I called a consultant who had done a large training project at work when I had been Australian Sales Manager. I had not spoken to him for two years. At the back of my mind when I called him was the thought that he had a lot of contacts with companies through his client base. He might be able to advise me, if, or rather when, I told my company that I would not accept their offer, how easy or difficult it would be to get another job as an Australian Sales Manager. In fact it is extremely unlikely that he would have been in a position to advise me on such a matter given his client base and the work that he did, but he said that he would be happy to talk to me.

We met at the Marble Bar in the Hilton for a drink. To my utter astonishment after we had debated the fact that working for a company one is always vulnerable to having one's life hijacked by events such as takeovers, re-organisations and mergers, he offered me a partnership and directorship in his training company. This was a significant departure from my prior work, especially in the sense that in a small organisation one is far more accountable, and I was to be responsible for creating my own client base and projects. While I was nervous about that aspect of it, I saw it as a good opportunity and I accepted, and we stayed in Sydney.

I enjoyed being with Charles, so that rather than not see him I was prepared to go with him to many of these family events since I was invariably invited. I am sure that most of the friends and family knew exactly the nature of our relationship (how could they not?), but it was never spoken about. I fortunately loved the homemade Lebanese food, the sweet cakes made with honey, pistachio and rosewater. Charles's favourite cake shop was run by Muslim Lebanese, opposite the Greek Orthodox Church at the back of Cleveland Street. Many of the Christians would not shop there, but Charles did. Quality came before any political or religious considerations.

Charles was a superb cook in his own right. He admitted that Lebanese food, just like Israeli food, did not really exist. It was all Turkish from the centuries of Turkish occupation that region had experienced. It was logical for him to have his own restaurant, and he invented some wonderful dishes, my favourite being fish cooked with *hummous*. He used to make yoghurt for us every week, and at the end of the week converted what was left into *labne*, by filtering it and letting it solidify.

The restaurant was tiring work, and he had decided that he really wanted to fly with Qantas as a flight attendant. I was not very keen on this idea because I knew it would take him away for much of the time. But it was what he wanted, and on the third attempt at applying he was accepted. He asked for my permission to take the job. I put aside my own preferences in the matter because I knew how much he wanted it, and told him to go ahead. I am so glad that I did.

Chapter 14 India calls again

Charles had always wanted to travel, and had been fascinated by the stories Gerrard and I had told of our previous trip to Asia. So at the end of 1981 we planned a trip to India with Gerrard, Toni, who would become his wife and with whom he would have two sons, and Julie who worked in the technical service centre where Gerrard was working at the time. Our first couple of nights in a Chinese hotel in Bencoolen Street in Singapore, long since disappeared on the tide of modernity, created a problem with the management. Julie was a late booker, and we had already booked two rooms. There was no problem with that, as there were three beds in one room and two in the other. They were just uncomfortable with two men in one room and one man and two women in the other, when clearly it should have been three men in one and the two women in the other. It was just not allowed. So after a bit of an argument, we finally agreed, took the keys and then just did what we wanted with the rooms.

We relaxed for a few days at the beach in Negombo close to the airport of Colombo in Sri Lanka, knowing that it would be far more relaxing than the next few weeks travelling around India. And then we hopped on a short flight to Tiruchirappalli in the south of Tamil Nadu, one of the most populous and conservative states of India. For obvious reasons it is also known as Trichy. The bank at the airport would not change Australian-dollar travellers cheques, but as we had enough cash in rupees, donated by a friend of mine, for a taxi ride into the city we did not worry much. They had told us at the airport that we would be able to change Australian dollars at the bank in town.

We first decided to find somewhere to stay so that we could drop our luggage off. We looked in the more modern part of the city, strangely often called the cantonment, although there were no post-Raj enduring signs of military presence. We found a most suitable modest place with rooms including ensuite bathroom for around five dollars a night.

It was early afternoon, and so we decided to stop off and get a liquor permit before heading to the bank. Tamil Nadu is a dry state, and to be able to drink alcohol at all, let alone buy it, a liquor permit was essential. In a couple of days it would be New Year and we wanted to be able to celebrate with some beer, so this was quite a priority. It also seemed as if it might be good fun. We located the correct government department and found the man who issued such permits.

One legacy of the British is a cumbersome civil service. We filled in the lengthy and detailed application form. The officer-in-charge asked for our passports. He looked at us very seriously and then said in a severe tone of voice, "It will be necessary for me to place a stamp in your passport in public view that you have been granted a liquor permit. Do you still want me to proceed?"

It clearly was thought to be an awful slur against our character, perhaps similar in our eyes to having a brothel permit stamped in our passports, and not at all the sort of thing that one would want to be available for public scrutiny. We summoned up the appropriate amount of seriousness for the occasion. "Yes", we replied. "Very well".

And the stamp was inked up and transferred into our passports, duly signed and dated, and we were ready for a beer. But not yet of course; we still had not managed the bank.

It was now well into the afternoon and we decided to address the money issue. The bank was a short walk away, and there were scores of people milling around outside, as they tend to in India. So our surprise to find that it was in fact shut was complete. The surprise turned into horror when we were further told that this was a religious festival and long weekend and that the banks would not open again for four days. We had about the rupee equivalent of three dollars left to last five of us for four days. Even with the modest accommodation we had found in the cantonment, it was clearly not going to work.

We hurried to what seemed to be the only large hotel in town, and went up to the cashier and asked if he could change our travellers cheques. "Not Australian, only US", we were told. We had a couple of American Express US-dollar cheques, and we would have changed these at the airport if only we had known. As it was, even the bank at the airport was shut now too.

The cashier was a man of principle.

"Are you staying at the hotel?" he enquired.

"Well, no we aren't".

"Then please go to the bank for changing money".

"The banks are closed for four days, and we have no money".

"Are not banks for changing money, and hotels for staying?"

"Well in principle yes, but …".

"Yet you come to a hotel for changing money but not for staying. You should go to a bank. Would you go to a bank for staying?"

"No. Of course philosophically you are right. But in this case we have no option. Please help us out".

After making us suffer a bit more he reluctantly agreed to change just one 50-dollar cheque. At least it would be enough to keep us alive, but we would be prisoners in Trichy until we could get enough money to pay the hotel bill. Places that charge five bucks a night do not have credit card facilities. And neither did the bus or train stations.

Somewhat dejected we walked around town debating what the options might be. Toni and Gerrard split off to have a look at something, and suddenly were back again excited that they had discovered that a bank was going to open for one hour that evening at six and that they would change our money. I was extremely sceptical about this news as it seemed so very unlikely.

Yet it turned out to be true. India is a country where you would never want to play "true or false"; you would always get it wrong. We changed our money, and enormously relieved we jumped into an auto-rickshaw to the old town and stopped at the foot of the temple.

There were two things I learned from this experience. One is that in India you must ask exactly the question to which you want an answer, otherwise it will not be interpreted, or your underlying need will not be addressed. They were happy to tell us that banks in town would change Australian dollars, but they did not bother to tell us they were about to close for four days. Some days later I overheard a conversation between a Dutch girl and a functionary at a ticket office for long-distance buses. She wanted to go to Chingelput, and asked when the next bus was going there. She was told the next morning. Nearly 24 hours to wait. Then in dismay she asked the question that gave her the answer she needed. She said, "You mean I can't get to Chingelput until tomorrow?" The answer was, "Oh yes, you take a bus to so and so, and then change to Chingelput and you will be there at four this afternoon. She should have asked when the next bus was leaving that would enable her to get to Chingelput as soon as possible.

The other thing I learned is that resolution of problems in India is totally independent of the energy you put into solving them. You might as well relax, take a deep breath and let the problem sort itself out. Every morning I used to wake up and think, "Today something will go wrong. It will probably not be the thing that you expect will go wrong. And when it does you must not work at solving it, just let it solve itself". It served me well.

And that epitomised India for me, the frustrations of trying to do anything like travel or change money on the one hand, and the most uplifting, almost spiritual experiences on the other. India changes you.

You may not enjoy it, you may feel threatened or revolted, but you will feel. It confronts your senses, your values, your morality.

From the flatness of the plains around Trichy, a steep hill rises above the town on top of which is a beautiful old temple. We went to the gates of the temple, removed our shoes and socks, and started the long climb to the top of the hill inside the temple complex. As we climbed the evening street bazaar was coming to life in the streets below, with its slightly distorted music wafting on the breeze, smells of incense and Indian perfumes in the heavy evening air, and throngs of people. It was the only hill for miles around, and at the top there was a magnificent view across the surrounding plains on one side and the now rather distant bazaar on the other. Birds were swooping low over the plains, surveying their kingdom. The plains were still, the ground almost invisible in inky shadows, the sun had set and the moon was already quite high in the sky. It was one day off full moon and was in a wonderful partial eclipse. The moment was one of incredible magic. It was serene, perfect.

The next morning I woke and turned to Charles. He was laying in bed with tears streaming silently down his cheeks. I was alarmed, and asked him what was wrong. He simply said, "They are so poor, I just can't bear to see them like that".

He never let that sadness show again, although I knew it was there. The Indians loved him. To start off with he looked a bit like them, and indeed he was asked on a few occasions whether he was from the north. But he was so relaxed and natural with them, they saw him as being one of them. He made them laugh, and us too!

We took the train from Trichy to Thanjore. Our First Class compartment was full. In those days smoking in Indian trains was allowed. Toni lit up a cigarette. Tamil Nadu is a state where men and women queue for tickets in different lines for modesty, and a man would never sit next to a woman who was not a relative or wife. We always made sure that, given we were five people, we apportioned the right gender to the odd seat so that Indians did not have to move or leave the seat vacant. Julie could never go and sit next to a man other than one of the three of us. And the boys could not sit next to a woman. So, for a woman to light up a cigarette on a train was a very bold act. One of the passengers expressed his disapproving shock. This at least initiated a conversation. One of the other passengers explained he was a Brahmin, and had been trained to heal. Charles quickly asked if he was any good at headaches. "Oh, yes, I am very good at headaches". Charles explained the awful, and completely manufactured, headache he had suddenly developed. Our fellow traveller got him to take off his shirt, and then opened a small metal box, and started to sprinkle white powders over the black hair of his chest, while mumbling and passing his hands over him. Charles sat there with a faint smile on his face, eyes almost closed, emitting from time to time not terribly realistic groans.

He paused. "Any improvement?" "Hmm. I am not sure, may be a little". The Brahmin continued with the treatment. Charles opened his eyes and pronounced himself cured, sporting a broad smile. The Brahmin sat back satisfied, beaming with pleasure.

On New Year's Eve we invoked our liquor permit and bought some beer to celebrate. We had a little party in our ITDC (Indian Tourist Development Council) bungalow. We had ordered some dishes of savouries to nibble on. The guy who delivered them kept knocking on the door asking if everything was alright. It was clear he wanted to join us and so Charles invited him. He got a little pissed after just two swigs of beer, and Charles started to question him. Was he married? Yes, he was. Did he have children? No, he had no children. Charles suggested that he did not know how to do jiggy jig (as he called it), the right way to make children, and then proceeded with a hysterically funny demonstration of the specific thrusts necessary for conception.

While we all laughed at Charles's antics, it coaxed out of this poor young man a dreadful story of how his wife did not want their arranged marriage, rejected him and ran off back to her family. As a result his reputation was ruined, his family insulted, and he was destined to remain on his own for the rest of his life.

We both loved the Indian English, the phraseology, the accent, and the movement of the head from side to side with the neck held still. When you understand it, it seems quite logical that this movement of the head means assent and understanding rather than "no". We wanted to buy some postcards at one shop, like the one they had in the window. "I am sorry, the postcards are exhausted", we were told. And they looked it. One time I asked to borrow a pen in an office to sign something. "I am sorry, the pens are all busy at the moment", was the reply.

Charles felt most at home with the Indian in the street, as it were. When they serve tea, they often pour it from one cup to another to either mix the milk or cool it, I was never quite sure which. The more experienced waiters would hold the cups a couple of feet apart while they poured the liquid from one to the other, in an extravagant show almost akin to art or juggling. Charles had to have a go at this. "Show me how to do it, show me, show me. Right, let me try, give me the cups". And he would do it. A crowd would gather and cheer and applaud him. He then, to the amusement of all, went and served some of the other customers. To have a foreigner serve Indians was a most unexpected event, and it caused a lot of laughter and amusement.

From Madras, where a sacred cow took a particular dislike to Gerrard and kept attacking him in the street, we caught the bus south to the beach at Mahabalipuram. We stayed in a small thatched bungalow on the beach, a wonderful position. One night a rat ran down the outside of the mosquito net presumably from its den up in the roof, and hit Charles on the head. Neurotic as I am, I examined him to make sure that the rat had not bitten him. In the centre of Mahabalipuram there is a temple right on the sea, the Shore temple to Shiva, which dates from the 8th century. It is largely abandoned and we were allowed to go right into the centre of the temple, the sanctum sanctorum, not normally allowed for non-believers. For reasons that I cannot explain I had a very strange sensation entering. My heart started to pound, and I felt both awed and frightened at the same time, my chest tightening so that I found it hard to breathe. The air in there was dense and stifling. Was it simply a lack of oxygen and the pervasive smell of incense?

We set off inland to what later became the centre of India's not-inconsiderable IT industry, Bangalore. In those days it was an exceptionally pleasant university city, well laid out and slightly cooler than the coast.

One night we splashed out and stayed in a maharajah's palace in Mysore, just a little way out of town on a rise with a sweeping view down to the valley where the town nestled. We had an enormous bedroom and a bathroom that was almost as large. There was a wide balcony where we sat at dusk sipping Indian gin and tonics and gazing out over the haze-covered town of Mysore with its famous incense industry. Charles made a real effort for dinner that night and dressed in a white cotton suit that he felt appropriate for the occasion. With his thick black hair and moustache, and the elegance of his white loose clothes, as he stood at the top of a sweeping staircase before we went to dinner he looked as if he might have been the prince who owned the palace.

That night I made love so passionately to him, and stupidly wore a metal cock ring, with the result that I was so hard that I burst a blood vessel when I came. It remains a physical weakness that I have endured as a memory of that night.

In Ooty, an old British hill station up in the mountains of Tamil Nadu, I spent the coldest night of my life. The low overnight temperature took us by surprise, and we had no warm clothes at all. We took the blankets off the bed to wear as ponchos when we went for a meal, looking like a plague of bats. Then, although we had two single beds, Charles and I slept together in one bed so that we could hold each other tight to keep warm and use the blankets from both beds on one. I used to love sleeping cuddled up with him. He once said to me, "Sometimes I think I am just your teddy bear". I told him that surely that was not so bad. I really found it very difficult to keep my hands off him, and that never changed. In the morning they brought us a metal vat of heated water in which to wash. It was heaven.

In the afternoon we took the steep mountain railway from Ooty down to the plains below, an extremely scenic trip. Our plan was to leave that night on the train from Coimbatore down in the valley to Cochin. But our plans were in disarray after learning that the train was coming from Delhi, and was running some 14 hours late. As often under such circumstances we divided up the tasks between the five of us. Toni and Charles were always sent to reconnoître for accommodation as they were the most fussy. If it satisfied them, the rest of us would be happy.

It was already early evening and we needed to know the options. Bus? Other trains? It seemed that the best was going to be to stay the night and take the train the next morning. I was on duty guarding the luggage. As so often happens in India, I was approached by a stranger.

"Come from?"

"Australia".

"Your profession, please?"

"Chemist". While this did not exactly describe what I did it was always a practical answer.

Just at this moment, Julie rushed around the corner having completed the task assigned to her.

"This is Madam?"

Julie was of course a work colleague, but that would have been hard to explain. "No, my sister."

"Ah! Profession please?"

Before Julie could answer I said, "She is also a chemist".

Then Gerrard turned up. Before the man had a chance to continue his investigation, I offered him the information he was sure to be seeking. "And this is my brother. He is a chemist too." Now Gerrard and I could hardly be any more different as two Caucasians. I am tall, in those days with dark brown hair, and rather olive skin. Gerrard is very fair, short and with blue eyes. However unlikely being brothers might have been, it never

ever caused any raised eyebrows or questions. On the other hand, neither did a claim once made by Gerrard that we were Chinese cause any protest.

"Ah, very good. Brother, brother, sister. Chemist, chemist, chemist!" looking from one to the other. "Yep, that's right", I said in a tone that I hoped expressed that we did not have time for idle chit chat.

The night was passable, and the next day we arrived in Cochin in Kerala State. Built on a series of islands around a large bay, with a Portuguese and Dutch colonial history as well as British, Cochin is one of my favourite places. It has a mix of architecture that belies its history, and the most common way of getting around is by boat.

We spent a few days in Cochin, speeding across the lagoon between the islands, enjoying the physical beauty of the town and the fascinating mix of architecture. The spice market was run by the White Jews of Cochin, who even then had dwindled considerably in number, and who were to our eyes not very white. But the mounds of aromatic spices, of cardamom and nutmeg, were still there. In the same street is a tiny synagogue that we were told is the oldest in the Commonwealth.

The cultural life of the state of Kerala is dynamic, and one of its main attributes. We saw Indian dancing, including the 500-year old dance drama of *Kathakali*, and enactments from the *Mahabarrata*. The active culture may well be in part a result of being the only state to have had a communist government; the rate of literacy and general education standards were also much higher in Kerala than other states.

We might have seen more of Cochin were it not for the *hartal*. This is the word for a general strike. Indians take their strikes very seriously, with the odd death or two during general strikes to be expected. Nobody is supposed to do any work whatsoever. In fact our hotel was kind enough to provide coffee and bread for us. For their trouble they had a brick thrown through the plate glass window from the street. In the morning the streets were deserted and the town was utterly silent. But in the afternoon, people relaxed a little and started to venture out for a stroll. By the end of the afternoon the town had more the aspect of a relaxed Sunday.

Our plan was to take the bus to Alleppey, stay the night and then catch the boat that meanders leisurely down the canals parallel to the Malabar coast some 120 kilometres to Trivandrum, as it was then known. Alleppey turned out to be a pleasant enough place for a night's stay. I recollect some shops selling fine cloth and fabrics.

I had steeled myself to accept that the boat would not run, for that was the rumour that was circulating in town. And in any case, as I have said, I tended to anticipate problems so that when they happened I was better able to ride them out. But we were rewarded for our exceptionally early start as the boat puttered into view shortly after six.

It was the most relaxing way of spending a day. Rural India was just waking up as we set off down the waterways, and we watched those people living on the banks under shady palms, get up, stretch and undertake their morning ablutions. As the heat of the day increased we sat where we could find shade and lethargically watched the green banks float by, lulled into a cat-like doze by the monotony of the motor, the lapping of water at the bow and the buzzing of a few flies.

Suddenly there was a jolt, and the boat suddenly stopped. We had hit a sandbank in the shallows where the canal crossed the path of a languorous river on its way to the Arabian Sea just a couple of miles away. A fishing boat of exotic design, looking as if it might have been sailing the Arabian Sea for hundreds of years, came alongside and took on board some of our passengers to lessen the load. The occupants of the other boat jumped out, and as the water was hardly up to their knees we could see how the problem had occurred. The strategy worked and they were able to raise the boat from the sandbank and it limped into a wharf close by. It seems as if the rudder had been damaged, and it was quite unclear how long it would take to repair, or even whether it could be repaired at all.

It was around two in the afternoon and we were still 80 or more kilometres from Trivandrum. It had been our plan to stay the night at the coastal resort of Kovalam, another 20 kilometres further. I remembered the lesson I had learned and sat patiently in the hands of fate.

It was getting hot on the boat, and the flies were beginning to annoy. Suddenly Charles leant towards me and whispered that a taxi had just arrived on the wharf. He slowly got up to avoid drawing attention to what he was doing, and then surreptitiously climbed ashore. He spoke to the driver, and beckoned to us. By this time others had noticed too, and there was a mad scramble for the taxi. The five of us managed to get in, together with another three or four – Indian taxis especially in such circumstances can accommodate a much larger number of people than in the west. Every day in India buses, taxis and trains look as if there is yet another attempt being made on the Guinness Book of Records. He took us to the main road a few kilometres away. There we assumed we would be able to catch a bus to the next town of Quillon.

But every bus was packed and did not even stop. We seemed destined to be stuck at the side of the road for eternity. Finally a jeep stopped and again we sought to break another record, with people hanging on to the sides and achieving a degree of intimacy many might aspire to, but with people we had not even been introduced to. We arrived at the next town of Quillon, where the jeep dropped us at the bus terminus. As we were waiting at the bus stop and examining the timetable, we were approached by a man in a taxi who explained that he had had a fare from Trivandrum to Quillon, and that he was going to have to go back empty. He offered to take us there if we paid just the same as the bus fare each. This seemed to be a good deal, and as he was available to leave immediately we got in the car. Taxis were all Ambassadors, BMH Leyland cars that looked like a Morris Oxford, made in India under licence. Some were newer and some were older. This one had had a long and hard life.

It laboured the 40-odd kilometres to Trivandrum and was on the point of expiring on several occasions. But there was one last hill that defeated it. The car stopped and would move no more. We were already close enough to Trivandrum, so we paid our fares, left the taxi driver and caught a bus to Trivandrum. From there we caught another bus and arrived in Kovalam exhausted, appallingly dirty and hungry. It was already almost dark.

We had not eaten all day, but decided that we should get accommodation before giving ourselves over to the indulgence of a nice curry. To our dismay Kovalam was booked out. After an hour or so we had managed to find just one room with a single bed, hardly enough for five people, but at least somewhere off the streets. At that time of night, it seems the matter was settled; we would never find another room. We were dead on our feet, demoralised and starving. So we decided to eat.

As I have mentioned, I did learn that the resolution to problems in India is independent of the energy put into solving them. And so it was that during the meal the waiter came over to us and asked, "Are you looking for somewhere to stay tonight?" It seems that somebody knew somebody who was looking after a house, and the owner was away. For a small sum we could have the house: three bedrooms, right on the cliff overlooking the ocean, and a boy to make tea for us in the morning. It was a superb property: modern, airy and clean with spellbinding views over the coast from the headland where it was situated. India had worked its charm once again.

It was here that Charles decided to shop for all the family, not an inconsiderable task. He engaged the services of a tailor and had clothes made from white cotton. Shirts and pants, blouses, shorts, culottes: it was a sizeable order, and was ready only just in time for our departure. I left him to his negotiations and investigated the therapeutic effects of ayurvedic massage.

Our last memories of India were the leaving formalities. Only about 70 passengers were on the flight from Trivandrum to Colombo. The Air Lanka plane had arrived on time from Colombo; even so the processing was so lengthy that the plane took off late. Additional to the information we had filled out on the form they wanted to know our profession, which the immigration officer then wrote in long hand on the form. Why did they need this information as we were leaving? Don't ask!

The English girl in front of us said, "Physiotherapist".

"What, please?"

"Physiotherapist", she repeated firmly and proudly.

"How are you writing that?"

We leaned over her shoulder addressing the official. "Nurse, she is a nurse".

"Ah, nurse!"

"No I'm not a nurse, I'm a physiotherapist", she objected with a pout of indignation at the offence.

We reasoned with her, "Who cares? What does it matter? All we want to do is get on the fucking plane. He can spell nurse. If he has to spell physiotherapist we might be here all day". We leaned over her shoulder again and said firmly again to the officer, "Nurse, just write nurse".

And we flew out to the outside world, richer by far than when we had arrived.

Charles and I travelled quite a bit together. In Austria once, as we travelled by train from Salzburg to Vienna there was one of the thickest hoar frosts I had ever seen. The twigs and branches of the trees were covered with white magic, perhaps one to two centimetres thick. Charles had never seen anything like it, and he ran from side to side of the carriage hardly believing the beauty of what he saw.

In Vienna I went to a concert before we left for Venice on the night train. Charles went to the sauna. I went to Salzburg for two days while he went to see a friend from Australia who was living in Cologne, someone I had never met or even heard of. In Pakistan he picked up a guy and brought him back to our room, suggesting we should all have sex together. And there was a charlatan who said he was from Fiji whom Charles said he had met at his restaurant. These were painful events for me. It was not so much that I was averse to having threesomes in principle, or that I would forbid him from having sex with anyone else, even if I had been able to. But I was worried by the reports of this strange illness that seemed to be affecting gay men. And in truth I felt less secure in the relationship than he did. Or at least it sometimes seemed more important to me than to him. He must have known how I felt about him by this time, and this allowed him to a certain extent to have his cake and eat it.

We went to California, London, Paris, Rome, Bangkok, Karachi and Singapore. But the one place we had always planned to go together was back to Lebanon. It was not to be.

Chapter 15 Enlightenment in Luzon

Charles and I had discussed going to Malaysia for a short break when his first holidays with Qantas came around. I even booked a flight. But then he had family issues to attend to, and he felt a bit tired, and so we did not go. However, I felt that I needed a break and decided at the last minute to go to the Philippines for a couple of weeks on my own.

"Good flight?"

"Yes, thanks".

"Where you come from?"

"Australia. Sydney".

"How long stay?"

"A couple of weeks or so".

"Business?"

"No, holiday".

This conversation between taxi driver and passenger occurs every day and all day long in taxis from the airport of any city. In this case the city was Manila. But it could have been anywhere. However, only in certain countries does the conversation develop further on a specific theme.

"Stay in Manila?"

"No, I am going up north to the mountains. Tomorrow to Baguio".

"You travel alone?"

"Yes, alone".

"You want nice girl to accompany you? No good travel alone. More fun with nice girl".

"No thank you".

"Much better with girl".

"No, I am not interested".

There followed a short silence while the driver assessed the situation and how he should proceed with his sales story.

"Perhaps nice boy. I can arrange very nice boy. You like?"

While potentially that did sound more interesting, that was not why I was in the Philippines. I wanted two weeks to unwind, read and think.

147

"No. I have plenty of books with me to read. That is going to be my company".

This was not an answer the driver either expected or liked. He laughed a little nervously.

"Books?" He laughed nervously again, and then fell silent.

The next morning I flew to Baguio, the main town in northern Luzon, surrounded by low mountains. I found a very pleasing bed and breakfast to stay. It was surrounded by flowers in a shaded suburban street, high above the road and with views across the garden from the main areas of the house. It was warm and comfortable, and about 20 minutes walk from the centre of the town.

Local newspapers are an excellent way of finding out about a new place. In Baguio it seemed that there was a certain level of violence that was being directed towards foreigners. Two Caucasians working with the local Catholic mission had recently been murdered. Indeed the young woman who owned the lodge where I was staying had advised me to be careful, even walking in town.

Baguio was a pleasant place to stay for a few days. There were a few churches and public buildings to visit, and the hilly nature of the town means that there are always pleasing views to contemplate. A short way out of town there are some thermal baths in a deep valley. I took the bus there and spent a pleasant day soaking in sulphurous pools imagining that it must surely be therapeutic. Although I did not want to admit it, there was also at the back of my mind the hope of a possible sexual adventure. There was certainly nothing doing in that regard, and indeed the baths were almost empty.

I had also planned the next part of my visit, which was to take the bus to Bontoc the capital of the Northern Province. From there I might go even higher into the mountains to Sagada, for a few days of peace and contemplation. Meanwhile on the Sunday morning I went to the park in the centre of town, and settled myself onto a park bench in the shade, reading my book and watching the local townsfolk enjoy their day off.

After a while a young Filipino man came and sat down on the other end of the same bench. I did not take much notice and kept on reading. After a while he spoke. "Hello, isn't it beautiful in the park?" He had a pronounced American accent, and spoke English comfortably. I looked at him more closely now. I imagine he would have been in his early 30s, was quite solidly built and well dressed.

He went on to explain that he had worked at the US Clarke Air Base, and that after serving a certain number of years such employees were given the opportunity of residence in the USA. He had taken up that offer and had gone to live in the States. He was now back visiting his family. He asked if I was Australian. He then told me that his sister lived in Australia, in fact in Sydney. She was a nurse in Balmain Hospital in Sydney. I told him that I was from Sydney and that I had had dinner with a friend in Balmain only a few nights previously. He said that his sister was also visiting the family in Baguio and that she had brought a friend of hers with her, an Australian girl, who also was a nurse at Balmain Hospital.

He stayed silent a few moments and then volunteered the information that they were thinking of taking their uncle's car and driving up to Bontoc for a few days so that the friend from Sydney could see some of the mountain scenery. I told him that I was also planning on heading up that way, but that I was going to take the bus. After a few moments he said, "Why not come with us in the car? There will only be me, my sister and her friend, so there would be plenty of room in the car for another person".

This was not exactly what I had in mind. I rather wanted to just be on my own. But he seemed pleasant enough and some company might be interesting, at least for the journey up to Bontoc, which by bus is some eight hours or so.

"Well, it could be a possibility, I suppose", I said. He replied, "Look, my family house is very close to here, and my sister and her friend should be there having lunch right now. It is one o' clock. Why don't we go and meet them and then you can decide if you would like to come with us?" I thought about it for a moment, and then decided that as I had nothing else planned, I had nothing much to lose. "Alright", I said, "Let's do that".

We got up and strolled across the park, and through the entrance on the far side. To my surprise he called a taxi. I had gained the impression that the house was close enough as to be within walking distance. We got into the back seat and the taxi headed off into the streets behind the park. In fact the journey was not a long one, and in less than five minutes we stopped in front of a pleasant and quite large house. My new-found friend got out and waited for me at a little distance from the taxi, which I assumed meant that he was expecting me to pay the fare. It was only a few pesos and I did not mind paying. But I was not sure that I felt comfortable with his assumption that I would pay.

We went into the house – the front door was open – and entered a dining room where the family was eating lunch. His father, mother, uncle and a friend were there, as well as a few other people whose relationship to the family was never explained. Neither his sister nor her Australian friend was there. Again I was a little surprised. I commented on this, and my friend explained that they would be along shortly. Meanwhile he brought a chair to the table for me and invited me to sit down and join them in Sunday lunch.

"What would you like to drink? Whisky? Beer?" The food did not look at all appetising, but at least I could see that they had all eaten it. I was now just a little on guard, and the thought of a drink, to which anything could have been added, did not seem like a sensible idea.

"No thanks".

"But you must have something to drink!"

"No, I really do not want anything to drink". A plate was placed in front of me and I helped myself to a little food.

"You know, there is just a small problem with my uncle's car".

"Oh?"

"Yes. It just needs a little repair. I thought it would be only fair if you are coming with us that we share in the expense. It is not a big repair and will not be very expensive". I did not commit myself. I forced a few morsels of food into my mouth.

"Have you been to the casino yet?" The friend of the family was asking the question.

"No".

"The old one burned down. I work at the new one. I can make sure that you win. It is very easy".

"I do not gamble".

"But this is not gambling. I am offering you a certain way to win".

"Even so, I do not gamble. But I appreciate your offer".

Just then a man came in from the back part of the house. He was wearing a priest's clothes. I was introduced to him. He sat at the head of the table and started talking about a forthcoming festival for which he was trying to raise money. The uncle immediately dug into his pocket and gave the priest some money. The father did the same. Then the uncle looked at me and suggested that I would no doubt wish to contribute as well. I responded by explaining that I would not for two reasons. Firstly I was not a Catholic and felt no involvement with the festival whatsoever, and secondly and more to the point, I had no money with me. While the latter comment was untrue, I felt that I delivered it with conviction.

By this time I had decided that things were definitely not as they should be and I was inwardly in a high state of alert, at the same time trying to keep a relaxed and unconcerned external demeanour. The many stories I had heard of tourists being ripped off, robbed and even murdered flooded into my mind. I glanced across the room to the entrance, and noted that the front door was still open. The street appeared quiet, but given that it was a Sunday afternoon, I figured that there would have to be people around.

Suddenly, I stood up, and moved rapidly to the door before any of them had a chance to react. I said, "I am leaving now", and ran out into the street. Once at the front of the house I turned left up the street and kept running for a short distance until I felt safe that they would not have followed me. I walked quickly into the next street, which was busier, and in just a few moments I found a taxi, and went back to the lodge where I was staying.

The woman who owned the lodge was in the sitting room. I told her what had happened and she expressed great concern. She told me that there had been many attacks on tourists and she begged me to go to the police. I told her that I did not want to complicate my life by going to the police. She asked me if I could find the house again. I told her that I was fairly certain that I could. She asked me if I would go with her driver and show him the house, and then she would go to the police herself. I told her that I was prepared to do that on one condition only, that she did not go to the police until after I had left for Bontoc. She agreed.

It was easier to find the street and the house than I had anticipated. We drove slowly past the house. Nobody was to be seen, The driver asked me if I was completely sure that it was indeed the house. I was absolutely certain. We returned to the lodge.

Later that evening the owner saw me and told me that she had been to the police, and they were going to follow it up immediately. Somewhat dismayed I reminded her of our agreement that she would wait until I had left before contacting the police. She simply replied that in these matters action was required sooner rather than later. I decided then and there that I would leave on the early bus to Bontoc the next morning.

I felt light and relieved as I left Baguio. The journey was long and uncomfortable, but the scenery was superb. In the evening we arrived in Bontoc, and I found a modest place to stay for the night. I have always found that poverty is more acceptable in warmer locations than cold. The easy access to nature outside blunts the misery of the environment. The poor of warmer climes seem happier than those of colder places, especially those in the mountains. Some of the most miserable places I have been to have been villages in the Peruvian Andes, where the villagers sit in rags, cold and dirty, expressionless and quiet. The same was true of Bontoc. Mud from the heavy rains and the limited sun as the mountains shielded the town from the life-giving rays, gave it a morose feeling.

I had heard that Mountain Province was one of the areas where it was possible to eat dog. I adore animals and if I stop to think, I would rather be a vegetarian. Like most of us, however, I manage very effectively to isolate the tasty morsels on a plate from the creatures with doleful looks in their brown eyes who might be the next ones to grace it. I am a non-practising "intellectual" vegetarian. I strongly believe in the sanctity of all life, and in the fact that it is far more productive for us to eat what can be grown on the land than feed it to an animal and then eat the animal. It also is probably healthier for most of us to avoid the animal fats that eating meat generally implies. But I relish a nice piece of beef steak with béarnaise sauce, and a leg of lamb with rosemary and garlic.

I assume that the fact that it is possible for us to believe one thing very deeply, and at the same time without any seeming conflict behave in the opposite manner, is due to the fact that the brain handles different parts of our cognitions in different areas. This it does without forcing moral judgments, or restraints of any kind, of one area onto the other. Very convenient! It may also be the explanation of why we are quite aware that worrying about something is unproductive. It will not influence the outcome in any positive way at all. Yet, even knowing this, many of us, and me in particular, are quite capable of investing enormous emotional energy into worrying. The word emotional may very well be the key. We worry with our emotional brain as it were, while recognising with our rational brain that to do so is a stupidity. "Stop worrying, it's not going to change anything" is a phrase often directed at me. It irks me since clearly I can work that out for myself. However, it does not change the fact that my emotional brain is quite impervious to the logic, and worry it will.

And what of the dog? Well, yet again there is a dichotomy. To eat man's best friend is utterly unthinkable. To experience as much as I can of what this earthly life can offer me (within limits we might discuss later) justifies most things. In this case I enquired at the place where I was staying where I might eat dog. It appears that the eating of dog had been pushed underground. Whether this was because of the pressure of tourism, the need for better public relations, or a shortage of dogs, was unclear. It was not on the menu of most restaurants underneath the chicken and noodles. I was directed to a place known to serve dog. There I was told that these were not domestic dogs; they were "sort of" wild dogs that were bred for this purpose. I did not care any more about the moral dilemma, for it seemed that I had the justification of trying that particular dog if I wanted to, on the basis that it was no worse than eating sheep or cows or pigs.

It was a disaster: tough and fatty, almost impossible to eat. I retired satisfied that I could join the ranks of those brave people who confess to eating dog, or even brag about it. There is bravado in travelling to exotic locations and recounting such stories, the "that reminds me of when I ..." stories. I have since heard people talk about eating dog and finding it tender and tasty. Maybe I was ripped off; who knows? But I can hold my head high when it comes up in conversation at cocktail parties.

The bus to Sagada leaves early in the morning from Bontoc. As I waited in the main street a bus from Banaue staggered to a halt, and a young American woman stepped off it right in front of me.

"Hi, I'm Diane", said the blonde girl, with a broad and friendly smile. She was heading to Sagada too, and so we sat together on the bus. Sagada had become a favourite destination for young backpackers, especially those of a rather more New Age bent. That suited me fine, as I was in the mood for thinking about things spiritual. This was reflected in my choice of books for this trip. They included two books by Fritjof Capra: *Turning Point* and *The Tao of Physics*. For a very long time I was aware that my scientific education had caused severe problems with my relationship with the Christian churches. But did that necessarily oblige me to abandon spirituality altogether? I was keen to learn about some of the Eastern traditions and investigate whether I could accommodate both science and spirituality, and if so on what terms. Actually the jury is still out!

The road led back down the narrow valley towards Baguio for a short way, and then the road to Sagada went off on a spur and immediately started to climb steeply up into the mountains. Eventually the road reached a low pass, where there was a police check, and then descended into the village of Sagada. Diane and I seemed to enjoy each other's company and we decided that we might as well look for accommodation in the same place. There are several simple lodges in Sagada. We elected to stay at a Catholic convent, run as a hostel. The rooms were small and simple, but adequate and clean. Mine had a single bed and a small window looking out over a yard with chickens and beyond to small paddocks. There was hardly room for my modest belongings stuffed into my blue faded backpack. Meals were available, wholesome and uncomplicated.

The several days I spent in Sagada were most rewarding. It is sufficiently high to be towards the tree line. Rather than the tropical vegetation one might expect at these latitudes, the hillsides were covered in pines. The village was small, and led down a valley. Above the village were hills with woods and superb views to the mountains surrounding. Often after breakfast I would take a book and climb above the village, find a secluded place on the edge of the woods and sit in the sun and read.

One of the attractions of the area, if one can call it that, is the hanging coffins. The Igorot tribe, whose descendants still live in Sagada, used to bury their dead in caves carved out of the limestone cliff faces. Even today the practice continues. Before they reach their final resting place the dead are left in chairs for two days in front of their house in the village, and then they are placed up in the caves where over time they merge with the elements.

One day I climbed over the mountains to some rice terraces in the next valley. It was a long walk and it took me all day. I have always been rather clumsy, I suppose, and I fell off the wall of one of the terraces into the paddy field, damaging the mud wall, getting very wet and muddy myself, and grazing my leg. The local villagers shouted abuse at me, justifiably from their point of view, although since it was quite unintentional, rather harshly I felt. In truth I was embarrassed.

Another day I ventured down the valley, through the tiny houses. I had almost reached the end of the valley when suddenly a violent thunderstorm sprang from nowhere. I ran back up the valley, and was amazed at how fit I was. In those days Charles and I both used to go to aerobics classes three times a week, and I often went jogging too, and indeed I was fit. I arrived back at the top of the steep hill of the village with hardly a gasp.

Diane and I did not spend a lot of time together in the day, but we did tend to eat together in the evenings. At night we would try out some of the other lodges, most of which were vegetarian, very inexpensive, and provided some interesting company. Diane was a product of the Californian New Age movement. I was not uncomfortable with some of what she believed in, but had serious doubts about others, especially the cult of Ramtha, in whom she seemed to be rather unhealthily involved. In fact she later worked for JZ Knight (Jayzee) typing up the transcripts of her chanelling sessions through him. The story goes that one afternoon JZ was in the kitchen contemplating the use of pyramid shapes to desiccate food (a well-known technique in certain quarters, I am assured), when Ramtha appeared to her somewhere between the double drainer sink and the dishwasher. It is quite unclear why Ramtha chose to appear then and there to JZ, but apparently he decided that she would make an ideal vehicle for channelling and communicating his wisdom to the earthly world.

The year following the visit to the Philippines I went to stay with Diane in a wonderful wooden cottage she was renting on Orca's Island, off the

Washington State coast close to the Canadian border. That was where she was typing the Ramtha transcripts. The cottage looked out over the sound to the snow-capped mountains of Washington, and what the locals referred to as "The United States". It was an idyllic spot. It was on Orca's Island that Diane gave me my first experience in a float tank as a present. It took me a while to get used to the total absence of any light, but gradually I did relax into the buoyant, salty warm water, totally alone with myself. The young couple who ran this business from their house were wonderful, gentle New Age people too. The husband was the prototypical SNAG (Sensitive New Age Guy). An exceptionally handsome young man, I knew that he was one of those straight men who are not threatened in any way by gay men. However, when we came to leave I offered him my hand, only to find it ignored as he embraced me and gave me a warm and affectionate hug. I was so astonished that I rewarded him by treading heavily on his left foot.

It was while I was staying with Diane that I heard some of the tapes of Ramtha manifesting through JZ, and certainly the quality of JZ's voice changed during these sessions to a deeper and rather gravelly one. But I had a few problems with the whole thing. Given that English was not Ramtha's language at all, it seemed odd that instead of using ordinary modern-day English, which is what JZ spoke, the messages came through in a rather contrived old form of English. This was to me both mysterious and I have to confess suspicious.

The fact that JZ charged US$500 for two-day Ramtha workshops and had purchased a Rolls Royce also seemed to be at odds with the wisdom Ramtha was revealing through her.

However, Diane was a delightful person and I enjoyed her company and the discussions we had.

At that time the NPLA were known to have some bases in the mountains in the north of the Philippines. They were an active, communist-inspired revolutionary group dedicated to overthrowing the government and the status quo with the ultimate aim of ensuring a better life for the numerous poor of the Philippines. There had been some dramatic high-profile attacks, and the government was very nervous. There were many roadblocks and searches on the main highways, like the control post coming into Sagada. Often in the day there were military planes flying overhead, presumably looking for signs of terrorists.

But it was at night that the noise of relatively distant gunfire was a little unsettling. One never could be quite sure where the next skirmish might take place. The police station in Bontoc had already been blown up in a daring attack. One night the gunfire was extremely close, but Sister Janet, one of the nuns in the mission, assured me that it was just the local police practising. I was not altogether sure I believed her.

Often at night I would sit in the kitchen with Janet, just the two of us chatting about life and about the Philippines. When I came to leave she asked me to hand deliver a letter for her. It was addressed to a priest in Bontoc, and I was to take the letter to a particular house, not the monastery or the church. She impressed upon me that the letter was very important and that I was to give this letter to nobody else and should look after it very carefully. I delivered it as she requested. I had no idea why she asked me to do this for her. It did cross my mind that she might have been assisting the NPLA. From our conversations I knew that that is where her sympathies lay, and I also knew that the Church was not always as independent in these matters as the Pope preferred (unless it was to do with Poland). I will never know.

After delivering the letter I went to the area where the bus for Banaue left. My next stop was to be the extraordinary 2000-year-old rice terraces spread over the hillsides beyond Banaue. The bus left in about half an hour, so I settled myself on a seat on the right-hand side towards the back. Gradually the bus started to fill up. An elderly woman, her daughter and granddaughter got on the bus and made their way down to the back where I was sitting. They sat in the row in front of me on the other side of the bus. The little girl was covered in nasty large red blotches suggesting some vile and highly contagious tropical affliction. I made a mental note to avoid touching anything she had touched.

The old woman sat by the window, which was open. She started coughing from deep inside, spitting out a white fluid into an aluminium mug she was carrying. She then emptied the contents through the window onto the street. This performance was repeated to my utter disgust every few minutes, both while the bus was stationary, and once it started to move. I looked at her with distaste, and she caught my gaze and looked back at me half-defiant and half-apologetic. Her daughter sat next to her while the girl ran around the bus touching and, I feared, infecting everywhere.

The bus left and made its way out of town, and climbing the long pass into the next province. It was a narrow and winding road, passing around the edge of steep rice terraces. At one point a man was standing on the side of the road looking down at the rice terraces below. He did not seem to hear the bus coming, and when suddenly it was upon him, it gave him such a fright that he fell forwards some 20 feet down the hill into a rice paddy. Someone shouted to the bus driver to stop, and then a couple of men rushed down to where the poor unfortunate man had fallen into the rice paddy, and helped him out. Amazingly he was uninjured, but a little shocked. Satisfied that no damage had been done, the bus started up the hill again.

The old woman was still spewing into her aluminium mug and emptying the contents periodically through the window. Eventually she seemed to settle a little and the daughter comforted her, placing her hand on the old woman's arm.

At the top of the pass, the bus stopped and the army came on board to make the standard check of passengers and ensure there were no guns on board. The bus started off again. By this time the old woman had settled slumped into the corner of the seat, and to my relief had stopped retching into the aluminium mug. The daughter was caressing her hand.

Suddenly I noticed that she was feeling the old woman's pulse animatedly, and became rather agitated. She stood up and by this time was frantic. She tapped the shoulder of the man sitting in front of her, and they exchanged some words. He then leaned over the back of the seat and took the old woman's wrist in his hand to check her pulse.

She had died. As the realisation dawned on me, I suddenly felt guilty that I had looked at her in such a scornful way. I had given her a withering look for offending me with her old, decaying body. How dare I!

The stop at which I was to leave the bus appeared after only a few more minutes, and I climbed off the bus. Banaue was another haven for New Age backpackers, and as I crossed the road a rather plump American girl was walking slowly towards me. She was dressed in flowing attire reminiscent of those stores in Sydney where tarot card readers have their cards in the window, and that smell strongly of incense.

"Hi", she smiled, with that dreamy expression which suggested either a condition close to nirvana or a substance.

"Hello. The woman next to me on the bus just died".

"You mean she passed over?"

"Yes, she passed over".

"Just like that! Wow".

Banaue was larger and far more commercial than Sagada largely because of the fame of its rice terraces. Diane had already visited the area and had returned to a remote village in the mountains to spend a few days. I planned to get to the area and see her before I left for Manila.

The only way to reach these remote villages was to walk there over the mountains. I met a Canadian guy and a girl he was travelling with and we agreed to hire a taxi to take us in the morning to the point where the path started up the mountain, and then to come back and pick us up in the evening. The ride to the start of the climb was quite a few kilometres. The climb was steep and the path rough, and it was very humid and hot. By the time we reached the top of the climb we were drenched in perspiration. The walk down the other side was easier, and afforded wonderful views over the rice terraces and the mountains.

Eventually we reached the village where Diane was staying. The streets were narrow and steep, the stone houses separated by just enough space for two people to pass. The streets themselves were just composed of large stones. There was no electricity, and life looked as if it was conducted exactly as it had been for thousands of years. The only sign of modern civilisation was the stand that an enterprising local woman had set up at the entrance to the village selling Coca-Cola to the odd tourist who ventured that way. She had clearly carried them all the way from the next valley from where we had come.

It might be sad from a tourist's point of view that this jewel of a bygone era will probably have disappeared by now. I am sure that electricity will have been installed and an easy access road built. This will no doubt have brought some clear benefits to the villagers. It will also have removed a fascinating showcase for people like me to visit. It was a real view into the past, like walking into your own Discovery Channel documentary.

The real test is what it will have done to their society, to their way of life, their relationships and their value systems, whether they were in fact happier in the days before even the tourists reached them, let alone the amenities that everyone takes for granted in the modern world.

Chapter 16 My love lost

When I first heard about the movie *Love Story* I went cold. Every cell in my body screamed at me that I did not want to see that movie. I never have. I was at the time not sure why I should have such a strong reaction, but intuitively it seems to me that I knew the parallels would be too close to my own life.

I have always worried about my health. I think perhaps it is to do with control. I would be far less concerned about having a heart attack, but I have a fear of something invasive and lingering. I am very bad at not being in control, and that is also no doubt the reason why I am apprehensive about using some recreational drugs. Furthermore, so many people have died from cancer in my family that it was always a distinct possibility that I would get it too. In fact I now have had treatment for two kinds of cancer, rare ones, but let me not get ahead of myself.

AIDS was the classic invasive illness for me to fear. I was first of all intrigued and then immediately alarmed in 1981 when I read the initial reports from New York in *Time Magazine* of an illness affecting gay men that caused them to have purple skin lesions and a strange kind of pneumonia. They all died. I had been to New York just after I met Charles in 1980, and I called a doctor in San Francisco whom I had also met on the same trip to find out what it was all about. He was not able to reassure me.

I remember in a way that is etched into my memory, a still frozen picture, vivid and bright, when I learned of the first case of AIDS in Australia. It was lunchtime, and the announcement was on a placard in front of a newsagent in a Sydney suburban shopping centre where two work colleagues and I were buying some sandwiches for lunch. "First Australian AIDS victim". My heart stood still. I was oblivious to all other sensory input, deaf and blind to the world around me as it resonated within me and slowly sank in. It was 1983.

It was that same year while Charles was still running the restaurant in the days even before he joined Qantas that he started to lose weight. I managed to convince myself that it was because of the long hours he worked. But I also noticed swollen nodes in his neck that I could never recollect being there before. I was becoming increasingly neurotic. How could we be affected by this monstrous disease? It was statistically virtually impossible. Nearly 20 million Australians, half male – let's say half sexually active. Take a percentage of men who have sex with men (as it is called nowadays – there are men who do have sex with men but are not in any way queer or gay) of say 7%: that means some 350 000. The chances of being among the very few to be affected was remote. Extremely remote. I did the calculation to try and reassure myself.

That was the logic. But again the emotional process was happening in a different part of the brain. I was scared.

We had never discussed fidelity within the relationship, but I felt that the time had come when we should. I broached the subject and suggested that with the advent of this strange illness they were calling AIDS we should agree to not have sex with other people. In those days little was known about this disease and how it was transmitted, and neither was there a concept of safe sex by using condoms. The only way to be sure then was to remain monogamous. Charles was clearly not comfortable with making such a commitment, and that worried me both from a health point of view and what it implied about the way he felt about me. I cared for him so much that I was somewhat vulnerable in the relationship. For me it was a very easy commitment to make. He did finally acquiesce, but I was never sure how serious his commitment was.

The restaurant was doing alright, but operated with the assistance of one of his sisters, and the interference of the family and all that that implied. He was tired and his voice had become very husky. The doctor said that he had a bad sinus infection, which despite treatment never seemed to clear up. He needed to get out of the restaurant.

The opportunity to join Qantas apart from anything else gave him a way out of the restaurant. Apart from my other reservations about him joining Qantas, I was not sure that I could trust him to be careful if he had sex with someone else, let alone be faithful to me.

I was relieved when he passed his entrance medical to Qantas without any problem at all. All seemed to be well with his health after all. It turned out to be rather difficult to extricate himself from the restaurant after it came to light that the financial arrangements the family had made when he acquired it compromised him and were not exactly what he had understood them to be. He insisted this time that I be present in the wrap-up discussions.

He adored his job with Qantas, and it was wonderful having him at home during his stand-down periods. But although his voice did improve a little he lost more weight. I used to drop him off at sign on and then meet him at the end of a trip in front of the building where the cabin crew signed off. I would wait anxiously, concerned that he might have lost more weight. I almost did not dare to look at him. He started to look so thin that it was agonising for me. He assured me that his eldest sister had also lost weight at about the same age and there was really nothing to be concerned about.

During one of his stand-down periods I had some work in Canberra and he came with me on the trip. On the way back in the car I told him that I was really concerned about him, that I loved him desperately and the thought that he might be ill and that he might have caught HIV from me was a constant nightmare I just could not get out of my mind. Although I was driving I wept uncontrollably.

My visit to the Philippines was in September. In October he suddenly had spasms in his left leg. On several occasions his leg shook uncontrollably for several seconds. He went to see our doctor who referred him to a neurologist. But the symptoms subsided after a few weeks and Charles put it down to a pinched nerve and cancelled the appointment. He was also suffering from bouts of diarrhoea and was often very tired.

One Saturday morning in November he got out of bed and announced that he wanted to buy a house for his mother to live in. We went looking and found the most delightful little Federation cottage in a quiet street in Strathfield, a rather well-to-do suburb in the inner west. It needed some renovation, but we both fell in love with it. It was a pretty house with lots of character. He made an offer and it was accepted. Then we arranged finance, involving re-mortgaging a studio apartment he owned and the flat in Coogee that I still owned. In effect I "lent" him $30 000, a significant sum in those days. Contracts were exchanged on the house, and we just waited for settlement. Charles always wanted his mother to feel that she had a place to live without having to rely on a landlord. I think we were both disappointed that the family was less than enthusiastic about the house than we both were.

My father was visiting my sister's house in California for Christmas that year, and I booked a round-the-world ticket for a quick trip there for Christmas and then to the UK for New Year. Charles returned from a trip the day before I was due to leave. He seemed to me to be even more painfully thin and was terribly distant and vague. I would talk to him and he would be very slow to respond. That afternoon I gave him a glass of orange juice and it just fell out of his hand on the floor. The next morning we were at the doctor's early. He said that Charles was running a slight fever consistent with a mild infection, and that it was probably not anything serious. That would explain his being off the air. I decided to leave as planned.

We said goodbye in the terminal, and I watched him walk slowly away, thin and exhausted. He looked a lonely and pathetic figure, a shadow of the old Charles. He was going to stay with his family for Christmas. As soon as I arrived at my sister's house I called his brother's number. There was no change in his condition. For the next few days until Christmas day

I called at least once a day. It was only when I got hold of Charles's sister-in-law, who was also his first cousin, that I managed to get close to the truth. She told me that he was far from alright. The day before Christmas they had consulted a doctor and he had been taken into hospital. At this point I called my own doctor who is also a personal friend and asked him to get involved.

On Christmas morning in California I called my doctor again and he told me that he had spoken with the hospital. He said that nobody knew what was wrong with Charles, but that he thought I should return to Sydney without delay. I picked up the phone again, booked a flight and left almost immediately for the airport.

The plane was empty and the night was long and lonely. I arrived at Sydney airport early in the morning, and my close friends and neighbours Dick and Jane met me and took me straight away to the hospital in the western suburbs where he was. They were just about to transfer him to Prince Alfred Hospital. He was unconscious, dressed in shorts and a T-shirt, and obviously had not been touched for days. He needed to be cleaned – a more fastidious man you could never find – and they had left him until he stank.

Once at Prince Alfred I was able to supply all the missing links in the puzzle, the symptoms that he was no longer able to describe. I told them that I thought he had AIDS. They agreed. By that evening they were able to confirm that he had toxoplasmosis, an opportunistic infection that had affected his brain. The twitching of his leg two months or more before had been the first symptom. There was a treatment, but it would require making up into a drip and would be administered intravenously. They could not be sure whether it would work – they were charting unknown waters. They cleaned him and put him in a room on his own, and I kissed him goodnight. By the time Dick and Jane took me home to sleep I was utterly exhausted.

Next day I was back early in the morning, and apart from a few hours at home periodically to keep my affairs in order, I spent my time by his side. I slept on the floor of his room; the hospital was kind enough to bring me a mattress. I touched him, I talked to him, I held him, I caressed him. His family came in the daytime. They never touched him at all, cowering on the other side of the room as far away as they could get, and let it be known that they found it offensive that I showed him affection. His mother had been recalled from Lebanon from one of her lengthy trips back home under the pretext that she had to sign some papers, so as not to frighten her. As could be expected her arrival was an emotional entrance. They did not tell her initially that he had AIDS.

I suppose it was predictable that the family would on the one hand blame me and on the other ask me why I had done nothing about it. They treated me as if I had seduced their reluctant little brother. Only his cousin, and sister-in-law, admitted to me that they had known in Lebanon years before that he had affairs with men, but that everyone chose to ignore it.

At night we could be alone together just the two of us. After two or three days – I cannot even remember – his hand twitched. That was the first sign of a slow recovery to consciousness. In those days not much was known about AIDS. I did as much of the nursing as was possible. Everyone but me had to don masks and gowns when they came into the room. It was more expedient for me to look after him in all but matters that required technical training, and I was pleased to do it.

A few weeks later he asked me why I had let them bring him back for all the suffering he was to endure. I did not know how to answer him. In truth I wanted him back, I wanted to tell him how much I loved him, I wanted to say goodbye. Yet, I do recognise that in some ways that was selfish. I could not ask them to leave him to die while there might still have been some hope. In hindsight those few weeks we had together were enormous learning periods for us both. For Charles they were strangely the most important weeks of his life.

He had lost much more weight and was skin and bone. Even so when I showered him – that was a task they allowed me to perform – my dick confirmed the sexual attraction I had always had for him, and always would. He started to eat and gradually gained strength. He would get hiccups quite often. Whatever medication they gave him would not stop them. But I discovered that by holding him and placing my head on his back and concentrating very hard I could get them to stop in just a few minutes. Even the hospital staff were fascinated. After about three weeks they allowed him to come home. It was agreed that he would spend the first night with his mother and then he would come home to me.

That first night was very painful for Charles. Although the doctors had been very clear that nobody would catch HIV from casual contact, his brother would not allow him to see his nephew and niece. Charles adored them both and felt a tremendous need to have contact with youth and renewal, with the young and healthy future of his family. But it was denied to him.

There was no way the family would admit to anyone that he had AIDS. That first night they took him out to see friends and family to disprove the rumours that he was dying. When I picked him up the next morning he had a fever and was unwell. I took him straight to the hospital. When I told them what the family had done they simply asked whether they had wanted to kill him.

The next few weeks were very difficult. I was very grateful that I had a direct number at the hospital that I could, and did, call. One morning Charles had a fever and could not stop shaking. On instructions from the hospital I got him into a hot bath and eventually it stopped. His mother often came over and spent the day with us. I was so grateful that I did not have a conventional nine-to-five job and was able to devote my time to looking after him.

Charles said to me that if he ever got over his illness he wanted to devote his time to helping others who were ill. He called his sister in Beirut, and a close gay friend now living in Bahrain. One day he cried and told me how much he missed his father. He felt that his family cared more about preserving their status within the Lebanese community than they did about him. He would only speak in English, except with his mother whose English was poor. He and I were never closer than in those days.

But he started to have difficulty breathing, and I had been warned to watch for certain symptoms, that being one of them. I took him back to the hospital, and as I helped him up the stairs to the street I knew in my heart that it would be the last time.

As he registered, they entered me as next of kin. They diagnosed CMV (cytomegalovirus) pneumonia, another HIV-opportunistic infection. They started treatment. The settlement on the house he had bought for his mother was to have been a day or so earlier, but it had been delayed. The family had given notice on their flat and had to leave the day settlement had been expected. As they had the key to the house to start cleaning and preparing to move in, they decided they would move in anyway even though they were not legally allowed to do so. This created more problems that had to be sorted out through the solicitor, who was a friend of mine. He managed to negotiate an acceptable outcome.

There was another issue that needed to be addressed, and that was Charles's will. He said to me simply, "You write it to make sure that your interests are protected. I want my mother to have the house. You take the studio apartment (there was no equity in it as we had mortgaged it up to the hilt to buy the house). You are the only one I trust". I wrote the will to make sure that I would get back my $30 000 invested in his mother's house. Both properties were left to me, but if his family paid me the $30 000 within two months of his death the house would go to his mother. It was the only way I could force them to pay me immediately and not to have the matter drag on for years. I kept the studio apartment and his personal effects, and everything else went to his mother. He signed the will and it was witnessed by nursing staff.

I had been at the hospital for several days without a break and I needed to go back home for a couple of hours one afternoon to attend to a few things. When I got back to the hospital the nurses rushed up to me saying that they had been desperately trying to contact me – this was before the days of mobile phones. Charles had suddenly had a very bad haemorrhage from the back passage and had lost a lot of blood, so much that he was blacking out. He was on the floor and I knelt by him to try and comfort him. That evening he had spasm after spasm followed by huge loss of blood. They tried to pump blood into him, but it was a losing battle. That evening I discovered in myself capabilities that I never dreamed that I could muster. I had always had a horror of things medical, but as I was the only person who was not obliged by hospital protocol to take precautions against contact with his blood, I could act faster than anyone else.

Late that night they operated. There was no option. They needed to find out why he was bleeding so much. The family was around; they attached a picture of the Virgin Mary to his bed to protect him during the operation. The next day it was still there but stained with his blood. I went with him to the doors of the operating theatre. We said our goodbyes, but he told me not to worry, he would come back. By then it was the middle of the night, and his family were in a room somewhere else. I waited alone in the corridor. One of the doctors who had been treating him passed by and stopped, asking me what was happening. I told her. She said to me that she had seen many couples go through hard times like this, but that she had rarely seen a couple closer than us.

Charles survived the operation. They found that his whole intestine was ulcerated from CMV infection and that was what had caused the haemorrhage. He had been returned into intensive care, and I had to abandon my bed on the floor of his old room for a chair, where I grabbed a few moments sleep. That day they managed to wean him off the oxygen, and he was burning with thirst. They let him suck an ice cube to ease his parched mouth.

During that evening the wound burst open. The doctors had already told me that there was absolutely no hope of recovery, his whole intestine was ulcerated, and it was just a question of time before another haemorrhage occurred. Charles and I talked.

He told me that he wanted to go, he had had enough. It was too young to die at 34, but he had no energy to fight any longer. I gave him my agreement. He told me not to stay on my own, that I should have someone to look after me. We talked about both going together, but I told him that I felt in any case that there were things I still needed to complete in this life. I asked him to wait for me on the other side, and he said he would. In hindsight I wish I had not asked him that.

We called the doctor, a tall, quiet man from PNG. We told him that we wanted only to continue treatment that would make Charles more comfortable, but to discontinue any treatment that might prolong his life. They detached some of the tubes and drips. The next day he slept much of the day and gradually changed colour. He became rather yellow, his sallow skin like paper. In the evening I went out for few minutes to get a sandwich, for I had not eaten all day. When I returned he was in a deep sleep. His sister, the one I liked and who had worked in the restaurant, was with him too. I sat by his bed, caressing his arm, stroking his hair and holding his hand. His sister was at the foot of the bed. His breathing gradually became slower and slower. For a while he was breathing only once every 15 seconds. And then he stopped breathing altogether.

His family came in amid a terrible wailing, but left quickly. I stayed with him on my own, the two of us together for the last time. The doctor in charge of intensive care spoke to me and told me what to expect in the grieving process, that my life would never be the same again, and then I walked quietly into the night.

I was in a kind of surreal daze, numb yet aware. I could feel the cool of the night around me, but I was not part of it. Everything was still: it was the early hours of the morning; the streets were empty and bathed in the yellow light from the street lamps. The pedestrian crossings flashed and in the distance the traffic lights changed colour. Dick and Jane came and picked me up and took me home. There had been times over the previous weeks when I had been so physically tired and so distressed at seeing him suffer, that I wanted him to go, and then felt an enormous guilt at even allowing such awful thoughts to enter my mind. Now he had gone and I felt, yes, perhaps in some ways relieved. I realised that I needed to devote some time to myself. But most of what I felt was an enormous emptiness, a huge void that I could not even get my mind around.

Those first few days I had tasks to undertake. The hardest was returning his uniform to Qantas. I went to the office, but I could not speak. They took me to a room, where I just broke down and wept. The funeral was his family's affair. I was not consulted or involved in any way. I had him in life and they had him in death. I sat towards the back of the Greek Orthodox Church, on the left side, together with my friends, for now I was nobody. His mother had several hysterical outbursts during the service. It was suddenly announced that the family invited mourners to the hall next door for refreshments, and that the family had ordered that nobody was to go to the graveside for the burial. They had decided to have him buried in Rookwood Cemetery, the last place Charles would have chosen.

They started on the last hymn, and his body was carried back up the aisle. I got up with four friends and rushed to the back of the church. The priest who had given him the last rites a few days earlier at the request of his family was there. I told him that we would go to the cemetery. He said that the family had decreed that nobody should be there. I looked at him and said, "You remember me from the hospital. I was his partner. He was more mine than anyone's, as you know, and I will be there to lay him to rest". The priest looked at me and then nodded slowly at the driver of the hearse.

Dick and Jane and Bill and Malka and I followed the hearse in a speed-crazed dash through Sydney to the cemetery. It turned out that the family feared that there might be problems at the cemetery because of the death certificate. They were terrified that the burial workers would refuse to touch the coffin, as had happened on a few occasions, and everyone would find out that he had died of AIDS. That is the reason they gave me for banning everyone from the cemetery.

But there were no such problems and I and my four friends buried him. I threw some earth on the coffin and said goodbye.

Those days following for me were awful, but a strange thing used to happen at night. I would wake from a deep sleep and be very suddenly wide awake. I would sit bolt upright in bed and have an incredible feeling of peace surrounding me. Never once did I cry at night.

After a week or so I went to stay with some close friends in New Zealand. They knew Charles, but we had never been there together. I needed to catch up, to adjust, to heal. I started jogging again. One day after jogging through the paddocks and across the country near the house, I had a shower ready for lunch. I was relaxed and not thinking of anything in particular. As I closed my eyes in the shower suddenly the image of the outline of a recumbent figure appeared. I opened my eyes and the image was still there, so I closed them again. Slowly a light started to shine from inside the abdomen of the figure. It got brighter and brighter and then gradually ebbed away. It lasted several minutes.

Not long after I returned to Sydney the family held the one-month memorial service. I think that was the worst day of all for me. I was just inconsolable. I left the gathering early and called two people I had known for many years and asked them if I could go around and see them. When I got there they told me that they could not accept my state of mind and they asked me to leave. Dick and Jane had left to go and live in England,

and I felt totally isolated. I went to the house of a gay German friend, and there met Marsail, a friend of his, for the first time. She just held me in her arms and I broke down and sobbed for what must have been an hour or two. I have never forgotten the unconditional love, understanding and compassion she showed me that night, and I will be grateful to her for the rest of my life.

The week that followed was the week of the moving paintings. First the large one above the bed. Then one of the suite of seven on the adjacent wall, and finally the one that fell off the wall with a loud bang. Later there would be crashing candles. I have always been the ultimate sceptic, but for these strange events I have never had a terrestrial explanation.

Then the problems started with the will and the family. "Mum is very upset. It seems as if you have everything. Everything!" I explained that the only thing I had was in fact the studio apartment, which had no equity in it. They had the house, the death payout from the Qantas superannuation, the car, his money. All they had to do was to pay me the $30 000 I had put into the house for the mother. They asked if I would accept payment over several years, like a loan. I told them that a bank would be a far better institution from which to borrow money. I had been prepared to lend it to Charles, but I was not prepared to lend it to them.

They explained that it was hard for them to get a loan. I could hardly understand why this might be so, they were not short of assets between them. I stuck to my guns. They did not pay me back in the timeframe the will had specified. I could legally have taken the house. But of course I did not. Charles wanted his mother to have the house, and I would make sure that happened, once I got my money. In the last meeting the brother tried to hold back $1000. Again I stood my ground.

They then asked me for a photograph of Charles as the mother wanted to have a kind of shrine to him in the house and they also wanted to build a mausoleum at the cemetery. Imported marble, very expensive. They wanted to give him so much in death that they denied him in life. I had scores of photos of him I had taken over the years we had been together. They did not have a single one. I gave them a photograph.

His favourite aunt invited me over to her house for lunch and I went. But I found it so distressing to be there without him, that although I really appreciated their wanting to keep in touch with me, it was just better for me not to. I had to try and get on with my life without him. It was going to be hard enough without the emotional strings that his family would pull.

I kept his personal items that were in the house. He had bought two Italian chains of gold in Bahrain; we each wore one around our necks. Since his death I have worn both of them.

In those initial days it was believed that only a small percentage of those with HIV would eventually get sick, maybe 3 or 5 %. Slowly it would become clear that that was not true. Eventually a blood test would confirm what I suspected, that I was HIV-positive too. The most likely scenario is that I contracted the virus in New York in 1980 before anyone had any idea that it existed, and passed it to Charles. I do not blame myself for that, for I could not have known, and never ever did or would knowingly have done anything to harm him. Now, not only did I have to adjust to having lost Charles, but I had to learn to face the consequences of my own illness.

ooOoo

More vivid and disturbing in many ways are my dreams of Charles. It is now over 20 years since he left me, and from time to time he is there in my dreams. He looks thin, and clearly is not well, but he is managing. Things are strained between us. He sees his family and sometimes he is living with them and sometimes not. He is not in a relationship with anyone else, but neither does he seem to want me. I feel hurt by this. We talk a little about our health, I want to be with him, but he rejects me. He seems to be quite happy living his life independently of me, and this is painful for me. The striking difference in him is the fierce independence he has created, not just from me but from everyone.

Then I wake and I know that it is not true. He is dead. It is on the one hand a relief and on the other a sadness. He is eternally mine for life, through death.

Chapter 17 Getting my life back

When Charles was dying he asked me to promise not to tell anyone he had died of AIDS. But because of my own situation, this was not a promise I would ever have been able to keep. During his illness and until his death my own health had not been of any consequence or importance. I almost did not care whether I was HIV-positive or not. Later in the year after he died I went back for another blood test, and it showed a marked deterioration over a short period of time in my T-cell count, considered a reflection of the strength of the auto-immune system and an indication of the damage the progression of the virus had done. It had gone from the lower end of normal to half that figure. The doctor said it was probably the stress of Charles's death. In those days there were no drugs available at all. It was almost better not to know what was happening to one's T cells, not to carefully monitor one's decline towards a slow and painful death, because there was nothing you could do about it. It seemed better to just try and put it out of one's mind and try to keep healthy and continue living for as long as possible, never knowing what might be around the next proximate corner. The same was true with respect to testing. Since virtually everyone was having safe sex by then, many figured it was better to live in blissful ignorance about their HIV status rather than be given a certain death sentence.

Gradually it became clearer that hopes that only a small percentage of those with the virus would go on to develop AIDS were false. As we learned more the facts hit me like a blow to the head. I read, "Scientists now believe that a much higher percentage of people carrying the HIV virus will develop full-blown AIDS". "Scientists predict that in time all those people carrying the HIV virus will progress to full blown AIDS, and die".

Knowing that I was HIV-positive severely impaired my sex life for many years, although I am happy to say that it did eventually recover. I believed that never ever again would I be able to have sex without exercising extreme caution and control, taking on myself the responsibility to make sure that my partner was protected. There is not much room for passion in that scenario. In those days I felt dirty and unclean, largely as a result of the stigma that existed both in the straight world and horribly too in the gay community. This is hardly conducive to maintaining a sense of solid self-esteem. Then even in the gay community there was a feeling that those of us who had HIV almost deserved it. It was seen as a disease of the highly promiscuous, those that engaged in some of the more exotic activities of gay sex, or the leather crowd. It was a while before people began to realise that nice gays got it too. Slowly people started to think that if they were not positive it was mainly because they had been lucky rather than anything else. Just one unprotected fuck with an infected person can be enough.

After Charles died I was emotionally and physically spent. The visit I made to New Zealand to stay with my friends helped me get back into a routine of eating, sleeping and exercise. I returned to work after that, but this was only a mechanical pursuit while I decided what I wanted to do next. I just felt awfully lonely and sad. I was alive but numb. I felt that I had to keep on living but had no real desire to do so. I went through the motions of life but with no taste or relish for it; it was more of an existence.

When I returned to work my business partner told me that if any client ever found out that I was HIV-positive he would get rid of me from the company. His wife called the morning I was to go to their place for lunch, saying that she had spoken to her sister, a doctor in England, and decided that she could not have me in her house because of the risk to their newborn child. Fortunately now there are laws that would not allow him to sack me for being HIV-positive, but it brought home to me that to stay in that consultancy was going to be problematical and that in time I had to find an alternative.

Meanwhile I was treading water in my life. I wanted sex but at the same time I didn't. The odd fleeting affair filled in the evenings; there was Phil, Robert and Kon. They each played a part in keeping me going, especially Phil who somehow was there making me cups of tea and comforting me when I most needed it.

By the time the end of the year came around I just felt that I needed to get away for a few months, somewhere where Charles and I had never been together, where I could think and come to terms with what looked as if was going to be only a few more years of life. I also hoped it might help bring the grieving process to a close, although I knew of course that getting away from my memories was not going to be quite that easy. I carried him in my heart and that went everywhere with me. At least my mind would be occupied with different things and places, and I had to break the cycle of the monotonous grief of the previous months.

In November I left again for a few days in New Zealand and then flew to Buenos Aires. I arrived in the evening tired and I just flopped into the nearest cheap hotel I could find. The next morning I went looking for something a bit more comfortable and found such a place just off the Avenida 9 de Julio. I walked down to the Argentinian Airlines office in Florida, the main shopping street, and made some bookings on my Visit

Argentina Pass. I planned to cover the country from Tierra del Fuego in the south to Iguazu in the north, and indeed I did.

The Avenida 9 de Julio is said to be the widest avenue in the world and carves a swathe through the centre of Buenos Aires, pinned at its fulcrum by a large obelisk. There are many different sized side streets that feed into it. I was walking along the north side of the avenue back to my hotel when I noticed that there was a young and rather handsome man walking along at my side. He was wearing reflecting sunglasses, and looked a little spiv-like, if I am honest. The pavement was very wide, and as we walked west I started to drift across the pavement to see if he would move with me. He matched my every move, staying close and looking ahead and down. There could be no other explanation than he was pacing me. After a few streets, we stopped at a red light at a small side street. Suddenly a deep sonorous voice enquired of me, *"Paseando?"* He said it without even looking up. He was asking if I was "out for a walk".

I spent the rest of the time I was in Buenos Aires with Miguel Angel. He was a warm, friendly and caring man, suffering hard times as were so many *portenos*, as the inhabitants of Buenos Aires are called. He was selling books on the street or in offices to anyone who would buy them, on a commission-only basis. He was spiritual, and had had a hard upbringing. He felt lonely and isolated, and we got on very well together, despite his being 12 years my junior. He was renting a room from a lady in an old house in San Telmo, an older suburb of Buenos Aires with lots of character, antique shops, galleries and more than its share of homosexuals. If he had been living in Australia I would certainly have wanted to continue to see him. As it was, he showed me that I was after all I had been through still capable of feeling something for another man.

I made a few excursions from Buenos Aires, but always went back to Miguel Angel. I flew south to Ushuaia, on the southern coast of Tierra del Fuego. I went to a *doma*, the breaking in of the new horses, in the middle of the island. Leather- and silk-dressed gauchos came from all over the island, their faces showing a wide ethnic diversity. Celts, Latins and Indians were all there. I walked on the lonely glacier above Ushuaia with clear bubbling water playing along its edge. I strolled along the waterfront close to midnight, with the sun still setting. I ate *centolla* mornay, a delicious crustacean dish, a speciality of the southern waters. I loved the empty streets swept clean and dry by a ruthless and noisy wind. I did not even mind when it snowed, even though it was already summer. Yet, Charles, I discovered, was not so far away from me. One night as I stepped out of the restaurant into the twilight, and walked by the water's edge, I was unexpectedly seized by helpless weeping. I had thought for many years after that it would be the last time I would cry for him, but I was even wrong about that, as a kinesiologist in Sydney brought me to realise 15 years later.

I returned to Buenos Aires for a few days and then left again, this time for Bariloche and the Andes. I took a trip to San Martin de los Andes, along the route of the seven lakes. These were clear crystal jewels dotting green lush mountains, undiscovered and unspoiled. San Martin was a Germanic hideaway, its houses steeply roofed, complete with ex-Nazi criminals. I took another trip across the border to Puerto Montt in Chile. There were about 20 of us on the bus. I was placed next to a young woman in the front seat. She turned out to be American, and had been living in Argentina for two or three years. She was about to leave and marry the man she was engaged to, back in Washington DC. Sometimes we spoke in Spanish, as that is how we started, and then sometimes in English. We both were equally comfortable in either language.

The journey took all day. We sat together in the front seat, and we seemed to like each other immediately. There was a moment of amusement when I left Argentina on my Australian passport for which I had an Argentinian but not a Chilean visa (required in those days for Australians). I had also a brand new British passport, and as I did not need a visa for Chile in that passport, I needed to leave Argentina on the Australian passport and enter Chile on the British. When I arrived 200 metres down the road from the Argentinian customs post at the Chilean border with a brand new British passport with not a single stamp in it, it would have been obvious to them that either I had been beamed down by Scotty or else I had left Argentina on a different passport. In fact they had a manifest on the bus of all the passengers and called me forward as *Señor Michael* (my middle name), *Australiano*. In Spanish the mother's maiden name is put last and the family name second to last. They assumed that Michael would be my family name. I stepped forward with another name and another nationality, but they did not seem to care too much.

To avoid complications, I told Adele, the American girl, my story in brief summary. The driver and his mate (they shared the driving) could not work out at all what the connection was between these two gringos. But they shared their *mate yerba* with us (this is a bitter tea drunk through a kind of metal straw from a gourd into which the hot tea is poured). We passed along the lake and over the border into Chile, stopping at Osorno, and then late in the afternoon arrived in Puerto Montt on the south coast of Chile. Adele and I had agreed we would stay in the same hotel. She was staying a day or so longer than me, but we wanted to do some sightseeing together. In the guide there was a place that looked ideal at US$25–$30 a night, and by the look of it quite comfortable. When we reached the terminus, the drivers asked us where we going. We told them what we had in mind. They suggested that as it was more or less on the way to the guesthouse where they stayed, they would drop us off there on the way. When we arrived at the hotel the taller of the two drivers jumped down, ran inside the hotel and returned with the sad news that the only rooms available were not $30 at all, they were $70. Seeing the look of dismay on our faces, the driver suggested that we see if there was room at their guesthouse. There was. It was clean and comfortable and only $15 a night.

Adele and I decided to go for a walk into town, maybe half an hour down a steep hill. On the way she confided that the taller of the two drivers had invited her out for a drive later that evening. In the bus! I suggested that as we had to walk past the hotel where we had planned to stay we should just check to see if what the driver had told us was true. She looked shocked.

"Are you suggesting that he dashed into the hotel and then lied to us about the accommodation so that we would go and stay in the same place as they were staying?"

"It crossed my mind. And now you tell me that he has invited you out for a romantic drive in the bus!"

"If that is what happened, wait until tonight and I will have a few words to say".

We both walked into the hotel. Yes, they had plenty of rooms for $25 a night. Adele looked like thunder. I was frankly not at all surprised.

I walked around the town while she returned for her romantic appointment. The town has some of the most unusual architecture I have ever seen. There are many strange wooden houses with swirls on the wooden tiles from which they are constructed. The wood is from a local tree and is very durable. The port is a treasure trove of fresh seafood, served straight from the cold waters of the South Pacific. I promised myself that Adele and I would eat there the following evening.

The next day Adele and I took a bus to Puerto Varas on Lake Llanquihue where a perfect conical volcano perched on the opposite shore. We had red-wine soup for lunch. It was good. Adele recounted how the driver had made a half-hearted pass at her once he had stopped the bus on a quiet section of the cliffs overlooking the ocean. She told him in no uncertain terms that nothing was going to happen. But it turned out in any case that all he really wanted was a shoulder to cry on about the fact that his wife had left him.

In the evening Adele and I ate down by the fishing port. The seafood was exquisite, and we talked about life, death, fears and love. I told her about my view of the universe. She told me she was not at all sure that marrying her fiancé was what she wanted to do. The next day we parted and I left for Bariloche. Of course we never have had any contact since. Such meetings provide the ideal situation where two people can be brutally, totally and splendidly honest with each other. It sometimes forces them to express their thoughts, and often hitherto vague emotions, coherently for another to understand, and helps concretise them.

I left Miguel Angel one morning after we slept together for the last time, jumping into a taxi in the Avenida 9 de Julio to go to the city airport of Aeroparque. I sort of knew I would never see him again, although I wanted to. He really liked leather and I left him with some of my leather, a kind of waistcoat, as a way of remembering me. We wrote a few times, and I even called him eventually once I got back to Australia. I know that if I could have made it happen he would have come to Australia, but I would never have been sure if it would have been for me or just for a better life.

From Buenos Aires I flew to Iguazu, and found a modest hotel on the Argentinian side from which to explore the falls. I stayed several days and took my time walking along the many walks with spectacular views of the falls that extend over 1.6 kilometres between Argentina and Brazil. I used to sit down reading and just being, listening to the dull roar of the water as it gushed over the rocks and plunged down into a foamy maelstrom below.

The damming of the Iguazu river at Itaipu between Brazil and Argentina had created a hydroelectric complex that supplied electricity (not all the requirements) to over 100 million people. It had also created a lake some 300 kilometres long, and completely changed the microclimate of the area. It had caused the water flowing over the Iguazu falls to change colour to a reddish brown as the soil was swept into the river by the deforestation. It utterly dwarfed the Aswan Dam on the Nile, and is one of the most amazing man-made sights I have ever seen.

I went to Paraguay to Puerto Stroessner, named after the dictator. By the time I got back there in 1995 it had changed its name to Ciudad del Este, and Stoessner had disappeared. It was a duty-free port that Argentinians and Brazilians alike fell upon with great exuberance. But it was poor and dirty, the mainly Indian population looking oppressed and for the most part asleep under trees in the heat of the day. I wondered why the country was called Paraguay when the Indian language was Guarani. The currency too was the *guarani*, as was the most ubiquitous drink. There was a store selling electrical goods run by Chinese. They had emigrated there from Taiwan, and I wondered what the process was by which they ended up in such a remote and unlikely place. There were all sorts of unsophisticated manufactured goods available, indigenous ponchos and other fabrics, stereos, TV sets, cameras, but nothing really exciting. I bought some sunglasses.

On my last full day in Iguazu I went to the Hotel Argentina, where I would stay nearly 10 years later when my fortunes had increased, in order to book a nature trip for the afternoon at the travel agency there. This was a trip in a glass-covered electric vehicle that allowed a close look at the jungle surrounding the falls. It sounded fascinating, and I was really looking forward to it. I was there in front of the hotel early at the place prescribed, but the time for departure came and went, and there was neither any sign of the tour operator nor for that matter any other punters. I went down to the travel agency again, where now there was a quite handsome young man working. I asked what had happened to the tour. "Oh, it was cancelled, didn't you know?" I was furious, and threw what I considered an appropriate amount of drama. He absorbed the onslaught, and then made me an offer. He could not get the electric car, but if I was prepared to walk he would be happy to take me into the forest and show me everything I would have seen on the excursion. He explained that he was a trained naturalist and quite able to explain everything to me. I accepted; it was after all a very generous offer.

We set off and walked into the jungle. I do not remember all the plants that he showed me but I do remember that a toucan flew overhead, and I was utterly delighted. I also remember the conversation. He told me that he was a *porteno*, from Buenos Aires, and that he had lived on the Brazilian side for the two years since he left Buenos Aires, together with his flatmate, a Brazilian hairdresser. He talked a bit about his life, and it became clear that he was trying to tell me that he was living there with his boyfriend. In the end he said that it was not always easy being gay and living with a lover, but at least it was easier in Brazil than it would have been in the much smaller town on the Argentinian side. I looked at him, and he smiled. "So, how did you know?" He laughed. "Only a queen would have thrown so much drama over missing a trip in the jungle", he said. We got on like a house on fire and chatted away for the rest of the afternoon. I was leaving the next morning to Rio, but he got up early to get back to the Argentinian side so that we could have breakfast together.

It was the first time I had been back to Rio in more than 10 years. It was just as wonderful as I had always found it. I found a room in a small hotel on the seventh floor of an office block above some shops just at the back of the beach. It was cheap. That night I met a guy in the street, and we spent some time together. He was an Afro-Brazilian, cute, but he became rather of a nuisance in the end, and I decided that it was just easier to take a trip up to Salvador in Bahia State.

I relaxed for a while on the west coast of the peninsula on the beach away from the centre of the city. The water was perfect, but it was an hour by bus into town and a bit lonely, so after a few days I decided that I would move into the city for the last couple of days.

Salvador has a fascinating African culture, more so than anywhere else in Brazil. The centre of the city is built on two levels: the upper city and the lower city joined by a massive elevator. The lower city is by the port, and there you can find all sorts of cultural activities including the *Capoeira*, which had its origins probably in Angola as a martial arts form, but was brought by the slaves to Brazil cloaked in the guise of an innocent-looking recreational dance. The upper city is where the old Portuguese colonial town was built, and I felt that the Praça do Pelourinho, or Pilgrim Square, was just like standing in a Portuguese town. I stayed in a hotel that took its name from the square, and whose balcony overlooked the lower city, the port and beyond the sparkling sea to the island of Itaparica, an ideal place to watch the sun go down. I took the boat over to Itaparica one day and walked along the shore in the hot sun, feeling free, at one with the beauty of the tropical waters, and content momentarily, before having to return to my life with HIV.

I had dinner with some gay guys I met – they are never far away in Brazil – and breathed the last of the warmth before heading to winter in New York and London.

Christmas was spent at a large house in Berkshire used normally by Nestlé for training purposes. Dot's son (this was the son who had lived in London and whom Dot had been visiting when she confronted me about being gay) ran the training centre and they had invited a few people for Christmas including my father and me. Dot and her son and daughter-in-law knew that I had HIV, and that Charles had died. Some of the other guests did not. When they started telling AIDS jokes an incredible embarrassment fell like a thick veil over the room. It was left to me to defuse the situation, as nobody else was game to say anything at all.

Although João and I had separated in 1972 at my instigation, we had remained friends. He once came to see me in Australia, and I even fucked him for old time's sake. I often thought about that later. After Christmas, in January 1988, I went to spend some time in London and obviously he was one of the first people I tried to contact. But he had apparently just disappeared. No answer from his flat, nor at work, and I knew that he was due to have been back from Portugal where he went for Christmas. Eventually when I called his work again, someone recognised my (by this time) Australian accent, and realised who I was. She had been to Australia and I had met her briefly during her visit.

She told me João was in hospital and seriously ill. I already knew in my heart what was wrong, I had already been there more than enough over the previous few years. I rushed to the hospital and held him and comforted him as best I knew. He had what is called PCP, a fungal type of pneumonia that is a common initial opportunistic infection as a result of AIDS.

His sister São, the one I was really fond of, and her army husband arrived in London after a couple of days. João asked me to tell them that he was gay, that we had been lovers and that he now had full-blown AIDS. This was quite a challenge, more so in that the message had to be delivered in Portuguese, as neither of them spoke any English.

João recovered enough to get out of hospital and he wrote a very beautiful letter to me in Australia thanking me for all the support I had given him. A friend of his called me a month or two after my return to Australia to say that just a few days before he had gone down to the street to buy a newspaper, come back up to his flat, sat in a chair and died from a massive heart attack. São had been with him when it happened.

It would not be long after my return that I heard that Enrique was very sick. He also had AIDS. A message was sent to me that he wanted to see me. I am ashamed to admit that I was so emotionally exhausted from the toll that AIDS was taking on my life and the losses of so many friends we all were suffering at that time, that I just could not bring myself to see him.

He died not long after.

Chapter 18 Treading water and the quest for knowledge

After the trip to South America and Europe I returned to work and to living with the knowledge that I was going to die from AIDS too. There were still no HIV drugs in those early days, and it was just a question of how long I could manage to keep going. I still was fit at that time and I used to jog around Centennial Park after work in the evenings. I was still able to run, although without Charles I did not have my heart in the aerobics classes any more.

I stopped going to see the HIV specialist as there was nothing he could do for me anyway. But everything that was wrong with me, from the flu to a stomach upset, put me into a panic as to whether this was the beginning of the end. I knew far too much about the progression of AIDS for my own good. I knew what to look for and I certainly did look for it. Every morning when I woke up, all day long and when I went to bed at night. Was this cough PCP? Was this stomach complaint CMV? Was this mark karposi's sarcoma? Was I getting retinitis? The fear of going blind was probably the worst.

I managed to do my work, and get on with life as best I could. Because I did not believe that I had many more years left, I had a renewed interest in a line of enquiry that had started several years earlier. I wanted to understand the human condition, what life and my life was all about. Is there any continuation after death of the body of some entity, a soul or spirit, consciousness of some form, or not? Trying to understand what life was about had been the driving force behind me going to university in 1980 and taking psychology and philosophy. I had some credits for my first degree from London, and so I needed only to do two subjects. In the end, although I really enjoyed the courses on psychology and generally I found them very interesting, they did not tell me what I wanted to know. I had to read more widely and spread my field of enquiry. My HIV infection gave more imperative to this search.

I was not brought up in a family that was in any way either religious or spiritual. Such things were never talked about. I was somewhat encouraged to go to church as a child, but my parents never attended and did not put much pressure on me to either. A combination of rationality and a scientific education led me to not accept the teachings of the Christian Church at face value, nor for that matter those of the Jewish and Islamic faiths. For years I had rejected both religion and spirituality because then I could see no difference between them. Although I could never believe in the concept of a personalised God, especially one that could allow such misery to happen in the world, neither did I feel entirely comfortable about a totally atheistic viewpoint, or at least an apparently meaningless universe. I needed to try and make some sense of it all.

Then one day a book called The *Wu Li Dancing Masters* by Gary Zukov seemed to fall off a shelf and hit me on the head. Shortly after, while I was in the Philippines, I read two books by Fritjof Kapra. These books suggested that it is quite possible to bring spirituality and science together, but not through the western religions. In fact it was only after reading some of the Eastern approaches to understanding existence that some of the teachings of Christ made more sense, as long as they were not interpreted literally as they are by the Christian religions. I think it quite possible that here was an exceptionally insightful man who had understood some of the secrets of the universe, but who had enormous difficulty explaining these esoteric concepts to what was essentially an uneducated agrarian population with little experience in such matters. He was totally misunderstood, and when he tried to explain the truth in terms that people would better understand, he was interpreted literally rather than through metaphor and symbolism. To my mind much of the Christian Church is based on total misunderstanding, and is in its practice often downright pagan. I think that Christ would be horrified at what is perpetrated in his name if he were to return today. I have no doubt that the prophet Mohammed would be similarly dismayed. The Buddha would not be too pleased either, I suspect, in fact I am quite sure.

Charles's illness and death caused an interruption to my enquiries, but in some ways the thinking that I had done before he got ill helped me both to help him and to cope with his illness. The fact that I grieved so badly for him suggested that I still had more work to do.

A month or so after Charles's death I attended two courses, one *"The Spiritual Tradition of India",* and the other *"The Meaning of Life".* The lecturer for the latter was an arrogant young Hungarian philosophy lecturer who believed that the only legitimate source of knowledge was that acquired through the scientific method. He set out to prove in eight lectures that there is no meaning to life, that we are each an accident that leapt out of the primeval soup, and that God does not exist. He chose four or five fields, including psychology, quantum physics, artificial intelligence and evolution, to prove his case. They were mostly fields in which I had at least a passing knowledge. It was partly his arrogance and dismissive attitude towards anyone who disagreed with him that bristled with the whole group, and there were some spectacular arguments. It was fairly easy for him to dispense with some beliefs about God. But he made the scope of his lectures so narrow that it was a far from satisfactory experience for everyone, and he left more questions unanswered than resolved.

By contrast the other series of lectures was an absolute delight, delivered by Sue Werner who is one of the most extraordinary people I have met. Around that time I also went to meetings of the Tibetan Buddhists. I even practised Transcendental Meditation, although I never believed the TM organisation should have tried to justify the benefits of meditation through what they promoted as scientific explanations. As far as I was concerned if meditation was beneficial, it should be accepted at face value rather than concoct a pseudo scientific hypothesis to underpin it. The most satisfying contact was with *Arsha Vidya*, a Vedanta group based in Coimbatore in India. What I found refreshing about Vedanta is that it deals with the nature of the universe and existence, whereas Buddhism deals primarily with the way to live one's life. Otherwise there are great similarities between the traditions. The Upanishad texts were written some 2700 years ago, and are the philosophical underpinnings of the later traditions of Hinduism, Jainism and Buddhism, although the connections to how those religions are practised today I find quite tenuous. I found the concepts of pure consciousness/awareness hard to understand. But in time I started to understand what was meant by words like "suchness" and other concepts that I had struggled with for years. Ultimately the existence of God as something separate from the "universe" is denied.

I never went to the ashram in southern India, but I attended a couple of retreats here in Australia and also went to their ashram in Saylorsburg Pennsylvania in early 1987. That was a strange experience after the rigid and autocratic ways of the western churches. I drove there on a cold and snowy night in February. The ground was solid, and there was a white blanket, stark against the bare black trees. But the welcome was as warm as the weather was cold. I was given a modern, comfortable room in the students' quarters, and then went for dinner. I was lucky enough to sit next to Swami Dayananda whom I got to know much better when he came to Australia. He is a warm and caring man, totally non-judgmental, with a wry sense of humour and an incredible modesty. He had an enormous sense of child-like fun. I remember him once leaping through high wet grass, holding his saffron robes high, laughing at himself as he got soaking wet. Yet at the same time this is a man with extraordinary wisdom, which he is willing to share with anyone who wants to know. It is hard to believe that as a young man he was a high-ranking member of the Indian Army.

In the morning when I left Saylorsburg, I asked how much I owed them for my stay. They were a little shocked. "Why, nothing!" If I insisted and wanted to make a donation, then that would also have been fine. I did, of course. At our retreats in Australia they charged only for costs of food and accommodation, and subsidised those for people on a pension.

Everyone helped with food preparation, serving and cleaning up. I never felt such a sense of community in all my life. Swamiji never ever pronounced how things were. He only ever told us what the Vedic texts said, and was always prepared to offer possible interpretations. He never once preached.

This contact led me to read some fascinating books. A couple of authors stick out in my mind, Ken Wilber and Allan Watts. Ken Wilber wrote that it is necessary to select the right tool for the type of knowledge you want to acquire. For example, he said, if you want to learn about the world around you, the sensate world, then discovery using the scientific method is the appropriate tool. A Popperian model of how science advances says that for a hypothesis to be valid it must be stated in such a way that it can be disproved, and remains valid until it is disproved.

But if you want rational knowledge, then you think about it, and argue it logically. There is no experiment that shows that two plus two equals four. That can only be concluded using rational argument and thought. When it comes to spiritual knowledge, he asserts, neither rational thought nor the scientific method are appropriate. You can never prove the existence or lack of existence of God scientifically, nor will you reach enlightenment by thinking. The only appropriate tool is direct experience, and techniques such as meditation can assist in achieving such direct experience. That is something I continue to struggle with.

I read Krishnamurti, and was fascinated by a book called *The Ending of Time*, which was a dialogue between Krishnamurti and the professor emeritus of physics from London University, David Boehm. From two quite different perspectives these two old friends argue that time does not have any fundamental existence. I also loved *Quantum Questions*, a collection of the spiritual and philosophical writings of the main players in the development of quantum physics.

Gradually I pulled away from organised groups and started to evolve my own beliefs. Krishnamurti has always said that the path to truth is an individual and a personal one, and that has also been my experience. I have to confess that I also read books about near-death experiences, books by Ray Moody and Michael Sabom, and later Van Lommel. I found fascinating books on paranormal phenomena including poltergeists, out-of-body experiences and distant knowing, such as those written by Scott Rogo, who worked out of Duke University. I also remember Swami Dayananda's words: "Paranormal phenomena may or may not exist. But in so far as they do exist they are no closer to absolute truth than your own present existence." At the same time I do find apparently discarnate phenomena fascinating. If the processes within the brain produce the illusion of self and the experience of consciousness/awareness, then how can phenomena such as perceptions and experiences that happen outside the body be explained? Are there instances that prove perceptions from outside the body? The nature of these phenomena is critical to what I can let myself believe.

Do recent advances of neuroscience in understanding the functioning of the brain (I still believe there is far more about the brain that we don't know than what we do) explain how consciousness/awareness and the experience of self are produced within the brain itself? Or do they simply explain a mechanism for how they are mediated? I just do not know, but I keep digging to try and find out.

Certainly at the physical level we are all from the same origin, we share similar DNA and are made of the same matter. If there were to be an element of the universe beyond the physical it is most likely that would also connect us all. Humans are very social animals and that has been central to who we are today. As part of that society there is a connectedness, an interrelationship that we cannot deny.

If each of us saw that we are all connected, then we would see that when we do something to injure another, or act in a way that benefits us at the expense of another, we are simply injuring ourselves. This view leads to love, compassion, consideration and respect. It seems to me these are the very qualities that are so lacking in the world that is evolving, and is one of the root causes of much of the misery we see around us. "Do unto others as you would be done by" is a wonderful rule by which to live your life.

The individualism of the Thatcher and Reagan years, the ideas of survival of the fittest and user pays, are all philosophies that I find utterly abhorrent for building a society. If we are all interconnected, just apparent individual manifestations of the same, we must all help each other rather than selfishly pursue our own agendas. We are all part of society, and as we take from it so we must give to it. This society confers upon us rights, and with those rights come obligations. I was born with the ability to generate more than enough money to live. Others were born into this world with far less ability to do so. Some are disabled or mentally ill. Others just do not have the ability to earn that much money, however hard they work. Why should I complain about paying taxes designed to assist those less fortunate than myself? Just because I do not have children, is it not still reasonable that my taxes go towards the education of the next generation? Now I need help from the state to get medication to keep me alive. Should those who are currently well resent that, because they do not need these expensive medications themselves? No they should not! Neither should they resent paying taxes for the benefit of society at large, but they often do. It is called selfish greed.

Financially it is, in my mind, the job of the government to collect taxes according to a fair and equitable system, and then to disburse those taxes fairly against the needs of the community and of people who make up that community. This process should be as efficient as possible, with little leakage or wastage, and it should be as immune as possible to being abused. Few governments if any achieve that. In my experience the worst of the developed world is certainly the USA, and the best in general are the wonderful democracies of north-western Europe.

A few years ago, I arrived at Bangkok airport. The hotel had sent a limousine to pick me up. The driver took charge of my trolley and steered me to the exit. He asked me to wait as it was 38 degrees outside, and he wanted to back the Mercedes up to the exit so that I could be spared walking 10 metres in the blazing heat. Very thoughtful. I slipped into the back seat of the airconditioned Mercedes. Waiting for me was an ice-cold towel soaked in cologne, and wrapped in a sealed plastic envelope, presented on a wooden platter. There was also a copy of that day's *Bangkok Post*. We slid out into the horrendous traffic and the scorching heat of one of Bangkok's hottest afternoons. On the way to the city the road passed through an area where tyres are handled. There were piles upon piles of those tyres, most used and dirty, and young men were working in the unrelenting sun, humping them around the yard. They were dressed in old ragged shorts, and their muscles rippled under brown skin, with rivulets of sweat running down their backs. As I stared at them out of the window of my limousine I could not answer the question as to why I was born into such a privileged and easy life. Why was I not Thai, humping tyres around in an inferno-like heat? While there was no answer forthcoming, and even though some may believe that it is "karma from a previous life", I was at least certain that my life had no more worth than theirs. I sat there in my white skin, in comfort, pampered, and by what justification? None that I can think of.

Racial prejudice has always been anathema to me. I do accept that there are differences between people. I like the way that Marian, a dear friend of mine from the USA, expresses it. She talks of tribes. We belong to tribes and these tribes transcend boundaries of race, ethnicity, wealth or sexual orientation. We feel comfortable with our tribe. But that does not entitle us to consider that one tribe is more worthy than another. They are just different.

Morally I am a committed socialist. When I lived in New York in the 1970's I know that were many there who considered me a communist. A name is a name. Since the collapse of what might be called centralised socialism in the 1990s, it has become accepted in many quarters that capitalism has been vindicated as the only system that works. Yet I believe it has many negative elements. People are abused and exploited, their lives are thrown into turmoil in the interests of returning more money to shareholders that they do not really need, on the money they had invested and which they did not really need either. I have never been able to see the fairness in that.

Unless there is strong legislation to protect the interests of employees, the employer is more than likely to be tempted to pander to greed at their expense. I have friends who have been dumped by the company to which they had loyally and in good faith given 30 years of their working life. They could not get another job at their age, and their superannuation at that point was not going to give them anything like the income in retirement they had expected. They were dumped either because at 53 they were considered as having reached their "use by date", or as a result of a takeover or merger, their position was duplicated and they were no longer required. There are some cases where this has enabled people to take an early retirement without penalty. But they are few and far between. When we talk of this happening in developing countries where there is little or no protection for workers, it can spell disaster for a family, however good it might be for the dividends and the share price of the fat cats in the rich countries.

I cannot for the life of me ever accept that some American can go to South Asia, file a patent on seeds the local people had been using for millennia, and then charge those same poor native people for using their own seeds, just because he filed a patent. Yet it happened.

Meanwhile I have still not come to any definite conclusions about the truth of our existence or what happens after it. After years of enquiry I have identified certain things I do not believe in, but on the central issues of existence the jury is still out! There are times when I feel the need to pursue my quest is more urgent, and then times when I concentrate on the more mundane aspects of life.

That period of 1987 and 1988 was one of more intense inquiry, and my head was full of matters other than work. I decided I needed to take more time off, not knowing how much I had left, and I went overseas again in 1988. This time I was away from March to September. The journey had been delayed a little when I got shingles in my hair and over my left eye. This was probably the first noticeable problem I had experienced due to HIV. But then again it might have been due to the stress of caring for a friend with some severe mental problems who was staying with me at the worst part of the crisis he went through. Fortunately he is now quite well.

I based myself in England and Amsterdam, staying with friends and my father. I went to Spain three times during the period, and to Portugal too.

It was really hard coming back after that trip and facing the reality of my life again.

Things at work were becoming less and less satisfactory for me, and I decided that I had to make some changes in my life. I had thoughts of setting up my own business, and perhaps to develop some stress management courses.

In the end it did not work out quite as I planned. I did leave the consultancy where I was working, and I did set up my own business, but I drifted into doing very much what I had been doing before. I tried to be careful not to step on the feet of my former business partner. But the matter was brought to a head when my largest client said to me, "We want to work with you. But there is one condition, that you do not pay any commission to the company you previously worked with". He knew that was what my ex-partner had insisted on, and a very large commission too! At least I never solicited business from his client base.

There were other clients who approached me and wanted me to continue working with them. Then I had a few breaks through some contacts and before I knew it I had a quite satisfactory training consultancy operating. I would in the next few years write two business books and use them as a springboard, and run public seminars starting in Australia, and then in New Zealand, in Asia and finally in South Africa. Out of these contacts my client work blossomed, but in a way that allowed me flexibility in my work schedules.

I developed an expertise in what is called Key Account Management, the way a company interacts with and manages their business with major customers. Even the client work became international with assignments in places as far apart as Korea, Brazil, South Africa and the UK. Travel started once again to be part of my work.

At the end of February 1989, a hot and humid time in Sydney, I went for a stroll one evening along the cliffs by the waters edge, the way one does, and met Warren, also, by the strangest coincidence, out for a walk. We seemed to get on well, and started going out after a few hitches. He was working for Qantas as a flight attendant in charge of First Class passengers, and so the first few months of the relationship were a little haphazard. He told me one night not long after we had started going out that he was HIV-positive, and he cried a little. I told him that I already knew, I had sensed it, our shared destiny seemed to throw us closer together. We drove to South Australia where his family was from, and then a few weeks later we spent time together in San Francisco while he was working and I was not. Although we had made it quite clear to each other from the outset that neither of us would ever live with anyone ever again, it became apparent that this was not going to be. We made plans for him to move in to my place in January. In December I had work in Wellington, New Zealand. I came home the long way around. I flew to Auckland and then to LA on the Friday night, and up to San Francisco on the next morning.

The next morning Warren and the crew arrived for a five-day slip (stopover) in Vancouver, and I walked into the hotel an hour or so after he did. He always said that nobody had ever formally "proposed" to him, and so one evening we dressed up, ordered a sumptuous dinner, and I went down on one knee and asked him to come and live with me. I then collapsed and fell asleep, more likely as a result of the wine than the jetlag! We stopped in Honolulu for a couple of days on the way back, and it was Christmas when we got home, and then January, and Warren moved in.

Chapter 19 Checking out the boyfriend

The Sydney Film Festival is always a fascinating cultural event. It takes place as winter starts to breathe its evening chill on a city ill-prepared for it. For winter sits uncomfortably on the shoulders of this summer city. It is a great few weeks of excellent films, both Australian and foreign. The opening night reveals a premiere, often of an Australian film but not always, and mostly of a novel or interesting film. It is always held at Her Majesty's Theatre, a superb and beautifully restored theatre built in the 1930s. There is also a cocktail party afterwards at a venue somewhere in the city, such as the Town Hall or the Powerhouse Museum. It is attended by film buffs, young trendoids, aspirant film-makers and celebrities of varied provenance. The only thing they all have in common is that they have paid quite dearly for the privilege.

That particular night the film had been about the life of Eddie Mabo and his fight for indigenous rights, which led, ironically after his death, to the land rights legislation that finally held that Australia was not a *terra nullis* when white man arrived. That *terra nullis* concept meant that white man had never recognised that indigenous people owned any land and thus it was all there for the pleasure of the invading colonisers. The legislation held that indigenous people who could prove a consistent association with land should now be accorded its title. The film was very moving, and at the end Eddie's widow, accompanied by her children, addressed the audience. She was not made for such fame, and had been pushed to the forefront of political struggle because of the advocacy of her now dead husband. My heart warmed to her immediately, and I was glad later that same week to have the opportunity of talking to her.

The party that year was held in the Powerhouse Museum. The Powerhouse used to provide electricity to run Sydney's trams, and then was acquired by the NSW government in 1970 and opened as a museum in 1988. It has been phenomenally successful with a wide variety of exhibits, many of them interactive, depicting mainly the technological world of Australia. The museum hires out its public areas for events such as the Sydney Film Festival.

Warren smoked at the time and the only place where smoking is allowed is outside in a small courtyard with some tables and chairs. It was rather cold; in fact I had on a couple of occasions gone dressed completely in black leather, but not on that night. We took our drinks and settled ourselves at a table close to some heating, grabbing the odd canapé or hot hors d'oeuvre as it swished by, and watched a world of which we were hardly part. Suddenly a young woman approached us with a slightly desperate look on her face.

"Do you mind if I come and sit with you guys? I am trying to get away from someone". "Of course not, please". We made way for her at the table.

She lit a cigarette and explained that she was on a blind date. The guy she had been paired with was, she asserted, a real creep, and kept annoying her. She felt that the company of a couple of older guys might scare him off. She pointed him out across the crowd, looking at her from the corner of his eye. He did seem a little spooky. Even at first sight and without knowing our charge it was clear that this was not a good match. Perhaps she had offended the person who had made the blind date, and revenge of a sort was being exacted.

Michelle introduced herself. She worked for the company that had made the Mabo film, and was involved on the sales side. We started chatting away, and found her very easy to talk to. Soon we were exchanging a few harmless confidences.

She revealed that she wanted to find a partner, as she was getting to the age where if she was going to have children it should be in the next few years. It was difficult to meet available men socially, and she had resorted to meeting men on the net. This was a world unknown to me in those days. When I wanted to meet a man, I just went out and met one! She told us that she had met someone over the net in whom she was quite interested. He was a young lawyer from New York called Robert. He had not been married, and seemed to have all the right attributes, at least as far as one could determine electronically.

They both were interested enough in each other to want to go to the next stage and meet. He was going in August with his mother and sisters to Italy where they were renting a villa in Tuscany for a month. He suggested that Michelle might like to join them, at his expense.

Quick with our advice based on common sense and intuition rather than years of training in psychotherapy, we expressed our horror. An inquisition in the form of a panel and jury of female relatives did not seem at all the right way of going about getting to know each other. We suggested rather a place that was halfway between them, and separate rooms so that escape could be arranged if required. A Waikiki hotel, we felt, might make the ideal venue, with adjoining rooms, but a lockable door between them if required.

We then volunteered the information that we were going to be in New York in July, in just about a month's time.

"Would you like us to go and check him out for you?" I ventured. "Oh would you? I think that would be most helpful, at least as a start. And then I could decide how best to take it to the next stage if he checks out alright with you two".

We chatted a little longer, and then we saw Michelle again later that week at a cocktail party held for the Mabo family. It was held at a Chinese restaurant, with a buffet meal. We sat at a table and had dinner with Gough and Margaret Whitlam. Gough was Australia's Prime Minister from 1972 to 1975, the first Labor prime minister after many years of conservative government. Both he and his wife are formidable people, enormous not only in their physical stature but also in their presence. They were tremendous company, and it was a memorable evening in many ways. But it did not really allow us to get to know Michelle any better. However, armed with what we knew and Robert's address and phone number, we set off for New York.

Michelle had let Robert know that two close friends of hers would be in New York shortly and might make contact. When we arrived in New York we called his work number and left a message. We normally stay with friends Ernst and Roger in Garden City on Long Island.

Eventually we managed to get hold of Robert and arranged to meet him at three in the afternoon at a bar on the Upper East side of Manhattan, on Third Avenue. It struck me as a rather strange time for a lawyer to be available, given that his office was located down in the Wall Street area. But he said that it was just around the corner from where he lived, and he happened to plan to be at home at that time.

We arrived a little early, the four of us, having driven into the city from Long Island in one of the Lincoln Continentals. The bar was virtually empty at that time on a weekday afternoon. We ordered a round of beers and waited. At the appointed time Robert arrived. He was clean-cut, quite a good-looking man, if not heart-stopping material. He would have been mid-to-late thirties I supposed, maybe a year or two older than Michelle. I introduced Warren and Ernst and Roger. I realised how intimidating this must suddenly be for him, to be confronted by four gay men, totally unknown to him, who were going to "check him out".

We must have all felt the same tension, and Ernst and Roger suggested that they would let us sit and talk and went off to the other end of the room, and Warren went to sit at the bar so that he could smoke. That left Robert and me together in a somewhat less contrived situation. I offered him a drink. He ordered a Perrier with ice, and we sat opposite each other with a small low table between us.

I suddenly felt rather apprehensive. We were misrepresenting ourselves as close friends of Michelle's. What if he asked me all sorts of questions that a close friend would know, and that I did not? Like what was her flat like, who were her other friends, how did she live her life? I realised how little I knew about her. I hoped that I could wing it if necessary. I need not have worried. To my surprise he asked nothing at all about Michelle. He did not ask how long we had known each other, or how we had met. He did not even ask how she was, whether she had any messages for him, nothing. I found this a little odd. If I were interested in pursuing a relationship with someone I had not yet met in person, I would be full of questions and keen to learn as much as I could about the person to fill in the gaps that electronic contact must inevitably leave.

I decided that talking about his work was perhaps the most neutral of ground, and yet at the same time a way of finding out a little about him. I needed to get him talking. Partly so that I could learn about him, and at the same time to avoid talking about the purported close friendship with Michelle.

He had mentioned that there had been some problems at work, and that had been why it had not been easy to find a time to meet. He explained some of the problems. The bottom line was that it sounded as if the law practice where he worked might fold. This was not a good start, but he did not seem to be particularly concerned.

I asked him which law school he had graduated from. When he said Brooklyn Law School, and the date was not long after I had left New York myself, I took a punt.

"Did you know Marty Kaufmann? He lectured in trust law."

He visibly blanched and raised his eyes to mine with a startled look bordering on terror. "Not Professor Kaufmann?"

"Yes".

"He took us for Business Law. He was a very hard taskmaster, we were all terrified of him".

I know that he was strict and rather gruff in his approach, I once saw him give a lecture in an auditorium somewhere near Penn Station, and he was impressive.

"So, how do you know him?"

"I lived in New York with him in 1974 and 1975. He was my lover".

The news that Marty might have had a social or intimate life quite clearly was a revelation to Robert. He now looked puzzled as he tried to conjure up another perspective on this university lecturer who had created such an aura of academic terror around him. I wondered if he could have imagined Marty as a chuckling man with a wry sense of humour playing mind games with me as he massaged my feet after dinner, a sexy man who was great in bed. Or as an obsessive-compulsive who would wash a glass for five minutes under the tap in scolding water, an addict of Carvel ice-cream and sleeping tablets. I could reconcile these images, as I knew Marty better, but I am sure that Robert would not have been able to.

Robert told me something about his life. He described a man who loved art and went to the theatre or to a concert at least once a week. He was devoted to his family and spent most weekends with his mother somewhere in Pennsylvania. During the week he applied himself to work and went to the gym to keep fit at least two or three times. He did not date, but was looking for a partner. He had never been married, but suggested that once he had had a long-term relationship. No details were forthcoming.

He was careful with his diet and looked after himself, preferring sobriety over excess. He sounded as if he was at the same time of exemplary credentials and as boring as could be.

We would have spent hardly more than 45 minutes chatting. He said that he had to leave, shook hands with the four of us, and walked quietly through the door and into the anonymity of the street. There was no specific message for Michelle. He did not look back, and was seemingly unmoved, unaffected by the vicarious proximity to the object of his intent, if not his passion.

I decided that either he was a crazed drug fiend who was trying to go straight, a mummy's boy who had been told to get a wife, or a closet gay who had not got the guts to be himself. The picture that he had attempted to paint of himself was too good to be true, and contrived. Surely nobody is like that, and if they were, would you really want a relationship with them? He gave no hint of having any sense of fun at all. Without that, what is the point? The truth was almost academic.

The vibes I got did not suggest that he would make a good partner for Michelle, or anyone else for that matter. And that was the point of the exercise, to determine whether he was worthwhile her pursuing to the next level of engagement.

I tempered my later report to her. I told her that he was a clean cut, at least on the surface decent, and quite an acceptable-looking young man. The story he told was one of a man without any apparent bad habits. I repeated many of the things he had told me. I added that I was concerned that he had asked virtually nothing about her, and that there had been no special message I was to deliver. I suggested that he might be suitable to pursue to a meeting but that she should exercise some caution.

We lost touch with Michelle after that for a while. But it seems that she did not pursue Robert as an option. But there must have been someone along the way as she now goes accompanied by her son, a gorgeous young fellow by the name of Josh, just the two of them together.

Chapter 20 Flying around

In the first few years that Warren and I lived together he was still working for Qantas. In the days before privatisation and deregulation the conditions of airline crews all over the world were far better than they are today. This was especially so with Qantas where in those days the stand-down time between trips was considerable. With the flexibility in my own work it allowed us to travel, do things together and make the best of the time we thought we might have. I had the choice of taking as few or as many client projects as I liked, and apart from the days I was working with the clients I could do my desk-based work when I wanted.

Although we might have had different perspectives on flying, being on opposite sides of the tray as it were, flying had been very much part of both our lives.

My life of flying started modestly in 1956 in a DC3, with a flight from Birmingham to Jersey. The plane flew at an altitude of 1600 feet, and I threw up. My first international flight in 1959 was also in a DC3. It landed on a grass strip at Knokke–Le Zoute airport in Belgium. Since then I have flown to over 120 countries and landed or taken off at well over close to 400 different airports, using well over 100 different airlines. Inevitably I have a few things to say about flying.

First of all intuitively I have a problem with the concept that you can place frail human flesh and blood in a heavy lump of metal, make it hurtle down a strip of concrete and then expect it to fly. It still sort of amazes me that it works. Aircraft are a wonderful combination of yin and yang. Grace and beauty combined with power and energy. To watch a plane make a sharp turn in the sky, almost hanging there on the breeze, its wings stretched out, its long fuselage nosing into the beyond, is to admire great beauty. Yet it once struck me at Barajas airport in Madrid, when a Boeing 727 turned its rear end towards the passengers waiting in the terminal, as it prepared to depart, that it was like peering up the backside of some giant animal, the three engines situated at the back of the aircraft black on the inside and fuming their excretions. I almost felt embarrassed to look. It was like an indelicate intrusion into privacy.

Before the days of aerobridges it was of course not uncommon to make one's entry in a rather graceless way up a ladder into the rear of the plane. The Caravelle, built by the French, was one such aircraft. It was this aircraft that set the tone for my flying experiences for several years.

One of the first overseas trips I made on business was to Spain. I travelled with Peter, our technical expert in application technology on our major product line. The fact of the matter was that he was far more welcome by the customers than I was, as he had something useful to say to them. I was there more to keep the local distributors honest. We travelled a few times together, and got on well. We were in Israel together in 1968 when troops were again mobilised in a period of great tension. That time we had to share a room in the Dan Hotel in Tel Aviv as they were overbooked. We both laughed when a few years later he visited London where our offices were and came around to my flat for a drink. I thought I had better explain to him the fact that I was gay and that I had a Portuguese lover living with me. It turned out that he also was gay and had a Portuguese lover. Sharing a room in Tel Aviv could have turned out more fun, if we had only known.

The Caravelle flight to Barcelona I refer to was with Iberia, the Spanish Airline. It was ironic that at the time they had an advertisement that said: *"Iberia, donde solo el avión recibe mas atención que Usted."* "Iberia where only the plane receives more attention than you." There was a picture of a spanner with a rose placed lovingly over it.

It was a perfect spring day in London, the sky was blue, not a cloud to be seen. The plane was half an hour late, considered more or less on time for Iberia in those days. I sat on the aisle towards the back and Peter sat next to me in the window seat. The plane took off and we headed towards the Channel en route across France to Spain. Lunch had not long been served when we crossed the French coast. It was still a spectacularly crystal clear day. I looked out of the window at the coastline below. "We're a bit low, aren't we?" I said to Peter. "I was just thinking the same thing", was his response. In fact rather than gaining height or even maintaining it, we seemed to be slowly losing it. Suddenly the plane started to "yaw", that is to move from side to side, one wing up and then the other. We were still losing height. Appetites seem to have been killed stone dead, and nobody was eating any more. Other passengers started to look nervously around them. The cabin attendants started to quickly scoop up all the lunch trays. One passenger asked a flight attendant, "What is happening. Are we going to crash?" She just said, "Direc' fli' to Barthelona", and scooped up the last of the trays.

We never saw the cabin crew again after that. We just seemed to be getting closer and closer to the ground. Soon I could easily see the detail of cars travelling along country roads, and people walking around. The pilot brought the nose up sharply and the plane was now flying at a very steep angle. The engine noise was enormous, a kind of screaming as power was being pumped out at maximum capacity. But the plane was still losing height. We all tightened our seatbelts even though there had been no instructions to do so. I looked down at the earth below and remembered thinking that it surely was not asking too much to just tread on that land again. It is hard to explain the sensation exactly. It was as if a summary of my life passed quickly before my eyes. But I did not really think I was going to die. I did think that the plane was going to crash, after all we were heading for the ground in a fairly determined fashion. But I thought that I would get up and walk away from the crash. Peter told me later that he was worried about his luggage. He never doubted that he would be alright but thought that he might lose the contents of his suitcase.

After what seemed like an eternity, but in fact could only have been a few minutes, I realised that we must be close to an airport. By now we were very low indeed. Suddenly the paddocks gave way to the open grass of an airfield. The screaming of the engine, for it turned out to be one only that was working, was phenomenal. The nose was high up, and with a thud we hit the runway at an extraordinary speed. It took the whole length of the main runway at what turned out to be Orly airport in Paris to stop. There were fire engines and ambulances racing alongside the plane. Only when we arrived right at the other end of the runway, did the engine scream subside. There was no sign of the cabin crew, and the plane had landed without either a "no smoking" or "fasten seatbelt sign". Now came the first announcement as we taxied away from the runway towards the terminal. "We xave yust made a full escale emeryency landin at Paris airport thank you".

We were taken to Gate 31, where we disembarked and were held in the transit area. Many rushed towards the bathrooms. They then gave us an explanation that might have been better left unsaid. "We are sorry that there were no announcements. The cabin crew did not know what was happening either. The pilot did not have time to communicate with anyone, he was concentrating on trying to keep the aircraft in the air. He did not think we were going to make it. We are all very lucky".

Later that evening they arranged to take us on the Iberia flight from Paris to Madrid, and made an extra stop in Barcelona to accommodate us. It was fortunately not a Caravelle, but a Boeing 707. On take-off I again sat on the aisle. It was easy to recognise the Barcelona passengers; they were tense and frightened. The man in front of me was gripping the arm of his seat so tight that his knuckles had gone white. I had heard of that happening, but had never seen it.

I flew a few days later to Bilbao in an ancient old crate, a DC6B or something similarly archaic. I was uneasy to say the least. That whole experience unnerved me and for years after that I was very nervous flying.

I never trusted Caravelles again. I noted that Air France had lost one mysteriously on a flight from Ajaccio in Corsica to Nice. It just disappeared. And there were other incidents too. TAP, the Portuguese airline, had one that took off from Lisbon that ran into the same difficulty, but was close enough to Lisbon airport that it managed to limp around in a circle and land.

I had to go to Barcelona quite often, but avoided that flight as if it were cursed. I found that for the same price I could fly Swissair via Geneva on a DC9 and that is exactly what I used to do. It was common to go on to Portugal after my Spanish trips, and of course our agents there knew well what had happened on the Iberia flight. They waited for me one night at the airport in the northern city of Oporto. I was on a Caravelle flight from Lisbon. To my relief the flight had been uneventful and we were on final approach. I saw the lights at the end of the runway and then suddenly felt a kick of full thrust as we aborted the landing and climbed steeply away into the night. The plane had the cabin lights dimmed and we headed out to sea, slowly droning away from the airfield. What had happened? Why did they abort the landing? Were we losing fuel for an emergency landing?

But there were no announcements. It was excruciating for me. Eventually the plane turned and came in for a second attempt. This time the plane landed without any problem. My friends on the ground were laughing when I got off the plane, as they knew that I would be traumatised. It seems that just as they were about to put the wheels on the ground there had been a power failure and all the lights at the airport went out, including those on the runway. The pilot simply aborted the landing and circled out to sea until they had managed to get the power on again.

For a couple of years I used to almost fly the plane for the flight crew. I got used to every nuance, every noise, every movement of the aircraft. I remember saying to my neighbour once as we were floating past the hangars at Heathrow and within a few seconds of landing, "Did you hear the landing gear go down?" He turned to me and said, "No, but I am sure the captain would know if it hadn't". I felt appropriately squashed, but he did not know the reason I was so paranoid.

Another evening I let my fears show was on leaving Madrid. I was booked on the BEA Comet 4B to London. It is true that the Comet had a rather chequered history as a result of metal fatigue, a phenomenon hitherto not known in aircraft. It had caused the dramatic crashes of a number of Comets and finally gave the race for supremacy in aircraft manufacture to Boeing and the Americans, at least for many years. However, I always found them comfortable planes, and the fact that they had four engines made me feel a little more secure.

The plane was late arriving in Madrid from London due to heavy snowfalls there. It was January and winter was always a bad time for weather-related delays in European aviation. Madrid had had problems for the previous few days with fog. As the sun set it was obvious that this afternoon was going to be another foggy one. The London flight arrived and they decided to turn it straight round without even cleaning it to get it off the ground before the airport was closed because of poor visibility. There was also still a problem with Heathrow, and it looked as if they would have to close that airport again due to snowstorms.

What was worrying me was that if we took off and could not get back to Madrid because of fog, and not land in London because of snow, would we be up there for several days while they sorted the problem out? Apologies were made about the dirty state of the aircraft, but nobody cared. The plane moved to the end of the runway, turned, accelerated and lifted off. Seconds later there was a loud bang above my head. I must have visibly jumped out of my skin. The guy sitting next to me was a Scot. He turned to me with a smile on his face and said in a thick accent, "It was the kiddy's balloon". When we arrived in London, everything was white and frozen. The airport was shut. They had allowed our flight to land, but other than that it was dead. There were no buses or taxis and it was in the days before the trains or the tube reached Heathrow. There was no way I could get back to my flat in St John's Wood. A fellow passenger took pity on me. He had called his wife from Madrid and she was there to pick him up. They took me back to their house in Surrey and I stayed the night.

Winter was bad. One night just before Christmas of 1967 I was flying home from Gothenburg in Sweden. There was a terrible winter storm and even though they kept de-icing the plane, it would just ice up again. This always made me nervous. Finally we took off, very late indeed. It was the night of our Christmas party at work. I was just between flats and staying with a work colleague for a couple of weeks. She was at the party, but I arrived far too late to go of course. The bus from the airport to the West London terminal broke down, fortunately close to a tube station, so I was able to catch the tube the rest of the way. I reached the terminus and decided to take a taxi to her flat as it was a long walk with luggage. As I was waiting for a taxi, a man collapsed right in front of me. We laid him on the footpath and put his head on my luggage. The blood stains on my suitcase from the gash on his head when he fell never came out. When I finally reached the house, there was nobody there and I did not have a house key. I got into my car, started the engine for a little warmth and made myself as comfortable as I could for what turned out to be a long wait well into the night.

The memory of the death of eight of the very popular Manchester United football team in Munich in February 1958 as a result of ice on aircraft wings made everyone rather nervous about ice. I made a daytrip to Antwerp once from Southend airport near London. It was a small propeller plane, and the morning was clear but very cold. Halfway across we suddenly heard a thump on the outside of the aircraft. We all pretended to ignore the first one. But the second and third bangs were harder to ignore. Eventually even the flight attendant was rattled and went to ask the pilot what it was. It sounded as if there was someone outside banging on the aircraft door to be let in. It seems that that morning the weather conditions were such that at the low altitude we were flying, and with the cold weather, ice was forming very rapidly on the fuselage and then falling off in great lumps and hitting the side of the plane.

Fog in winter was one of the worst nightmares in Europe. I was once due to leave on a flight from London to Paris for a night, work the next day in Paris, and then fly on to Milan the following evening. When I reached the airport for the evening flight to Paris I discovered that it had just closed due to fog. I was invited to rebook for a flight the next morning. That was always a gamble; with so many cancelled flights that night all the flights the next morning would be fully booked. You had to try and guess at what time the fog would lift the next day so that your flight would leave. If you tried too early there was a chance that it might get cancelled again if the fog had not cleared. If you left it too late there would be little point in going; the day would have been wasted.

I made an excellent guess, and mine was about the first flight to leave for Paris the next morning. I went about my business and headed out to the airport in the evening for my flight to Milan. I went to check in, but was told that I was not on the flight; it was overbooked, and my name did not appear on the list. The check-in lady asked if I had reconfirmed my flight, suggesting that the whole thing was my fault. I pointed out that I had been in Paris for less than 12 hours and was not required to reconfirm. She did not answer that, but told me that there was nothing she could do; I would have to go to the departure gate on the air side and see what I could negotiate. She did check my suitcase for me, and gave me some paper that would get me through immigration as I did not have a boarding pass. Those days were far more informal than nowadays.

I went straight to the departure lounge where there was a great degree of turmoil. I made my way through the crowd to the desk, and presented my ticket. The plane is full, no seats, was the message I was given. When I insisted that I had a confirmed, "ok" status full-fare ticket, I was told that I had left it too late to check in. I pointed out that I was at the check-in desk land-side well within the required time. At that point a woman with a handful of tickets lent across me saying in French (this was Air France), "Here are the tickets for the group". I grabbed them out of her hand – she should have been less rude and more careful – and looked at them. They were for a large group booked on another flight and on discount tickets.

By now I was angry. I told the woman at the counter that it was quite clear what they had done. They had taken a group from another flight and put them on this flight, but in so doing it meant that several people with full-fare tickets would have to be bumped off the flight. I ranted and raved but to no avail. They took all the passengers from the group and left some dozen booked passengers on the ground. The desk closed and we were redirected to the transit counter of Air France.

We were told that the next available flight to Milan was the next afternoon, and good night! At this point two decided not to travel at all, three decided to take the train, and all the rest but an Italian couple from Milan and me decided to wait until the next day. I was determined to leave that night somehow, and the Italian couple sensed that I might be on a winning streak, so they stuck with me.

The transit staff said that there were no connections at all that could get me to Milan that night. I did not believe them and demanded the ABC international flight guide. They passed it to me and within three minutes I had found a connection via Rome. Somewhat sour about my discovery they checked with Alitalia and agreed that it would work, and reissued the tickets for the three of us. I asked them to get a message to Milan airport to the people waiting to meet me about the changed arrival details. They never received the message.

The flight to Rome was bumpy, but immigration was quick and we arrived in time for the domestic flight to Milan. The plane took off and everything was looking fine. The only problem was that there are two airports in Milan. My luggage, I assumed, had still been on the original flight and would have arrived at Linate. This plane was going to arrive at Malpensa. But half an hour into the flight they announced that there was fog at Milan and the plane would probably divert to Turin for the night. Exactly what I needed.

At the last moment it seemed that Milan did clear and we landed. Not at Malpensa after all, but at Linate. Ours was the last flight in and everything was closed. I could not even change any money, but the Italian couple who had stuck by me all this time were so grateful for my efforts that they exchanged some francs for lire for me, at least enough to get into the city. My luggage was nowhere to be seen. Neither were my associates and I decided to head straight for the Sonesta Hotel at the city air terminal.

The next morning several phone calls failed to locate my luggage. I strolled into the terminal next door to make a report about my lost luggage, and there on the floor was my suitcase with a pile of other cases. I just took it and left.

But that is not quite the end of the story. Two years or so later I was checking in for a flight in Paris, and the check-in agent and I recognised each other. She had been the one at the gate where I seized the tickets of the group, and made such a fuss. She told me that she remembered me because she had felt so sorry about what happened. My assessment of the situation had been spot on. They had bumped us to put on this large group, and she had had to follow instructions from her supervisor. She apologised to me, and I sort of felt sorry for her. We parted friends.

Weather is often a reason for concern in flying. After all, how often do we read after an air crash something about "poor weather conditions"? It is reasonable to be more concerned when the weather is bad, and in fact that is about the only time when I believe the pilots earn the large sums of money most of them are paid.

I once made the pilgrimage to Grand Canyon, and even arose before dawn to see the sun peep over the horizon and light up the rim and then gradually the depths of the canyon. I am not able to tell you what it was like as that particular morning an enormous storm front had moved in from the south-west. The dawn was simply a gradual lightening of the bank of thick cloud. Dejected I set off for the airport after breakfast. By this time the storm was really threatening, the clouds had become darker, and one could tell by looking at them that they contained immense quantities of pent-up mayhem.

The Fokker Friendship F28 for Las Vegas hopped cheerfully out to the end of the runway. The engines were revved while keeping the handbrake (or whatever) firmly on. The plane squirmed a little on the runway, pulling at the leash to be away. The pilot let go and we were off, tearing up the runway.

But suddenly the pilot slammed on the brakes, and we all were forced forward in our seats. "Ladies and gentlemen, I just aborted the takeoff as we were not developing enough power in the right-hand engine. So I am going to turn around". I heaved a sigh of relief as I imagined the next set of words about getting the thing sorted out, cowlings off, engineers doing tests, electronic pressure monitors, whatever it takes. "And go back to the end of the runway, and try again", he continued.

I was hoping like hell that it would not pass muster and we would get it sorted out properly. This time he revved that engine to a deafening roar, and the plane was straining heavily to break free. What seemed like several minutes went by, and then suddenly the plane lunged forward down the runway and into the air. It did not take too long before we were in the middle of the storm. We were being tossed around like a leaf in a gale. The lightning was flashing all around us, but the worst part was the lurching in the unstable air. I was wondering what the power looked like in the right-hand engine right now.

After a while the pilot came on the intercom and said that he had tried to climb above the storm but it was so massive he just could not get high enough. He told us that he had requested permission to drop to 12 000 feet and try to fly below it in less turbulent air. I was furious that I had not concentrated more on American geography trying to recollect whether there were any peaks in that part of Arizona above 12 000 feet. We landed in Las Vegas eventually, in one piece but rather shaken up. I walked straight past all the one-arm bandits for the bar and ordered a double Scotch.

Winter weather has always been stressful for me, more so than summer storms. The low-pitch drumming of a plane slowly dropping height through what seems like an interminable cloudbank can appear to last a lifetime. It seems that so much time has elapsed that surely the airport has been passed a long time ago, the passengers all silent staring out of the window waiting for some break in the featureless cloud. And then to suddenly drop through the cloud, as I did in Geneva once, and find the plane in a blinding whiteness of a snowstorm and only a few feet from the ground.

The heart races and the imagination flies, and after all there may have been no danger at all. But it is the emotion of the moment that creates the effect. And it is not assisted by comments from the crew themselves. On the Grand Canyon flight the flight attendant said as she staggered around, "This flight can often be rough, but I have never ever seen anything like this". On another flight a captain told everyone, "There is a little red light on the panel here saying the cargo door is open. But we do not think that is true. We believe that it is a malfunction in the panel and we are going to take off anyway". Or once on an old DC8 a flight attendant who could not find where the oxygen mask was located in the seats confided to me, "This plane is so old, I never saw one like it, and the oxygen masks are in a different place". They may all be true but it does not have to be said. All of these three incidents were in the USA of course where aviation-wise there is a tendency to let it all hang out a bit more. Or at least there used to be in those days.

There are scary airports, scary airlines and scary aircraft types. You reduce the risk by trying to avoid all three. There are some well known scary airports. Best known was the old Kai-Tak in Hong Kong, where the approach is made low over Kowloon, a steep bank to the right, and passengers can see whether the local inhabitants are eating chicken or beef in their noodles in the old tenement buildings, before slipping precariously onto the runway, and then stopping short, usually at least, of the harbour at the other end of the runway. I never landed at the airport at Gibraltar, I only walked across it as the main road in and out of Gibraltar crosses the runway, but that must be like landing on an aircraft carrier.

Ushuaia on the southern tip of Tierra del Fuego in Argentina had one end of its rather short runway in the water and the other at the foot of a small hill (it has since been relocated). It would not be so bad if they took off over the water and then climbed to get up over the forbidding mountains of rock and ice that surround the town on the other side of the bay. But my flight made a straight-line ascent, and cleared the mountains by such a small distance that any loss of power would have had us hiking on the glacier.

Wellington in New Zealand is renowned for its windy weather and scary airport. It is a formidable combination as the weather screams through Cook's Strait. There are mountains all around and again water at one end and a small hill at the other end of the runway. I have had a few aborted landings there and some takeoffs that lasted just a few seconds before the headwind forced the plane airborne like a rocket. Wellington is the only place I know where the buffeting by the wind and the turbulence causes discomfort while the plane is still at the gate!

Escarpments are also nail-biting scenarios. It has been abandoned at least by jets now, but the city airport of Congonhas in São Paulo in Brazil was the one I dreaded most. The plane would come in low over houses and you could look out of the window at the escarpment jutting out over the city. Sometimes it even seemed to be above you, which had it been true would have been a disaster. It was always simply an optical illusion, and even though I knew from previous landings what to expect, I was always glad when I could see runway under the tyres rather than houses.

In the early 1970s I got to know Congonhas airport rather well. Every weekend while I was in Brazil it was an unwritten rule that I spent the weekend in Rio. I fell in love every weekend. The first time I went to Brazil I had spent the week working in São Paulo with their sales guy, Bernardo, who in fact lived in Rio. He explained to me that he did not have a car, otherwise he would have driven up from Rio and we would have had transport to visit customers. We both were frustrated at having to try and get a taxi to go anywhere. The second morning he turned up with a car. I enquired if he had rented it. No, he had bought one the previous evening after work. Inflation was such that it was stupid to have money sitting in the bank, and he needed a car. Cars were generally a little cheaper in São Paulo than in Rio, so it made sense to go out and convert his spare cash into a car that would hold its value better than the cash.

Perhaps it was this that distracted him from getting around to have the office book my flight to Rio on the Friday afternoon. By Wednesday he told me that it was too late anyway, the flights would all be fully booked. However, I should not worry. I did.

On the Friday afternoon we headed out to Congonhas. The airport was frantic. I was instructed to stand still while Bernardo rushed off somewhere with my ticket. He came back about five minutes later, grabbing my suitcase and told me to stay where I was. Another five minutes passed. Then Bernardo appeared out of the crowd, handed me my ticket and a boarding pass and baggage receipt, and told me to rush right now to Gate 2 and board the plane, adding that my luggage might be on the next one rather than this one. I did as he suggested. It was free-seating and there were not many seats left on board. I grabbed one. A few minutes later a man was walking up and down looking for a seat, waving his boarding pass. But there were no seats left. There was one passenger and one boarding pass more than there were seats available, and I knew why. Poor guy had to get off.

There were often problems with these flights. On a Monday morning I was booked on a flight in the other direction, from Rio to São Paulo, the *Ponte Aereo*, as it was called from the Santos du Mont downtown airport. That was another scary airport that takes only turbo props as it has a very short runway with water at both ends. In fact when it rained heavily they closed the airport and all traffic was diverted to the far more distant Galeao airport. This particular morning I turned up for the flight only to be told that I had been removed from the flight list as I had failed to reconfirm my flight. I pointed out that I had arrived from Caracas late on Friday night, tried to reconfirm the flight on Saturday morning, but had not been able to get through to their office. They were sympathetic but not inclined to help. I marshalled further armaments. I told them that I was a travel agent in the USA (I was living in New York at the time and my ticket was issued there). Was I to assume that any of my clients I booked with their airline and who arrived at such a late hour so that they could not reconfirm their flights, would likewise be offloaded? And if that were the case then surely I would be better advised to book my clients with their major competitor? While none of my story was true, it did get me a seat on the flight.

I used a similar ploy when I was refused entry to the off-limits Forbidden City Hotel in what was then Bophutatswana, a South African homeland. This time I actually presented a business card with my name on it from a travel company in the USA for whom I had done a favour. I not only gained access but I also received an apology and a personally guided tour.

As well as scary airports there are scary airlines. The names of some of the airlines I have taken hardly inspire confidence. Iraqi Airways, Nigerian Airways, Mozambique Airlines. But in fact flights with those airlines turned out to be totally uneventful. Libyan Airlines got me to Tripoli from Cairo via Benghazi in one piece, but not without its own special way of doing things.

I called the airline in the morning to reconfirm my flight. There was a little shuffling of paper and hesitation before I was told that everything was in order but that I should arrive very early, very early indeed for the flight. When I arrived I checked in without any problems. The plane was of course late. There were quite a few Europeans on the flight including a guy from the UK who it appeared had a name very similar to mine. Later on in the departure lounge he explained that he had called the airline that morning to see if he could get a seat – he was booked on a flight the next day. He knew that the plane was normally booked solid, and was quite surprised when they told him there was a seat for him. In fact they seemed to think that there was already a booking for him. Then when he got to the airport to check in there was a problem.

Of course I realised what the problem was. He called the airline before I did. Because of the great similarity in our names they thought that he was me, as it were, and confirmed his seat. Then when I rang to reconfirm my flight half an hour or so later, they must have realised their mistake. That is why they told me to get to the airport very early, to make sure that I was the one to get the one seat allocated now to two of us. In the end they managed to accommodate him, and we both had a laugh about it.

But the plane was severely overbooked. It was a Boeing 727 with First and Economy configuration. They took all the foreigners, many of whom, like me, were booked in economy and found a seat for us in First Class. Then in economy they placed four passengers in each set of three seats, by putting up the armrests and abandoning luxuries like seatbelts. It was only a short flight and the plane would still have been under weight requirements.

To my surprise they served alcohol in First Class in those days, especially given that in the Libyan airports it was so Islamic that there was not one single word of anything but Arabic, which made it quite difficult to know where to go. One of the flight attendants was a very camp French guy, who was long suffering of all of the irregularities that working for Libyan Airlines implied. When the plane arrived in Benghazi they pushed the stairs up to the front door. They had still not been secured to the aircraft when a local ground-staff man started up the stairs. The French flight attendant screamed at him to wait, but to no avail. He reached the top of the stairs at the side of the aircraft, but they were so unstable that they started to sway and he fell off them between the stairs and the plane, falling the three or four metres to the ground. The French guy looked at me and shrugged his shoulders in the way only a gay guy can. As far as we could see the man who fell was alive and able to move!

Iranair is not an airline I would have chosen to fly, but did so once. I was living in Australia but back in Europe on holidays. I went away with my father on an early spring holiday to the Greek Islands. We checked in for the flight back from Athens to London with British Airways only to find that the queue suddenly stopped moving a few people in front of us. The plane was overbooked, and even though we had tickets, there were no seats for us. About 20 people were in this situation. The British Airways staff was quick to distance themselves from the people who were responsible for the mess. "London is the fault". After the indignation subsided and we were faced with the reality that no matter how much hopping up and down and remonstrating we did, it would not expand the number of seats on the plane, we had to try to find an alternative. I looked at the arrivals and departures board. There was a Qantas flight due in three hours that then went on to London. Ideal. But no, British Airways said this was not possible. Instead they selected an Iranair flight via Paris. The most vocal amongst the crowd was a middle-aged woman who sounded exactly like Mrs. Slocombe in Are You Being Served?. She firmly announced in her flat north-country accent, "I'm not flying with that there Ayatollah!" But there was no real choice, so we proceeded through immigration to the departure lounge to wait the four hours before the plane was due.

Mrs. Slocombe decided to while away the time getting to know the other passengers. "You're from Australia, aren't you?" she perceptively enquired. She confided, "I have a nephew living in Cape Town you know". I was not sure whether she realised that Cape Town was not in Australia, but at least she did not ask me if I knew him. She continued, "It must be an awfully long flight from Australia. How long does it take?" I told her nearly 24 hours. She turned with a degree of alarm on her face. "Doesn't the pilot get tired?" she asked anxiously. I explained the concept of crew change at intermediate stops. She looked at me sympathetically and said, "You must get dreadful jetlag". I agreed. To express her empathy of what it must be like she said, "Me and me 'usband went to Austria for our 'oliddies last year, and I was jet-lagged for a week".

The Boeing 707 finally arrived, and took off for Paris. In Paris the plane refuelled, and the transit passengers were required to remain on board. I was most concerned that during the refuelling process several of the Iranian passengers were smoking. The doors were open of course. I approached one of the English flight attendants and expressed my concern. She said that she was worried too, and that they had done the same thing at each stop. She had tried to stop them smoking but they would not listen to her. She had given up. Great!

Lloyd Aereo Boliviano is one of the strangest names for an airline, I have always felt. Maybe it was the name of some Welsh immigrant to Bolivia who established an airline. Their base is at La Paz, the highest airport in the world at over 4000 metres. This means that both landings and take-offs take a very long time because of the rarified atmosphere. We had arrived in La Paz from Iquique on the coast in northern Chile. When people walked off the plane and desperately tried to adjust to the sudden change in altitude, they staggered. It reminded me of the scene in the film Close Encounters of the Third Kind , when the earthlings walked out of the spaceship back onto terra firma, slowly, staring around them, unsure of their earth legs.

The evening before we left La Paz we had been in a small village on the shores of Lake Titicaca. That day had been proof that it is not only air travel that can be dangerous. In the morning we had taken a fairly large boat into the lake, and then transferred to a small boat that had, because of its smaller keel, access to the uninhabited island where we were to have lunch. This part of the Andes was not only home to the ancient civilisation of the Tihuanacans, but also of the humble potato. We had a picnic on the island based on a variety of potato species. Then we went for a stroll to see the ruins of an ancient temple. The Tihuanacans had lived on the Altiplano from 3000 BC (or BCE as it is now more sensitively known), and their civilisation lasted for almost 4000 years. It was amazingly advanced and to our astonishment had extraordinary similarities to the ancient Egyptian civilisation. There were magnetised blocks of stones with fields that converged at a spot some hundreds of metres away, and to this day nobody seems to understand how it was done. There are ancient carvings of people of all sorts of ethnic types, and one wonders how on earth these people knew of their existence.

Apart from the history of the ruined temple, the island was beautiful in a wild and rugged way. A storm was brewing across the lake, dark blue-grey clouds in a bank were gradually filling the sky. The wind was sharp and cold and the retreating sunlight bathed the landscape in crystal clear images of an intense colour. The water looked like indigo, pristine and freezing cold; there was snow on the mountains in the distance. As the wind swept down from the mountains it rippled the surface of the lake and ruffled the reeds on the shores of the island. It cut into us like knives.

We decided that the time had come to leave the island and get back to the larger boat. There were about 15 in our group and we clambered aboard. The boatmen cast off and started to move the boat out into the lake. But the wind was very strong and it blew the boat onto some nearby rocks. They tried to push it off, but the wind was more powerful. There was a crunch, and rocks appeared through the floor of the wooden boat. It was taking on water badly. The boatmen continued to try and push the boats off the rocks, but we all shouted at them to stop. If the boat was going to sink, better that it be on rocks jutting out of the lake than in deeper water. It was quite clear that we had only a few minutes to abandon the boat. There were no life jackets at all on the boat, and in any case the water was so cold that one could have survived only for a few minutes. We were able to climb off onto the rocks and pick our way to the relative safety of the uninhabited island. We were very lucky that just a few of us, including Warren, got our feet wet, but nothing more serious.

However, by this time the lightning was streaking down from the sky and the thunder echoed around the mountains and across the lake. We were not dressed for such weather. I felt a hollow of foreboding in the pit of my stomach. We took what shelter we could in the lee of a stony hill.

Our guide had a cell phone, but there was no reception. The larger boat was a long way out in the lake and signalling would have been a waste of time; they would never have seen us. The island was uninhabited and we were stuck! The immediate problem was to try and keep warm and protect ourselves from the rain that was bearing down on us in a large mass of impenetrable grey.

Suddenly we noticed a small motorised fishing boat streaking across the lake to safety. We stood on the shore and shouted and waved. They slowed down and approached. The guide explained our predicament and offered them a large number of American dollars to ferry us to the large boat, four or five at a time, for the boat was very small. The negotiation was completed and they agreed. The first group set off. By the time the boat returned it was starting to rain. They had taken some life jackets off the large boat and the next group put them on for the journey across the lake. By the time the boat had come back for the third group it was raining heavily, and the wind was fierce. Warren, who never imagined when we met all the adventures that were in store for him, and I were in the third group. It was raining so heavily that the fishermen threw a tarp over the boat and we all cowered underneath as we set out for the large boat, the helmsman trying to hold the rudder steady as he also sheltered, blind, under the tarp. After a while I peeked out only to discover that the helmsman had let the rudder move and we were just going around in circles. I shouted across at him, and he emerged from under the protection and adjusted course for the boat again.

We all eventually arrived safely on the large boat and headed for the village where we were staying. In the evening a local shaman came to the place where we stayed and we were invited to address questions to him. The process was that the questions were submitted to him via a translator as he did not speak any Spanish, and then he would consider the matter deeply before throwing coca leaves on the floor. He would then study where the coca leaves fell to divine the answer to the question. Warren asked me if I was going to submit a question but I felt that I did not particularly want my coca leaves thrown in public. A couple of questions about the future of various relationships of the children of two couples in the group were dealt with. The shaman gave us a special blessing for our journey the next day. It is quite unclear whether it had no effect at all or saved us from a worse disaster.

It snowed over night and the mountains close to the airport were covered in a soft white mantle. The aircraft for our flight to Cuzco in Peru was a 727-100. The plane was so old that it did not even have overhead bins, just a shelf for coats and jackets. The takeoff was as expected a lengthy process. I counted the seconds down the runway and the time to be airborne was at least twice that at sea level. But the plane climbed into the air and we relaxed. In fact it climbed to the extraordinary height of 41 000 feet. The view over the Andes was awe inspiring. Just as we started the descent there was a loud bang from the back of the aircraft and the whole plane shuddered.

Warren and I looked at each other. He said, "What the fuck was that?"

"An engine", I said, "I think we lost an engine".

"I never heard a noise like that on Qantas". His experience with them spanned over 20 years.

"You wouldn't, that was Qantas. But I am sure it was an engine".

We looked again at each other. "Who is going to look after Stumpy?"

Our wills are all in order but the one thing we had never taken care of us what would happen to our furry feline child Stumpy if we were both to die together. We both adored him, and he was emotionally very dependent on us.

While we were deliberating this conundrum one of the passengers asked the flight attendant what that noise was. She told them it was a bird that had got into the engine. At 41 000 feet this was a pretty impressive bird. An alternative story was broadcast shortly by the captain. Just a little engine stall, quite normal, happens all the time. Maybe it does happen all the time with Lloyd Aereo Boliviano, but not with other airlines.

A particularly worrying combination is a scary airline with a scary aircraft. This is what you get with companies flying old Russian jets. Like Cubana, for example. We took a flight from Santiago de Cuba at the eastern end of the island to Havana. It was a clear, beautiful morning when we checked in for the flight. The YAK 42 sitting on the runway did not inspire much confidence. Shortly after an announcement was made to the effect that a delay would be necessary due to poor weather conditions in Havana, we saw the mechanics set about the front door to the aircraft with a heavy hammer. Some well-aimed thuds appeared to correct the problem, and the weather in Havana cleared sufficiently to enable us to take off. One could either have taken the view that with two accidents in the previous six months killing all on board, statistically a third was remote, or a pattern was emerging.

The Yak 42 is a sturdy machine. It has three jets at the rear, which are necessary to lift this aging hulk into the air. The doorway is low, and you have to stoop to go inside. We sat three rows from the front. Shortly after take-off the woman sitting in front of us opened the bottle of rum she had brought to make the journey more fun and less memorable. She shared a little with the young girl sitting next to her. By the time the plane was on descent into Havana, which had enjoyed superb weather all morning, the woman was exceptionally at ease with the world. The plane was in final descent when she suddenly realised that nature had overtaken her and she needed to rush to the toilet just in front. She clambered past the young girl, and staggered into the toilet. Not more than a few seconds had passed when she was out again whispering frantically into the ear of the young girl. The girl just as frantically picked up her bag and started rifling through it, producing a stream of toilet paper within only a few seconds. The woman grabbed it gratefully and rushed back into the toilet. By the time she emerged, trees and bushes were drifting past the window and she had hardly sat down when a heavy thud announced that the flight had been successfully completed.

Our next encounter with a Yak was its smaller sister the Yak 40, of Air Kyrgystan. The plane was to take us from the capital of Kyrgystan, Bishkek, to Osh, a market town on the other side of the mountains and close to the border with Uzbekistan. It is a tiny version of the Yak 42, with some 40 canvas seats, two each side of the aisle. The cabin is small and you enter from the rear. Warren and I sat in the last seat but one. Luggage was piled up at the front of the plane and at the back in the aisle.

The hostess stood in front of us in the aisle towards the front of the plane, in her neat 1960s style bright red uniform and pillbox hat. She spoke in Russian first. Then staring at a point somewhere above our heads she mechanically said, "Flight time 55 minutes. Have a nice". She then walked down the aisle to the back of the plane, opened the door into the small rear compartment where the toilet was situated, and shut the door behind her. Warren and I looked at each other. We assumed that she had got off the plane, and wondered if she knew something that we did not.

The plane seemed to be the only one moving. It slowly passed the carcasses of some dozen siblings that were permanently being cannibalised for spare parts to keep a few aircraft in the air. We took off and then slowly, very slowly, climbed in circles until enough height had been reached to cross the mountains. Despite the three rear engines this plane was clearly very underpowered. The views over the snow-capped mountains not far below us were dramatic, white humps stretching into the distance with the occasional peak that jutted above the rest. I wondered how such an extensive range of mountains could exist and not be well known. The plane tipped its nose towards Osh. As it landed it was clear that with all the luggage in the back compartment as well as at the front of the plane and in the aisle at the back, it was back-heavy. Once it hit the runway it started to slew from side to side, and for a few seconds I was terrified that it was going to pirouette on the runway. The captain managed to hold it on the runway and we came to a halt. The flight crew left the cockpit and made their way down the aisle over the suitcases and tried to open the door to the back compartment, But it was blocked. The luggage had all fallen over behind the door and blocked it. Fortunately it turned out that the stewardess had not got off the plane after all. Rather she had been behind the door trying to hold the luggage piled up in the toilet. When it slewed on the runway after landing, she failed to hold it in place and it all fell on top of her. But she now managed to climb out from under the suitcases and open the door. Looking a little dishevelled, and trying to adjust the red pillbox hat that was now sitting sideways on her head, she smiled at us with a plastic smile attached to her face, as we stepped down the rear stairs and into the Fergana Valley.

In fact our next flight was from the Fergana Valley airport to the capital of Uzbekistan, Tashkent. Even though it was in an ancient Antonov, the like of which I had not flown since an internal flight in Poland with the biblical LOT in 1972, it was uneventful. As Antonovs seem to have a less catastrophic reputation than either Tupolevs or Ilyushins, and as it was a propeller aircraft, it seemed to create less fear in me. On the other hand the Turkmenistan Airways flight from New Urgench to Ashgabad, both in Turkmenistan, in a Tupolev 154 was a different story.

Somehow we had received word that the flight would be several hours late, by what we had been told was "government decree". Clearly the other passengers had not been so fortunate, and having not been warned, had been waiting for five hours by the time we had whiled away the afternoon and arrived at the airport. Whiling away the afternoon is in fact not that easy in that part of the country. We amused ourselves by visiting a cooperative, now renamed something less socialist-sounding but to all intents and purposes the same, then dropped in for tea to a house in some village on the way (we suspect that they must have been friends of our local guide and would have been paid for their kindness), and then had an early dinner at a desolate nightclub with a yard full of what looked like Hills hoists.

The forward cabin of the Tupolev 154 had to be loaded first to stop the plane falling back, literally, on its tail. A Gulag-trained guard wearing a flight attendant's uniform stood at the foot of the stairs barking at the threatening throng of would-be passengers. With expressive lunging and snarls she managed to keep them at bay until the cabin was prepared. The scramble for the seats was made more risky by the fact that the carpets in the aisle were not attached to the floor, causing a considerable amount of sliding. But eventually everyone was seated and the refreshment service began. The meal was sparse, very sparse. But it was followed shortly afterwards by a slightly better repast, at a price. There were no takers. That being so, they closed the doors and we took off.

By this time it was late at night and the only thing to do was to stare at the flattering photograph of Turkmenbashi, the mad dictator, on the wall at the front of the cabin (the day that he dyed his hair black they had to rip down thousands of old posters of him all over the country that adorned almost every vertical surface, and replace them very, very quickly). There was also the cabin wall decoration, which was very reminiscent of the furry wallpaper in an Indian Restaurant. In this case the plane landed in the right place and in one piece. Sadly 38 sister Tupolev 154s did not make it, and the few that are left continue to crash. As I am not sure how many were made I do not know what that puts the chances at. But in any case for the equivalent in local currency of seven US dollars (black-market rate, that is) for an hour's flight in a jet, maybe you can't expect too much.

Flying has changed so much over the years. It has become a commodity on the one hand and onerous because of the increased security measures on the other. I fly nowadays more than Warren. But neither of us looks forward to it any longer. I fear the good old days of flying are gone forever.

ooOoo

There are dreams where I fly. Not for a while now, but before, I used to fly unaided. I could stand on the ground, and pushing my hands firmly towards the earth several times, as if I were flapping wings, I could rise above the ground. Sometimes I would achieve a height of 50 metres or more, well above the trees. And then I would be able to glide over the countryside, swooping over paddocks and streams. I never flew over towns or villages, only over countryside, lush green pasture rather than dry and parched land.

My flying dreams to do with towns were not unaided. Then I was in an aircraft. So often they crashed and I always survived. Sometimes the plane would taxi along streets. Sometimes it would take off and hardly clear the roofs of the city. Then other times the take-off was slow and difficult, along a runway that dipped deeply, or curved like a motorway snaking through the city. The plane would lift off slowly, but not gain sufficient height, and career dangerously between the buildings, until finally it would give up and drop to the ground in an explosion of fire. At this point I wake and everything is calm around me.

Sometimes I am on the plane, and it is large, almost like a flying cinema. I walk around the aisles, looking for the toilet. I get more and more frantic, and then suddenly wake up aware of the erection that a straining bladder has caused. The overwhelming waking experience in most of these dreams is relief. How strange that when the waking lives of most of us seem so fraught with problems, we are unable to create dreams that give us any more peace. The terrors of the dreaming mind are often far more disturbing than the waking state.

Chapter 21 Living positively

I am aware that my pulse is racing. 120 is far too high. I would not even dare to imagine what my blood pressure is. Why do I put myself through this every time? Why? Because it is a matter of life and death, that is why. Mine.

I have gone through in my head what will happen in a few minutes so many times. I have dreamed it, rehearsed it, tried to work out logically what the results are likely to be. I have set a figure above which it will be alright. And then, just like waiting for exam results where one thinks that imagining that one has failed might lead to a better mark, I try to prepare myself for the worst case.

At the same time I know that physically I will be and feel the same when I walk out of the doctor's room as I was when I walked in. The only difference is that I will have been faced with the truth of what is going on in my body. Or will I? We still know little about this illness. The doctors work off the numbers, and on that basis I am eligible or disqualified for trials of new treatments. In most cases I am disqualified. "The viral load must be below 10 000. Yours as you know is over a million".

Not only has Charles died, but so have both João and Enrique, all of AIDS. I lost not only ex-lovers, but friends too, dear, wonderful friends who slipped away into skeletons and turned into old men 40 years before their time. So many people, such awful loss and sadness. I wonder when my time will have arrived.

Warren had the opportunity to take an early retirement from Qantas in 1991. It was not an easy decision to take, and indeed if we could have seen into the future with the advent of a new range of drugs becoming available in 1996, probably he would have stayed. But as it was, with the facts as we knew them at the time, it seemed like a good opportunity and he took it.

While I continued to work in my own consultancy Warren did some part-time teaching and took on most of the responsibility of the day-to-day looking after the house. In 1992 we also decided to go back to the doctor and have tests done. By this time AZT had appeared, and there was more reason to not just let things take their course. Before there was any treatment at all there was no real argument either in favour of monitoring T cells or even getting tested, but the advent of some treatment, however ineffective it would turn out to be in the long run, changed all that.

Warren's results were not bad. Mine were of grave concern. The T cells were well below what was considered the danger point of 200. Below that figure one is at significant risk of developing one of the opportunistic infections that generally are the cause of death. I started taking AZT. But there was not a great improvement in the counts. In fact that was been the pattern for 15 or so years for me. I had never had a count higher than 220 since 1986, and it has been down to zero probably due to chemotherapy I took in 1996.

I was told in 1993 that maybe I had a couple of years left.

Virtually all the early medications appeared in the USA first of all. In 1995 I went to the States to see a doctor in LA to see if I could get inscribed in a trial of a new drug called 3TC. I was accepted, but not before the clinic gave me a very thorough, frighteningly expensive and totally depressing full examination. It showed that I was positive to CMV and to toxoplasmosis, both of which can blossom in immune-compromised people into a fatal illness. Charles had had both of them and in fact died from CMV. These infections are now somewhat easier to treat than they were then.

I managed to get onto the 3TC trial, but again it did not do dramatic things for my counts. Not too long afterwards more new products started to appear, and again I managed to be among the first to be offered them. We now know that starting treatment with monotherapy (just one drug) sets people up for resistance and that is exactly what happened to me. We all thought it was the right thing to do at the time, but now know better. It could be argued that without the AZT and the 3TC I might have died anyway. We will never know. I just envy those people who were able to delay treatment until later when they could start with triple therapy and be far less vulnerable to resistance. But what is done, is done.

One night in 1995, after we had been out to dinner, I was getting ready for bed, and noticed a mark on my left leg. When I looked again, I could see another one. My doctor thought that it could be karposi's sarcoma, a form of cancer that affects immune deficient people. Then there were spots on my left hand and they started to appear on my arms too. They were quite distinct purple lesions, sometimes raised, and often starting as a lump just below the surface of the skin. The diagnosis was confirmed, but I was assured that it was not normally something that was in itself fatal.

My ankles started to swell first, and then my feet and my whole legs from the knee down. The KS, as it is called, had got into the lymph system and caused what is known as lymphoedema, caused by retention of fluid when the lymph glands are not working properly. A new form of chemotherapy had just been approved on a trial basis, and I was among a handful of patients to be given it. At times I was very tired, and once or twice I needed blood transfusions. I was also allergic to the drug, and had to be given an anti-allergic injection before they administered the chemo. Those days when I had the chemo I was a wreck, but mainly due to the Fenergan they gave me for the allergy.

Shortly afterwards more new HIV drugs came along, new classes altogether such as the protease inhibitors. They also started to be able to measure viral loads. This is a reflection of the amount of live virus in the body. If it can be kept low it suggests that the virus is being controlled and is just sitting there doing little damage. If it is high it means that the virus is active and gradually destroying your T cells. As they say, the viral load tells you how fast you are moving to the edge of the cliff, and the T cells tell you how far away from it you are.

My viral load had always been so high it beggars belief. It was a terrible frustration for me to hear friends talking about how their viral load is undetectable, and how their T cells have shot up to 500 and 600, while mine was so high they could not even measure it and the T cells so low I might get an infection any time. There is a popular belief that with the triple combination therapy that became available in 1996 HIV is like diabetes, an inconvenience but a chronic disease that can be controlled. That may be true for many, but with those first combinations not unfortunately for me. I sometimes used to feel that I ought to be capable of doing better. And I feel that it is not fair. But then most of us early ones are dead. After all we estimate that I contracted HIV in New York in 1980 before anyone knew about it.

About the same time as all this was happening, I suddenly developed what is called peripheral neuropathy. It was almost certainly a side effect of a drug that was quickly taken off the market, affecting the nerve endings below my knees. As a result the feeling especially in my feet is not normal. Sometimes I feel pain, at times there is numbness, or the feeling that wax from a candle has dripped and dried on the skin. Usually the condition reverses after you stop taking the medication. In my case it did not. The two afflictions of my feet and legs, the neuropathy and the lymphoedema, are permanent and irreversible. I have lived with them now for well over 15 years.

On the brighter side those triple combinations did push the KS into remission and the marks on my skin virtually disappeared. But I have always been at the front of a wave of new drugs. The pattern was until recently that each one lifted my T cells a little, and then over six months or a year they gradually declined pushing me back into the danger zone again. It was like living on a roller-coaster, with periods where I fetl a certain relief and knew that at least for a few months I was secure, then I dropped again into that dark area where I was vulnerable to infection and possible death.

The poor counts have also precluded me from trials. Warren managed to get onto some trials of a product called Interlukin. It is administered either intravenously or by self-injection over the course of a week. You feel as if you have a really bad dose of the flu by the end of the week. But in his case four or five treatments boosted his T cells well into the normal range and they stayed there for a couple of years or more. Then he just topped it up from time to time as required.

I was not eligible for the trial, but purchased Interlukin in the USA and the hospital administered it to me. It cost me thousands of dollars, and made no identifiable difference. I probably would have needed to take it for a longer period, but with a high viral load any increase is expected to be very transitory. Interlukin illustrates the point that HIV medicine is still at the cutting edge and we still do not know long term what will happen, The trial Warren was on was interrupted because the results clearly showed the benefit of being on Interlukin. Those who were the control group were offered Interlukin. But ten years later when they looked at clinical outcomes they found that Interlukin had had no positive effect on health outcomes at all.

In 2001 both Warren and I had a cancer scare. It turned out that his was a more serious problem than mine. It seems that long-term HIV patients are more susceptible to certain cancers in general and especially anal cancer, which is a skin cancer of the squamous cell type. In my case they operated and decided that it had not advanced very far at all. But in Warren's case it had, and he had to have a six-week radiation course. Fortunately it seems to have been cured. But it seems to me that in time we will see more and more of these problems, either due to long-term immune suppression or due to the drugs themselves.

For if the disease does not get you, the treatment very well might. The side effects that I have suffered are not at all pleasant. There is a redistribution of fat in the body. You lose it from your cheeks (all four of them), arms and legs, giving you a sunken look. The veins stand out on your limbs, and your arse collapses into something reminiscent of ruched curtains. As if that is not bad enough for the self-esteem of the average gay guy, the fat is redeposited in places like the abdomen and in my case the back of the neck and shoulders as well as the abdomen. Many of us have pot bellies, and in my case I was so jowly at one stage that I needed shirts with a neck size of 46 centimetres or 18 inches, and the fat build-up on my neck and shoulders made me look like Quasimodo. That has recently improved. Whether it is due to a change in drugs, the suggested natural products my naturopath prescribed, or a change in diet, I am not sure. (Fortunately for those who were lucky enough to not start treatment until more recently some of the physical side effects I have described seem to escape them. This is primarily a result of better drugs.)

Your muscles ache. You are constantly running to the toilet with bouts of diarrhoea. The function of the pancreas is affected. Cholesterol goes up as do sugars and triglycerides. A heart attack or stroke is a stronger possibility, and has occurred with five of my friends; one of them died at the age of just 40. Your sleep patterns are disturbed. You feel tired.

And yet, after all that and despite everything, we are alive, I have so far outlived Charles by over 24 years, suggesting that different people are affected by the same virus to a differing extent. The host is a critical factor in the progression of the disease; you can have lucky or unlucky genes. In all that time I have tried hard not to let HIV stop me from living my life. I do sometimes feel sad, even resentful, that HIV took from me what could have been the some of the best years of my life, from when I was 42 until I was in my 50s, when some of the newer triple combinations became available, and although my counts did not improve, I did a bit better on them. Those years should have been some of the best in my life, but they were marred with worry, stress and poor health. It was not until I reached 60 that far more effective drugs came along and finally my counts started to improve somewhat as well. I have felt better in the last 5 years than in the fifteen years prior.

On the other hand despite that Warren and I travelled while we could. We have taken Concorde from New York to London, cruised to Alaska and the Caribbean, toured South America and Central Asia, and gone on safari in Africa. As well we have been to Madagascar, Mauritius, Zanzibar, Bali, Barbados, Havana and the Arctic Circle. Some of it was related to my work and some pure holiday. Sometimes I travelled on my own and sometimes Warren and I travelled together. In the chapters that follow I recount some of the stories of these journeys.

Chapter 22 Letters from Lesotho

In 1995 Warren and I went to Club Med in Bora Bora, Tahiti. It is surely one of the most stunningly beautiful places on earth, with a lagoon of colours that defy description, white sandy strips lapped by crystal clear water, and the island itself serene and green majestically rising from the centre of the lagoon and reigning over the beauty below. We swam with manta rays, escaped to secluded beaches with an outrigger, ate and drank like royalty, and felt like we were in paradise.

We also met friends there who have been with us ever since. There were Jacky and Alexandre from Paris, and Marian from Milwaukee. Marian and I in particular became very close, and during many of my travels I have written her letters. These were the days before common usage of emails, and I printed out the letters and mailed them to her. They serve as an account of many of my travels from 1995 for a few years. Then later when emails became widespread I included a wider circulation.

Africa September, 1998

Dear Marian,

One of the things that is good about a computer is that you can go back and write something at the start even when you have already finished the main text, a bit like a Russian history book. This letter has turned out to be a collection of my thoughts and experiences over a period of nearly three weeks that I have been travelling in Africa. I wanted to capture them before they faded into obscurity. They were very real as they occurred, and I suppose rather personal. I found it easier to write down my thoughts in the form of a letter, and I am sending it to you, even though in some ways it was written for me as much, or even more, than it was for you. I hope you understand.

Right at the moment I am bored out of my mind with another 4 hours 38 minutes before we land in Johannesburg. The route takes us south-west from Perth towards the South Pole. There is nothing at all for thousands of miles, it is really quite unnerving. Just the odd whiskey sour. It seems a bit self-indulgent in a way to be going off on my own knowing that out of nearly three weeks away there is only one week of work, and time for me before and after.

I am planning on hiring a car tomorrow and driving to Lesotho. There have been some problems with election results, and a reporter was killed in front of the royal palace last week. But I figure that if I avoid the capital

Maseru and especially the palace, I should be alright. I will see when I get there. The other thing I am planning is a little trip to Maputo, which you will recollect is the capital of Mozambique. It is quite a nice thought that the choice is mine, to go where I want, almost on the spur of the moment.

***

I was surprised that things worked out as smoothly as they did. I did have great difficulty trying to find out what the political situation is in Lesotho. I tried the embassies of the UK, Lesotho, USA and Australia. This was a very frustrating exercise, as no-one was available and all I got was recorded messages, apart from Lesotho where the number was always busy. In the end the Australian Embassy was the one who came up with the goods. They said that they had no more information since the army and the police had had a gun battle over some demonstrations in the capital a few days earlier. There were elections in May, and despite the fact that there were 150 foreign observers who said that everything was above board, the opposition parties cried foul. There had been problems with the ballot boxes, they claimed. More votes were cast than people. It turns out that there were in fact irregularities, and the international observers had not picked it up.

The guy at the embassy said, "Isn't there anywhere else you would rather go?" "No!" "Well, there are no instructions not to go, so go!" I called Bev at Amex Travel (she's a friend of Trish), took a cab around there and organised to hire a car and to book a trip to Mozambique. I left the British passport with them to apply for the visa for Mozambique; then they dropped me back at the hotel, I checked out, rang Sandy in Cape Town to let her know my plans, Avis dropped the car around, and by 12.15 I was off into the Jo'burg traffic, still a bit jet-lagged.

Running south from Jo'burg is the N1, which is basically a strip of bitumen that runs for kilometres across the high veldt. The first part – a freeway, quite badly maintained, but even so a good road – passes through Jo'burg itself. It is strange to pass signposts to Soweto. The road goes through the urban area of Jo'burg itself, which is just about the ugliest city I have ever seen, with mounds of dirt left from the mining, and a mist of pollution hanging over soulless suburbs. Then it gives way to the high veldt, flat and rather featureless. I drove for four hours, wondering whether I was going to start to feel too tired to drive, but in fact I was alright. I reached Bloemfontein, the judicial capital, and the capital of what was originally called the Orange Free State. This is very conservative Afrikaans country. I looked up a guide of country houses, and called a place in Ladybrand (great to have the mobile!). I reserved the last room, and set off for the last 130 kilometres.

What a gem this place was. Close to the border with Lesotho, it is a small village, and the house is a sandstone home dating from the end of the last century. I had a whole cottage to myself, beautifully furnished, almost fussily so, with details like a pot pourri inside the tissue box. It was a luxury to have a sitting room, a little kitchen and a bathroom as well as the bedroom. The bed was all in white, with enormous country pillows and lace pillow cases.

Dinner was excellent and served in a very cosy dining room. There were a few other guests, mainly South Africans who were heading to Lesotho for work. This morning I headed off towards the border. Because of the problems I decided to enter the border at a post further south than the capital. The road runs down the South African side of the border. By this time the plains had given way to vast mountains, mesas stretching into the distance. There was no traffic as I passed through Wepener to the border. In stark contrast to the smart glass windows and neat uniforms of a western border post, this one was sordid. There were rotting trucks and cars, rubbish everywhere, and tumbledown shacks with tin roofs. The echo of Warren's voice about "Third World toilets" resounded in my head.

I parked the car and got out of South Africa without much trouble. A few metres further on at the Lesotho barrier, there were a few more problems. Firstly my passport is so worn they could not work out which country I was from. Then there was a dispute about whether I needed a visa or not. After we finally agreed by referral to a higher authority that I did not need one, the next hurdle was that there was no room for any more stamps in my passport. Finally they found a corner that suited them, and I was on my way.

Lesotho, the mountain kingdom, is described as one of the poorest countries in Africa, but its future is a bit brighter because of water. South Africa is desperate for it, and Lesotho normally has it. The whole country is rugged, with bare mountains, shocking roads connecting the sparse villages. There are domestic animals like cattle and sheep all over the place, often tended by a young shepherd boy with a blanket wrapped around him to keep out the biting cold wind from the mountains, and a wooden staff for keeping the animals in check.

I drove carefully, half an eye on the amazing landscape unfurling in front of me, and half on the animals, blanketed shapes and other hurdles on the side of the road. At one point I had to drive off the road as there was a car overtaking a truck on my side of the road. Just as well I was going slowly. The villages are poor, the people dressed in brightly coloured clothes, but still with the Basuto blankets wrapped around them to keep out the wind. I took the only main road, which is surfaced for 40 or 50 kilometres, and then at a sordid little village I set off on a dirt road towards Malealea Lodge. The road was shocking and I had to drive carefully. There were men on horseback, little villages with prim but modest primary schools, and gradually the mountains became more and more grand. After 35 kilometres the road just terminated, and there was the lodge, owned by a white guy who is third-generation Lesotho. (Actually the natives are called Basuto, Masuto in the singular. They speak Sesotho, and live in Lesotho, which is pronounced "le Sutu".)

And that is where I am right now. Just after the gate there is an area where all the ponies for the treks are situated. The lodge is a collection of small cottages. Mine is simple, clean and comfortable, with ensuite that actually has hot water. There is power in the evening from six until half past nine.

There is a restaurant of sorts. Ample food is cooked for everyone by Agnes, large warm and motherly, with no menu of course; you get what you get. Since it costs less than $30 for room and three meals a day, one can't complain. There are a few other people staying here. A Dutch couple on honeymoon, pleasant but rather boring and uptight, and a German-born man who has lived in Africa for 30 years, and now lives in Zambia. He used to live in Lesotho. His partner (wife?) is a charming and very attractive lady from Zimbabwe. I suspect she is Shona. Last night she consulted with the local Sangoma, who is a traditional doctor and fortune teller. He told her that she gets headaches and occasional backache (the German reckoned that was due to the afternoon pony trek) and that she is going to be very wealthy…

There are three people from across the border, one of whom is the owner's father-in-law. And there is a Japanese lady, an anaesthetist, who arrived on a public bus; well it took her four buses to get here actually. I asked her if she had been to Yufuin in Kyushu. Ah yes, it's beautiful, full of old spas and lovely old buildings. "You should try the public bath, but as westerner maybe you not like to bathe with lot of other men". I decided it was not the moment to mention The Steamworks in Melbourne, so I just said that I was sure I could cope.

I showed the Japanese lady the Southern Cross. At half past eight the sky was wonderful, the milky way so bright it looked like clouds. Soon after, the moon came up and the sky was filled with light; you could see the mountains even though there was not a light for miles.

I fell asleep with the noise of the wind in the trees; it was wonderful. I woke early as I am still jet lagged. As there was no power, I just laid in bed with my thoughts, but at dawn I got up, showered, and set off to a secret place I found yesterday. Out of the lodge and through the few houses of the village, there is a path behind the tree, which leads up to the top of a ridge. Yesterday when I went up there, there was just the noise of the bells around the necks of the sheep, and the shepherd boys sometimes sitting and sometimes walking, with their sticks, goading the animals to fresh pasture. It was so tranquil it felt as if time had stood still. I returned this morning. The sun had just appeared over the top of the mountains, the distant ranges misty and mysterious with shadows. Closer there was smoke coming from small clusters of houses perched on the ridges. The villages have stone houses, many of them round, some made of just earth, and with a thatch roof. I counted nine ranges of mountains from the most distant to the closest.

I found a rock ideally matched to my body, and I sat with just my own breath as company. In front of me and down the hill was a clump of bushes or small trees, their light green leaves contrasting with the barren hills. I thought about Cobus. He is good for my self-esteem, gentle and passionate, unexpected in an Afrikaaner I thought. I listened to the wind. It was cool, with chilly gusts and then a warmer breath with a hint of a warm day to come. I noticed the movement of a stalk of grass in the wind. It was minute and perfect. This was the closest to peace I have felt for a long time and I could have stayed there for an eternity; it was almost a moment to die.

Then the clouds moved over, and a chill sprang up. Shafts of light fell through the clouds on the mountains. I walked on down the hill, and returned around the foot of the mountain. A hearty breakfast of eggs and bacon was waiting for me, and now I am ready for a pony trek.

***

A few hours later ...I once went around a lake on a pony in the south of India. The poor thing was half-starved, and the owner was keen to make sure that it did not exert itself too much. This was different. My trusty guide was called Belmont, small, extraordinarily good-looking with long eyelashes, a brilliant smile, and a large ring in his right ear. And apparently an itchy arse that required constant and detailed attention! At 27 he is married but his wife left him and went back to her village.

We set off out of the village, and tracked up over a hillside following a narrow path. The villages are all connected by these paths, and the villagers either travel them on horseback or walk. It is hard to tell whether the figure wrapped up in a blanket, with just a little part of a face showing, is male or female. When they get close there is a gruff exchange of greetings and the truth is revealed. Sometimes the men wear a large floppy hat, especially the younger ones, and they quite like to wear a moustache. They are very black, and certainly not the original inhabitants, who were in fact Bushmen. The Bushmen are not as dark – rather they are rather yellow in complexion – and theirs are the languages that gave the strange clicks to modern Xhosa. The modern-day inhabitants of Lesotho are 90% Basutos, and indeed many years ago the country was called Basutoland.

We passed three people on the path, and my guide stopped. He said to me, "This man very sick, we must help". He got off his horse, and helped the man to climb on. He appeared to have some lung problem; Belmont said it was from working in the mines. (Out of a population of 1.6 million, over 125 000 work in the mines in South Africa. The conditions are dreadful, but for many it is their only chance of work. Even so, many mines are now closing and people are losing their jobs.) He was obviously very sick, and spat quite a lot – not in my direction, I was keen to ensure. He probably has TB, which is rife in Africa, and more likely than not it would be co-infected with HIV. He had come home to die.

We made a detour to his village to drop him at his house. The path down was very steep, and this was a real initiation trial for my skills on horseback. I managed to stay on, but I suspect with elevated blood pressure. The village was composed of about 20 huts scattered over the hillside, all made from stone, and most round with a thatch roof. There is no electricity, sewerage, or as far as I could see, running water. There may have been a well, but I could not see it. The huts are very small, no more than 15 feet in diameter, and would house a family. They have a minute front door, and a window about one foot square.

After we had dropped off the poor old guy – he was 48 I found out – we headed back up the hill and across the ridge with spectacular views of the mountains. I thought back to the mountains of Luzon in the Philippines, to Sagada. I remembered the rural feeling of Nepal. But this was different. Belmont told me, "Beautiful country, but no good. No work", He drew my attention again to the dryness of the land. The rains are due to start in a few weeks. They need to. Shortly we arrived at the top of a ridge and looked down into a deep ravine with an apology of a river crawling along the bed. We started down into the ravine, again so steep that the horse missed its footing a couple of times. No wonder I had to sign my life away at the post office (don't ask why the post office) before I set out. Actually the post office is a desk in a metal shack inside the compound. We stopped, tied up the horses, and then clambered down the rocks towards the Bushmen's paintings. It was very steep, and as you know I do have some problems with my feet, peripheral neuropathy thanks to HIV medication. I persevered as far as I could, but in the end the mountain side was so steep, and the path so narrow, that I decided to give up. I have seen plenty of bush paintings around the world. I felt I could live without this one.

On the way back I learned that my instructions on driving the horse were not complete. It decided it wanted to get home fast and set off at a canter and I did not know where the brake was. This was all a bit scary, but I managed to stay on until we came to a hill, and I found out that pulling up on the reins slowed the beast down.

And so back to the tranquility of the room. The battery on my laptop is getting low, so there will be an interruption until power resumes at dusk this evening and I can charge it.

***

Power is on. The German is fascinating. He advises on agriculture, and knew some of the local farmers when he used to live in Lesotho. Nikki, his wife, is Shona, as I thought. His first wife was also from Zim, but she took him to the cleaners and left him with an enormous loan to pay from a business in Liberia that failed. He has two sons. He lamented that there was one living in Germany and who was supposed to be getting a job. He told me that a coloured boy wearing dreadlocks was going to find it hard to get employment in Germany. I agreed.

They had invited a local lady to lunch. Her husband had been a very progressive farmer until he died last year aged 82. She now manages the farm with some of her sons. An elegant, charming lady, she spoke excellent English.. She used to be a teacher, and now must be around 70. We had a traditional lunch today of maize meal and vegetables, with some steak, which I suspect is a not very traditional luxury. We ate it with our fingers. Nikki managed to do so much more elegantly than I was able. The German resorted to a knife and fork.

The Dutch couple returned late from their pony trek. The one horse did not seem to like the other, and kicked. Unfortunately the girl's shin was in the way. Nothing broken but badly bruised. Such are the perils ...

I will take the Japanese anaesthetist to the border tomorrow. She then has to go back to Bloemfontein where she left her airline ticket in a safe by mistake. I will head back across country for Jo'burg, the airport and a flight to Cape Town. It will be to literally move from one world to another. One assumes that one knows which one is best, but I fear it is not quite that simple. I have been captivated by this little kingdom. Today I thought that this is where we should have come together instead of Japan, but it would have been complicated. Going to Yufuin will be just fine.

I will drive through Maseru to the border tomorrow. Things seem to have settled down, and I can avoid going through the town centre anyway.

A group of local kids, teenagers and early 20s I guess, have formed a choir, and they came to sing for us before dinner. They were magnificent as only a young African choir can be. Two young Polish ornithologists turned up after a few days out on a trek.

In the morning Handa and I set off to the border. We had to drive through the middle of Maseru as it happens. Nothing to report except that I now learn that at that very moment some junior army officers arrested the chief of the army and forced him to resign, together with 28 senior officers. The capital is an exceptionally boring, dirty and ugly town. Once we got over the border, I said goodbye to Handa and set off through the Free State. I took the back roads, with no traffic, tearing along at 130–140 kilometres per hour. I reached Jo'burg in six and a half hours from Malealea Lodge. It is just an amazing thing to imagine two worlds more different – the aggressive South African drivers tearing around the freeway system, and the tranquil rural villages of Lesotho.

As I waited in the Business Class lounge I was pondering that South Africa really is like two different countries that are intertwined yet totally separate, almost like two serpents locked in combat but coiled so tightly around each other they cannot even strike. In the lounge there was a sea of white faces. Only later did a very well-dressed and handsome black enter. Then a couple of Indians. But this is a bastion of the old order, and I fear its days are limited.

It also made me wonder about femininity. There was a black woman who delivered some ice to the bar. She was elegant, tall, graceful in the European sense of the word. Native women from the country do not have this type of femininity. Is it learned? How did it evolve? Is it natural in a more urban than rural setting? Surely not! Is it an embellishment of natural femininity, an exaggeration, an extension of female characteristics? I have no answer. Some input, please?

***

And now a few days have elapsed. The weekend in Cape Town was a return to the way we normally live our lives, comfortable and easy. We went out and had lunch, friends came over for dinner, we went out to brunch. The topics of conversation are always the same. The sagging economy, the violence, the exodus. People no longer have the heart to delude themselves. Some express a forlorn hope that maybe the country will follow the path of Botswana or Namibia. But no-one really believes it will. Mandela makes an uncharacteristic gaffe from the comfort of a meeting in Mauritius. He said that liberation had liberated criminals to move into white areas. He said that "real" South Africans would not flee the country because of crime. This has prompted an outrage in the press.

"Should we all wait until we are murdered in our beds?" A large survey of senior business and professional people has shown that 74% are considering leaving the country.

A very cluey coloured guy on my course raised the question of the problems that affirmative action legislation was causing in recruiting people – there are very few competent people to fill the quotas – and in the motivation of competent whites who can never hope to get promoted. In fact the whites are finding it increasingly difficult to find a job at all. The SA economy shed 100 000 jobs last year, yet the population is increasing rapidly. Many believe it is now close to 50 million. And less than 10% white. Home mortgage rates are 25%. The stock exchange plunged from 8000 to 4800 in the last four weeks, and the economy is on the edge of recession. Black unemployment is somewhere between 25 and 45%, no-one is quite sure. What a mess! The only other time I have ever come across an intelligent, educated people who are so politically aware and who talk so openly and with constant concern about their problems, is in Israel.

***

I am back in Jo'burg. Trish and I went to the house of Bev and Roger for dinner last night. Wonderful, kind, warm, welcoming people. They live out in the country on a small property, but even there they were forced to put in gates, alarms and an intercom. As we drove past a couple of squatter camps, at 11 at night, doors locked, the mobile on within easy reach on the console between us and the emergency number dialled ready, neither Trish nor I voiced our concern, but I was aware how vigilant we both were. The list of carjackings, hold-ups and murders in the paper this morning (and every morning) is testimony to the fact that our concerns are well placed. She sometimes calls her security service to meet her at the gates of her fortified block of town houses, so that they will ensure she is not attacked as she waits for the automatic gate to open.

Today is Wednesday, and due to their total ineptitude, the local office – the people I am working for here – have failed to make any appointments for me, so I have a free day. This morning I did some work for when I get back (for Honeywell), and this afternoon I took a trip to Soweto. There were just six of us: two British, two French, a Dutch lady and me. The driver and guide were black. The guide in particular was brilliant, vibrant, extremely eloquent, and exceptionally funny. It was utterly fascinating. We saw the squatter camps, the original matchbox houses built by the government, and the more up-market Orlando West section where Desmond Tutu and Winnie Mandela live. It is awfully depressing. The better off blacks are in just the same situation as the whites in that they have to protect themselves by alarms and razor wire too. The poverty is

231

abject and pervasive. The guide's estimate of national unemployment is 45%, the upper figure bandied around. Not many of the three or four million people who live in Soweto have a job. Even those who do have a hard life. The environment is desolate, with scrappy bits of waste land, and full of litter. While some of the houses are quite pleasant, most are not. Worst of all are the squatter camps with shacks of corrugated iron without facilities.

Soweto (South-West Township) is best known of course for the riots that started on 16 June 1976. Unarmed students were peacefully protesting the education system, and the fact that they were forced to study in Afrikaans. The authorities started firing, and between 600 and 700 people died. There is a scrappy monument and an exhibition housed in mobile freight containers of photographs and newspaper clippings. The photographs were extraordinary, portraying excruciating pain.

Before I start working again I am half listening to BBC World. There was an interview with Bianca Jagger. I knew nothing about her and confess to being utterly seduced by her and the work she does for Amnesty International.

***

It is Saturday night in Mozambique, and I am determined to keep awake for another hour to digest dinner, even though I am tired. It is almost comforting when names and words from the past gradually emerge into one's consciousness. Renamo, Frelimo, Samora Machel, even Lourenco Marques. It is hard to imagine that in this place only 30 or 40 years ago – who knows when it ceased to exist – stood Lourenco Marques. It was the place where the comfortable whites of Rhodesia and the Highveldt of South Africa brought their families for the summer holidays. Geoff told me about his childhood memories – king prawns, the beach, families on holiday – but that was not Maputo, the ugly capital of Mozambique today, that was Lourenco Marques. Someone last week told me that this is the 6th poorest country in the world, whatever that means. What is clear is that the country has suffered incredibly from a Marxist dictator and a civil war that finished only six years ago.

How strange and arbitrary is the hand of fate. I have always felt that the thing that most strikes me when I travel is the other lives I might have had, the other people I might have been, the other cards that I might have been dealt. I am sure it is this that causes me not to have a racist bone in my body. The people I have met here in Mozambique are kind and gentle, they have dignity and grace in lives that had neither of those things. What must it have been like to live through a civil war like that, entirely at the mercy of history being written? I look at the older waiters in the hotel.

There is a tiredness about them, but no apparent bitterness in their faces. They are my age, with a few wisps of grey in the dark tight curls, and a stiffness hinting at arthritis and backaches. And I love them.

It is alright to believe that you are not a racist. But it is a great comfort to meet people of other races and be able to live that truth. I think of Victor and Walter who were on my course on Thursday and Friday last week in Jo'burg. They are alive, intelligent, responsive, for God's sake, no different from the other delegates except for their physical looks. And in the case of Victor I have to confess that his looks were a problem. Those gorgeous clear brown eyes, the long eyelashes, the high cheekbones and the pointed chin. His moustache was neat, and even though he was well shaved the shadow of his beard showed dark in his jaw. I went weak at the knees at the thought of him!

But I digress. Maputo. Even before the plane touched down I could see that "Third World toilet", the phrase so eloquently coined by Warren, was going to be a pale description. One always can tell something about countries where there are police, army and security guards everywhere. While waiting for transport to the hotel I exchanged a few words with a Portuguese woman from the World Bank in Washington DC. She told me she felt guilty that she had been on aircraft for two days and had not done a stroke of work. She'll get over it.

Out of the decaying buildings, the scrappy bits of dirt, the stunted trees, and the pervasive rubbish, rises the anachronistic Polana Hotel. It ranks with those great hotels of tradition: Raffles in Singapore, The Peninsula Hong Kong, The Strand Rangoon, The Victoria Falls Hotel and maybe The Nelson Cape Town. It is no mean feat to create such an oasis of charm and elegance in a town like Maputo. It was built in 1922, and of course only recently renovated, by South African developers. It is stunning, with white, classic lines, tended gardens and an extravagant pool. Inside, the grandeur of the marble, columns, high ceilings and Gumps furniture is spectacular. Even the lift is the old open-cage type. The hotel is built up high overlooking the Indian Ocean so that as you look across the gardens out to sea you are not even aware that there is some small sordid scrap of Maputo between the hotel and the shore.

The guy at reception bundled me onto a tour of Maputo, which was just on the point of departing at the instant I arrived. In fact he held it up for me for which I am grateful as it was great. In three hours I got to see everything there is to see. If you look really hard you can see under all the decay some streets that must in the colonial heyday have been very pleasant, with large spacious villas hiding behind wafting tropical shrubs and trees. But very few of them have found a keeper they deserve. Most are broken, rotting, falling apart. The streets are in a terrible state of repair, with most of the cars bent heaps of rust. Some of them have been just abandoned where they finally gave up the ghost.

The windows in the most unassuming cathedral I have ever seen are all smashed. Another church offered us a wedding, African singing and the trilling of the women in rejoicing. They are the occasional sparks in an otherwise dismal scene. Along the beach to the north are hollow skeletons of hotels either abandoned by the Portuguese or more recent ventures that never came to fruition. The beach is sad and unappealing. In the centre of town one can hardly see any vestiges of the old Portuguese town. More prevalent are buildings from the 1970s that have spent themselves already. Statues and monuments hint at the Marxist recent past. They still have embassies from places like North Korea and Cuba, where many of their doctors are from. They also need to rename a few streets. Kaunda, Nyerere, Nkrumah, they have all been sacked, and I am also a bit doubtful about Avenida Kim Il Sung and Avenida Mao Tse Tung.

On a brighter note the guide was gorgeous. He kept pleading with us to not leave the hotel with even a watch on, saying that one of the guests yesterday was attacked right around the corner from the hotel. Nearly everywhere we went he described as being very dangerous. He is tall, very slim, with long delicate fingers accentuated by the way he moves his hands. Eighteen years old (we chatted away in Portuguese and he revealed a few personal details), he has a beautiful colour, *café au lait*, obviously mixed blood, and the most sensuous mouth I can remember. Furthermore, from my considerable experience in these matters, I am sure that he is gay.

On that note I will take to my bed. I have left the window open and can hear the wind gently caressing the palms. Tomorrow I take the boat to Inhaca Island.

***

An hour can be a long time. The ferry was in fact a speedboat. The driver, Sergio, Portuguese, was born here, left for several years and was now back again, young, confidant and eminently presentable. The boat was full with an interesting mix of people. I sat inside the cabin with the locals and Sergio. He put on a tape. Out of all the colonial languages Portuguese has lent itself best to being blended with music from tropical climes. Suddenly I am transported to Brazil, and I can feel Portuguese memories in me awakening again. After a rich deep melody full of seduction, sensuous rhythm and nasal vowels, the unmistakable twangs of the Portuguese guitar announce a somewhat upbeat but not quite disco version of one of the most famous *fado* songs. *"Amalia Rodrigues vai cantar!"*

I say to Sergio. They all laugh. Suddenly I am in Alfama, in a *fado* bar in old Lisbon, sipping rough red wine and eating spicy sausage. I remember how I have always been captivated by the *fado*. I could see myself putting the shawl around my shoulders as tradition requires and standing up, eyes almost closed, singing those melancholy aching songs about life, about fate – *o fado*.

Then I am in the farmhouse nearly 30 years ago, the 600-year-old *quinta* owned by João's parents, at Torres Vedras, with the wide entrance of stone steps decorated with terracotta and stone pots and a profusion of flowers and plants. I am in the house, upstairs in the dining room looking through those windows with tiny seats each side, across the vineyards that produce the rich, full red wine his father makes, to the village of Matacães in the distance. His sister São is there in the dining room, kind and gentle, with her deep velvet voice. She deserves the man she will marry, a fine general in the Portuguese army who has served many years in Africa. He is a little older than her, commandingly handsome, yet kind-looking. He has served enough time to be able to retire in Portugal on a generous pension, and São is relieved that, unlike many, he has returned with his life.

Then I remember that lunch after a freezing dip in the Atlantic near Porto Novo, the banquet of fish and seafood served on a long table, the kittens again delicately picking their way between the lavish leftovers from the seafood. I remember the afternoons at Ericeira with the Oliveira family at their seaside holiday house. The relaxed lunches with fish and salads with juicy olives and ripe tomatoes. And the rainy Saturday afternoon in December I stopped in Lisbon to buy some shoes and catch up with the Oliveiras before taking the night flight out of a cold and dark winter to arrive bathed in warmth and brightness in Recife in Brazil.

The boat jolts as the sea gets rougher, and I am back in Mozambique. In the distance is the silhouette of Maputo. I wonder if I have been a bit harsh in my description. I reconsider it, and decide that as a compromise I will admit only that it looks better from a distance.

By now we are having a rough ride. Those who were sitting in the open on the back of the boat are no longer smiling. The spray has drenched them, and the good-looking Italian man is not looking well at all. He takes off his glasses. *"Um pasageiro vai vomitar"*. Sergio can see what is happening. The poor man is terribly sick, not once but over and over again, moaning in desperation as his body convulses with vomit. I am now focused on my own *faiblesse* in this regard, and much as I feel for him and want to help him, I have to look the other way to conserve my breakfast.

Another 20 minutes. Three times Sergio stops the boat to attend to the Italian, but the swell is so heavy it makes it worse. I urge Sergio to just keep going. The last complication is that it is very low tide, and we cannot get the boat in. We all have to get out and walk the last 3–400 metres, through shallow weedy water. When the tide comes in I will get my jeans and shoes back again. Some kind guy carried my computer and light bag.

An hour can be a long time.

Now what can I tell you about the self-indulgent few days on Inhaca Island? The island is quite large, some 30 kilometres long. There are no roads and just a few villages. The resort here was reopened just a few months ago after being "reissued", and is almost empty. They are still trying to get their act together. It is very relaxing, palms wafting in the breeze, the generator switched off for half of the day giving peace and quiet, and no traffic at all. The speedboat from Maputo does not come every day; it just depends on the demand.

The seawater pool is pleasant, but you cannot swim off the beach here, it is too shallow. The locals fossick around in the shallows looking for things to eat. The tide is very high here and moves very fast. What is wonderful is Ilha Portuguesa, 10 minutes ride away in the powerboat just opposite the hotel. It used to be a leper colony (why are many of the best beaches in former leper colonies? I assume because they are isolated), and is now totally uninhabited. I go over whenever I can, and set off on my own along the shore. The beach is wide and sandy, and the ocean clear, gently shelving and not too rough. The water is cool, but very pleasant. Since I am utterly on my own, I do what I have always loved to do: take all my clothes off and saunter along the shoreline, sometimes going for a swim, and sometimes just walking. I find the combination of water and light intoxicating, exhilarating. This is where I feel complete and quite free.

The trips back and forth to the island are fun. The boat is one of those flexible twin-hulled ones with very powerful twin engines. The ocean between the islands is very choppy, possibly because of the strong wind, and provides for an exciting ride. We all hang on like grim death while Gunther, the young and not at all shabby South African driver in his tight little Speedos, alternatively floors it and eases off, riding the swell. We arrive drenched, always.

In between the eating and swimming I have been working on the project for Novartis that I have to have finished by this time next week. I find it hard to bridge the mind-set gap. I am usually glad to climb under my mosquito net and fall asleep.

***

Just two hours and I leave for the airport in Jo'burg to go home. I am glad. It has been great, but I am ready to go home, and I am looking forward to seeing Warren.

The trip back here was relatively uneventful. The speedboat trip was jarring to the spine, and transfers to the airport in Maputo a little disjointed, shall we say. What a miserable place Maputo is. My first impressions were absolutely right. The flight with LAM was uneventful despite my concern. They fly to a total of three international destinations: Jo'burg, Harare and Lisbon. Old traditions die hard. I just wonder what plane they operate there. This one was a Fokker 100 tiny jet, quite new by the look of it. Didn't Fokker go bust last year??

Today was a First World day. A walk to Sandton City and a mini shopping expedition that was successful in its entirety, and a haircut. I look tanned, my white hair all spiky and quite trendy for someone on the way to 60! As I walked back the 15 minutes to the hotel (safe in the day, but I am the only white who walks), I walked past a teenage girl and a woman whom I assume was her mother. The girl suddenly started to sing, "Jesus, I want to be with you". I wondered what had prompted that.

Trish came over, dropped the big suitcase and we went out to lunch under the sun shades. It is very hot today, unseasonably so. It was a First World lunch with a fine South African wine, excellent food and not a hint of indigenous Africa ... Trish is facing moving to Sydney to be with her brother. She knows she has to go, but it is an awful wrench from friends and her environment.

It is just as well I went to Lesotho when I did. This week it is a disaster. The political intrigue is too long to explain here, but I strongly suspect that the South African government rigged the Langa report on the last election in May. It was late, the pages did not match up, it was released to the South African parliament before it was released to the Lesotho government, and it equivocated. "There seem to be indications of irregularities in the election, but without firm proof ...". The opposition parties erupted. The army, or part of it, mutinied, and the PM requested South African military intervention. They provided it. The result: at least 60 dead, including 8 South African military, and the capital is in ruins with all the buildings in the centre set on fire and every single shop looted (possibly a vast improvement based on what I saw). All the foreigners have fled, leaving the hospital virtually unattended, and there are hundreds of refugees streaming over the border. King Letsie has complained, saying his permission had not been requested for the troops that "invaded" and he had not been informed ahead of the invasion. The Lesotho opposition were very well armed (with South African–made weapons) and very determined, and have now fled to the mountains from where they are expected to carry out attacks. Nice one, South Africa! I was right to be cautious and at the same time very fortunate in the timing of my visit.

The sun is setting, and in the morning when it rises I should be well on the way to Perth. So it is time to turn off the computer and try and get some sleep.

j

Chapter 23 Letters from Bali to Malawi

Zomba, August 1999

Dear Marian,

It is a cold morning here in the tropics, high on a plateau (nearly 6000 feet) in the south of Malawi. I do not like radiator heating, and prefer to sit here with my leather jacket over my Bora Bora T-shirt. The Ku Chawe Inn is on the top of the plateau looking 3000 feet down to the valley and Zomba below. It is just past eight in the morning, and I am showered, have had breakfast and am planning the day ahead. I am of course also jet lagged, which is why I have achieved all these things so early in the morning. Every time I come to Africa from Australia it is the same story; it takes days to get over the time difference. I fall asleep exhausted by mid-evening and then am wide awake in the middle of the night.

But I get ahead of myself. Perhaps I should start with Bali. What a wonderful week we had! This time we stayed in Kuta, which is the best known of the beach locations. It used to have a bad reputation as a haunt for drunken Australian surfies. That seems to have faded now, with most of the visitors from Italy, Netherlands, France and very much middle-class Australia.

Kuta has a very good surf beach, with a strong rip (undertow), so that care is needed, but it is refreshing and a more real-life feeling than the pool. The hotel we chose was recommended, and a good tip it certainly was. The hotel is right in the centre of Kuta, but quiet, with a superb large pool, and just 20 metres away is the beach, not even a road to cross. We took a bungalow, right in front of the pool, in traditional red brick with large panels of ornate stone of a light cream colour. The gardens are luscious and well tended. Once out of the front door of the hotel you are in the middle of all the bustle of Kuta: the hawkers and the shops, restaurants and cafés.

The hotel is of course patrolled by security guards. One of them can arrange anything for you: taxi, car hire, massage, pedicure, and in my case a haircut. The security guard takes his cut of course, and appears to be exceedingly busy with all these arrangements. I did not have time to get my haircut before I left and it was in need of some heavy-duty trimming. "The hair dresser is quite a long walk away, but maybe one of the women on the beach ... let me see what I can arrange". A lady came to see me, but then the security guard changed the arrangements and a hotel gardener stepped out of nowhere brandishing the largest pair of scissors I have ever seen. Well, yes, they might have been gardening shears, I am actually not quite sure. He placed a chair in the garden under a tree and in 10 minutes performed a quite acceptable job for a very acceptable price. The event was considered by the others as intriguing enough to warrant several photographs.

Bali! I have to confess that part of the attraction was the generous passing parade of gorgeous young bodies scantily clad, full of vitality and blessed with the freshness of youth. On the other side of the glass window was the juxtaposition of my own youth, gone, hardly even accessible to memory, and the evidence of what the passing of time will in turn inflict upon them.

In fact the week was a rounded combination of so many senses and experiences all wrapped into one. Bali is special; that was recognised by "The Beautiful People" and the wealthy or adventurous years ago. It is a Hindu island (92%) of three million people in the middle of an archipelago of over 200 million Muslim Indonesians. The Balinese have their own language and alphabet, and their own culture and look, different from other Indonesians. They have high, pronounced cheekbones, beautifully tapered to small chins and mouths with generous sensuous rounded lips, ready to break into a genuine welcoming smile. Their eyes are like almonds, kind and steady.

Their music is different too – light, tinkling, delicate. Some find it monotonous, yet with attention and more familiarity the western listener will find melody and harmony.

The island is dominated by some large volcanoes, some still smoking, a gentle reminder of the respect they deserve. From the coast the land rises very gently but steadily in a classic volcanic slope towards the peaks. It is on these slopes, in the villages, where the real beauty of Bali is to be found. There is abundant vegetation everywhere: flowers, creepers, bushes and trees. Along the side of the road are small houses of stone, some with their own Hindu temple. At every doorway is the traditional offering of flowers in a little basket of palm fronds, and at the foot of the frequent small shrines on the side of the road, even in towns, they are usually also accompanied by burning incense sticks.

There are high walls along the road giving privacy to the homes behind, the ubiquitous red brick with inlays and carvings, sometimes showing their age gracefully as they bend and deform, crowned with creepers and flowers. The villagers are busy without being hurried. Certain villages specialise in specific activities. There are woodcarvers, furniture-makers, weavers, jewellery-makers. In some areas rice is grown on small terraces, giving a bright green aspect to the hillside, then on others coffee, or the spices for which Indonesia is famous – cloves, nutmeg, cardamom and vanilla – as well as fruit such as pawpaw, passion fruit, mango and pineapple. The smell of incense burning at shrines and the cigarettes with cloves is never far away in Bali.

One morning we hired a car with driver for four hours to go to two such villages: Mas, famous for its woodcarvers, and Ubud, a centre of art and galleries. The journey cost 70 000 rupiah, just over $10! *Mas* means gold in bahasa (a most convenient coincidence for what used to be called Malaysian Airlines System, MAS). Emiel and Paul had been to this particular gallery before. Inside the doorway is a large courtyard of trees and open workshops where Balinese carvers have worked for years cross-legged on the floor patiently carving and sanding. The sanding was almost like a meditation for them, it seems. The gallery is in some way connected to part of the Balinese royal family. There are waterfalls, pools with fish, bamboo, and then the gallery itself. What treasures there are! Part of a fallen branch had been carved into a score of leaping deer. It was exquisite.

And then when I least expected it, for this was a day of appreciation and drifting, not a day of shopping or acquisition, I saw a carving. The head and shoulders of a Balinese dancer, so elegant and delicate, in a light wood (satinwood I think it is called), that I caught my breath. And then I could not take my eyes off her. I would walk away, look at something else, but my gaze always returned. I picked her up again, and did not want to put her down. I decided that I did not have to, for an investment of just US$400. You will see her where she already sits on the display cabinet in the dining room. (This is of course an outrageous price by Balinese standards, where most people earn between 120 000 and 200 000 rupiah, or US$20–30, a month. However, this is the best gallery in Bali, and when you see it I am sure you will agree that it is worth every cent, or every rupiah out of the more than two million it cost.)

Meanwhile back at the beach it is lunchtime: *Tom Yang* spicy soup, or a lobster bisque followed by crabmeat fried rice, in an open restaurant right on the edge of the beach but part of the hotel. As such the hawkers can wave their wares at us, but may not come and pester us. The sun glints off the Indian Ocean, the massage women pound in their oils in the shade of the trees, and the Speedos saunter past. Another dip in the pool, half an hour laying in the sun, feeling heavy, sinking into the beach towel, watching the palms sway lightly in the breeze, and the white fluffy clouds drift across a clear blue sky, with the background comfort of the ocean breaking on the shore. A siesta followed by a shower and then gin and tonics on the balcony before heading out to dinner.

The evenings were rather social for us. Manfred and Judy, who owned and sold our favourite restaurant, Spot On, saw me walking along the beach. They had been in Bali for a few weeks and certainly knew the places to go. And for that matter the real price for a Cartier, Rolex or Rado watch, so perfect a copy that a casual observer, and sometimes even professional ones, could never know. It is about US$8.

Two friends from Adelaide, Lalla and Pam, our age also, arrived a couple of days after us. Rarely therefore did we eat dinner just the four of us. There are some narrow winding lanes connecting the road along the beach with the next parallel street. They are attractively called Poppies Lane One and Poppies Lane Two. Both Poppies Restaurant and Un's are in a courtyard through a narrow doorway in the lane. The tables are under trees, with neat white tablecloths, and a frozen sorbet–like drink of tropical fruit juices on arrival. The food frankly is alright, but Bali is not a mecca for haute cuisine. We tend to eat local food where possible on the basis that we can eat European food any day. Indonesian food is not really that varied, but we ate well and inexpensively.

Judy had discovered Hula's Café in Legian, the next beach community that merges with Kuta. They have a show there four nights a week starting at 11 called *"Cocks in Frocks"*. It is run by an Australian, and it is so nice to think that culture is a two-way street, and in our own little way Australia has embellished the cultural life of Bali. It is of course a drag show, and is enormous fun. The Balinese are gorgeous as boys and spectacularly beautiful as girls. I am glad to say that it is just a show, with not a hormone or surprise mound on the chest in sight. But it was beautifully executed, the mannerisms and movements a wonderful parody. I am not frankly normally into drag, but this was excellent entertainment. The elegance of the dainty Balinese was offset by the Aussie sending up the whole process gutless by his own tasteless and at times obscene performance, with enormous eyelashes and exaggerated bosom that at one moment collapsed into an enormous puddle on the floor!

The bar is small, packed, and was full of every possible representation of the world community: straight and gay Australians, Europeans, Indonesians, men, women, and even a few children. Italians and Dutch guys draped their arms around Balinese boys, and very straight beer-guzzling Australians were being caressed as part of the show by cheeky versions of Whitney Houston. A barely trusted favourite is the snake "lady", who wears her pythons around her neck, puts their heads in her mouth, and up the trouser legs of anyone in shorts who gets close to the stage.

Now that is the positive side of globalisation! A world community in harmony; I adore it.

But there is a negative side too. There are many Australian gays who criticise Asians who, they say, form a relationship with a white guy just long enough to get their residence in Australia through the gay immigration loophole (about dependent partners), and then dump them. This does happen in some cases, but generally I feel that it is the Asians who are vulnerable in relationships with Europeans. We have the money, and are larger, stronger, and more experienced in life. Thus in a relationship we tend to hold most of the cards, especially if we are visiting their country. It is a positive step that internationally binding laws have been enacted such that predatory, usually older, men having sex with under-age boys can now be arrested in Australia for crimes they committed in other countries. Underage needs of course to be defined. There are plenty of 16-year-olds who know exactly what their sexual orientation is, but the law concerns boys far younger than that. There are, however, still many foreigners who use vulnerable young people (it happens of course with young girls as well) with scant regard to their emotions and with no real respect.

Black and white. The beach is a centre of cultural life in Bali too. One morning I heard the rhythmic beat of drums and then the tinkling of music. From the town a line of people emerged like a twisting snake towards the waves, and then turned to the left and walked along the sand, heading towards a kind of altar that had been built on the beach. There were groups of women, dressed in white brocaded bodices, with immaculate hair and make up that accentuated their small mouths. They carried round things, made of leaves, bamboo and flowers, and would eventually place these in front of the altar. The men wore the traditional sarong, with neat well-pressed white linen jackets. They provided the music, using cymbals, drums and other instruments I could not identify. There were many children, also beautifully dressed, exact miniature copies of their parents. The women walked with each other, as did the men.

Once they arrived at the altar, the musicians sat under trees, and the others sat around the altar. Some priests performed a number of ceremonies, at times ringing small silver bells, and spraying the crowd with water from a metal bowl. There was a bird sitting by one of the priests. I am not sure for what he was destined, but I think I would have crept away, just in case the sacrifice and offerings went a bit beyond flowers.

This was the white ceremony, as I call it, and was for purification. They hold it twice a year. It seemed a happy event.

Surprisingly, the black ceremony was not really sad either. On Friday several cremations were held on the beach. The deceased may have died some time ago, and the ceremony waited for auspicious indications. Again the line appeared from the town, this time suddenly and moving fast. Everyone was dressed in black. The pallbearers carried a tall structure on poles of bamboo, in bright reds and yellows, with a canopy over the coffin draped in white, and a young man keeping the dead person company, perched uneasily on the top. The beach is steep in parts, and the structure at times seemed to lean dangerously until the large group of bearers moved quickly around in a circle, almost like ants, to bring it upright again. The procession was accompanied again by music, this time more paced and serious.

The pyres were lit on a section of beach about 200 metres from the hotel, and gradually the mourners dispersed, making way for the next group. I say mourners, yet in a religion that incorporates reincarnation, it is more a question of seeing the dead off to rest a while before being born again for another life of learning and striving for the ultimate. There was no crying, and in fact the moment did not even seem to be particularly sad. What was more sad I feel was that this important journey was observed by a whole load of curious, semi-naked European beach lovers, who did not always keep the respectful distance that would have been appropriate for the occasion.

***

I was really not ready to leave when on Sunday I had to catch the plane to Perth. I stayed the night with some friends who live there, and then on Monday morning trekked out to the airport again for the lunchtime flight to Johannesburg. The strong headwinds gave us a tedious flight time of 11 hours. It makes for an exceptionally long afternoon, and there is absolutely nothing to see out of the window.

I arrived on sunset, tired and feeling a bit flat. I stayed the night at the Holiday Inn Garden Court at the airport. I was just considering falling into bed at around half past seven when the phone rang. It was Hans Peter and André from Switzerland who had just arrived in Jo'burg from Cape Town. I had emailed them with my plans when I knew they were coming to South Africa, where André comes from originally. We had a quick dinner at my hotel. I was so tired I could hardly stand up, but it was great to see them and catch up on all their news, considerable as it turns out. They had bought a new house. HP was the operations manager for a regional airline and confronted his boss with a charge of corruption over aircraft leasing arrangements, and was promptly fired!

At 10 I collapsed. At half past two I was awake again! Bright and full of the joys of spring I did some work, and then listened to a worldwide public broadcasting radio program run by the BBC and Whateveritis from Boston. Great. I would rather have been asleep!

And so at eight in the morning back to the airport again, this time for the two-hour SAA flight to Blantyre in Malawi. As the plane circled the airport at Blantyre it revealed a soft rural undulating landscape, a few villages hiding in the trees, empty dirt roads, clear and red, and then we landed. The airport terminal including the international arrivals hut is no larger than my house. The process of entry is slow but cheerful. Silvester is waiting for me outside to take me the nearly two-hour drive to the Zomba plateau. He is bright and intelligent, speaking extraordinarily good English with an astonishingly broad vocabulary. Perhaps even more importantly he drives the diesel 4WD carefully, as the roads are very narrow, poorly surfaced with potholes everywhere, and unfinished at the edges. Along the roadside there are always people in Africa. They saunter, they sit, appearing generally morose. There is not much to be elated about in these countries.

Malawi used to be called Nyassaland in the colonial era. It is a landlocked country spread along the shores of the lake with which it shares a name. It borders Tanzania, Mozambique and Zambia. With 11 million people and a life expectancy of around 45, literacy for men less than 50% and for women less than 25%, Malawi ranks about 175th of the 196 countries listed in my Encarta in terms of GDP per capita, at US$150 per annum.

Dr Hastings Banda, a medical GP who lived in the UK until he was about 60, rescued the country from the Federation of Rhodesia and Nyassaland, created by the British as a construct of independence, but destined to have a very short life. Dr Banda was then not much more than 60, and he assumed power, and was made president for life. The trouble is that no-one expected him to live to the age of 96 (at least, for he may have even been older than that). He was totally senile and demented by the time he was just 93, and although the country was more or less being run by his mistress, who had the title "Official Hostess", and was over 40 years his junior, he was ousted. Democratic elections were held, or at least what passes for them in any country where hardly anyone can read or write, but not much will have changed. Silvester told me that even now very little is known about this strange figure, and some claim that he was not even from Malawi, but rather from the neighbouring country of Zambia. At least the wealth he amassed he left in Malawi instead of depositing it in a Swiss bank.

The villagers eke out a meagre existence subsistence farming. The houses are poor and sparse, not even in any way quaint or picturesque. The African landscape is dotted with rot and litter. The towns are sullen, with any attempts at beautification, such as a flowerbed, such an abysmal failure that it makes things even worse.

Silvester is an excellent travelling companion. He is married, has two children, one 5 and one 10, and says that is enough. His father has asked him if there is something wrong with him that he only has two. It is considered selfish and greedy to have few children. We talked about Africa, about religion and forms of government. We both agree that although the separation of the judiciary from government is enshrined in constitutions, the fact that it is not respected is a big problem in Africa. He asked me how we manage to keep this separation in western countries. I found the answer is not quite that easy. But it has something to do with the fact that our nations really live democracy rather than pay lip service to it. We all buy in to democracy, it is the way we live our lives. And the fact that the military upholds the constitution before the politicians! What would happen if the Australian prime minister were to say, "I am not going to call an election, I will just stay here"? I suspect he would be arrested, or taken by men in long white coats, and put in a home for the bewildered for the rest of his life on the basis that he had totally lost his grip on reality. We would probably feel sorry for his mental state.

He was shocked to find that few Australians ever go to church. He feels that religion, for all the ills and excesses of the Church, provides people with a value system in Africa. He said that it assists in preventing the whole continent slipping into anarchy. How can a country like this produce such an independent thinker, especially when he has never left Malawi? And only 29 years old.

I hope that Silvester is the one who will take me on Friday to the lake, another two and a half to three hours drive. Meanwhile here I am perched on the top of a mountain! There are pine forests all around; it is a conservation area. By African standards it is an achievement. We would not pay it much more than a passing glance. Nice view down to the valley, but ...

Yesterday I read a 150-page report on Category Management, the way that supermarket chains ought to be managing their business in the late 1990s. I need it for the program I am running in South Africa next week. I will need to make a few more overheads later today. And of course, I started this epistle. I am sure you realise that it is a way for me to record, as well as to share with you, my experiences, far more vividly than the camera can capture. At least for me!

***

The second night here was even worse than the first. A live band was playing until late for the Americans (see later), and the curtains in my room do not close. I slept little and fitfully, and was wide awake at 5.30. There was no hot water and then the electricity went off! I expect this in

Africa, but then I don't expect to be paying US$110 for a room for the pleasure. And I have the sniffles and a sore throat!

Ku Chawe Inn is not really a resort hotel, rather a business hotel that happens to be built up on the plateau away from the car-jackings and robberies of Zomba in the valley below. Zomba used to be the capital until just a couple of years ago when it was transferred to Lilongwe. Parliament only moved this year. Zomba still seems to be an important commercial centre. The dining room in the evening is predictably a place that raises more questions than it answers. Who are these people, why are they here, how come that they are in this unlikely location?

On the next table is a local man with a thin neck and an earnest look. He is discussing a construction project with the man opposite; they need three concrete mixers. The man opposite him across the table is an Arab, to judge from his looks and the heaviness of his accent. He wears a black-leather jacket, long floral shorts that flap around his legs, grey ankle socks and black slippers. He limps somewhat, causing his sex to swing noticeably inside his shorts. I learn they are faced with a problem of access during the coming rainy season.

Next to them is a mysterious lady whom I would have liked to have talked to. White hair flowing, she is solidly built without being fat, with a casual swing of the hip as she walks confidently to her table. Wrapped around her she has an ample, brown wool shawl, and she carries in her hand a comb-bound report, which she studies carefully as she eats her dinner and sips a glass of beer. Government business? Education perhaps? United Nations? Her first language is English. She is not American, but it is unclear where she is from. Probably British.

On the other side of me are two men who are connected through business, and nothing else it seems. The one is a local man, probably about 50, although it is not easy to tell. He sits quietly and comfortably, looking ahead of him towards where his companion is sitting. The companion is European, maybe German or Swiss, also past 50, slim, even gaunt, sitting back in his chair and looking sideways, never towards his table mate. He appears bored, totally disinterested, especially in his workmate opposite him. Finally he mutters, "Start tomorrow at seven", but neither of them moves and no other words are forthcoming.

There is a quiet Filipino who has lived in Tanzania for 10 years, an engineer who is supervising the construction of a cotton-processing plant. His wife and two daughters, both at university, have always remained in the Philippines in their home province of Locos Norte. He goes home twice a year for a month each time. He tells me that he could easily get a job lecturing at the University of Manila; in fact they have pressured him to take up an appointment. But the pay is nowhere near as good as his current job. I wonder whether he has made a tremendous sacrifice for the sake of the education of his daughters, or whether there are other dynamics. What would he do for sex? Is he careful to protect himself against rampant HIV?

Behind me is a long table of some 30 young Americans, spending their last few days in Malawi after a two-year teaching project as part of the Peace Corps. I interviewed a lady who turned out to be a nurse with the group. I always had been led to believe that there was some connection between the Peace Corps and the CIA. From what she said I saw no evidence at all to support that view. She was charming, sincere and realistic. At night there is a live band to entertain the group, but I decided to retire to the tranquility of my room.

***

While there was no electricity in my room this morning, and the battery on the laptop was going flat, I decided to take another walk, this time through a small village and to the top (well, almost the top) of the nearest peak. It was very demanding, and I remembered your great effort at climbing Uluru.

The village was the sort that might appear in any serious travel program or newsletter on African poverty. It had mud huts with grass roofs, no electricity, possibly a water tap down the hillside. Cooking is performed in simple aluminium pans over a wood fire. There are kids everywhere, with runny noses such a part of their life that they do not even notice. Their clothes, their rags, make the place look like a Hollywood set for Charles Dickens. Urchins is a word that comes too easily to mind. They ask for biscuits or money, but without enthusiasm. Maybe Warren is right after all about "Third World toilets". I guess I look for knowledge and experiences when I travel, not necessarily pleasure all the time.

It is my last morning before heading off to the lake. I am full of cold, and feeling miserable. At least the telephone service has been reconnected, and this morning there was hot water and electricity.

***

Club Makokola – Lake Malawi, August 1999

Yesterday was not really a good day. I was as sick as a dog (do dogs get sicker than humans, I wonder?). I arrived here after a three-hour drive, and slept most of the afternoon. The one bright spot was that Silvester was the driver. He is such a bright young man, a real pleasure to be with. There is hardly any traffic in Malawi. Given that the Nissan Patrol we were driving costs $US90 000 plus and the wage of someone working as a waiter in the hotel is $20 a month, this is not altogether surprising. I asked Silvester whether the clothes people wear are made in Malawi or imported. He said that they are all second-hand clothes donated by other countries – not exactly the answer I was expecting.

We passed through rural areas. Closer to the lake there are more Muslims. Apparently they came as traders across the lake. Each village has a modern mosque, certainly built by money from the Gulf States. Some of the men are dressed now in long, pristine white robes and the pillbox beret typical of the faith. Everywhere in Malawi there are missions and overseas-funded projects, most of them sponsored by religious organisations of some sort. I can see where Silvester is coming from when he says that he cannot imagine what Africa would become without religion.

Closer to the lake the houses tend to be of deep red bricks with a thatch roof, small and square, made up of just one bare room. I asked Silvester if the roofs leak. He says, "Yes. The roofs have to be remade every year. But all these houses are temporary in nature."

Education is now provided by the government free of charge for children from 6 to 14. But secondary school is expensive and not many families can afford it. Hopefully literacy might be on the way up.

Security here is a problem. He says that the car thieves are well organised and almost certainly come from outside Malawi. They will mark and stalk a car they are interested in. He says that if he ever has to spend the night in Blantyre and he has the company Nissan Patrol with him, even though it has an alarm, he worries about where to leave it to be safe.

The lake is serene, with mountains in the distance and a pleasant, but I assume artificial, sandy beach. It is at last warm here. I note that even though many say that the lake here is free of bilharzia, the water borne snail that enters your skin and makes you very sick, no-one gets into it! There is a reasonable-looking pool that I might try out later.

The other event of note last night was the Supermodel Zimbabwe competition. This is the lead-up to the finals in Vic Falls in October. I saw these models around the club yesterday. Both women and men just gorgeous, as indeed one might expect. The whole event was filmed for international television (Zimbabwe and Malawi??). They modelled clothes designed by two Zimbabwean designers, Debbie and some guy who looked like a freaky dwarf; he had long ringlets and was dressed like a bag lady. Both are white. The clothes were tremendous. There were seven themes, each one distinctive and attractive. The astonishing thing is that the guy looked such a dag and produced these amazing clothes for others. I could impute some deep psychological process here to do with his lack of self-worth, causing him to express his talents totally outwards and project them on to others more beautiful than he is. But I won't.

I have never been interested in fashion modelling, I confess. But this was an original and vibrant show. There were 18 models, all from Zim, 12 women and 6 men. Over half of the women were white (compared to their representation in the total population of 0.75%), whereas with the boys, four were African, one white and one Indian (he is an absolute drop-dead beauty, but I suspect that he knows it).

It was quite an African event really. It started an hour late – just as well the TV was not live – and then the power went off in the middle and they had to call for a 10-minute break! There was a raffle, one prize being won by a black guy from Manchester! He had this really heavy, North-Country English accent, and was as thick as two short planks.

Two of the female models were very young, 15 and 16. Terrifying! They were mature, sensuous experts at tantalisation and comportment – provocative, even raunchy. Imagine as a parent having to manage that! I find it hard enough to parent Stumpy (who by the way is never far from my thoughts. I miss him putting his little paws over my arms and coming up and nuzzling me).

You might consider investing in a book I am reading called *Made in America* by Bill Bryson. It is instructive, entertaining and a must for anyone interested in language or the history of language. He has utterly quelling things to say about the early American historians and how they ascribed sayings to people who never said them – Patrick Henry, for example. He dismisses Thomas Paine with a deft thrust of a sharp word, and claims that the early history of the American Revolution as it is taught in schools across the USA is just fantasy! The Boston Massacre was no such thing. Maybe you have already read it? Comments please! Interestingly he refers to one of your words, "varmint", which was a spelling of the word "vermin" that occurred simply as a result of the way that word was pronounced in those days.

I have been laying low trying to get over my cold and to prepare myself for a rugged week of work ahead. In places such as this, where there is really not much to see or for that matter to do, the entertainment comes from the people one meets and the conversations one has. For example, I had a long chat with the dwarf I referred to earlier, who looks just as freaky up close as at a distance. He is certainly Jewish (and the other designer, Debbie Katz??) and possibly gay too. He has been designated fashion designer of the year of Zimbabwe for the last 10 years. He was telling me that he had received interest for his clothes from the USA, but that there was no capability in Zim to make a reliable and repeatable quality, or meet deadlines.

The producer of Supermodel Zim is a worn lady with a cigarette growl, a keenness to have the first drink of the day, heaps of energy and really good fun (Warren would have liked her). She was accompanied by her husband who works in advertising. They all were quick to tell me that Zimbabwe is utterly wrecked. The exchange rate of four years ago of Z$10 to the US$ has fallen to 40, and is expected to plunge to 80 within weeks. They say that everything they have worked for is worthless, and they are stuck. No way out. Her husband is bitter and angry and annoyed with himself that he did not take the chance to get out in 1980 when he had it.

Security is getting worse, and even though they have lived there for generations, they are considered as foreigners and are not allowed to keep the land they own. Everyone from Zim says the same; Mugabe has absolutely no support from any section of the public, it would seem. He never takes his own private plane (I read this in The Economist), but rather just turns up unexpectedly for a regular flight. He never announces any appointments, and is rarely seen in public. This way he is more likely to escape the assassin's bullet. He has turned what at independence (or at least the start of the civil war between the whites and the blacks after the whites declared UDI, Unilateral Declaration of Independence, from the UK) was a well run and prosperous country into another African basket case.

A pleasant couple are farming in Zambia. He is from Zim and she from South Africa. Their contract is expiring and they do not know what to do. They love Africa and farming, but want children, and fear for the future. She says that she is totally unrealistic, does not listen to the news, and prefers to think everything will turn out alright in the end. He knows the score but hangs on in hope. I suggested that their lifestyle is repeatable in countries like Australia and New Zealand, and they should consider moving now while they are still young. Then there is the problem of being separated from and worrying about parents who stay behind. In some ways it is like a Jonestown scenario. They are good, genuine people, and I feel terribly for the plight they are in through no fault of their own. In fact one of the disasters of Zim is that the government forcibly acquired the largest farms, which produced most of the country's foreign income, and then split them up and gave them to their cronies, who of course were not even farmers. Foreign income plummeted.

And so the Supermodel affair is even more important than a fashion show would normally be: proof of an ability to do something of quality. Last night was the second and last night. It started an hour late again. The marketing manager from Air Zimbabwe got to his feet again, demonstrating for a man in his position an extraordinary lack of both English and intelligence. He very unwisely referred to the Federation of Rhodesia and Nyassaland, and announced that now all servicing of Air Zim planes is done in Harare. He was naïve enough to think this would be a selling point!

The clothes were tremendous, the bodies admirable, and altogether it was a very pleasant way to spend an evening. All 37 of the group left this morning at five, and the club seems deserted. Today is overcast, a surly sky threatening storm, but Zane from Zambia tells me that it will not rain, the season is not right. I keep thinking I hear rain, but it is the wind in the leaves that always confuses me in the tropics.

Snatches of conversation from other tables fascinate. "So if 80% of people arrested for crimes get off, why wouldn't you?" "There have been a few assassinations in Harare recently in car-jackings". "They just say they died from malaria rather than AIDS, it is easier". "My sister works as a teacher here, and they asked me to bring lots of antibiotics from Ireland for the hospital. They do not have enough". "Africa is a lost cause". It is always negative, invariably depressing.

My houseboy Billy has been irksome. To start with the lock on my cottage is so worn that this morning I could not get out. There I am bleating for help through the flyscreen on the louvered windows, a forlorn little voice wafting across the gardens. Billy has introduced himself to me several times, and asks when I am leaving. He mentions that he has brought me water, towels, a locksmith, and so on. I gave him 50 *kwacha* to shut him up, for this is of course what he wanted all along. One is always caught between the knowledge of how poor they are, the need to not upset the current balance too much, the fact that at least he has a job, and the annoyance of being asked for money, several times! I felt 30 *kwacha* would have been a better balance point, but he got lucky because K50 was the smallest note I had. There are 43 to the US dollar.

He asked where I was from, and then how he could get to Australia. He was somewhat crestfallen when I told him, at his request, how much the airfare would be. It is after all at least four years salary! I felt it wise not to mention the Business Class option.

Tomorrow I leave. Silvester is not able to take me, so Isaac will drive the Nissan over the "bad road", which is about 150 kilometres (100 miles) shorter. I am ready for Durban. Wow! It is raining. Light and gentle, the rain is sprinkling on the leaves, comforting and refreshing. If it were not dusk, when the malarial mozzies sneak out, I would probably go and stand in it.

I think I am done with Africa, for a while at least. I have been here 23 or 24 times over the last eight years. Twenty-one African countries is a fair go. It is time to focus somewhere else. Or just enjoy the house. And snuggle up to my Stumpy!

j

Chapter 24 Stopping work

As the 1990s drew to a close I continued to fail on regime after regime of medication. Or maybe I should say that the regimes failed me. It was so frustrating to see everyone else responding so well while my counts just slowly kept getting worse. Whenever new drugs came along, often on a trial basis, my medication was changed in the hope that something would work better. But it didn't.

In July 2000 my HIV specialist told me that in order to try to give the drugs the best chance of working for as long as possible, I should stop work. My counts were dangerously low and he felt that the pressure of working and having deadlines to meet and seminars to conduct was causing my health to deteriorate. I had been running my sales and marketing training and consultancy business since 1989, and I was tired and also felt that the time had come to stop. I was not even sad about it. For most of the time I operated the business I had enjoyed what I did tremendously. It was varied because the client base covered all sorts of industries and included some of the largest and most successful companies in the world. I enjoyed the fact that I knew my subject area well, had a wealth of experience, and was recognised as an expert in my field. I liked the travel all over Australia and the world. But now I no longer had the same enthusiasm and passion for my work as before, and that certainly is the time to stop and take stock. I agreed to take the advice of my doctor and stopped work that month.

I have never been ambitious towards money, but my work has paid well enough for me to have never wanted from a financial point of view. I would be comfortable rather than wealthy and could manage without generating income. While my working days were over, I did not want to just sit in a rocking chair and watch the world go by in the hope that my T cells might recover. I think in fact they would have deteriorated more if I had done that. Rather, I felt that the time had come to try and give back some of my good fortune to those less fortunate than me. And with my background and experience I wanted that to be outside Australia, in the less developed countries. I looked around for opportunities to get involved in some volunteer work that would meet my needs.

Friends of ours were members of a medium-sized Australian NGO (non-governmental organisation) that was established nearly 40 years ago, and does development work in some of the poorest countries of the world. It is called AFAP (The Australian Foundation for Peoples of Asia and the Pacific). Through them I became involved, and one thing led to another and I was suddenly Chair of the Board. The agency does work such as food security, water sanitation, eco-agriculture and environmental programs, and disaster relief. But the jewel in the crown is the dengue fever reduction program that was pioneered in Vietnam and Cambodia. It is an approach that does not involve spraying of chemicals and is thus far more environmentally friendly. We work through partners on the ground in most of the countries where we operate with the exception of Vietnam where we have our own office. The countries where we have concentrated to date have been the Pacific, Sub-Saharan Africa, PNG, East Timor, Nepal and Sri Lanka, as well as our large programs in Vietnam. The organisation has expanded considerably over the last few years largely as a result of the very talented and committed staff. I have been very keen for the agency to develop more programs in HIV and the staff and Board wee very much in agreement. Obviously I am very much involved in that. While there is always plenty to think about and do and I love my involvement, the fact is that I devote more of my time to the two other organisations I am involved with.

APN+ (Asia Pacific Network of People Living with HIV) is the regional peak body that represents the interests and advocates for the needs of the HIV+ (the "positive") community in Asia and the Pacific. Its membership is all the HIV+ organisations and groups that represent PLHIV (People Living with HIV) in 30 countries of the region. When I was involved with the international work that the Australian positive organisation (NAPWA) undertook for a few years I served my full term of four years as the Australian representative to APN+. Since then I have been an Advisor to APN+. For the last three years together with two other Australian positive colleagues I have been implementing a capacity development program for APN+ funded by the Australian government's overseas aid program (AusAID). Apart from that I do what I can to help in terms of governance and institutional strengthening, running training sessions, developing proposals for funding, mentoring, whatever! I work with amazing other positive people from all over the region, each with their own stories and challenges they have had to face. Most of them are far younger than me of course and refer to me (I trust affectionately) as papa John.

The other organisation has as its goal access to treatment for PLHIV who need it wherever they live. This is very close to my heart as I know that without treatment I would have died years ago. I believe that it is quite reasonable to spend the extra time I have as a result of that treatment trying to ensure that others less fortunate than me have the same access. The organisation is called the International Treatment Preparedness Coalition (ITPC) and it operates all over the globe. It works at the global level on advocacy issues and at the grass roots level with small community groups all over the world. My personal interest is in those issues that affect access such as drug pricing, patents and generics, availability of good rather than cheap regimes. The cheapest regimes can in the long term be less cost effective because of their tendency to cause resistance and the need to go to more expensive regimes, and because of side effects. It is a hard battle. I am currently on the Board of ITPC and again do what I can in the areas of governance, institutional strengthening and advocacy.

I often speak at meetings and conferences and provide whatever assistance I can to work towards a better life for positive people wherever they might live, but specifically in the Asia-Pacific region, the main focus of the work. The decisions about treatment are generally made at a country level by the government. It is important to ensure that the PLHIV organisations have the skills and knowledge to lobby the people who make decisions that affect their lives. This requires working with the PLHIV and their organisations operating at the country level, and so that is where much of the work is done. That has led to my undertaking nine or ten trips overseas every year for the last few years. I intend to continue doing it for as long as I can.

I feel passionate about this voluntary work I do and am totally committed to it. This has been an extraordinary change after being in private enterprise for so many years. It took me two years to learn most of the acronyms without which you can hardly understand a conversation. At times it is frustrating the way things are done. For profit organisations run more efficiently and it is easier to get things done. But the people I work with nowadays are like my family, and that was never the case before.

At this stage of my life, I have nothing to lose by speaking my mind on issues surrounding HIV. I am of course very open in public forums about my HIV status, as my positions dictate. I stand up at meetings and conferences, both in Australia and overseas, and say what needs to be said about access to treatment for positive people, stigma and discrimination, and what is called GIPA. GIPA is the greater involvement of positive people in all aspects of the response to the HIV epidemic including policy-making, strategy development, implementation and evaluation. It has been shown time and time again that is an essential part of all successful interventions to address HIV.

I have adapted my basic skill set to other areas, and I would find it very hard now to go back to where I was ten years ago. I love what I do, I get enormous satisfaction from it, and I will keep doing it as long as my health and energy levels allow me. The fact is that the situation in HIV outside Australia and the developed countries has improved in some areas and some senses but not in others. Although there are more people on treatment now than ever before it still represents worldwide only a third of those who are estimated to need it. The regimes most people are on are not good. Furthermore the need for treatment will continue to rise dramatically as more people are infected and tested, and those who are taking treatment are living much longer and will continue to need it. Just at the same time as the need increases the funding for it is slowing instead of increasing. The reasons for this are complex and justify a book in its own right. There is so much that needs to be done, and sometimes one feels that the fight is almost hopeless. In the end I have to believe that there is a chance that humanity will come to its senses and do what is necessary to address this epidemic. We have the technology, we have the resources, but what is lacking is the political will of those who have the power to act.

When you have HIV yourself and you have been lucky enough to live as long as I have so far, then it is not surprising to feel that you want to do what you can to avoid other people going through the same torment, recognising that the agony and misery most people suffer from HIV and AIDS in the developing world is far, far worse than anything I have ever had to suffer.

ooOOoo

By coincidence, as I was writing this section of the book and thinking about dreams I had the most disturbing and bizarre dream of Charles I have ever had. I had fallen into a deep but restless sleep after a horror flight on the non-stop service to Johannesburg from Sydney. The first part of the dream is a classic example of misfiling of previous waking experience. A few days before this dream I had received a text message on my mobile phone. In fact there were three, and they all were of strange characters, not letters, and of course totally unintelligible. The number of the phone from which they had been sent was at the top of the message and so I had called to say that I had received a strange message and would they call me on the landline. The person did in a couple of days. It hardly cleared up the mystery as he was after a house guest who had been staying with me, and claimed never to have called my mobile at all, just the landline. That mystery can remain such as it is, only marginally connected with the dream I want to talk about.

In the dream my mobile phone indicated that I had received a message and there was a number but no message. I called the number having no idea at all who it would be. To my astonishment Charles answered. This was a great surprise to me as he was in Geneva (another misfile as I was contemplating calling a few days earlier a contact in Geneva about a problem connected with UNHCR and a manager in Hanoi who worked for the NGO where I am Chair of the Board.)

But Charles was in Geneva and he answered the phone. I recognised his voice immediately of course and I said his name. He of course also recognised my voice but at first denied that it was him. I insisted and after a few moments he "came clean" that it was indeed him, and we spoke together, in French. It was unusual for us to speak French when just the two of us were alone, although we had when it was dictated by being in the company of people who did not speak good English. In this case I recalled and recognised his words in French rather than just my own.

It was obvious from some other conversations in the background that he was in the middle of conducting some business. He spoke very sharply to me. He was angry that I called him. I tried to placate him, but we argued. I asked him why he was angry with me. He said it was exactly because of calls like this.

I was so taken aback that I couldn't even ask him how he was. I was just getting ready to recompose myself and ask him about his health when the phone went dead. I thought of sending him a text message to avoid any conflict, but then realised that the phone I had called him on was a landline, not a mobile and so I couldn't. So I called back after a few moments. This time he answered in English by simply saying "hold on", and then continued with a conversation he was having with someone else about business. The business was some kind of not-very-legal lurk, and it involved some Chinese guy. I noted that his accent in English seemed more pronounced than it had been. While I was waiting, I planned what I was going to say. I wanted to explain how it had happened that his phone number had appeared on my mobile and that was how I had called him in all innocence, and not to harass him. I wanted to ask him if he had a lover; I both wanted to know and at the same time I didn't. I realised that I was not going to be able to ask that question.

And then suddenly I was awake, and I was in Johannesburg and slowly it dawned on me that there was no phone call, and that he was still mine, just as always. I was relieved.

Chapter 25 Tales of a summer in Europe

Europe August 2002

Hi everyone!

I have made numerous attempts to get a generic email out since I left home over a week ago. I might finally make it with this letter.

I started in Singapore with a schedule that was crazy. I met with several HIV groups, and that was in fact very interesting. Whatever any of you might think about how nice Singapore is because it is clean and tidy and it is illegal to fart, just be aware that their policy is that treatment of HIV-positive people is not a priority; the view is that they ought not to have caught it in the first place. So, there has up to date been no government-subsidised medication. On the one hand the government berates NGOs in the sector for not doing more to educate men who have sex with men, and at the same time refuses to consider decriminalising such behaviour. The NGOs protest that they cannot work in an area that is illegal. A suggestion that all Singaporeans returning from overseas should be tested for HIV raises amazing questions of logistics let alone the ethics (not in the official lexicon) or whether it might be in any way useful.

I stayed in the new Fullerton, which in a previous life was the GPO. In those days the decor was less luxurious, but I suspect the service was better. Today there are thick pile carpets, chandeliers hanging everywhere, and marble lavatories, and the rooms have bathrooms with mirrors that give a perspective of yourself that you had never imagined and certainly did not want to be confronted with. Often hundreds of these images stretch into infinity in a terrifying sequence of horror.

I had to do severe battle with the Fullerton, despite it being the new Singapore darling of hotels (the PM tends to dine there). A power failure for hours meant they could not find me a room when I arrived. When they did find one there was a gap between the windows that let in all the din of buses, taxis and scooters screaming past the window on an elevated road. Once in the new room they moved me to, they advised me they had lost my credit card details and demanded that I check in again to process the credit card. Then they charged me a fortune for several items from the mini-bar that I had not used. On the last day they offered to extend my room checkout time for free because they took a meeting room we had been using away from us early because they wanted it, and then they tried to charge me for the extension anyway. In the end I went to the airport several hours early as I felt I would be more welcome there.

And indeed I was. The next time I might stay a week in the Singapore Airlines departure lounge. It has a constantly available and wide variety of food and drinks, internet connections that work, and a lounge with massage chairs for a sleep. It compensated for the mongrel of a time — the flight was due to leave for Johannesburg at 1.20 am.

From the minute I checked in I knew that this was going to be another Jo'burg experience from which I would itch to flee. As I walked through customs at Jo'burg I asked myself, are these guys the customs officers? They look like the same people I had previously seen in Sandton Mall cleaning shoes. Same uniforms too. In fact they are the same people … The tall one chewing gum says, "Hellu, Baba". I winced. He must have thought I was in arthritic pain and let me go. I am told that this was simply a sign of respect and recognition of experience and maturity. Yeah, right!

Japan, which I adore and where I was recently, is tidy, safe, clean, egalitarian, exquisitely tasteful and wonderfully subtle, but expensive. South Africa is exactly the opposite. For example, I had been booked into the Montecasino in Fourways, north of Jo'burg and in a low-risk murder and mugger belt. It is so far away from anywhere that nobody would want to go there, including the crims. It carries the name Intercontinental. But in South African style, the hotel business centre shuts at seven in the evening just when everyone wants it, and is closed Saturday afternoon and Sunday. The attendant is often not there anyway and the centre is closed during her long and mysterious absences. When she is there she conducts long and urgent business on the phone in Xhosa. Furthermore the computer is ancient. The lack of speed ensures a high revenue as the charge per 15-minute block is the highest I have ever come across.

The hotel is built in a pseudo Italian style, and it is next to the Montecasino Tuscan village. The village dates as far back as early 1999. It has narrow twisting streets with cafés, restaurants and boutique shops, devoid of customers, offering but not selling trendy international clothes and accessories. The synthetic ceiling is a pale Mediterranean blue except where the casino is, where it is a more appropriate night sky with millions of stars. It has the charm of a plastic-moulded washing-up bowl.

But it is safe. Guards on every door use modern technology to frisk every visitor. Guns may be placed in the strange oxymoron of a place called "gun safe". It is important to be able to recognise the metal guns. Outside on the tables in front of the "Village" are all sorts of plastic ones. There are life-size ones for lighting cigarettes, toys for little boys and girls so that when they grow up they will not be spooked when they have to play with a real one. Of course on the far table a nice, motherly Afrikaans lady is selling gorgeous replicas of AK47s.

I went to see many of the contacts I normally see in Jo'burg. They are predictably the same, wringing their hands about how awful things are. Business is hard, they cannot see any future, but they are far too depressed to do anything about it. Thank heavens at least that the close friends I have there are more cheerful. I did the drop of the drug run I operate when I can, whereby we take ARVs (anti-retrovirals for HIV treatment) "surplus to requirements" to contacts who make sure they are put to good use in South Africa. We had a chat about the constant battle against the South African government to get acccss to affordable treatment for all South Africans. This has been an amazing cooperation between lawyers and activists brave enough to take the government to court. At least in South Africa it is still possible to do that.

Wednesday I hired a car. It is better to choose a reputable company just to be on the safe side in places like this. You don't want to break down in Jo'burg, so I thought that I would be alright with Avis. The man who brought the modest but neat-looking South African—made Golf to the hotel gave me the keys and left quickly. Just enough time to give me instructions on how to get onto the N1. I know Jo'burg well enough to be suspicious of his advice. In fact he told completely the wrong direction. I started the engine. It was firing on three cylinders. I was headed downtown into a "you really shouldn't go there" area. Just my luck, I thought, for the wretched beast to expire leaving me a sitting mugger's and execution target in some forlorn road. But it kept going; I even managed to get up to Pretoria to see the Australian High Commission (where the AusAID office is located), which was astonishing in its efficiency in comparison to the rest of South Africa.

I zoomed down the back way to the airport (R21 for those who know), only being hooted and almost forced off the road a couple of times because I was exceeding the speed limit by only 10 kilometres per hour, not anywhere near fast enough. But then there is always the risk of being squashed between a BMW driven by a blonde-haired young woman with attitude, streaking like a bullet in the fast lane, and a black taxi belching out a blue-and-black fog of diesel, crawling along in the slow lane overloaded with people such that it seems like another attempt is being made on the Guinness Book of Records.

I arrived at the Avis counter to settle up the hire charge. The pleasant young man smiled sweetly as he ripped me off blind. When I yelped at the final bill, he looked a little hurt. The first thing I noticed was that he had manufactured 25 kilometres I had not driven. There were a few muttered apologies and when he reworked the bill, the total came to only about two-thirds what it had been a few moments earlier. I told him that the car was a heap of shit. He looked most taken aback saying that it was brand new. It had, he pointed out, only 1760 kilometres on the odometer. I told him I noticed that and assumed that it was on its second time around.

I relaxed into the buzzy atmosphere of the Virgin Atlantic Business (they call it Upper) Class lounge, and heaved a sigh of relief. I had managed to get out of Jo'burg a day early!

The desperation of Africa slipped quietly below the menu of kingclip, steak, soups, salads, baguettes, sandwiches, cheese platters, ice-creams and fruit plates from which you could choose. The ingenious seats lower into an almost flat bed. You can either change into a sleep suit, or cuddle up in the duvet, and wait for dawn over Sardinia.

Heathrow's Terminal 3 looks forlorn at any time of day, but possibly is at its best at half past six in the morning. It has presumably been left as it is, so as not to vulgarly thrust the wealth of Britain into the face of passengers arriving from all manner of Third World countries. It succeeds. The carpet must boast the greatest concentration of international bacteria in the world. It ought to be an UNESCO heritage site, perhaps to be donated for microbiological research.

And so I am back in some sort of civilisation ...

Time to attend to washing and a little shopping expedition – CDs and books are what I like to buy in London.

Watch this space.

***

The sharp wind rustles the leaves, the gusts causing the few brave people in the street to narrow their eyes against needles of rain. Umbrellas turn inside out, the pavements are awash, paper litter is sodden into the ground. The cold strikes deep into the flesh. Inside thermostats awake, and central heating comes to life. Summer has arrived in London.

I cannot fathom the British economy. The powerhouse darling of the pink pages of the Financial Times is nowhere to be seen in the streets. Everyone will tell you that manufacturing has had its day. The oil and gas money was squandered years ago by that Thatcher woman, and the cash inflow is more of a dribble. The offices of the IT estates are empty; the yuppies have lost their jobs and have evaporated into thin air, leaving behind static nylon carpets, glass partitions and blank screens at workstations.

Has it become a service economy? Londoners will swear that there is none, and all the evidence supports their view. What about finance? Ah, there are a few executives in the city earning phenomenal salaries, or being paid them even if they do not earn them. But nobody is sure if they actually produce anything.

And yet, there is money. Housing is booming, restaurants are full, rents are cruel. A round of drinks in the pub will cost twice what it does in Sydney, and the pub lunch has deteriorated into a microwaved restoration of a prefabricated portion that has been transported frozen from a factory in Essex. Transport is far more expensive than in Japan, and of a quality more reminiscent of a Third World country. Even the underground in Tashkent is looking good in comparison.

The UK petulantly stamps its feet at the water's edge in Dover looking at Euroworld in the distance. It has never really believed in "Europe", and I get the impression that it has overinvested in its relationships – political, cultural and trade –with the USA over many years, at the same time pretending to a large degree that Europe did not really exist. The battle against the adoption of the euro is being mounted in England as I speak.

But the British stoically put up with anything, just as they did in the Blitz. It is in their genes (except that the British are now several shades of colour darker). For example, the Tube! I cannot recollect the figure of how much has been thrown down what is probably the longest drain in the world, the Northern Line. Seventy-five million pounds was it? Or 750 million? Well, whatever it was it has disappeared. The only sign of the expenditure is that they are now able to make announcements about all the disasters so that passengers are better informed. "Due to a signal failure services on the Northern Line have been interrupted." "There will be no service due to urgently required maintenance between Morden and Kennington. Tickets will be honoured on the bus." "Please note that the next train will NOT be going via Charing Cross after all. And neither will the next one, or the one after that." "This is the driver. Sorry about being stuck in this tunnel. I do not know why we are stuck. It seems that there is a problem getting into Stockwell." "Due to reduced services on the Piccadilly Line passengers should take other alternatives as necessary."

Sometimes they do not make announcements and just wait to see if you notice that the train arriving at the platform is not going to where the sign says it is. And then there is the game they have played for years at stations like Camden Town and Kennington, where the next train is going first from Platform 3 and then from Platform 4, and then again from Platform 3. This provides exercise for the passengers as they clamber up and down the stairs linking the two platforms, and at the same time it seems to make the long wait time go quicker.

The trains are disgusting – full of litter, newspapers, empty bottles and cans, half-eaten sandwiches (seems that the taste of Poms does after all have some limits), wrappers. I wondered whether there was a possibility of suing London Transport for damage to hearing from the screaming of the rails that happens on the Victoria Line between Stockwell and Vauxhall. But as many of the passengers are in a catatonic state, with earphones connected to their CD players at top volume, jammed into their ears, chewing gum and staring into space, I doubt whether a case could be brought.

Most people feel that the great advantage of London is that it has excellent connections to everywhere else, in the same way that a prison is a good place to escape from. And escape they do. Colin has his house in France, and so does John. Fred and Marianne have their place in Sarasota. Others have already left altogether. Some have retreated to the country. Plans are afoot for others to flee as far as Australia. At least it will leave a little more room for the people arriving on foot through the Channel Tunnel. Good luck to them.

***

Travel in reality often does not measure up to the expectation. At least Holland was pleasant enough despite the cold and the rain. One wonders whether they invented the word bourgeois. Everything is so nice. Nice buses and trains, nice department stores serving nice open sandwiches. Even the charter flight to Barcelona was nice.

Barcelona was as attractive as ever, a compact, well-laid-out city full of charm. And hundreds of tourists. The memory plays tricks but in the end I did manage to locate most of the old restaurants I used to frequent all those years ago! Las Ramblas is still wonderful with its flowers and cafés. But it is also full now of those tedious living statues and pickpockets. The locals are very easy on the eye, which makes for a pleasant stroll down the avenue. The old quarter has some superb boutiques that did not exist before, but otherwise not much has changed.

I guess you may have heard something about the International AIDS Conference . It was very badly organised in a conference centre that is well past its use by date. The Community Forum (for positive people only) seemed to me as if it had been organised the previous day over coffee. The PLWHA (People Living with HIV and AIDS) lounge was a disgrace, located in what looked like a storage area, with food that was cheap but totally unsuitable for people living with HIV. The opening ceremony was full of long speeches of self-congratulation and was very poor compared to the opening of ICAAP in Melbourne. It was not in the least inspirational.

My skills-building session was a great success, said with due modesty! I met most of the people I wanted to from all sorts of countries. But not much was achieved. The truth is that the rich world does not have a serious problem with HIV and therefore does not see it as a priority. The poor world has a terrible problem and one that gets worse every day, but they have no money or resources to do much about it. The people who could have made a difference studiously ignored the whole conference. Yes, there has been a little progress, but in relation to a problem that has got much worse, and the overall situation has deteriorated considerably. The war on terror and winning elections, which means subsidies and appealing to the electorate's xenophobia and lack of charity and compassion, mean, I fear, that nothing will change. You all know that only a quarter of the Global Fund promises have been delivered.

Brazil and Thailand are the shining examples of countries that have made progress. That's despite everything the USA could do to protect the shareholders in its pharmaceutical industry. The US administration has so much to answer for. In the closing ceremony Maire Bopp du Pont from the Cook Islands actually got Clinton, with whom she shared the podium, to partially accept her criticisms of the USA by silent assent and finally by clapping his hands. Pity he no longer has power.

So, flat and dejected I left to Vitoria to see Carmen after 14 years. It was not a good few days, and I was desperate to escape.

Funny the people you meet. A strange woman got on the train in San Sebastian. She was pushing a pram with a dog in it She came up to me and started to speak excellent but accented English She said she was born in Uruguay and brought up in the USA, and now lived on the French side of the border close by. She was dirty with old clothes and shoes, her jumper in holes She had beautiful grey eyes that had dulled over the years She told me she was a Swedish citizen and out of a dirty pouch produced a crumpled passport that suggested she was indeed a Swedish citizen The only thing that I thought strange was that it was all in black and white like a photocopy. She told me she had been bitten by a snake in the USA and showed me an awful wound on her arm Then she asked me for a euro for a coffee. I gave her two. She confided that she had been married to an Arab but that he was no good. She laughed and added that he only liked to give it up the arse, and shrugged her shoulders fatalistically. She showed me how to get to the El Topo to cross on the rail to France. You know something? I really liked her.

And now I am in France with all sorts of other problems. Like the fact that I could not find a hotel in La Rochelle last night. What a misery, but I have found one this morning, and still have to decide what to do and where to go next.

You see it is not always the fun that you hope and expect it to be.

Have you ever wondered how it is that a leaf knows when to stop growing? There comes a time when the organism "decides" that it is big enough and all the cells stop reproducing. How and when does it decide? Well, that is the thought for the day.

***

Meanwhile, France.

If I were faced with doing an Elba, and had to be exiled from the country where I choose and love to live, there is no doubt in my mind that the best alternative would be France. It is the quintessentially European country. It has an abundance of physical beauty and variety, from the wild Atlantic coast to balmy Mediterranean beaches with rich colours and bougainvillea hedgerows growing against whitewash walls. It has the highest snow-capped peaks in Europe, grand lakes, verdant rolling countryside, wide lazy rivers, vast solitary forests, and areas of craggy rocks with ancient villages perched on top. It has soaring cathedral spires, old castles full of turrets, sprawling palaces. It has sleepy villages whose timeless houses sit comfortably in the heat of the afternoon. A deserted lane leads around a corner from abundant fields and intoxicating growth of the summer season, past neatly trimmed grass edges into the village. The long shutters are firmly closed against the heat of the afternoon and the inhabitants are nowhere to be seen, apart from the odd dog that wanders aimlessly into the street from a dusty yard and flops down panting in the shade of the plane trees. In France more than in any other European country, there is an accommodation between the new and the traditional. Rural France is timeless, undisturbed on the outside, but behind those closed shutters there are all the interior niceties of modern living. The French have never been ostentatious about their comfort and wealth, for to do so might invite the need to pay more taxes. There are plenty of old broken-down barns with a Mercedes inside.

And then there is Paris, surely the most consistently perfect of all cities. You only have to stand on the Arc de Triomphe to see the perfection of Napoleonic planning radiate out and filter away towards the river. There are none of the jarring shoe boxes of 1960s London that agonise that skyline. There is instead a flow of grey slate roofs, shutters and metal balconies, in summer with little window boxes giving colour and life. It is integrated, complete and just right. Then at street level there is a culture of cafés and restaurants, of corner *épiceries* to ensure that the basic necessities of French life are available. Access to a morning baguette is more sacred than access to things like motorways, schools and supermarkets. Yet at the same time France is the most modern of nations with its power grids, fast trains and industry. France has even evolved a modern fashion, integrating new materials to serve its needs, but not in a garish or intrusive way. The trains are plastic inside for the most part, as are the chains of comfortable hotels. But these new polymers have been used in a way that makes them stylish rather than utilitarian. Plastic has evolved from convenience to fashion.

And the French have class. Where other countries may have class distinction, they in fact have no class. What they have is groups based on different types of vulgarity. But in France there is an elegance that has to do with its great past and at the same time its ability to integrate it into its present. And as long as you are prepared to embrace this Frenchness, you are free to become part of it. Racism in France was never based simply on colour as it was for example in England. It was also based on the degree of Frenchness that a person was willing to adopt. There is no doubt in my mind that that is why the French culture of the colonial days in places like Mauritius endured long after the British took charge, and even after a hundred or more years of occupation, the British never managed to leave their mark, other than overturned laws and systems of government.

It is of course more difficult for anglophone countries to arm themselves against Americanisation. France has tried, and perhaps succeeded, better than most countries to repel this hegemony, with the possible exception of Spain.

What I like about France is that it fosters conversations about these issues underpinned by realism and a variety of views, and a passion that explains easily the French Revolution and the fact that the country is already on to the Fifth Republic! Yes, the world owes France more than we give credit.

So it was with pleasure and anticipation that I fled my weekend in Spain with Carmen and headed for La Rochelle. What a most pleasing small port this is with its narrow winding streets, ancient houses, history galore and one of the most imposing ports anywhere.

I took a boat trip to the island of Aix, where there are no cars, and sleepy cottages with the most enormous weeds in front of them, testimony no doubt to the torpor of the local life in summer.

Having considered going further north, I changed my mind at the last minute and headed south again to Narbonne, where Liz, a friend of ours from Australia, has recently installed herself. The area is one of peaceful canals flowing slowly from village to village. I spent three days in a most suitably lazy way, slowly ambling along the canal banks, and sitting outside at cafés and restaurants enjoying the local food and wine. It was extremely hot, and even in the grand old house where I stayed it was uncomfortable trying to sleep.

I them jumped on the TGV to Paris to stay the night with our friends Jacky and Alexandre. Then yesterday I completed the train part of my trip with the Belgian train, the *Thalys* from Paris to Brussels and Amsterdam. Now there is something about the Belgians. They have an amazing knack of looking shabby, and making sure that their transport is the same. The *Thaly*s is like the miserable experience that flying Sabena used to be, before it landed its last. Dowdy, worn, and with staff who were born to put their noses in the air and make sure that you know they wished that you and they were not there. The train was made in 1994; how on earth can it be in such a shocking state? But then, that is Belgium. If I had to live there I would probably be surly and disagreeable too. Beer cheers them up a bit, but not much else.

I arrived in Holland as I had left, in cold wet weather everyone was grumbling about, but that for me was a welcome change. After a quick dash to Scotland I flew back to Birmingham and then took the train to London. The train was a predictable disaster. Nobody at the ticket office knew what time it was due to arrive in London, which I imagine is a way to make sure it is not late. It was supposed to take 2 hours 12 minutes, I eventually discovered. This is a considerable improvement over the 1 hour 30 minutes it used to take in 1965 for a slightly longer journey from Birmingham city to London. This is progress adjusted for inflation. It cost 30 quid.

In fact I was so tired that just before Northampton I fell asleep. During that brief moment of repose I must have slipped through an Alice in Wonderland–like wormhole, because I woke up in Africa. Well, I say I was in Africa, but the train looked much the same: the same garbage all over the floor and seats, those blue dirty uncomfortable seats. But all the passengers were now African. After a while I was able to look into an underground train pacing us on a parallel line, and that was in Africa too. The strange thing is that when I looked at my own skin, I was still the same colour.

So how do I feel as I sit contemplating that diabolical journey home? It is for me an awful feeling the morning that I wake up and realise that the next time I will be in a bed will be on the other side of the world. No-one in their right mind looks forward to that. I just want it to all be over and I am looking forward very much to being in Australia again.

j

ooOoo

When you have lived in various places there seems more of a confusion in your identity of place that at least in my case manifests itself in dreams. I dream that I am in England. I had been living in London and for some reason I do not understand I had moved to Birmingham, the city where I was born and from which I was so grateful to be able to leave. I am torn between living there or in London. I do not want to live there, and I could move back to London if I wanted to. I think that I moved to Birmingham to look after my parents.

And then I suddenly miss where I really want to be, which is my home in Sydney. So I get on a flight home to feel in my own environment, and it is such a relief to be back in Australia. But then I have to get straight back on a plane and fly to London again.

Chapter 26 Manila to the Mekong

Vientiane, April, 2003

Hi everyone!

Thursday was rather stressful. I had kept an eye on the Manila flight through the staff travel website, and knew there would be enough seats on a space-available basis, and so I cancelled all the other full-fare options when the time for ticketing came. When I got to the airport and I was told that the flight was weight-restricted, I felt as if my day was about to go badly wrong. In the end I returned to the counter 40 minutes before the flight was due, and they had weighed the plane again, and decided to let me on.

I relaxed in 3C (best end of the aircraft), and decided to do a little work. I switched on my laptop, which I needed for all the work I was going to do in Laos, only to find that it emitted a distressing beep and did not want to do much more. I switched it off, and then on, and then repeated the procedure. Then I discovered that there was a little button on the side at the back poking out. It must have been pressed during the security check at Sydney airport. I pressed it in, and all the problems were solved. And so I was quite relieved to arrive in Manila relaxed and operational.

Cities change so fast nowadays. But I was getting panicky that there was absolutely nothing I recollected of Manila, no familiar landmark or street corner that jogged the memory. There was a vague recollection of a large open square next to a stretch of exceptionally fetid water, with a few girlie bars. Eventually I came to the conclusion that that had been Manila Bay and the area had been Ermita. But a visit there the next day for a meeting did not bring back any memories at all.

That of course was back in Marcos's days. The NPLA was far more active then. Nowadays the insurgency is almost purely of a militant Islamic nature. Like the bomb last week in the airport in Davao in the south that killed 23 people.

The area where I stayed did not really exist a few years ago. Pasig has grown out of the ground, pushing tinted windows and shopping centres sporting world brands before it. The Philippines has not seen the same growth as Thailand or Malaysia for example, but some money has poured in. This has assisted in the achievement of Manila's ranking of the third most polluted air in the world after Mexico City and Shanghai. Well done!

Ahmet had already arrived a few hours earlier from Hanoi, and we met and had a chat ready for the next day of meetings with the Asian

Development Bank. An Australian writer, Shirley Hazzard, wrote a book many years ago about the UN, based on her experiences of working there. It could as well have been the ADB building. It was constructed in 1994 as a squared figure eight with six floors. Security was tight, although the wooden stick used to probe bags and the personal space of some visitors looked less high-tech than I would have expected. We went to the fourth floor, unaccompanied, which turned out to be against regulations, in search of room 4260. No expense has been spared in the concern for Asia's poor. And to be fully representative of the donor nations, materials and styles from the wealthiest countries have had the most influence. Japanese screens run along every corridor, marble adorns every set of lifts and stairs. It is exceptionally easy on the eye. The trouble is that the whole building looks exactly the same; you could stand anywhere in the building and have no distinguishing reference point. In the foyer in front of the East Core lifts there is one useful distinguishing feature that makes it recognisable. It is a blood pressure monitoring machine.

There are rows and rows of workstations and offices, all of which look identical. The offices are signed with the number and the name of the occupant. We discovered however that if you are in the North Core and ask someone sitting at a workstation casually, "Where is room 3540?", they go all glassy-eyed and look at you bewildered, frightened even. Many people seem to have never been out of their own core. Perhaps they do not know that there are other cores beyond the borders of their own set of Japanese screens.

How odd to move from office to office (we had seven meetings) chatting to people from Stuttgart, Coventry and Baltimore, all trying to imagine that they actually lived in Asia. They leave the filtered air and static electricity of the clean grey carpets, and go home through foul traffic and unsavoury smells to a maid that does everything for them except play tennis.

After the ADB I had a meeting with PAFPI. Now the areas where I work are so full of acronyms that I still have trouble with them myself. Don't worry about what it stands for, suffice it to say that they are a group that works with HIV-positive people in the Philippines and I have been asked to deliver a plenary at their conference in May. Bobby swished through the doors of my hotel to take me on the lengthy trip to Ermita to meet their Board and a few other associates. It was actually not long in distance, just time. We struggled along the painful street known as Edsa, and chatted in the back of the taxi. He recognised me from ICAAP Melbourne 2001. Quite clever really as I am sure we all look the same to them.

The purpose of the meeting was to agree what I would talk about and get an idea of the program and where I would fit in. Seems that I am the opening plenary that will set the scene for the five-day meeting.

He dropped me back in Pasig, then Ahmet and I went out to dinner to chat though some AFAP (the development NGO of which I am Chair of the Board) issues, and I called it a day at just before midnight. And this is retirement?

The new airport at Manila is supposed to be magnificent. It has been completed several months now but will not open until at least later this year. There is a court case going on over non-payment of the contractors (a French/German consortium). So we had to struggle that extra distance to the old one. After the recent bomb attack in Davao they are a bit paranoid over security. There are three security checks before check-in, and then three between passport control and the aircraft. Fortunately Thai Airways are less concerned, so if you have any metal knives removed at any of the checks, you get one with your meal to make up for it.

It is about four years since I went into the centre of Bangkok. The tollway extends right to Sukhumvit nowadays making the journey quite quick. The BTS sky train has been built on an overhead track with about the same charm as the monorail in Sydney. But on the other hand in Bangkok, what did they really have to lose? The city was never of such breathtaking beauty that a cogent argument could have been mounted to stop it.

Robert, my co-worker for Laos, and who lives in the north of NSW, arrived around midnight and the next day we made a shopping excursion to a centre called MBK, accessible easily on the sky train. All Asian cities have these mammoth shopping centres, multistoried, airconditioned and with hundreds of shops, and they are a mecca for both locals and tourists alike.

In fact I prefer to browse the street markets, but even Pisspong (did I get that right?, oh yep, Patpong) is so busy nowadays in the evening that all you can do is shuffle past the stores so slowly that every store owner can be intimate with you before you struggle past to the next trestle of bargains. That evening we had dinner with representatives of the Australian Red Cross and a guy who works for one of the positive groups in Bangkok. We had Lao food, just what we needed to prepare us for a week in Vientiane.

The flight the next morning required a 5.15 wake-up. Retirement?, I hear you ask yet again. Despite the ease with which we managed to get our visas on arrival in what is a brand new and very pleasant airport, no doubt supplied by some wealthy country – I suspect Japan or France – it was late morning when we arrived at our hotel. The P&B hotel is just half a block from the banks of the Mekong, and despite a 40-year-old appearance, I was assured that it was brand new. The delegates had already arrived from Yunnan and XinGiang in China, and from Vietnam, Cambodia, Indonesia and Laos. Quang from Hanoi was coughing rather a lot. We kept our eyes on him until we assured ourselves that he did not have SARS pneumonia!

The hotel was fine for me. I had my insecticide spray so that the gaps around the windows in my room did not matter; it was clean, had an ensuite bathroom, and an airconditioning unit. At US$17 a night, it was a good deal, I thought. The first thing we needed was a kip. In fact for 500 baht we got so many kip we could hardly stuff them in our pockets. There are 10 000 or more kip to the US dollar and the most common note is 2000, or 20 US cents.

The only problem with the hotel was the training room. We had a choice of either the airconditioned one that was very small on the ground floor, or the roof. The roof was open at the sides, and had commanding views over dilapidated houses, backyards of rusting metal and other surplus articles, and in one direction the roof of a temple. It was also hot, light and very noisy. We tried both options, but in the end the 39-degree heat on Tuesday beat us back to the airconditioning. This was requested by the Chinese and Vietnamese, big wusses that they are. We organised a vote from which we both abstained, showing that democracy may appear to be dead, but there are some of us still fighting.

Robert and I discovered Vientiane gently. It is that sort of place. It is like a sprawling village along the banks of the Mekong, so unpretentious that it is utterly unremarkable. No buildings are more than a few storeys high, most old and falling down. The Thai invasion over a hundred years ago ensured that no history would remain. If you peek behind a few palms you might see the vestiges of French colonisation in the form of a shutter sagging at a window. Other than that, the twin curses of Asia – neon lights and plastic everything, placed in many cases on dirt floors – is the rule of the day. The centre of the city is three blocks long; even at an amble it is covered in 7 minutes 23 seconds. Then come the suburbs of twisting laneways between tropical gardens and heaven-knows-what nasties. Dengue and malaria are endemic problems.

We commandeered a Red Cross vehicle for a quick city tour. This included two temples, driving past various government buildings, of which the Cultural Hall was the only one that looked attractive, the golden *stupa* and the Victory Arch. The latter dates right back to 1962. That was it. We tried desperately to give the economy a nudge by a visit one afternoon to the morning market (don't ask!), but frankly it was a challenge.

The official name of the country is the Lao People's Democratic Republic. It is one of the very few communist countries left. But there are few signs of totalitarianism and military control. The streets are full of young men in saffron robes, doing their rounds to receive food, chatting and laughing together. It really should be renamed the Buddhist Socialist State of Lao.

We had dinner one night in one of the more pleasant eating houses (restaurant would have been too pretentious a name) with suspicious items on the menu like "backpacker burger" as well as Lao and Indian fare. After dinner we strolled up the road a block or so to a fountain in a modern nondescript square. We were quickly assailed by two young lads who wanted to know whether we had girlfriends and if not would we like a boyfriend, at least for half an hour or so. Bold as brass!

We thanked them very much for flattering us with their teenage youth, but decided to head home. There had been lightning during the evening, but now a wild dust storm gathered speed, leaving swirls of grit through the main street. Within minutes it was deserted, and we were the only unfortunates struggling against the dust, eyes narrowed, and trying not to trip over the broken side of the road, which could not really be called a footpath. It was like a movie set from a 1950s Hollywood movie. We made it back to the hotel as the rain hit.

The workshop went very well, and we were surprised that the plans we got each country to write about how they would interact with positive groups were quite good. Language was a challenge, and although we had a few people translating, the Lao language's lack of consonants at the end of words provoked some strange misunderstandings. Like the discussion on 'human rice', and how these rights should be protected.

The Lao team asked of the Vietnamese while we were reviewing the plans, "Why you only have sick people?" A good question I thought, as I scanned the plan again trying to find the reference. "We start with more but expect to end up with sick". And how am I to know that "Key?" in fact was supposed to be "May I clean your room now?"

On Friday the meeting finished at lunchtime and Robert and I rose to the challenge of getting rid of several hundred thousand kip. It wasn't easy, but a stone box solved much of the problem. Then we set off to the airport for our Lao Aviation flight to Bangkok. They use European-made ATRs and so it was a far less scary experience than central Asia for example.

The frenetic city of Bangkok was a distinct gear change. Drinks in the hotel foyer, dinner with Greg and Bev over strategy for the APN+ AGM (see what I mean about the acronyms?), a meeting with the Red Cross the next morning, and it was all over.

Saturday night's flight looked bad and so I opted to try for the Sunday night one. When you receive this it means that I will have got on it, and I will send this from my home email address on Monday. At least no more travel until May (apart from Melbourne).

j

Chapter 27 Glimpses of Estonia

Estonia, July, 2004

Hi again!

They are a dour lot, the Estonians. In a circumcision-like rite both sexes appear to have the muscles of the mouth enabling them to smile, severed a few days after birth. On the other hand one might argue that after a thousand years of occupation by the Swedes, the Germans and more recently the Russians, they would not have too much to smile about. None of those is exactly known to be a barrel of fun. The more recent Russian occupation from 1944 to 1991 was the one the Estonians were most keen to see the back of. Even as a Baltic state they clearly stand with their back to Russia and look westward across the Baltic. Surely it is significant that they called themselves Estonia; relative to the world they aspire to be part of, they are on the eastern edge. Had they felt more Russian they might have been Westonia.

Estonia has been quick to embrace their second independence. The first was in only 1918 and lasted until the Germans arrived in 1941. The second was in 1991. They celebrate two independence days. In many ways it is a poor man's Scandinavia. There should be no doubt that this is a Nordic country. When you turn the engine of your car on, the headlights come on automatically, the permitted blood alcohol level is zero. And the people have that Nordic look, a kind of sunkissed skin colour with no blemishes that might have developed through laughter or crying or other not-permitted emotions that could affect the skin, and topped by real blond hair.

On the surface there is hardly a vestige of the former Soviet days. There are none of the really desperate apartment blocks that still exist for example in other former Soviet states, such as Uzbekistan or Tajikistan or mother Russia itself. The suburban sprawl of Tallinn encompasses middle-class, substantial homes with neat gardens. Even in the country the farmhouses look wholesome. Apart from the odd village with tin roofs, no doubt a legacy from the Russian utilitarian days, the country looks comfortable. There is a generous smattering of Hapsburg yellow houses, with a modern car parked in front. The roads are good, well signposted once you get out of the city centre, and the whole country is dotted with bus stops. These are visited at least from time to time by modern green buses painted with flowers. In the city there are even bendy busses, and the only hint of former transport is the odd Soviet style tram. Perhaps the most surprising thing of all in the country are the road signs telling you that there is "Internet in 200 metres". And as for mobile telephones, they are ubiquitous. Mind you, of course, for a country without a strong landline telephone structure you might as well go straight to a mobile network. Nokia is imprinted in mirror image on most Estonian ears.

The European Union has crept in early here. The currency, significantly called the *kroon* and sounding very Nordic, is already pegged to the euro. European cousins down the muddy and rather uninspiring Baltic have helped out where they can. When the bridge from Copenhagen to Malmo was opened, the ferries running from Denmark to Sweden were no longer required and were passed to Estonia to operate from the mainland to islands such as Saarema. Did I travel these same ferries in 1967 when I used to pop over from Halsingborg to Elsingor for dinner and a change of herring? Maybe.

We spent a pleasant few hours on the Saarema Island, with its beautiful sleepy main town of Kuressare, really little more than a village, but boasting its own castle and moat. The island is a popular holiday destination for Estonians who can manage even a short weekend break here quite easily. The beaches are really non-existent, but you can cycle, walk or just hang out in a forest. Estonia is covered with forests, mainly pine as far as we could see, giving rise to the largest single industry, timber. It is hardly surprising given all the other climatic circumstances that Estonia is the home of amber. A tiny piece just two or three centimetres long can run you up to 500 bucks (those with non-AUD currencies should make the conversion of this horrifying sum into their own currencies). It all depends on the clarity of the amber and the rarity of the insect trapped in the original sap. I went for something slightly less clarified and a more pedestrian insect.

I get the impression that insects might play a vital role in the enjoyment of Estonians. I believe that they would have some of their best fun pulling the wings off flies. But look at what they have to put up with. Summer lasts just a few weeks, and you hardly get any sleep during that time until you fall into a stupor around five in the morning as a result of alcohol. The grog shops do a brisk business and are open 24 hours a day. It does not get dark at this time of year. The sun sets for a few hours but the sky is always light. At three in the morning the cheery globe is piercing its rays through the most unsuitable sheer curtains they fit to make sure that you do not miss out on the daylight, because it does not last that long. In the winter the reverse is true. Just a couple of hours of lifting light at lunchtime, and for the rest dark, freezing cold and covered in snow.

Alcohol plays an important role in Nordic society. It is almost like a forbidden fruit, priced in such a way that it cripples you. The change in sensation must be the proof of their sentient being and doubles as the conviction that they must be having fun.

The language does not help. Estonian is basically the same as Finnish, a Finno-Ugric language distantly related to Hungarian. It requires high cheekbones for the vowels to be properly enunciated. When Estonians speak English, their accent usually renders the message they are delivering exceptionally boring with a monotonous droning, interrupted by final staccato of double consonants. For example their word for stop is "stopp" and the double "p" is forced out in a rather aggressive explosion.

We took a city tour of Tallinn comprising an hour in a bus riding around the area surrounding the old town, followed by a walking tour of the old town itself. The guide clearly felt the heavy burden of responsibility to deliver herself of minute details about her country. "One million, three hundred and sixty two thousand inhabitants with 67.9% Estonians, 25.6% Russians, 2.1% Ukranians, 1.2% Belarussians ... In Tallinn there are 370 000 inhabitants, which means that one in every four people from our country are from capital. In our stadium there can sit 300 000 people, which means almost all the population of capital, or also means one in four Estonians. Here is the highest skyscraper in capital and in whole country at 113 metres high [more of a tickle than a scrape, I feel], and opposite the second highest building in our country with 108 metres". The guide pauses to look at the audience to see whether this fact has had the desired effect of education and wonder. Many of them have fallen asleep in the warm bus. What is clear is that a terrorist attack on this type of high-rise would be more effective with a bicycle than a highjacked aircraft.

However, the old town is a jewel, with narrow winding streets and beautifully restored old buildings, many from medieval times. The upper part of the steep town is crowned by the Alexander Nevsky Russian Church and is truly magnificent. Most of the churches are, however, Lutheran, with severe and frightening pagan symbolism in their art, most likely to frighten young children into submission. Pretty stairways lead from one cobbled street to the next until you reach the Town Hall Square with the wonderfully restored medieval town hall faced with limestone. There are cafés where you can sip a beer or a bottle of overpriced Chilean wine, listening to a band from Norway demonstrating solidarity with their Nordic cousins.

Tourists abound: there were three million visitors last year. Mind you they nearly all came from Finland, just 1 hour 40 minutes away on the jetcat from Helsinki. Even at the extortionate prices they charge, the grog is much cheaper here in pseudo Scandinavia than the real place. And the Finns can come here and let their light blond hair down and get pissed much cheaper than at home, and without anyone recognising them, or at least they would be able to were it not for the fact that the rest of Helsinki usually has the same idea.

There are plenty of places to eat. The traditional Estonian restaurant interested me. I started with the curd and cod's liver, and then moved onto the Estonian black pudding with plum sauce and sauerkraut. John, my travelling companion, was disappointed that the wild boar was "finish". We might try again tomorrow. In fact it is in the restaurants that one can see the glimpses of the past. There is absolutely no dedication to service at all. Many of the staff are young and female, and consider themselves exceptionally beautiful, as they stand with a pouting look on their faces, in their tight jeans and clinging tops, revealing more of their cleavage than the weather conditions would indicate is wise. A kind of Estonian Spice Girls look. They can with some effort be cajoled into taking an order, but as a result of a combination of very bad English comprehension and an unwillingness to work, often the order suffers fatal flaws on the way. It often seems that as the transition happens from a Soviet type of economy to a capitalist one, many people think that wealth happens automatically without the intervention of something called "work".

At the other end of the scale, as it were, another pseudo Scandinavian trait is the roughness of their toilet paper. Scandinavians have always enjoyed, yes maybe really enjoyed, scratchy toilet paper. It demonstrates the hardiness of the race compared to their soft neighbours mollycoddled by more temperate climes to the south.

On Sunday we drove to the south and to the east of the country. This time I was intrigued by the old soviet apartment blocks right out in the country miles from anywhere. They are not entirely abandoned today, but in their heyday they housed the people who worked in the rural industries. From time to time old decaying factories appear and disappear, gradually fading back into the landscape from which they emerged in the 1950s and 1960s.

We stopped and had lunch in a small utilitarian town called Viljandi. There was a supermarket with a reasonable selection of food, but no fresh meat and few vegetables, a clothes shop, a hairdressers (they are also obsessed with having their nails attended to, it seems), and a few stores selling more generalised rubbish. We ate in the restaurant belonging to a Business Hotel. It was clean, the food was good, but the whole place had a soulless atmosphere about it. Was it Soviet or Finnish? Hard to tell the difference!

We drove to Tartu, the second largest town in Estonia, a pleasant enough place but one can imagine how terminally boring it would be to have to live there, and then to the western shore of Lake Peipsi, which Estonia shares with Russia. There was a strip of dirty sand spread like a handkerchief between some scrubby bushes and a few piles of litter, and I assumed from the fact that there were a few hardy locals sitting there in swimmers, that it must have been a beach.

We headed back to Tallinn arriving in the early evening. It was when we got back to the Hotel Metropol that it suddenly came to me that Estonia is still slightly like slipping into an episode of Goodnight Sweetheart, except that it is the 1960s rather than the 1940s. The décor, the dress, the lack of buzz. To its merit you have to look carefully to notice it. In another few years the past will have disappeared without trace.

j

Chapter 28 Ten "mirrion"

Seoul, April 2005

Hi everyone again!

I am at the domestic terminal waiting for a flight to Po'hang. It was easier than trying to find the bus terminal, and at only a few dollars more than the bus journey, why not? Everyone, including me, seems surprised that I am heading for such an off-the-track place as Ullungdo Island. I have been promised amazing peace and tranquility. We will see. That would make a good change from the frantic life of Tokyo and Seoul.

Tokyo was fun even so. Claude and Nigel, with whom I was staying, live in a great part of Shinjuku. It is a quiet neighbourhood (can you believe it?) with narrow roads and small neat houses and little restaurants. It is also very trendy. It is the only place I have ever been where the lampposts play classical music for your enjoyment as you shop. Tiny little dogs with bows in their hair and dressed up in coats sit in baskets, and do no doubt for the most part what other dogs do.

A good meal can be obtained for less than 10 Aussie dollars – as long as you are prepared to point. I even had a whole sashimi meal, little dish at a time, yum cha–style for less than $12..

The underground is easy once you have worked out the system. I managed to get to the gay-bar district on Saturday night. Frankly it was not that interesting, except that there was quite a jumpy pub with people spilling into the streets, almost London-style. I did take a trip later to the bars, after a bit of direction, and found that far more fun. Many of the bars are in basements or the upper floors of buildings and occupy something akin to office space. One of the bars I went to even had a backroom, one of those dark rooms with no furniture and where people feel rather than see.

The trip from Tokyo to Seoul took eight and a half hours, appalling for such a short distance. On the way to the station Nigel took me in the car to Asakura where there was some kind of festival going on. The streets were packed, and oddly clad people, many wearing precious little (they could have died with the secret), pushed or carried floats shoulder-high through the streets. I left the temple until the return visit, as the streets were far more fun.

Yesterday I was busy all day in Seoul meeting people, and then in the evening I was treated to a rather rushed banquet as I had arranged to meet the guy who runs the local HIV-positive group at nine. The banquet was great. We had sort of green things in a red sauce, meaty things, soupy things, bits of raw fish, and a myriad of dishes that could have been anything at all, and were better to be left in the "unknown and unidentifiable" category. It was great, as far as I could tell.

Then I rushed into the metro system for the rather long journey to Korean University. Now, I am not sure if I am not looking the best, but twice people got up on the train and gave me their seats. It may be another example of the Zanzibar "Babu" (grandfather) effect, which I managed to convince myself was due to the (premature?) white hair. They imagine I must be much older than I am. Well, that is what I am hoping is the reason.

Anyway I met JJ and we had a long chat and a beer in one of the local drinking holes. He is utterly charming, a 38-year-old PhD graduate lecturing in art. The trip back was just as easy. They Koreans seem much more light-hearted than the Japanese, chatting away, exceptionally well-behaved and polite, giving the odd smile. People stopped to ask me if I need help (God, I must look decrepit). There are even fewer round eyes here on the metro than in Tokyo.

Now, I thought that we were mad with mobiles in Sydney, but not in comparison. They all have these appendages protruding from the ear wherever they go. And tiny little appendages they are (the only appendages where small is a status symbol, I suspect …).

And so the Korea of 1974 when I was last here has disappeared. This modern, middle-class, very pleasant, but a little smog-bound, society has emerged where there was not much before.

And so I am off to Po'hang and from there tomorrow with the ferry to the island. I have not established yet whether they have electricity so you may or may not hear until I get back to mega-civilisation again.

***

It has now been several days since I saw any sign of a foreigner. In fact the last one was at Gimpo airport in Seoul. After a pleasant Asiana experience I set to finding a yogwan to stay in Po'hang. This town is (for David R) the Korean equivalent of Gijon in northern Spain, without the gay entertainment! It is a utilitarian and rather functional-looking port with little superficially to recommend it. In places where there are no signs in English at all, no plastic mouldings or pictures on the menu for food, and nobody, but nobody speaks English, life for the foreigner can be taxing.

For example last night I thought I had ordered dinner. Seems I had not! Eventually I did get something. Today more careful studying of the bible that is Lonely Planet has made life a little easier, depending on whether you like pickled cabbage with chilli as an alternative to the vegemite and toast for breakfast.

But back to Po'hang. I found a suitably priced (cheap) *yogwan*. It took a little while to work out the etiquette of how to use the room, but I managed. There were serious issues of which footwear to use in which part of the room. Then I jumped on a local bus to Kyong Ju, which as you all will recollect is the old capital of the Shilla dynasty. In fact it is the only place I have seen in Korea with old houses and traditional roofs. It is perhaps more famous, I hear you saying, for the tumuli of the buried emperors that erupt like a pubescent acne all over the town. I returned to the sordid splendour of Po'hang's port ready for the sea trip.

I took the fast cat (Australian-made, but it has totally cut all ties with its origins) for the 135 kilometres to Ullungdo, out in the Sea of Japan way off the east coast of South Korea. What a gem this place has turned out to be. Mind you, without the help of Johnny, my contact in Seoul, and a guy at the ferry terminal who called ahead and booked a room for me here, I don't know how I would have made it. The problem is that as they never see foreigners, they are not used to trying to communicate with sign language, unlike the Japanese, thus communication is exceptionally difficult.

Ullungdo is a mountainous island, sparsely inhabited and covered in forests. The cliffs rise sheer from the cold clear ocean. The small main town, Todong, is comprised of two or three narrow parallel streets winding steeply up from the harbour. There is plenty to buy, as long as you like seaweed, dried octopus and other unidentifiable things neatly packed in polyethylene packs.

The *yogwan* where I am staying in Todong is a bit more upmarket than in Po'hang, and will do me fine for the stay here. The village is charming with old houses, spectacular views and even a couple of traditional bathhouses, one of which I investigated. The bath tradition in Korea is similar to Japan's, but in this case was about a meticulous personal scrubbing rather than a social occasion. In five minutes you can be out on the headland alone watching the ocean caress the rocks, not quite up to the Atlantic crashing onto the coast of Maine, but still a deeply satisfying and comforting experience. This morning I took a taxi (they are all 4X4s) along the coast to Namyang. The Lonely Planet guide advised that in that area one is likely to get stared at. I am used to that, for whatever reason.

I sat on a stony beach and read a few chapters of a novel about life in Bombay. I also have managed to do a bit of writing, while listening to

Andrea Boccelli and Cesaria Evora of the Cape Verde Islands. Is this globalisation, I ask myself?

The weather is perfect, around mid-twenties or seventy-fivish for those old non-metric people. Well, I am off to do some more discovering.

***

Of course you can get them, coffees I mean. They cost 400 won from a little machine, in a tiny paper cup. As the instructions are in Korean the risk versus the payback is too high. I did manage one once – it was lukewarm and had sugar in it.

There has been a significant change in the last few days. People have started to come up to me and want to talk. This is thwarted from the start as most do not speak a word of English. But there have been a couple of exceptions. One is a "Businessman" from Seoul who was useful in being able to clarify a few details about Ullungdo for me.

Yesterday I took another taxi; in this case the terrain really demanded a 4X4, to the foot of the Pongae waterfall (called pok po in Korean should you ever be in a Korean restaurant somewhere and suddenly feel the need for a waterfall). I tackled the one-kilometre steep climb to the base of the falls. I was happily reading my book when a very attractive young lady appeared. She explained, haltingly with a bit of guessing and prompting, that she was in the army. Now there is always a nervousness here about "the North", and let's face it, it would not be that hard to take Ullungdo, as it is about as close to the North as the South. But I was taken aback when this delightful young woman looked at me sternly, and as she wrote down a telephone number said seriously, "Wiv emerchency telephone polis wiv dis numba". I nodded soberly and folded the paper placing it carefully in my wallet.

The next visitor was a bit more fun. He bounded up the steps, a bandanna strapped to his (rather loose) wrists, and a counter-culture diamond stud in his ear, explaining that he was a university student from Seoul. "Engineering?", I enquired. "No, make ceramics", he replied. Aaaaah!

I have done so much walking and climbing, I must be fitter now than I have been in years. The weather still is perfection. This morning I took the cable car to above Todong village. As always the views were wonderful.

Now a few things I may have forgotten to mention. The first is about food. Slender metal chopsticks are the hardest of that entire species to master, especially when a piece of slithery seaweed is just inviting to be popped into the mouth. In fact the easiest thing to eat with them is the *kimchi*, gorgeously prepared with chili and garlic, and I should mention that it is also fermented. The ease of picking it up is I am sure why I have eaten it, there can surely be no other reason.

Another catch is drinks. In the stores you see a nice bottle in the fridge with some fruits on the label. Nice fresh juice, two bucks, about right. Uncap it, take a swig. And die. It is vodka of uncertain aristocracy, with a smidge of fruit taste. The next time I was more careful. Avoid the screw cap, plastic ones surely will be alright. No, try again, this one turns out to be rice wine. One does not have to worry too much about the public image of being inebriated as a result of these confusions as many of the locals have been swigging such stuff all day long by the look of them.

On a more genteel note, this village is a centre of bonsai. There are heaps of little bonsai shops up the main street. More popular seem to be the local produce for presents. Decisions are being made every moment. "Do you think auntie would prefer the dried seaweed, or the octopus?" "Should we get granny some pumpkin taffy? She can always take her teeth out and suck it".

Well, tomorrow the ferry goes back to Po'hang and then I make my way via Seoul to Tokyo until Saturday. Hey I just discovered that if I hit this key on the computer ¹Ì¤Ó ™" ¤ ¸ °¼»þ¤Ì¤¾ all the writing goes funny.

***

Instructions in the hotel in Po'hang advise that for the security of the nation there will be an emergency drill every 15th of the month. If you are inside, stay inside. If you are outside, immediately run to the nearest air-raid shelter (presumably only signed in Korean so that if there is not enough room, we know who won't make it in time). If you are driving, pull into the right and stop. Then get out of the car and rush into an air-raid shelter. Finally, if the drill is at night, turn all lights off immediately, close the curtains and hold your breath.

Hmmm. I would love to have been a part of all that, it sounds enormous fun.

Well, I am luxuriating (yes) in the Star Alliance lounge at the new Incheon Airport Seoul. The best thing about it is that it is a Singapore Airlines lounge. I fell first upon the scrambled eggs and bacon (well, I did get up at 5.15 in Po'hang to catch a domestic flight to Seoul), and then immediately after on the congee, one of my weaknesses, and indeed I have been known to brew some at home in the rice cooker – another story. It was a hard choice as to which to go for first, but deprivation drove me to the western breakfast. Then I snaffled down a couple of sambos while I was at it. And coffee!

289

So this is the end of this trip to Korea. Did you know, he asks politely of the audience, that one in five Korean men has a problem with alcohol? With the confusion between fruit juice and vodka so easy to make, it is not surprising. Well, most of that 20% were on the ferry back to the mainland yesterday afternoon. By a masterful stroke of stupid design, the way out to the "food hall" where people can dance, sing, eat, drink and throw up to their hearts' content, is through the First Class area (where I happened to be sitting). At one late stage in the voyage these drunken hordes erupted through the door in a conga formation, terrorising more reserved compatriots and renting the relative calm asunder. This was too much for the rather sensitive man in front sporting the seasickness patch fashionably behind the left ear, and he called management. By this time the conga was back in its cage, leaving behind only a drunken prostitute who in a dreadful error of judgment thought she might have found a punter in me.

Today I saw a Caucasian. And then another. I was back in Seoul. Ah Seoul! A big bow, deep and low.

***

Seoul June 2005

"Ten mirrion", said Mr. Chung. "Fir tin", corrected Mr. Lee. However many millions live in Seoul, it is far too many. Some of the apartment blocks are a little old, but many are new. Ten stories high, and called Building 302, or Building 635, with the motif of a *chaebol* on the end wall without any windows. You can't go far in Korea without being in contact with a *chaebol*, the humungous companies that dominate Korean industry, politics and everyone's life. The Korean Times announced today that the richest Korean is a Mr. Lee Kun-hee, the boss of Samsung. He is worth 1.73 trillion won. Now, a won will not buy you much, but a couple of trillion will. Over five billion Aussie dollars, for example. And anything else you might fancy.

The drive from the relatively new Incheon Airport is nearly 80 kilometres to central Seoul. It would have been far more sensible to have built a fast train like in Hong Kong at the same time as they built the airport, but they did not. The expressway assures that you can cover the distance in only an hour. Or two. My translator, Mr. Park (but call me Walter), assures me that it is in hand. The new train will be ready in 2008, he beams. (I wonder why, when Asians adopt English names for commercial transactions with westerners who struggle with Chinese and Korean ones, they seem to choose the most bizarre ones. Justin, Clement, Harvey, Brenton.)

The traffic is rather chaotic despite the wide avenues and the lack of farm clutter that plagues other Asian cities like Delhi or Jakarta. I wonder whether crunching gears is a feature of Korean cars. Last night's Kia taxi crunched and so does Mr. Chung's Kia four-wheel drive. The answer was provided the next morning when Mr. Lee drove Mr. Chung's car. No crunching. But Mr. Lee is much taller than Mr. Chung, and I suspect that the short Korean legs of the last generation have not quite grown into the distance to the clutch of cars built for the next generation.

I can't help thinking back to my first visit to Seoul in 1974. It was a different country in those days, still miserably poor, and very underdeveloped. Those old factories with dirt floors are a laughable contrast to the modern economy and society of today. But the people do not quite fit their new business suits yet, although the minuscule mobile phones sit comfortably in everyone's ear. There is still a lot of the "country boy" in them, and maybe a roughness that the awful years of civil war stamped on them. And to make matters worse the men have flat arses and the women often have bandy legs.

Of course the language does not help. The script is intriguing, with circles and lines, almost like cartoon characters playing with balloons on sticks. But spoken it sounds like Turkish word endings interspersed with the attempted ejection of a glottally entrapped pubic hair followed by a sneeze that has gone wrong. No wonder their English is so bad, and hard to understand, even that of the relatively accomplished speakers.

Their food is indicative of a difficult history of survival. Not only have they had the Chinese and the Japanese to contend with, but vile cold winters with little fresh food. The meat and fish are sparse, and the vegetables are prepared to last for months, by pickling and fermenting them in earthenware pots. Fish comes in small portions with nasty bones in them. I have never been skilled at deboning fish, but having to do it with thin metal chopsticks requires quite another level of skill. Meat is stringy bits often cooked with vegetables like the Japanese *shabu shabu* in a large shallow wok creating a tasty soup from the ingredients, and which you drink after extracting and then slurping down the cooked food. The dish is called *shinsollo*, and is as good as Korean cooking gets.

Raw garlic, pickled radish, fermented cabbage with chilli and ginger, spicy octopus: this is hardly a gentle cuisine for those of delicate palate. And that is just breakfast! The tradition of this food must go back centuries. I bet the habit of rushing off to the bathroom with toothbrush and toothpaste after lunch is a bit more recent.

Korea has not surprisingly been influenced heavily by the USA. This creates sad sights, like a pretty girl, beautifully dressed and presented, chewing gum with a vacant look on her face. They know their society is badly American. Awful cheap movies on the local TV, advertisements everywhere, even in the middle of the video route map sequence on the Asiana aircraft. There seems to be a lot of anti-American sentiment. Partly this is due to the description by the US president of the North as being part of the axis of evil, just when the South was making some progress in thawing relationships. Most Koreans, especially the young ones, want a reunited Korea and resent the American administration trying to pour cold water on it.

Some have a specific and good reason for their antipathy. I went with Walter to a party and met the people with whom he normally works. Their company used to be Swedish going way back. Now it is American. And it has just been bought by another American company. This will allow the new owners to get rid of most of the local Korean staff and save a hell of a lot of money as they merge the two local operations. Soon there will be higher profits for the mother company in the USA. This will be useful for all the American investors in their stock. Let's face it, they have seen their paper fortunes decline over the last year or so, so a boost will be welcome. But in this case many of the people I met at the party will lose their jobs and find it hard to get another. There will be no generous payouts, no unemployment benefit. This is after all a country where you only get three days annual leave a year to start off with. After a couple of years you start to add one day's leave for every year you work.

Walter's wife is expecting their first child so he is very worried. Justin will find it hard to get another job at his age, but cannot afford to retire. So as you all feel a nice warm comfortable feeling when your stocks go up, just ask yourself who is paying for it in some far flung land. Long live the Capitalist Dream!

But the Koreans are a hardy lot, and they will probably survive. Mr. Lee's wife (I think that was DL, but it could have been JH or maybe it was Mr. JY Lee, to be honest I am not quite sure) has a pharmacy on the island of Jeju. They will be alright. In fact out of all of them, I think he has the best lifestyle of all. Anything to escape this monster city with its however many millions there are.

And I am going to do the same, check out and head for the airport for the 11 hours tedium to Sydney. I blanche and stagger a little at the 1500-buck hotel bill for three nights and three breakfasts, even though I half expected it. The Grand Intercontinental looks forward to welcoming you back again soon. Yeah, right!

j

Chapter 29 The "Z" and "U" of Africa

Uganda, April 2006

Hi everyone!

The flight from Sydney to Jo'burg stretches a day as far as the body would want to endure. It leaves early, lasts 14 hours direct, and arrives late in the afternoon. You do not want to sleep as it is daylight all the way, and arrive exhausted and jet-lagged. There is little to see on the way. Surprisingly the air map at the halfway mark shows only the cities of São Paulo and Santiago. Our flight went down to the 61st parallel, on the edge of the polar ice cap, which unfortunately was obscured by cloud, and the tip of South America lay just the other side of the ice.

Waz left out of breath as we rushed for his flight to Cape Town, the connection imperilled by the late arrival of our flight from Sydney. I had an overnight stay before heading to Zambia the next morning. Just enough time to catch up on the latest scandal to beset the South African government, with the former deputy president Jacob Zuma accused of raping an HIV-positive activist, and having unsafe sex with her. The statements that he has made show appalling ignorance of HIV transmission, are right out of the cave, and generally set a disastrous example for South Africans. I also noted that South Africa has the highest incidence of road rage in the world, and twice the world average of road deaths.

The view of Victoria Falls from the air was spectacular from my window seat for once on the correct side of the aircraft, as we came in to land at Livingstone. Tadeus met me and we joined the rest of the group at the falls. I had arrived just in time for the one recreational event of the week of the AFAP conference on managing a five-year program covering five countries, whose emphasis this time was on HIV. Tadeus generously got totally drenched with me as we made a quick trip to the Zambian side of the falls. After the good rains this season the flow over the falls was massive, in fact to the point where there was so much water and spray that the experience was frustrating and wet on the one hand, yet exhilarating and impressive on the other. We then took a leisurely lunch and cruise on the Zambesi spotting an elephant wrecking the trees on the banks of the river with determined application, and a group of hippos peering at us from the safety of the river.

We then set off for the over 300-kilometre drive through the flat and for once relatively green Zambian bush to our accommodation. Without the interventions of various churches one gets the impression that there would be few services at all. Schools, hospitals, clinics and churches are all intertwined. The mission where the conference was held did not have sufficient space to accommodate the 20 or so people who comprised the group, and so we stayed an hour's drive away over the most appalling dirt road at another Jesuit institution called Kizito Pastoral Centre. Christine and I shared the Bishop's "house" (in fact she slept in the Bishop's bed), a dreary concrete blob with very basic features. The one feature that it did have was hot water, the only accommodation to have such luxury. At eight dollars a day full board, one could hardly feel justified in complaining. But the Mozambicans and I noted that to just put a "sh" in front of the Kizito turned the word into the almost accurate description of "strange" or "weird" in Portuguese!

Friday was the day where we reviewed issues around HIV. I got to make the opening presentation. A few local dignitaries joined us including the doctor in charge of health services for the whole region. The fact that he arrived at nine in the morning drunk, made an utter fool of himself, and kept popping out for what we assume was a top-up, did not inspire much confidence. Tadeus made a note to "fix" him.

There was a traditional lunch, some dancing and a sale of dyed fabric made by positive women as part of an income generation project funded by AFAP. Their production technique is improving but they still have a few things to learn about marketing. I felt obliged to make a heavy investment.

There was some interesting debate over things like volunteerism, and I found myself at odds with the AFAP team and siding with Kenya, Mozambique and Malawi. Overall it was a very interesting and useful day. Some of the group had a little difficulty with English, yet I mused over the fact that however limited their language skills they all seem to manage words like "sustainability" and "mitigation" easily. Of course that is NGO-speak rather than English!

I have mentioned Tadeus a few times, and I have to confess at being most intrigued by this extraordinary Pole. He looks very young for what must be his 45 or so years, boyish even, masculine, and yet very gentle. I could not have guessed apart from the small cross around his neck that he is in fact Father Tadeus. He has lived at Chikuni for 24 years. I tried to imagine how his life is, and how it might otherwise have been, and what brought him to be the man that he is. He certainly says that he loves what he does. There is a sensuality to him that I found a little unnerving, and I wondered how or if he ever gave expression to it.

In fact those foreigners who either give their time for nothing, like the very competent HIV doctor from Italy, Claudia, or those in the group who devote themselves to development work to eradicate poverty, from Croatia, Italy and England, are all in their way extraordinary people.

The greatest sympathy went to the team from Zimbabwe. The WHO has just announced that it has now the lowest life expectancy in the world, having dropped from 57 20 years ago to just 36 now. The wealth distribution across the border with Zambia has completely reversed. The inflation rate is the highest ever recorded in the world. Dinner costs a million dollars in a currency that used to be as strong as ours, so you can imagine the implications for the elderly and their pensions or little savings they might have had. A small bill requires literally armfuls of notes.

Not so the Zambian *kwacha* (pronounced in a strangely similar way to *"Quatsch"*, "rubbish" in German). Why it has strengthened so much against the US dollar is a total mystery to everyone. Is it the record price of copper? Or is it really a manipulation of the government ahead of an election? The fact remains that petrol is still US$1.50 a litre, and that in a country where the per capita GNP is only a dollar a day creates a crushing burden.

As might be expected there are few cars on the roads, and very few roads either. On Saturday we had to get up for breakfast at 5.45 to make sure we got to the airport 250 kilometres away in Lusaka at 10.30. I made it in time.

I had a couple of hours in Nairobi airport which caused me to again wonder about "femininity" as we understand it in the West, and to what extent it is innate rather than learned. This is a subject that had engaged my interest on previous occasions in Africa. In the villages the women do not generally show the attributes that we normally would describe as feminine in their comportment or behaviour, as indeed is true all over the world. And yet here in the airport there are stunning-looking young Kenyan and other African women teetering along in high heels, swinging their hips and exhibiting all the attributes of "femininity" that we would identify with in the West. So is this adoption of femininity modelled on the western concepts, and where did these paradigms come from? No answer came to me before the flight to Entebbe in Uganda was called.

The plane landed after dark, and the first images of a country can be so different between night and day. The drive of 40 minutes to Kampala the capital, nestled higher up in tropical valleys between rolling hills, revealed the place to be so different from Zambia. The streets were full of people, out walking, at roadside markets, with music blaring and the dust in the air giving an almost surreal look to the scene bathed in dim street lighting. Standing out were the neon signs of the petrol stations with their standardised world branding for who knows what marketing advantage or cost. It looked almost middle-class.

And yet Uganda has hardly recovered from the civil wars, murderous dictatorship of Idi Amin, or the misplaced policies of Milton Obote who followed him. It is described still as one of the poorest countries in the world. Museveni, the current president, has become a darling of the west. It is true that the economy seems to be growing strongly and the record on HIV, if it is as stated (and some dispute this), has been impressive.

I now have to go out and discover Uganda in the daylight. The lack of hot water in the hotel and the fact that the phones do not work and the power tends to go off have alerted me to the fact that my impressions last night might need to be modified. I will let you know.

***

My second intuition, or rather suspicion, turned out to be right. Kampala by night is a different story than by day. The hotel (owned by Asians) where I am staying is a 10-minute ride by cab to the city centre. Kampala is built over a series of seven hills, like all self-respecting cities starting with Rome. And in some senses it is either like a city in a garden, or rather a city that has fallen apart and been taken over by the unrelenting march of vegetation. There are hills for each of the main religions: a Catholic hill, a Protestant one, a Muslim one and so on. Each crowns its hill with the mark of a church or a mosque. These hills are often connected by unsurfaced roads with deep ruts, and often slippery with mud now that the wet season has started.

The city centre is built on a deep slope down into one of the valleys. Even on a Sunday there is lots going on in the markets and most of the stores are open. The city centre is run-down, falling apart, dirty and full of goods that nobody seems to buy, and that I could not imagine why anyone would want. The buildings are blocks of concrete or brick with broken and barred windows, decaying to the point where it sometimes is hard to tell whether they are still inhabited or abandoned.

I sauntered around the busy streets aware that I was being stared at constantly. I am not so naïve as to think that it might be because of my great beauty, indeed it was just that I was the only white face around. Even in the city centre the roads are full of mud and potholes, and I could not manage to stop my jeans being splashed with the red sludge that pervades the city. There were very few buildings of note. A church, an Indian temple and a sky-blue glass walled modern creation that belongs to a bank. In fact the key stakeholders of the country!

Although there was really nothing more to see, I felt unjustified in returning to my hotel so soon and as I was a little tired from dragging myself up the steep hills, and still not sure how I would go about finding transport back to my hotel, I decided to stop and have a drink at the trendiest café I could find. The transport problem was solved when another white face came and sat down on the terrace of the café. Leone turned out to be a Belgian who works for the US government doing governance work on their behalf, and specifically with the Ugandan electoral commission. She is charming, grew up in the Congo, has great insight into Uganda, and is a tremendous conversationalist, so we had drinks and then dinner together. The tips she gave me on what to see have been invaluable. Her knowledge of Ugandan politics has been spicy. As is so often the case when strangers meet who will probably never meet again, it was easy to talk freely about our lives. She described some dilemmas in her life, and revealed some sad events that unfurled over the last few years. We just get on like a house on fire, and will meet for dinner again on the night before I leave. Such encounters are the jewels of travel, far more than any temple or museum, and they are more prone to happen when one travels alone.

I took Leone's advice and hired the private taxi driver who took me to the city and works from the hotel, to take me to Jinja and the source of the Nile the following day. Sam was an excellent choice, despite his English being a little hard to understand. The fact that he mixes up his "l"s and "r"s, rather like an Asian, complicates comprehension. But when I realised that loads and livers were roads and rivers, it was somewhat easier.

Sam took me first to the tombs of the Bugandan kings, or Kabakas, on Kasaubi hill. Young George, the local guide there, filled in the history in a surprisingly interesting manner. We then headed for the Baha'i Temple. I have to confess that I had heard about the Baha'i but knew little about them. The free-of-charge booklet (no, sorry you cannot make a donation, only Baha'i are allowed to donate) explained who they are and what they stand for. It seems to be a rather eclectic approach not dissimilar to the Cao Daists of Vietnam, but far less loony. Perhaps it has more in common with the Theosophical Society formed in Madras by that Blavatsky woman, although the Baha'i did have a messenger from God. In any case the temple is charming, the gardens superb and a real oasis in an otherwise rather oppressive city.

The road system in Kampala is utterly chaotic. It was raining in the morning and the going was really rough over the appalling roads. They are going to build a highway, funded by the World Bank, to avoid much of the city, but they have only just started. Traffic is diverted over waste areas where no road exists at all. At some points we could not even get through because of flooding. Sam took me through slums so wretched that even he commented on them. The way these people exist is an outrage that none of us should allow to happen. Yet, even though they live in hovels, they are all immaculately turned out in clean very presentable clothes. How they manage to find the dignity to do that given the way they have to live is beyond me.

Finally reaching the main road to Jinja is only a partial relief. This is the main highway that leads from Rwanda and the Congo, and of course Kampala, to Kenya and the port of Mombassa where most of the goods arrive and leave by sea for these landlocked countries. The trucks are old, overloaded, grinding up the long hills spewing out clouds of black diesel. The passenger buses from Kenya and the minibuses that are the main mode of transport in Uganda are too impatient to observe the solid white line. They overtake on blind corners just to get around these juggernauts no matter what the cost. Sam explained to me that the cost was often that of many lives, especially when one of the overloaded minibuses collides head on with one coming in the opposite direction. Sam's best quality for me is that he is a very cautious and conservative driver.

Sam is turning 40 this year. I asked him how he felt about that. "Wonderful!" he said. He told me that it meant he was grown-up. I found it hard to identify with his sentiments on the issue. I later learned that his father died at 49, his father-in-law at a similar age. I wondered if he was telling me the real truth about how he felt. Sam is a candidate for a heart attack. He is a solid boy and I do not believe that he weighs only 85 kilograms, as he claims. Today we had lunch at the slightly ageing Windsor Lake Victoria Hotel at Entebbe. He chose the buffet and I was astonished at the amount of food he managed to put away. Just when he surely must have reached his limit, as an afterthought he threw down a cup of tea and two generous slices of cheese cake.

We drove through the protected forest of Amavenda, now dotted with factories owned by Asians pleased to get some cheap virgin land, and squatters who were happy to get out of the pollution of Kampala and to get some fresh forest air. Tea and sugar cane plantations follow in a land that is so fertile that anything would grow.

Sam knows his Jinja. We had lunch at the Source of the Nile Resort, a sprawling place with bungalow-style accommodation perched on the banks of the Nile. There was hardly any sign of life there. We then took in the barely impressive Bugajali Falls, and the hydroelectric scheme at Owens Falls, opened in 1954 since when it has managed to provide electricity for Kampala and totally wreck the eco-environment of the whole area.

Until two weeks ago Jinja was the accepted source of the Nile, being the only point at which water runs out of instead of into the massive Lake Victoria. Two scientists somewhere or other, presumably desperately doing a PhD, have now claimed they have found the real source of the Nile on the other side of Lake Victoria. As far as I can see the whole thing is entirely arbitrary and of interest only to those who have a stake in the tourist industry of the area (owned by Asians).

We proceeded to the "actual place" where the source is supposed to be, discovered by some bloke called Speke in 1863, and looked at what appeared to be just like any other stretch of water from the discomfort of a run-down café where they had few drinks available and no change. Somewhat more intriguing for me was the fact that this is also the exact place where Gandhi requested his ashes, or some of them at least, to be scattered, and there is a rather smart monument to record the fact.

I was hoping that I might be able to catch up with Lydia, a rather formidable activist who seems to have managed to encourage the government to act on the misappropriation of a couple of hundred million dollars of Global Fund money by three ministers. But her mobile is not answering and I fear she is away. But let it be said that Uganda has done a creditable job on HIV. All over the place there are signs for places where HIV treatment can be given, and leaving Entebbe there is even a "Thank you for visiting Entebbe" sign sponsored by the national AIDS care and support group TASO. With Botswana they seem to have the highest percentage roll out of ARVs in Africa. People openly talk about HIV and admit they have lost friends and relatives from AIDS. They seem to have done a better job than most in education and treatment and possibly as a consequence in reducing the stigma and discrimination around HIV. So full marks to Museveni. Or almost.

I heard him speak at Kobe last year, and it seemed to me that there has been a shift in his approach. This always had included a strong concentration on condom promotion. But in the last few years he has moved away from this, putting abstinence first. In fact there are large posters, and I do not think I have ever seen a country with billboards larger than those in Uganda, stating that to avoid HIV you must adhere to abstinence. So what changed? Well, I gather that Mrs. Museveni has become a BAC (Born Again Christian) and in embracing the PEPFAR money (Bush's finger at the Global Fund) they have to promote ABC (Abstinence first, otherwise Be faithful, and in the last resort use a Condom).

Whether this has had an effect on the previously reduced rates of new infections is hard to say. Official statistics suggest that it hasn't, but there are plenty of people who dispute this. More independent figures show at least a levelling off in the new infection rates and some believe they have started to rise again. All I can tell you is that religious hegemony is omnipresent. On the cable TV in my room over half of the channels are given to evangelical Christian stations that spout garbage, both American and home-grown African, guaranteed 24 hours a day. Fortunately there are the Indian stations (Asian-owned) which have the only news I can get most of the time. They also have wonderful programs debating in an Insight style format issues such as the allocation of a percentage of university places free of charge to those from the lower castes and hence the poor. The dialogue is passionate and wonderful and demonstrates why the Indian democracy actually works even if it takes a very long time to get anywhere.

Another concern that I personally have with Museveni is that he has stated that there are no homosexuals in Uganda. That is what generated the provocative idea of putting the camp into Kampala. I learned from Leone, my Belgian friend, that when she was assisting in the drafting of the current constitution of Uganda by Museveni's team about 10 years ago, they insisted on ensuring that homosexuality was to be illegal. Of course HIV is now a totally generalised epidemic and so the original vectors (probably female sex workers connected with the main truck route from Mombassa) are irrelevant. However, there is never any talk of education with groups normally considered at risk such as sex workers or men who have sex with men. This was also strikingly true of all of the discussions that were held in Zambia about HIV education last week. Presumably these activities are illegal and therefore do not exist.

I decided that after all of this thinking, I needed a bit of relaxation down at Lake Victoria at Entebbe. Now for most of us I imagine that the word Entebbe conjures up the story of the audacious rescue in 1976 by the Israelis (in the days when the rest of the world respected and admired them – what a sad slide that has been) of the hostages on an El Al plane that had been hijacked by the PLO. It was an amazingly executed exercise as they crept in over the lake not even noticed by the Entebbe control tower (probably owned by Asians), and managed to rescue all but three of the over 100 people held at gunpoint on the aircraft. Well the fact that the control tower did not notice might not have been all that surprising really on reflection. The plane is still there, dragged away to a close by paddock.

The Botanical Gardens were very pleasing but I decided not to visit the zoo. I have a bit of a problem with zoos, especially in Africa where there are such things as game reserves. And apart from those two things there really is not much at Entebbe at all.

I reflected on the road back to Kampala that while I had not seen the gorillas in the mist or some of the highest peaks in Africa on the border with Congo, the things that really should be seen in Uganda, I had at least obtained an idea of what the Uganda that most Ugandans inhabit is like. I noticed that the best presented constructions in the country are petrol stations. At US$1.20 a litre petrol is a price that Ugandans find hard, and the petrol companies and the government must be making a killing. But then the stations are individually owned (mostly by Asians).

So what is with this "Asian-owned" shit?, you will be asking. Remember that one of the most contentious things about the Idi Amin reign of terror (why are the British such bad judges of character in these matters? – no don't even mention Mugabe) was his expulsion of Asians (mainly Indians brought here by the British originally) who were not Ugandan citizens. Eventually many of them returned to Uganda and reclaimed the houses and businesses that had been taken off them and given through a government commission to needy African Ugandans. At that time they just had to give them back to their original owners.

Uganda is now back in a situation where almost everything is owned again by the Asians, from beer plants to water-bottling plants, hotels and restaurants, the wood industry, construction, trucking, well just about everything! The good thing is that they employ people, well Africans! But they pay them as little as they can, barely a subsistence wage, and treat them appallingly. So the resentment that Idi Amin acted on is alive and well.

Now it is time to move on, to go and relax in South Africa where life is more comfortable but where it is just not as easy to have the sort of relationship with black Africans that I personally feel you can in all the other countries of Africa. But that tension between the races in Africa is another subject altogether.

Was it worth coming to Uganda? Hey, give me a break, this is the first new country I have added to my list in over a year! That makes 143, still a few to go …

j

Chapter 30 Q and A!

Doha and Tirana August 2008

Hi everyone yet again!

So what do Qatar and Albania have in common? Yes, of course, they are two countries that until this trip I had not visited, now bringing the total number of countries I have entered (passed through immigration) to 145. Those omissions are now remedied. Apart from that fact linking them there can surely be none other!

Qatar is a few years behind Dubai and the United Arab Emirates in spending big but as their huge gas reserves are bringing them unprecedented petro dollars they are fast embarking on a massive investment program. It is hard work walking round Doha the capital. The temperature was still a blistering 42 degrees in the day and well into the 30's at night. I stayed in the centre of the city, the only feature of note being a refurbished old area of narrow winding streets with white houses full of charm and blinding light. Like all these countries the labour force is made up of migrant workers from south Asia and the Philippines. They are given a visa for one year and never are allowed to own any business or get permanent residence. There are no Qatari restaurants, the wealthy eat in expensive western hotels and the rest (including me) eat Indian food. The *biryani* in the hotel was more than acceptable.

Before I set out to discover Doha as gently as I could given that I had arrived overnight from Bangkok and was tired, I set in motion a plan to break the laws of Qatar for the second time. The first law I had broken was the one banning people with HIV from entering Qatar. But I do that in a lot of countries. The second Law I hoped to break was about having sex with another man. One of the advantages of the era of the internet and email has been huge changes in the way people meet each other for all sorts of reasons including sex. In preparation for visiting both Qatar and Albania I had already done some investigation on one of the sites dedicated specifically to gay men looking for hook ups. I had a mobile telephone number and nothing more for a man about whom I knew only that he said he was in his early thirties. I had seen a photograph of part of his torso.

I called him from my mobile just after I got to my hotel, around 8.00 a.m. as we had agreed. He was a bit vague and offhand. I shrugged my shoulders, it did not really matter. But half an hour later he called me on my mobile explaining that he had been at home when I first called and he was not able to talk. Now he was at work. He said that he was not feeling too well, something to do with a change in the weather. Maybe a drop in temperature from 45 to 42 degrees I speculated to myself. He suggested that perhaps I should call him later in the day to see how he felt.

This was not necessary as I had just got back to my hotel room at around 4.00 p.m. when he rang me again on my mobile. Was I in my room? Could he come round? Just for a chat, not for anything else. Fine I said. He knocked on the door in fifteen minutes. I looked through the spy hole in the door and saw a handsome young man dressed in a *Thoub*, the white Arab dress worn by the Qataris with a black band (the *Ogal*) to hold the white head covering in place. I opened the door and he came in. I felt somewhat underdressed in a T-shirt and boxer shorts. The hotel was a cheaper Indian owned establishment in the centre of the old town and the room was small, with little space. I motioned for him to sit on the bed and offered him a fruit juice from the tiny refrigerator. He accepted. I also sat on the bed but at a discreet distance from him.

He spoke excellent English. He had studied engineering at Oxford and worked in the petrochemical industry. He was married with a little boy who had been born prematurely and had survived only because of the excellent intensive care facility at an international hospital in Doha. He was devoted to his son who was then three years old. I got the impression that he was extremely well connected and that money was abundant.

He turned to me and asked if I minded if he took off his headdress as it was quite hot and tight. I looked at him and said "You are welcome to take anything off, in fact everything if you want". And he did. He was exactly the sort of man I find sexually very attractive, and he clearly had not had satisfying sex with a man for a while. The sex was intense, passionate, urgent almost. He fucked me. And I was really glad that he did.

We tried to get together again but it proved too difficult. He clearly had to be exceptionally careful with whom he had sex. It could only ever be a foreigner who did not know his name or who he was. It had to be in a hotel where he could pass unnoticed. I thought about what he would have to give up if he wanted to life as a gay man: his country, his family, his work, his privilege. It would not have surprised me to find that he was part of the extended royal family. However much one might want to live true to one's sexual identity, there are limits to what can be forsaken to do it.

The next day I decided to hire a driver to show me around in airconditioning if not comfort. Baba is from Sri Lanka and has lived in the Middle East for 22 of his 43 years. He went to Oman before he even got married. Short trips home allowed him to father two children, but he has rarely spent time with his wife. He sends nearly all his salary home to support his family, about $500 a month. He drives for the hotel where I stayed but as this was the weekend he supplemented his earnings by taking me round in his weathered Hyundai. We set out first to Sealine Beach some 60 kms through the desert to a small and rather dirty beach with a delicate green/blue tepid sea inhabited by more jelly fish than people. The resort demanded a $40 entrance even to have a coffee. We left. Outside the resort are rows of dune buggies for those who relish dicing with death, from dehydration if not turning over, up and down the nearby sand dunes. The desert is complete, not a bush or a scrubby plant, just stone and sand, and through the dust and haze the extraordinary site of the odd gas plant and a plastics factory. They seemed more like mirages than real.

Doha itself is a massive construction site. There is a corniche around the bay and about 50 skyscrapers in various stages of completion towards one end. The architecture is adventurous, surprising and in many cases very pleasing. Emulating Dubai's reclaimed Palm development, Doha is constructing a similar luxurious Pearl development. The new area of the city comprises massive hotels, offices, apartment blocks, totally excessive for a city that is supposed to have barely 500,000 people. On Friday afternoon we visited the shopping mall. The Qataris must go straight from the mosque to the very expensive and elegant shops. By evening the streets of the city that were totally desolate in the morning as religious dues were paid, are full of people and the local market, very ordinary compared to most bazaars, was packed. The strand of Islam practiced here is a form of *sunni wahabism* but not as extreme as Saudi Arabia. On the other hand try to get a drink!

The hypocrisy of course is that they sell alcohol in duty free and serve it on board Qatar Airways. It is just that you can't take it into the country. There are not many women in the street, and those that are of course are veiled. Migrant workers generally cannot bring their wives. The indigenous Qatari men are actually quite light in colour, smallish and many very good looking. They all wear the startlingly white robes and head dress with a black cord holding it in place. The undergarments are also loose fitting and white. As of course I just happen to know.

Qatar Airways has won all sorts of awards for its service. It is in fact the best product I have ever experienced. Even the menus come in a leather compendium and there is a choice between hot and cold towels. The aircraft are beautifully, even lavishly, appointed. But what they need is the training and discipline of Singapore Airlines to deliver the product.

The contrast with England's transport system could not be more stark. I arrived there to be greeted with late, expensive and dirty trains which would not process 'foreign' credit cards and lifts that do not work on either side of the platform requiring dragging heavy luggage up and down 25 steps. I was there just a couple of days but even that was depressing.

It is always a relief to get to France and especially the area where John now lives in the Lot et Garonne with its charming villages, rolling hills and superb food. Our trip to Albania was made easy by a flight from Toulouse to Milan connecting with an Alitalia flight direct to Tirana.

We had selected, John and I, a modest family hotel in the centre of town called Villa Tafaj. Neither of us was quite sure what to expect. We knew that Albania takes its name from the Albans of Roman times even if in Albanian the country is called *Shqiperia*. It was under Turkish rule for 400 years and by the time the communists banned religion in the late 1940s some 70% of Albanians were Muslim. Now that religion is allowed again it is interesting that not very many people have taken it up. Albania used to be bigger, but after 1913 Kosovo was taken from it. I think they plan on getting it back.

King Zog 1st was self appointed, and ruled from 1928 to 1939 when Mussolini invaded them when they weren't looking over Easter. They never really have trusted the Italians since. Enver Hoxha led the communist resistance and at the end of the war established the communist government. He was a western educated school teacher, and retained a Stalinist doctrine far longer than even Moscow. In fact Albania fell out with the Russians over their move away from Stalinism and then flirted with the Chinese for many years. The legacy of that period can be seen today in the appalling tenement apartments, an economy in tatters and an ecological nightmare. Significant minerals and chrome extraction allowed Albania to build up a considerable military presence. The extracted minerals were exchanged for lots of Migs, a submarine base on the south coast housing 12 submarines in a closed arsenal built under a mountain – we saw the huge doors off a narrow inlet– almost like something out of a 007 movie. But the best is the 600,000 bunkers they built all over the country and especially on the coast, looking like half buried daleks. They are all still there today. Some have been converted into beach huts.

The industries that were established from chemicals to textiles have all closed. We saw one that once employed 20,000 people. It is in a paddock rotting alongside the tenements that house the unemployed people. It is hard to know what Albania produces today. The answer seems to be not much. I was told they are desperate for foreign investment and hope to join the EU. But since the collapse of communism in the 90s the political situation has swung from right to left and back again, the only thing uniting the governments being their complete corruption, lack of effectiveness and disaffection by the electorate. Only 50% voted in the last election. It is generally accepted that Albania has a long way to go before it will meet the criteria required for EU application. They prefer to deal in Euros than their own disgustingly dirty *lek* notes, but nobody is fooled. Not many people are taking the risk to invest there.

So Tirana awaited us. It is a mystery why they moved the capital there and did not leave it at the nearby major port of Durres. It has few buildings of note, some wide avenues, a couple of huge squares with shoe box like communist buildings including the Opera House. But to be fair it has a pleasant relaxed feel about it. The student area is almost charming and on every street corner there is a café. We decided that to visit more of Albania than Tirana we needed a driver. The hotel recommended Fredi. This turned out to be an excellent choice and we kept him for four days.

I generally prefer to hire cars and be independent, but I have never been more glad that we didn't. The roads are the worst in Europe and the driving in Albania is by far the most chaotic and bewildering I have ever experienced. We drove nearly 1,000 kms over most of the country. The number of flowers and crosses at the side of the road marking deaths was terrifying. Literally there was one every few hundred metres. And that is just the Christians! (I asked Fredi if the Muslims were better drivers, or did not have cars, but he said they simply did not mark fatal accidents in the same way Christians do.)

They drive on the wrong side of the street into oncoming traffic, especially in the city, make U turns anywhere and without warning, ignore solid white lines, overtake on bends, do not stop on red lights, which in any case only exist in the capital. Pedestrians wander everywhere, and once I even saw a legless beggar sitting in the middle of a highway at dusk begging. Roundabouts are a free for all, people often park exactly where they want, even in the middle of the street. The explanation? In communist times the only people who could drive were high ranking government employees and military. Then after that there was no driving test until recently, and the licence can be easily purchased without one. Although there are very strict rules and police everywhere controlling papers and jumping out from bushes with a large stop sign like a red lollypop, bribes are far easier than paying fines and much cheaper. Fredi is a magnificent driver, and good company as well. He knew where to eat and where to stop and have coffee and we agreed to let him arrange the four days. It included a long trip to the very far south and an overnight stop in a coastal town called Sarande. But it started with a visit to the castle at Petrala and lunch at the top of a mountain called Dajti.

There are various castles we saw apart from Petrala, one at Kruja, another at Berat and one at Gjirokaster in the far south. They are all ruins with little to commend them. Two had museums but they were closed as there was no power, a very common occurrence in Albania where most of the power is hydroelectric. A combination of little rain and incompetence means that in most places the power goes off for several hours a day.

The construction is different from what I expected. The communist tenements falling apart and looking as if they have already been condemned were no surprise. But the fact that there are very few interesting old buildings did come as a surprise. In some of the mountain villages like Kruja and Gjirocaster there are a few old stone houses, but that is it. On the other hand there has been an attempt at more modern construction. In fact I have never seen so many partly finished buildings in my life. In some areas every other house is either a skeleton or has only a few walls completed. "There is no money to finish them" was the explanation given by Fredi. This may be true. The so called pyramid scheme backed initially by the government at the time (which paid the ultimate penalty by being thrown out), was a massive scam. People were told that if they invested a sum of money they would receive 20% interest a month. Too good to be true? Yes, of course, but Albania had been under communism for many years and the people did not know better. As more and more people put in all their savings it worked at first using Peter to pay Paul, and that encouraged others to follow suit. And then of course it all collapsed after a few months and everyone lost their money, often all of their savings. The banks are a bit more cautious now, and that may also be a reason there is no money available currently.

But there are some new buildings that have been completed. Many, especially businesses, hotels and restaurants, have the brightest and most garish colours imaginable. They all have huge balconies and columns, and they are often a different luminescent blue, green, yellow or orange from the rest of the building. Imagine a bright orange building with startling blue balconies! Or lime green and scarlet, the combinations are several. Shops and showrooms have huge windows often taking up a whole wall. This must create enormous problems for temperature control.

Along the coast apartment buildings are being built at a great speed. Most are empty. Ones that were built right on the waterfront in Durres are only five years old and already falling apart. Similarly the hotel we stayed at in Sarande was brand new, very spacious and modern. But already cracks were appearing in the walls, the plumbing did not work properly and it is clear that in just a few years they will be as bad as the communist tenement buildings down the road. Many say that now is a good time to invest in Albanian property, and it might be, if you are patient and are prepared to take risks. One complication is that land was taken from individuals by the communist government in 1945. There are huge claims in the courts on behalf of people who now claim it back. Meanwhile the land has been occupied by other people for nearly sixty years and houses have been built on it, in many cases illegally and without any planning permission. Fredi showed us land he hopes to reclaim soon on behalf of his wife, a spectacular tract on the coast in the south. He has apparently won the case in the courts but still not managed to get his hands on the title.

The most spectacular drive was south of a town called Vlore right along the coast, climbing to 1,200 metres at one point, and looking straight down into the Ionian Sea below. On the climb up the road has been refurbished but the descent is narrow and dangerous. The views are amazing. The few villages are poor and rather dismal. But there some empty beaches inviting development of tourism. Its inaccessibility may keep it pristine at least for a while.

Sarande in the south has quite a Greek influence, and indeed it overlooks Corfu only a few kilometers away. The town is built on a bay, attractive and looks by far the most prosperous place we saw in Albania. I was sad we did not have more time to spend there strolling along the waterfront or having a drink in a café overlooking the small port. We did manage dinner by the water looking at the lights of Corfu twinkling in the background.

At least the far south and the interior does not look as much like a garbage tip as the rest of the country. The litter everywhere in the entire centre of the country is appalling with azure polyethylene bags drifting along in the breeze. The sides of the roads, even in the country, look as if they are deposits for garbage in the absence of any formal disposal facilities. Old cars are abandoned in fields. Most cars in Albania were bought second hand in Germany, Belgium or Switzerland and taken to Albania where they are run into the ground over the dreadful roads and then dumped, The favourite is the Mercedes, accounting for maybe half of all the cars on the road. Their reputation for resilience is what makes them so popular. Many of them would have been near the end of their normal life expectation before being sold again in Albania.

And what about food? In restaurants there is a strong Italian influence. The coffee is good and there are small cafes everywhere and seemingly well patronized. With Fredi we normally had lunch at about 3.00 p.m. which is the main meal of the day when for most people the working day finishes – they start early in the morning. There are salads to start with and then a meat dish followed by fruit and dessert. There are some quite acceptable local wines. The quality of the food is mediocre for the main part, but at least a step up from *shashlik* which is the national dish under various names from Serbia to Iran. Service reflects the history of the country, at best slack and sometimes downright surly. Surprisingly however, the toilets everywhere we went, even in small towns, were clean and equipped with most necessities, even toilet paper.

Albania has a reputation for being unsafe, but I never felt threatened and there was little evidence of street crime. I think the problem is one of a much higher order where the mafia style operations clearly dominate much of the movement of money.

I mentioned earlier that I had lined up a couple of 'little adventures' on the net for both Qatar and Albania. As I have discovered over the years one of the added benefits of such liaisons is meeting people from the country I am visiting who can often give me an insight into what life there is like, especially for other gay men. Tirana provided some encounters with anything but typical Albanians.

The first encounter was with a man who came to my hotel. He spoke very good English and was exceptionally tall, a man around 30 years old but carrying a few more pounds than a man of that age should. He told me that he had married an American woman who had gone to Albania for work. They had elected to stay in Albania as they wanted to contribute to the development of the country. Their motivation seemed more to be to assist than to make money from their work; they worked in education. He told me that he had already had sex with his wife that evening but that he had not enjoyed it. He never did. I was the sexual satisfaction for the evening for him. I can hardly same the same in return.

The second encounter took me to a trendy area of Tirana near the university. The house I was going to was hard to find and so I met the guy on a street corner and then he took me to the ground floor of the house which he rented. He was Thai and had been living in Tirana for nine months. He was a trained masseur and had applied for a job at a health spa in Tirana. He found the city rather dreary and boring. After Bangkok that did not surprise me. He said he was waiting for a friend with whom he lived to join us. The friend was on his way from the airport after a business trip to Russia. He turned out to be the third person I had been in contact with on the net, and of course I never expected there to be a connection. So we had a threesome.

Was going there worth it? Of course, it was! It was a fascinating experience of a country with a unique history. Would I go again? No, there are still too many other countries yet to be ticked off the list.

Chapter 31 The wrong solution

Dili Timor Leste, May 2009

Hi intrepid readers!

It's not difficult, it does not require any particular skill. You just have to be very vigilant. You dare not let your concentration wander for even one second. After a while you can pick the signs that there might be a huge hole; on the broad flat flood plains the culverts are usually bad, or where a bridge starts and finishes there are often chasms that will at least jar the vehicle badly, even if it does not break anything. Often the holes are so big you can see them from a long way away, but other times they are in the shadows of trees and invisible until the last second. There is always the risk that as you swerve to miss one a goat or child appears in the space you had intended to use. Most of the time the road on the three hour drive to Baucau snakes up and down short cropped hills and often clings to cliffs with the deep blue Banda sea below, and the going is slow, but even when there is a straight section you should never do more than 60kph.

The villages are simple, the houses have walls of wooden poles or planks, and roofs of grass, only a few seem to have foundations of stones. Electricity? Generally no. Water? Judging by the use of streams for washing and the women carrying water on their heads, certainly only communal at best. The countryside is exceptional. Villages are almost hidden in the luxuriant undergrowth sheltered by the low rolling hills with sparse trees, and behind them mountains with dark grey clouds capping them, and a promise of rain although the wet season should have finished two months ago.

I am often at my happiest alone driving in another country – hiring cars is never a luxury for me, it bestows an independence to go and see what I can find, and to turn the contents of my experiences over in my mind. But I do feel guilty on this occasion. There are two reasons. Firstly I know I ought to have stayed in Dili and started work on the IPPF project that has to be completed in another three weeks. The title is uninspiring today, 'Promoting shared responsibility to avoid transmission of HIV', for use in India. The other reason is the cost of the trip and what else I might, perhaps should, have done with the money.

Timor Leste represents amongst the worst value for money in the world. Many poor countries have two or even more economies operating, so I do not expect to pay 50 cents for a meal. But the developed economy here is terribly expensive for generally exceptionally poor quality. The food is appalling and dear. There are few hotels, so it is a fact of life that for USD $60 a night you get no hot water in the hand basin and a trickle of warm water in the shower, most things broken (in my room in Dili this includes the TV, the air conditioning, the power socket, the switch for the ceiling fan, the tap in the bathroom hand basin and the flush on the toilet). Beds sag, white towels are not white and never changed, rooms are not cleaned very often. Car hire is very expensive. There is no third party car insurance in Timor Leste so when you hire a car you are liable for any damage whoever inflicts it. But you can reduce your liability to only $2,000 for USD $28 a day. The sparkling white brand new RAV4 is cute and appealing, and worth stealing apart from anything else. I pay the money.

Shit, this weekend is costing me a bucket. And my mind wanders back to Bairo Pite Clinic on Friday. Alarico is always barking at me about the extreme poverty of most of the people with HIV. "You know how important nutrition is, John, they are starving, can't you help?" I list off all the things I have been trying to do for him in Australia and in Timor Leste, because I known he is right. But so far I have not got any commitments to help. He looks at me and says nothing for a moment. "Well, before you go, come and see A....she is now so thin she can hardly walk. She has been in the hospital for a week now". I do not look forward to this. To my shameful relief she is not there in the room but her husband is, he is also positive. We shake hands, he avoids looking me in the eye. Alarico explains that they both stopped taking their medication and they both got sick. "Why? Why do they stop? Is it because they do not understand that they must take them, and take them for ever? Or do they not want their family to see them taking pills? Or is because of the side effects?" Alarico shrugs.

"I am worried about O..., as well", I tell him.

"She is not eating. Swollen stomach, no appetite."

"What does Dr Dan say?" Alarico shrugs again.

"I don't think he knows what it is. She has gone to the districts, she will take traditional cure".

I am sceptical. I turn to Ines, "You have to get O.. to come back to Dili and to insist with Dr Dan. Last year Armando died and I worry she is going to just give up if she gets sick too." Ines nods in agreement.

I justify my present indulgence by thinking that even if I had given Alarico the money I have spent it would not be sustainable. Next week there will be another crisis. But I know I am just rationalising and it is a cop out. I get on with my trip anyway.

The old Portuguese *pousada* (inn) in Baucau is a large inappropriately Mediterranean pink colour, high on the hill looking down to the sea over the various small villages that make up Baucau. The typical double flights of stairs reach up from the street to the reception area that is also in the Portuguese style and looks rather elegant. The bedroom is almost austere, but the restaurant has a hint of faded European sophistication. I ordered the *caldo verde* (how Portuguese can you get?) and a pasta dish, and splashed out on half a bottle of a Portuguese red wine, a Douro. The restaurant was almost empty. I went to my room, read a little and then put out the light. At eleven my phone started to ring. I awoke and staggered across the room groping for the telephone, half asleep.

"What's your name?"

"Who is this?"

"I am Baby and I am in Room 3".

I missed the opportunity to do some outreach work, and said I had been asleep. Clearly someone in the hotel would have helped her identify who was male and alone. Was she really in Room 3? Too many questions with no answers.

I have a weakness for tropical beaches. The previous evening I had driven down the hill to the local beach, the rough road snaking through small villages almost obscured by banana tress and magnolias, and was greeted with a superb sunset. I went back in the morning for a swim. On the beach I noticed something that I had not seen the night before, a yellow sign warning of crocodiles. There was no-one around to ask. I contented myself with a quick and shallow dip and headed back towards Dili where there was a superb beach that I had noticed on my way down. It was easy to find again by the UN 4X4's parked under the trees there. I swam, I walked in the edge of the water the whole length of the golden beach, I laid in the sun, and I thought about Timor Leste.

No-one will deny it is a mess. National expenditure was four times revenue until the gas revenues started to flow just recently. Even Ramos Horta (why are the leaders all so European looking in a country of people who are not?) recently asked the question in parliament as to why given the huge amounts of aid poured into Timor Leste since 1999, there are so few signs of improvement? He asked "Are we Timorese stupid or is there something else wrong?"

Two obvious major problems are the official language and the currency. The official language is Portuguese even though only really elderly or highly educated people speak it. Their own language *Tetum*, a kind of local language and Portuguese mix, is not a consistent written language and they were not going to choose *Behasa Indonesia* (which everyone speaks). What were their options? And adopting the US dollar makes everything very expensive especially at the lower end of the market, adversely affecting poor people. Suddenly the lowest currency value went from 500 Rupiah (5 cents) to the odd coin of 25 cents, but most things are rounded off to a dollar. But again, what other options did they have? They wanted to replace the rupiah as soon as the Indonesians left, and they did not have the time or the money to invent their own currency. The US dollar was adopted and now it is too late to change it.

The Norwegians have helped them establish their investment fund, the petroleum reserves will last for only ten years. They want to build the capital and invest, that is spend, only the interest. But where does it go? The government promised to pay the salaries of people from Bairo Pite clinic, but there appears to be a problem. We at AFAP have been supporting them for years, but our funds have run dry and their government has to live up to its obligations. They were due to start paying these salaries in February and now it might be June. Meanwhile doctors and staff are working but not being paid.

Public schools are not free, most of the positive people cannot afford to send their children to school. Health is still very poor. In Dili both malaria and dengue are endemic. Tuberculosis is a significant problem. I can of course speak more about HIV than other areas. Half of the Global Fund money in the last grant went on hiring Indian HIV specialists, so I was told. Do they see patients? No, they work in the ministry of health. There are no tests for basic indicators for managing HIV (CD4's) let alone viral load. The medication used to come from Brazil as a gesture of solidarity to Portuguese speaking nations. But many drugs were arriving after their expiry date, supply was haphazard and now they are using Indian generics, a step in the right direction at least. Most HIV patients see Dr Dan at Bairo Pite, an eccentric American who speaks *Tetum* and whose patients adore him. He takes risks in most of what he does. I cannot criticise him, even there have been some appalling mistakes along the way; he probably does as well as anyone can under the circumstances. I waited to see him once at the clinic, he spent on average just a couple of minutes with each patient. Inevitably the care is deficient, but when the chips are down Timor Leste is probably better off with him than without him. He just won an award in last week's Independence (which one?) Day honours.

So if there is slow progress on health and education, where does the money go? Infrastructure, I was told. Most of the roads in the country are still passable only with 4X4's. Even in Dili the roads are atrocious. Agreed the city was virtually destroyed in 1999, and there have been some sackings of buildings as recently as 2008. But Dili is still full of shells of buildings, and even those standing are for the most part falling apart. There is now an uneven footpath along the road in front of my hotel, the 'corniche!', but at night it is unlit and has huge deep holes in it, presumably drains. There is a very small number of new buildings, the most notable one being the lavish new presidential palace. Outside the main area people live in shacks in what one can only call close to being shanty towns.

The mobile phone coverage is fair in main towns, but it was installed by Portuguese Telecom, is outrageously expensive and bad. As few people use landlines, and there is no directory of mobiles, getting in touch with people even for business depends on knowing what their mobile number is. The internet is so slow that I can only operate very slowly with webmail, and sometimes it is so bad I cannot even get my homepage up. I have tried downloading emails directly but the system is too slow.

Unemployment is huge, and there seem to be no opportunities on the horizon for that to change. Whatever the government is doing with its money it is not creating jobs for local people. Foreign aid is not doing much better. The economy seems to run on the money the ex-pats spend. The police force is run by the UN, NGOs are full of ex-pats, some paid developed world salaries, many of them volunteers with a stipend. Even the government seems to use foreign consultants. Some businesses are benefiting no doubt, like restaurants, bars, car dealers, and probably sex workers, but I have never believed in the trickle down effect. In any case many businesses are owned by recent Chinese immigrants.

So how has Timor Leste got to this point? It is interesting to look at what the various colonial powers left as a legacy. Generally the French left a language, a religion and a culture, even the British lengthy colonisation of Mauritius never displaced the French patois. The Spaniards pretty much the same, they just left earlier and with their hands full. The British left full coffers and an attempt at a functioning government when it could. Interestingly the only situation I know of where there is virtually no sign of the colonisers is in Indonesia. The Dutch did not leave even words let alone a language, no culture, no religion, just damned canals, never a good idea in the tropics where they quickly turn into festering breeding grounds for awful afflictions. The Belgians of course left bloody wars. And then the Portuguese. They left their genetic imprint being more prone to create attractive coffee coloured children than other colonisers. What else? Well, not much.

I wonder why they stayed here so long, there were scant resources, not even enough to plunder. They did nothing with Timor, just left it as a forgotten backwater until the fall of Salazar in Portugal in 1975 caused the Portuguese to start divesting themselves of what was left of their fragmented and decayed empire. Should Timor Leste really be part of Indonesia? The people of Timor Leste are different from the rest of Indonesia, but I assume this is also true of the western Indonesian end of the island. They are believed to have a dash of Melanesian in them. They are darker, and some have tight curly hair, and are hairy. They do not have the high cheek bones and seductive lips of the Indonesians. They have an overlay of Catholicism on top of their animist beliefs. So Timor Leste is different ethnically and culturally but then so are many other parts of Indonesia, West Papua, Aceh, Sulawesi. Sadly Indonesia never tried to learn how to make a confederation of its various components, with tragic consequences, not just in Timor Leste.

The fact is that after the annexation in 1976 the Indonesians treated them as inferior and discriminated against them. Instead of trying to resettle people, if only they had allowed them some level of self determination within Indonesia and been prepared to invest as much in East Timor as they did in the rest of Indonesia the story might have been very different. A peek over the border to Indonesia today shows a far better standard of living, even despite Indonesia's relative poverty and other problems. Was it really worth losing so many people in the civil war of 1999 (nobody knows how many people perished but there are estimates that as many as 30% of the population of about 900,000 at the time might have died) for what they have now? A struggling virtually failed state that despite all our efforts seems to make little headway.

Well in the meantime the wet season has still not given up and probably as a result of the torrential rain this evening the electricity went out for an hour here in Dili. It was a very Dili dinner. The special on the menu was chicken at seven dollars. I had a diet coke. The bill should have been $8.50. She gave me a bill for $9.50. "No, look at the specials board", I said, "Chicken $7!"

"Oh", she said, "Made mistake".

She then went to the specials board, rubbed out the $7 and wrote $8 in its place.

Chapter 32 Looking to the future

Retirement is a risky business, because you never know how long is it going to last. You do not want to spend all your money and then live another 10 years in poverty and misery, and yet neither do you want to stint yourself and then die leaving a vast fortune to those who do not deserve it and probably have little idea how to enjoy it. At least being gay and having no progenies, I do not feel that I owe it to my children to leave them most of my fortune.

In my case the future is even harder to guess. Should I take the view that if I have managed to live with HIV for 30 years, then I can live another 20 years or more? Or do I take the view that after 30 years I am already living on borrowed time and the end must be nigh? I now also have Type II diabetes most likely as a result of the side effects of the medications I have been on for so long. There would appear to be a higher incidence of cardiovascular problems and some cancers with long-term HIV patients. We are finding that HIV in some way causes premature aging. It is unclear whether it is due to the medication, the virus, or as recent studies suggest inflammation in the body that could be due to co-infections with things like cytomegalovirus. There continue to be so many unknowns in HIV. But generally I take care of myself, and I take my chances, as do we all.

In 2004 I started to take an injectible drug for HIV, making up the solution and injecting myself twice a day into the stomach. There are friends I have who think they could never manage to do that, but I find that the limits of what one can or cannot do are not understood until they are tested. Survival and love are both amazing forces in humanity, and for both of them I have found I have been able to do things I never would have thought myself capable of. There are more new-generation HIV treatments on the way, and for the last year or more I have just been back on tablets again. Although a vaccine is years away the outlook generally for treatment is probably better now than for the last few years. I have been in what is called "salvage therapy" for some time now, and although some of the counts remain disappointing, I am here, I am alive and I am living my life as fully as I know how.

I am now over 65 and heading to 70 of course, but I am not ready to be old yet. There is so much in the areas where I volunteer my time that needs to be done, and so much still to see and to appreciate and enjoy. I tend to live my life with concrete plans and the odd dream with a horizon of six months to a year but not much more than that. This has been the case for many years now. I do not preclude a long life into old age but neither do I really expect it, or even less bank on it.

I have absolutely no regrets about being gay and it shocks a little when straight people suggest that my life has been cursed in some way by being gay. It has not. But I wish I did not have HIV.

When I look back over my life so far I am amazed at how fast the world changes, with the speed of that change accelerating all the time. Not long after I write something about a place, including this book, it is no longer true. Events and situations slip quickly into history, rarely to be heard of again. Who talks about SARS nowadays? I wonder when we will be able to say the same thing about AIDS.

I have tended to become more reflective than I used to be. I listen far more than I did and talk far less. I am frightened for the world and feel that my generation should be ashamed of the legacy it will leave the next one.

In my travels I have always been struck by the incredible natural beauty of our planet. It is our home, and it is hard to not feel, when we allow ourselves to just be with nature, that we are anything but separate from it. We now know from a more scientific perspective that this is literally true, we are symbiotically connected with Earth. How can we therefore show our home such disrespect in the way we treat it? We ourselves have invented an artificial construct called money, which has no inherent existence independent of us, and we honour it by placing it above the very environment that makes our life possible, even above humanity itself. How can any sensible person refuse to sign a protocol on reducing carbon emissions because it would reduce the number of jobs available in our country and add to the unemployment rate, even if it were true, which it most probably isn't? Politicians the world over have replaced the priority of serving their people and the world community by their desire to get re-elected. This engenders short-term policies and thinking that do not extend beyond the next election. It discourages global thinking and cooperation between countries.

We have to do something about global warming and the media has a responsibility to make sure that this issue is constantly put under the noses of the people, since in today's world they seem to have more power than anyone to influence opinions. When the democratic principles were being developed by the ancient Greeks nobody had any notion of a media that could exert such influence over the people.

The other phenomenon that frightens me and that I really do not understand is the evolution of religious fundamentalism. Is this fundamentalism at least in part driven by the failure of materialism to deliver what people want from life? I have no idea. I suppose it is naïve to believe that a state can ever be totally secular, given that political leaders always bring to their job a set of values, and many of these are tied up with their personal belief systems. But if countries are not to be divided on the basis of dogma often based on religion, both internally such as the USA at the moment, or globally such as the cleft being driven between Christians and Muslims, then we must strive to make them secular.

If the Age of Aquarius is going to come it had better hurry up!

I have some confidence in our youth that they will do a better job than we have. At least in developed countries young people have benefited from extraordinarily diverse experiences. They travel, they are worldly and have a degree of self-assurance that is sometimes frightening. I love the creativity and enthusiasm of youth, its passion and its wisdom. We have to trust in their independence of thought and spirit, and that when necessary they will choose principles over the transient comfort of material consumption.

And as for me? There will no doubt be more enquiry and more learning. I will continue to observe and experience this wonderful world for as long as I can, and where I can influence it for good I will do so. Life it is to be lived, for otherwise it has little value. I have trodden a long path from the semi detached two up two down in a nowhere suburb, but there is still a way to go.

Chapter 33 Dreams

Dreams intrigue us all. For we all have our private worlds both waking and dreaming, but rarely do we share them. Many of us are only vaguely aware of this other world. I have friends who assert that they never dream. I lean back on my psychology studies at Sydney University and tell them that they do in fact dream, they just do not remember. Since everyone's experience is their own truth, they tell me again that they do not dream, I am wrong. So be it.

At times the dream experiences are vivid, more vivid even than real life, yet at the same time elusive. The snapshots are clear and in focus, while their connections are vague and obtuse. Memories are etched in clarity in parts, but not as an integrated image. There are gaps and mists of vagueness. The images pass across our awareness like a veil of mystery across the eye of perception.

And these people I know in that other world that seems real in the moment (for I cannot fundamentally know which is real and which not), do they act on their own behalf or mine? Surely I manipulate them like marionettes, either taking into account who they are, or not. Are these reverie figures similar to the people in the waking world? Do they say the same things and do the same things, or are they just actors whom I have created at a whim, playing the parts I want and without consideration of what they would really do or say?

It is my world and nobody shares it, as I share the dream world of others only if they wish to tell me. Sometimes Warren whimpers in his sleep. I know that he is being pursued again, cornered, threatened, and he is afraid. I know that because he has told me. For years they have chased him like this, with knives. I used to wake him gently by calling his name – I read somewhere that it is dangerous to wake someone from a deep sleep by touching them – so that he can escape the torture to which he is being subjected, maybe the torture he inflicts on himself.

Have you woken in the night, suddenly, and remembered a dream vividly? Perhaps it has brought you an idea to be captured for the waking world. Or maybe the dream was so bizarre you wanted to tell others for their amusement, or perhaps an insight. But despite your determination, in the morning the only memory is of the fact that you had to remember it. The picture frame is there but the picture has gone. Even if you rehearse the dream in your waking mind, knowing its vulnerability to be swallowed into the great never, believing that to rehearse it actively may store the memory in a safer set of neurons, placing it on a different shelf in a different place and on a different level, on waking you discover it has been stolen back even so. The only security is to take it away altogether, safe from tricks. You have to get up and write it down right then and there.

Certainly dreams have fascinated us for all of humanity. So what do our dreams mean? I was recently reading a book in which the author asserted that they had no meaning at all. I am not so sure that I agree. I believe that there is a hierarchical dream structure.

At the most superficial level there are dreams that are simply a mix-up in the filing, and accessing of older files, as we put away more recent information. It is as if you have been tidying up the office. There is some filing of thoughts from that day. As you place them in a file, you glance at files adjacent, and the contents become mixed up. This gives rise to strange connections and amusing impossibilities. Sometimes the resultant stories are bizarre and even hysterically funny as the files become integrated. Fantasy based on fact. Sometimes items from your "to do list" fall into the mixing pot too.

In the same category are pre-living outcomes that are on our minds, such as exam results. I often receive the test results from the HIV specialist the day before my appointment.

The second level is dreams where there are messages that are encoded. Interpretation of dreams has been a tradition as old as dreams themselves. Look at the popularity of the writings of Jung and Freud. I always liked Freud, not so much because I think that his theories are exact explanations, but more because I admired his boldness in confronting basic elements of human experience that others refused to talk about. And because I also think that sex and the knowledge of our own mortality, and the consequent fear of death, do indeed dominate much of human behaviour.

These are the dreams that were used to discover the bases of neuroses and mental disturbances. The codes are not as simple to read as some of the popular books on the interpretations of dreams, or even Freud, would have us believe. But for people who are in touch with themselves, insights can be gained from thinking about their own dreams and asking themselves what the metaphors and allegories mean. And competent and insightful therapists can, I believe, help people to understand the significance of their dreams, and through that understanding gain more peace in their waking life.

And then in what might be called the highest level of dreams, I also believe in very rare cases there are insights revealed, whereby in the dreaming state some people are connected to a wider whole, outside of themselves. They become aware of knowledge outside themselves. I have not had this experience myself, but I have several friends, whose judgment I trust, who have. One friend of mine used to have vivid dreams of terrible incidents, often just before they happened. When he realised that these dreams came to pass in the waking world shortly afterwards, he became so disturbed that sometimes he was afraid to go to sleep.

So what of this dream world? Could it not be that the difference between our dream world and what we call reality is not as clear as we suppose? To what extent does reality happen only when probabilities are observed and become manifest? We know that at the subatomic particle level that happens. Could our joined consciousness cause the world that we know to emerge from an ambiguous soup of probabilities? Perhaps the real world in which we think we live is just a consensus dream experienced by all humanity. Or is our consciousness only a small fragment of a greater universal consciousness, a kind of holographic fragment? The secrets of the universe appear to still not to be ours to know. Will they ever be I wonder?